Karl Barth and Evangelical Theology
Convergences and Divergences

Karl Barth and Evangelical Theology
Convergences and Divergences

Edited by
Sung Wook Chung

Paternoster: thinking faith

Baker Academic
Grand Rapids, Michigan

12 11 10 09 08 07 06   7 6 5 4 3 2 1

First published jointly in 2006 by Paternoster Press in the UK and
Baker Academic in the USA
Paternoster Press is an imprint of Authentic Media
9 Holdom Avenue, Bletchley, Milton Keynes, Bucks,
MK1 1QR, UK
285 Lynnwood Avenue, Tyrone, GA 30290, USA
OM Authentic Media, Medchal Road, Jeedimetla Village,
Secunderabad 500 055, A.P.
www.authenticmedia.co.uk

Baker Academic is an imprint of Baker Publishing Group,
PO Box 6287, Grand Rapids, MI 4951606287
www.bakeracademic.com

Authentic Media is a division of Send the Light Ltd., a company limited by
guarantee (registered charity no. 270162

British Library Cataloguing in Publication Data

A catalogue record for this book is available from the
British Library

ISBN-13 978-1-84227-354-8
ISBN-10 1-84227-354-X

Library of Congress Cataloging-in-Publication Data
Library of Congress Cataloging-in-Publication Data is on file at the
Library of Congress, Washington, DC

ISBN-13: 978-0-8010-3127-4
ISBN-10: 0-8010-3127-3

Design by James Kessell for Scratch the Sky Ltd (www.scratchthesky.com)
Printed in the United States by Versa Press

Contents

The Editor

Dr. Sung Wook Chung is Associate Professor of Christian Theology at Denver Seminary, Littleton, CO., USA. He is a native Korean and received the M.Div. degree from Harvard University and the D.Phil. degree from the University of Oxford. He is the author of many professional articles and academic books. He has authored *Admiration and Challenge: Karl Barth's Theological Relationship with John Calvin* (New York: Peter Lang, 2002) and edited *Alister E. McGrath and Evangelical Theology: A Dynamic Engagement* (Carlisle, UK & Grand Rapids, MI: Paternoster & Baker, 2003) and *Christ the One and Only: A Global Affirmation of the Uniqueness of Jesus Christ* (Milton Keynes, UK & Grand Rapids, MI: Paternoster & Baker, 2005).

Contributors

Henri Blocher is Professor of Systematic Theology, Wheaton College. Formerly Professor of Systematic Theology at the Faculté Libre de Théologie Evangélique in Vaux-sur-Seine (where he has also regularly taught Hebrew and philosophy), Professor Blocher is widely recognized as a careful and profound theologian and an evangelical statesman. He has lectured or taught in schools in Europe, Australia, Africa, Canada, and the USA. He was a member of the Lausanne Committee on World Evangelization (1975–1980) and has also served the World Evangelical Fellowship/Alliance in a number of capacities over many years, including (since 1993) their Theological Commission Task Force for dialogue with the Pontifical Council for Promoting Christian Unity. He has recently assumed the presidency of the Fellowship of European Evangelical Theologians. He has authored a number of books including *Original Sin: Illuminating the Riddle* (Downers Grove, IL: InterVarsity Press, 2000), *Evil and the Cross* (Downers Grove, IL: InterVarsity Press, 1994), *In the Beginning: The Opening Chapters of Genesis* (Leicester: Inter-Varsity Press, 1984).

John Bolt is Professor of Systematic Theology at Calvin Theological Seminary, Grand Rapids, Michigan, USA and an ordained minister in the Christian Reformed Church. He has degrees from Calvin College (B.Sc.), Calvin Theological Seminary (B.D., Th.M.) and a Ph.D. from the University of St. Michael's College, Toronto, Canada. He is the editor of the new four-volume English translation of Herman Bavinck's *Reformed Dogmatics* (Grand Rapids, MI: Baker, 1996).

A frequent contributor to the *Calvin Theological Journal*, which he edited from 1991–1999, his major publications include *Christian and Reformed Today* (Brescia: Paideia, 1984), *The Christian Story and the Christian School*, (Grand Rapids, MI: CSI, 1994), and *A Free Church, A Holy Nation: Abraham Kuyper's American Public Theology* (Grand Rapids, MI: Eerdmans, 2001).

Sung Wook Chung is Associate Professor of Christian Theology at Denver Seminary, Colorado, USA. He received the M.Div. degree from Harvard University Divinity School and the D.Phil. degree from Oxford University. In addition to numerous professional articles on systematic theology, he authored *Admiration and Challenge: Karl Barth's Theological Relationship with John Calvin* (New York: Peter Lang, 2002) and edited *Alister E. McGrath and Evangelical Theology: A Dynamic Engagement* (Grand Rapids, Michigan/Carlisle: Baker/Paternoster, 2003), and *Christ the One and Only: A Global Affirmation of the Uniqueness of Jesus Christ* (Grand Rapids, MI & Carlisle, UK: Baker & Paternoster, 2005). Besides, he also authored in Korean *Christian Theology Made Easy* (Seoul: Hong Sung, 2005), *Christian Apologetics Made Easy* (Seoul: Hong Sung, 2004), *The Cross Theology and Spirituality* (Seoul: Revival & Reformation, 2005), and *The Key Words of the Reformation* (Seoul: Revival & Reformation, 2005). He also translated the works of Paul Tillich, Jonathan Edwards, and Alister E. McGrath into Korean.

Oliver Crisp is Lecturer in Theology at The University of Bristol, UK. Previously, he taught at the University of St. Andrews, UK (2002–2004) and held the Frederick J. Crosson Research Fellowship at the Center for Philosophy of Religion, University of Notre Dame, USA (2004–2005). He has also been a visiting lecturer at Regent College, Vancouver, BC. He received the Ph.D. degree from the University of London. With Paul Helm he co-edited *Jonathan Edwards: Philosophical Theologian* (Burlington, VT & Aldershot, UK: Ashgate, 2003) and has written two monographs, *Jonathan Edwards and the Metaphysics of Sin* (Burlington, VT & Aldershot, UK: Ashgate, 2005) and *Divinity and Humanity: Issues in the Incarnation* (forthcoming).

Gabriel Fackre is Abbot Professor of Christian Theology Emeritus at Andover Newton School of Theology, Massachusetts, USA. He received his Ph.D. from the University of Chicago and is an ordained minister in the United Church of Christ. He is past President of the

American Theological Society and the author of numerous books and professional articles. Among his major publications are the *Doctrine of Revelation: A Narrative Interpretation* (Edinburgh, UK & Grand Rapids, MI: Edinburgh University Press & Eerdmans, 1997), *The Christian Story* (Grand Rapids, MI: Eerdmans, vol. 1, 1996; vol.2, 1987) and *Restoring the Center: Essays Evangelical & Ecumenical* (Downers Grove, IL: InverVarsity Press, 1998).

John R. Franke is professor of theology at Biblical Seminary in Hatfield, PA. He holds the D.Phil. from Oxford University and is the co-author of *Beyond Foundationalism: Shaping Theology in a Postmodern Context* (Louisville, KY: Westminster John Knox, 2001); the editor of *Joshua, Judges, Ruth, 1–2 Samuel* in the *Ancient Christian Commentary of Scripture* (Downers Grove, IL: InterVarsity Press, 2005); the author of *The Character of Theology: An Introduction to Its Nature, Task, and Purpose* (Grand Rapids, MI: Baker Academic, 2005) and *Barth for Armchair Theologians* (Louisville, KY: Westminster John Knox, 2006); and currently serves as the chair of the Evangelical Theology Group of the American Academy of Religion.

Timothy George is the founding dean of Beeson Divinity School of Samford University and an executive editor of *Christianity Today*. He holds degrees from the University of Tennessee at Chattanooga (B.A.) and Harvard Divinity School (M.Div.; Th.D.). He has written and edited numerous books including *Theology of the Reformers* (Nashville, TN: Broadman & Holman, 1999), the New American Commentary on *Galatians* (Nashville, TN: Broadman & Holman, 1994), and, most recently, *Is the Father of Jesus the God of Muhammad?* (Grand Rapids, MI: Zondervan, 2002). George is a member of the editorial boards of *Books and Culture*, *First Things*, and *Harvard Theological Review*. He also chairs the Theological Education Commission of the Baptist World Alliance and is a widely sought-after speaker on matters of Christian higher education, theological and biblical issues, and cultural trends.

Veli-Matti Kärkkäinen is Professor of Systematic Theology at Fuller Theological Seminary, Pasadena, CA and Privatdozent of Ecumenics at the University of Helsinki, Finland. A native of Finland, he has also taught in Thailand. An author of ten academic books in English, his latest titles include *Trinity and Religious Pluralism: The Doctrine of the Trinity in Christian Theology of Religions*

(Burlington, VT & Aldershot, UK: Ashgate, 2004), *Doctrine of God: A Global Perspective* (Grand Rapids, MI: Baker, 2004), and *One With God: Salvation as Deification and Justification* (Collegeville, MN: Liturgical Press, 2004). Currently, he is finishing a book for WJKP on the doctrine of the Trinity at the global level. He is also the co-editor of the forthcoming *The Global Dictionary of Theology* (Downers Grove, IL: InterVarsity Press).

Frank D. Macchia is an ordained minister in the Assemblies of God. He serves as Professor of Theology at Vanguard University of Southern California. He earned the M.Div. at Union Theological Seminary in New York and the D.Th. from the University of Basel (Switzerland). He serves on the Faith and Order Commission of the National Council of Christian Churches (USA). He also serves on the Pentecostal team of the international World Alliance of Reformed Churches/Pentecostal Dialogue (now in its eighth year). He has served as President of the Society for Pentecostal Studies and now edits the Society's Journal, *Pneuma* (which is published by Brill). He has offered papers at numerous academic and professional societies and published articles and essays in various journals and anthologies. His most recent book is, *Baptized in the Spirit: A Global Pentecostal Theology* (Grand Rapids, MI: Zondervan, 2006).

Alister E. McGrath is Professor of Historical Theology at Oxford University. He studied at Oxford and Cambridge Universities, and holds first class honors degrees from Oxford in chemistry and theology. He was awarded an Oxford D.Phil. for his research in molecular biophysics, and an Oxford D.Div. for his research in historical and systematic theology. His particular interest is the interaction of Christian theology and the natural sciences. His recent major publications include *A Scientific Theology* (3 vols, Grand Rapids, MI: Eerdmans, 2001–2003), *Dawkins'* God (Oxford: Blackwell, 2004), *The Twilight of Atheism* (New York: Doubleday, 2004), and *The Order of Things: Explorations in Scientific Theology* (Oxford: Blackwell, 2006). He is also the author of the best-selling theological textbook *Christian Theology: An Introduction* (Oxford: Blackwell, 2001), now entering its fourth edition.

Kurt Anders Richardson is Professor in the Faculty of Theology, Department of Philosophy, McMaster University, Ontario, Canada. He received the D.Th. degree from the University of Basel, Switzerland. His current research and writing include the above as well as giving theological lectures in international venues in Europe, the Middle East and China. He has authored *The Epistle of James: New American Commentary* (Nashville, TN: Broadman & Holman, 1997) and *Reading Karl Barth: New Directions for North American Theology* (Grand Rapids, MI: Baker, 2004), *Christ and Empire: Apologetics of Political Christianity* (Grand Rapids, MI: Brazos, 2006, forthcoming), *Christian Theology: 21st Century Teaching and Learning from Nicea* (Zurich: Chalice, 2006, forthcoming).

Kevin J. Vanhoozer is Research Professor of Systematic Theology at Trinity Evangelical Divinity School. Previously, he was for eight years Senior Lecturer in Theology and Religious Studies at the University of Edinburgh. He holds the M.Div. degree from Westminster Theological Seminary (Philadelphia) and the Ph.D. degree from Cambridge University. He is the author of *Biblical Narrative in the Philosophy of Paul Ricoeur* (Cambridge: Cambridge University Press, 1990), *Is There a Meaning in this Text? The Bible, the Reader, and the Morality of Literary Knowledge*, *First Theology: God, Scripture, and Hermeneutics* (Downers Grove, IL: InterVarsity Press, 2002) and *The Drama of Doctrine: A Canonical-Linguistic Approach to Christian Theology* (Louisville, KY: Westminster John Knox, 2005). He has edited several books, including *The Cambridge Companion to Postmodern Theology* (Cambridge: Cambridge University Press, 2003), *Dictionary for Theological Interpretation of the Bible* (Grand Rapids, MI: Baker, 2005), and *Hermeneutics at the Crossroads* (Bloomington, IN: Indiana University Press, 2006).

Foreword

Evangelicals—those who stand in the tradition of the Reformation and the movement of revival—are giving increased attention to the theology of Karl Barth, for they are beginning to see in his monumental work a viable alternative to fundamentalism on the right and liberalism on the left. Yet there are lingering reservations among evangelicals as to whether Barth's theology is truly scriptural and fully evangelical. Among theologians, besides myself, who belong to the wider evangelical movement and who evince a marked appreciation for Barth are Bernard Ramm, G. W. Bromiley, Gergory Bolich, J. I. Packer, Thomas Torrance, Donald Dayton, Donald McKim, Kurt Richardson, Frank Macchia and Timothy George. Evangelicals who have viewed Barth fundamentally as an adversary of true faith include Cornelius Van Til, John Warwick Montgomery, Francis Schaeffer, Edward John Carnell, Norman Geisler, R. C. Sproul, Charles Ryrie, John Gerstner, Gordon Clark, Carl Henry, Harold O. J. Brown and Clark Pinnock. The last two are more moderate in their criticisms and see promise as well as dangers in the Barthian enterprise. Evangelical critics of Barth on the European scene include Klaas Runia, Helmut Thielicke, Adolf Köberle, Paul Althaus, Karl Heim, Walter Künneth, Adolf Schlatter and G. C. Berkouwer.

Barth himself maintained a mixed attitude toward pietism, the seedbed of modern evangelicalism. Among his criticisms of the pietists was their individualism and subjectivism. Yet Barth manifested a growing appreciation for pietists after he embarked on his *Church Dogmatics*. Pietists whom Barth viewed positively include Philip

Spener, Nicholas von Zinzendorf, A. A. Bengel, F. A. Tholuck, H. F. Kohlbrügge, Johann Christoph Blumhardt and Christoph Blumhardt. It should be also be noted that Barth was profoundly influenced by S. Kierkegaard, whose voluminous writings abound in pietist sentiments. Barth did not remain with Kierkegaard, however, since he saw the need to tie faith more closely with rationality, to base faith on the message of redemption as well as on the Redeemer.

Barth has been upbraided by evangelicals for his alleged universalism—that all will be adopted into Christ's kingdom by faith. Yet Barth takes pains to distinguish between the universal dimensions of the atonement, which he affirms, and the teaching of the universal restoration of the whole of the human creation, which he denies.

Emil Brunner, who was at one time an ally of Barth, has with some justification accused Barth of objectivism—locating salvation completely outside of human striving and experience. Barth has similarly been called a Christomonist, since he appears to see the drama of salvation entirely enacted in the life, death and resurrection of Jesus Christ. Yet his critics err when they discount the crucial role of the Holy Spirit in Barth's theology. For Barth it is the Spirit who enables us to reach the goal of Christian salvation—the renewal and sanctification of God's people. Barth, moreover, is correct in contending for the priority of God's reconciling work in past history over the decision of faith, however necessary human involvement may be in the plan of salvation.

Barth's questioning of the sacraments as means of grace has also earned him the criticism of his more orthodox peers. For Barth, in his maturity, the sacraments are best understood as signs of the person and work of Christ in history rather than conduits of grace in Christian experience. Barth's break with sacramentalism has been deplored by many of the devotees of the Reformation, especially those of Lutheran and Reformed lineage. I too have difficulty with Barth in this area, though I completely support his effort to maintain the freedom of God in all of God's relations with the human creation. In my opinion we need to listen to Barth's fresh appraisal of the sacraments, since it manifests an underlying concern for personal faith and obedience, thereby attesting his kinship with pietism.

Where I have personally benefited from Barth's theology is in his emphasis on the gospel before the law, divine revelation over human reason, dogmatics before apologetics and theology over ideology. My reservations lie in his objectivistic and universalistic slant, which he nevertheless strives to hold in balance with his concern for vocation as the third element in salvation—after justification and sanctification. I also have difficulty with his tendency to reduce evangelism to a witness to salvation rather than a means of salvation—the Holy Spirit bringing the knowledge of Christ's redemption to people caught up in the morass of sin.

We can all thank Barth for exposing the anthropocentric theology of neo-Protestantism, which recast theology as a human quest for God rather than a faithful witness to God's saving work in Jesus Christ. Barth has enabled evangelicals to treat Holy Scripture with the utmost seriousness without denigrating the legitimate claims of historical criticism. He has also helped evangelicals to recover the mission of the church—to proclaim Jesus Christ and him crucified to a world lost in sin as opposed to making the gospel palatable and credible to its cultured despisers (as in Schleiermacher and Tillich).

Barth has provided us with a theology of the Word of God that is at the same time a theology of the Word and Spirit. We cannot follow him all the way, but we can identify with his pilgrim theology—always being reformed through the new light that breaks forth from God's Holy Word. This is not a new word from God but an illuminated word—the Spirit acting upon the text and at the same time renewing the human heart so that we can see, understand and believe.

Donald G. Bloesch
Professor of Theology Emeritus
University of Dubuque Theological Seminary

Preface

Karl Barth is undoubtedly one of the most influential Christian theologians in the twentieth century. However, the evangelical reception of the theology of Karl Barth has been complicated. He has been a hot potato for evangelicals. Some evangelical theologians rejected his theology outright, arguing that Barth's view of Scripture is not consistent with the historic evangelical view. Other evangelical theologians accepted wholeheartedly Barth's emphasis on the Word of God and Christ-centered interpretation of the gospel.

For the last twenty years, Karl Barth studies have had a renaissance in English speaking world including America, Canada, Great Britain, and Asian countries in the Pacific Rim. A number of young generation scholars have presented a new interpretation of Barth's theology, and their interpretation seems to demonstrate that Barth's theology is more consistent with the historic evangelical faith than evangelicals have ever thought. However, it is true that more conservative evangelical theologians still have serious reservations about Barth's theology as well as its new interpretations.

Why do we have a variety of responses to Barth' theology? It is because evangelical theology is increasingly becoming a diversified, not a uniform, movement. Under the umbrella of "evangelical theology", we can include not only traditional theological systems such as Calvinistic Reformed theology, Arminian-Wesleyan theology, and dispensationalism but also conservative evangelical theology, postconservative evangelical theology, and ecumenical evangelical theology. However, we need to remember that in spite of rapid diversification of evangelical theology, there are core family values that all evangelicals cherish and have allegiance to. In the context of evangelicals' mixed responses to Karl Barth, this book aims to be a balanced attempt to appraise Karl Barth's theology from a consensual evangelical perspective. Thus, the primary purpose of this book will be exploring the substantial convergences and divergences between the theology of Karl Barth and the historic evangelical faith. On the basis of that exploration, this book will present ways for evangelicals to dynamically engage with Barth's theology for the benefit of the entire evangelical Christianity and beyond.

One of the most valuable features of this book is that the representative theologians of various evangelical theological trends contribute to this book. For example, John Franke is representative of postconservative evangelical theology, and Gabriel Fackre is representative of narrative evangelical theology. In addition, Oliver Crisp and Henri Blocher are representative of conservative Reformed evangelical theology. John Bolt represents a Dutch Reformed attempt to integrate Barth's theology into evangelical theological construction. Frank Macchia is a Pentecostal theologian who attempts to integrate Barth's theological insights. Another significant feature of this book is that the contributors demonstrate the maturity and dynamics of evangelical theology by thoroughly engaging with the new interpretations of Barth proposed by mainline Barth scholars for the last twenty years.

I hope that this book will be a helpful reference point for both evangelical theologians and Christians in their assessment and appropriation of Barth's theology.

Sung Wook Chung
Denver Seminary

Easter, 2006

1

Revelation

Gabriel Fackre

Karl Barth is called the "theologian of revelation." evangelicals also bring revelation center stage. What then do we make of Barth's thought on this doctrine? Evangelical commentary has been extensive and the views varied.[1]

Evangelicalism today is constituted by core convictions, but ones that manifest in multiple ways.[2] The interpretation and evaluation of Barth's teaching on the doctrine of revelation in this chapter will be from the point of view of "evangelical narrative," one that follows Scripture's journey of the triune God from Genesis to Revelation—creation, fall, the universal covenant with Noah, the particular covenant with Israel, the incarnation and atonement of Jesus Christ, the birth of the church, the coming of salvation, the

---

1 For a helpful review of points of view, see Philip R. Thorne, *Evangelicalism and Karl Barth: His Reception and Influence in North American Evangelical Theology* (Alison Park, PA: Pickwick Publications, 1995) and the earlier Gregory Bolich, *Karl Barth and Evangelicalism* (Downers Grove, IL: InterVarsity Press, 1980). For the most intensive evangelical engagement with Barth's teaching on the subject, see Carl F. H. Henry, *God, Revelation and Authority*, vols. I–VI (Waco, TX: Word Books, 1976–1983), esp. I, pp. 203–12; II, pp. 40–8, 143–7, 158–62; III, pp. 224–9; IV, pp. 148–61, 196–200, 257–71, 298–303; V, pp. 39, 53, 97, 299, 366–70.

2 See the author's entry, "Evangelical, Evangelicalism," in *The Westminster Dictionary of Christian Theology*, Alan Richardson and John Bowden eds. (Philadelphia: The Westminster Press, 1983), pp. 191–2.

consummation of the purposes of God in the resurrection, the return of Christ, final judgment and everlasting life. [3]

Given not uncommon misunderstandings of Barth's view of revelation, citation from his writings will be extensive, especially so from his mature work in volume IV/3/1 of his *Church Dogmatics* (hereafter referred to as *CD*, IV/3/1) in which the doctrine of revelation is interpreted in terms of the *munus triplex*, and specifically the *prophetic* office of Christ.[4] In this exposition, Barth clarifies earlier ambiguities, speaks to his critics, and introduces some new themes. Thus revelation has to do with:

> Jesus Christ Himself in His prophetic office and work, as He confesses and makes Himself known as the humiliated Son of God and the exalted Son of Man, and therefore as the Mediator between God and man, and therefore as the One who restores fellowship between them and accomplishes the justification and sanctification of man.[5]

God's reconciling deed in Christ—the priestly work of humiliation—receiving the judgment on sin, and the royal work of exaltation, victorious over death and giving life to humanity—must be *made known* to the world. In Christ, "reconciliation is also revelation."[6]

1. Objective and subjective revelation

Barth is known for his "dynamic" understanding of revelation, the occurrence of the Word as that Word reaches the hearer.

> For me the Word of God is a *happening*, not a thing. Therefore the Bible must *become* the Word of God, and it does so through the work of the Spirit.[7]

---

[3] See "Narrative Theology in Evangelical Perspective," in Gabriel Fackre, *Ecumenical Faith in Evangelical Perspective* (Grand Rapids, MI: Eerdmans, 1993), pp. 123–46 and *passim.*

[4] The balance of this chapter includes a version of material from the author's section "Karl Barth" in *The Doctrine of Revelation: A Narrative Interpretation* (Grand Rapids, MI: Eerdmans, 1997).

[5] Barth, *CD*, IV/3/l, p. l80.

[6] Barth, *CD*, IV/3/l, p. 165.

[7] Barth in John Godsey (recorder and ed.), *Karl Barth's Table Talk* (Richmond: John Knox Press, n.d.), p. 26.

The *address* to us, received through grace by us, is a critical accent in Barth's teaching, bound up with a wariness of all attempts to deny the freedom of God. But this emphasis does not stand alone: the fundamental *fact* of revelation is the first-century *act* of revelation in the life, death, resurrection and ascension of Jesus Christ. Revelation does not depend on its subjective reception. God's reconciling deed in Jesus Christ is, as such, revelation.

> For as it takes place in its perfection, and with no need of supplement, it also expresses, discloses, mediates and reveals itself . . . It displays itself. It proclaims itself . . . Its donation sovereignly precedes all reception on our part . . . it is not dark and dumb but perspicuous and vocal, that it may and will therefore be received, but is independent of our actual reception . . . reconciliation is indeed revelation . . . In itself it is the basis of knowledge even when it does not correspond to the knowledge of a single man . . . It is out-going and self-communicative, even before it attains its goal in the creaturely world . . . This objectivity of even its revelatory character must be emphasized so expressly because misunderstanding can so easily creep in . . . it is necessary to hold fast not only to the objectivity of reconciliation . . . but also to the objectivity of its character as revelation, to the *a priori* nature of its light in the face of all human illumination and knowledge.[8]

The objectivity of revelation, therefore, is Jesus of Nazareth teaching, preaching, healing, serving, suffering, dying, rising, ascending—the Word of God incarnate.

Barth's stress on the objectivity of revelation is yet another way of underscoring the "scandal of particularity" so central to his theology. He does not want revelation to be confused with anything else, in this case with our *reception* of it, even with the enlightening work of the Holy Spirit that enables us to hear the Word. Here, and here only, in the enfleshed Word, the free God discloses who God is. Neither the freedom *from* nor the freedom *for* us can be taken in tow by our subjectivity, as is done by the modernism that traces all things to our general experience, or the pietism that grounds faith in our religious experience:

> Jesus Christ is *the* light of life. To underline the "the" is to say that He is the one and only light of life. Positively, this means that He is the light of life in all its fullness, in perfect adequacy; and negatively,

---

8 Barth, *CD*, IV/3/1, p. 180.

> it means that there is no other light of life . . . outside and alongside the light which He is. Everything which we have to say concerning the prophetic office of Jesus Christ rests on this emphasis . . . "Jesus Christ as attested to us in Holy Scripture is the one Word of God whom we must hear."[9]

The repetition of this note in IV/3/1 is a response to those who appropriated his earlier stress on the *moment* of the Word's action in existentialist terms,[10] and to those who accused him of a new form of "liberal" subjectivism.[11] These criticisms do have a point to make, but their validity does not lie in the association of Barth with experiential reductionisms. The "objectivity" of the Word made flesh in Jesus Christ, therefore, constitutes the primal meaning of the prophetic office of Christ. Here is the heart of Barth's theology of revelation, Jesus Christ, the "one and only Word of God, spoken as preceding "all reception on our part," reconciliation *as* revelation.

1.1 *The trajectory of revelation*

Barth's christological concentration cannot be separated from the entire sweep of the drama of God's deeds. He tracks the revelatory reconciliation in the historical event of Jesus Christ back to its origins in the inner-trinitarian Life, and then follows the course of the electing Love there present forward into the covenant with creation, the call and expectation of Israel, to the Word enfleshed—and from there again to the witness of Scripture, the recollective

---

9 Barth, *CD*, IV/3/1, p. 6.

10 As in *CD*, I/2, p. 518. While he sought to correct in IV/3/1 the subjectivist impressions left by his earlier emphasis on the appropriative act, he did not describe the "happening" and "becoming" of the Word stressed earlier in terms of the work of the Holy Spirit. Responding to a student's question as to why the Holy Spirit does not appear more explicitly in the section on the "revealed Word" in *CD*, I/2, Barth says that in 1932: "I wanted to place a strong emphasis on the objective side of revelation: Jesus Christ. If I had made much of the Holy Spirit, I am afraid I would have led back to subjectivism, which I wanted to overcome" (Barth in Godsey, *Table Talk*, p. 27). The "objectivity" thought to be to the fore, however, was so shaped by actualist assumptions that it was open to the charge of subjectivism that had to be repudiated in the volume under consideration.

11 So Carl Henry, *God, Revelation and Authority* vol. IV (Waco, TX: Word, 1979), pp. 196, 200, 270–1 and *passim*.

life and tradition of the church and finally to the full light of eschatological radiance.

1.2 *Triune Self-revelation*

Barth's description of the Trinity as "Revealer, Revelation, Revealedness" indicates the grounding of the doctrine of revelation in the divine Life Together, as in his initial treatment of revelation in the discussion of the Trinity in *CD*, I/1.[12] The act of Self-disclosure in Jesus Christ is an expression of the character of God as intrinsically self-disclosive. What God does in the missions of the economic Trinity is who God is in the immanent Trinity. While there are reaches of mystery in the divine being, God does not tell us "one thing in history while being something else in eternity. His secondary objectivity is fully true, for it has its correspondence and basis in His primary objectivity."[13]

God *as* the Word incarnate *is* God the self-revealing One. Whether Barth is consistent in the application of this assertion of the primal self-disclosivity (found in his fertile idea of the social nature of the *imago Dei* as well as here) is a matter of debate. Critics find modalistic tendencies in his thought which would preclude the revelatory coinherence of the Persons suggested by the "primary objectivity" of revelation in the inner-trinitarian Being.[14] We shall return to this question.

1.3 *Little lights and free communications*

Barth categorically rejects "natural theology" or whatever he considers its equivalent, such as the Reformed tradition's "general revelation," or Emil Brunner's "point of contact." Jesus Christ alone is "Revelation." Yet in *CD*, IV/3/l, a line of argument appears that has prompted some to think that Barth has altered his views. The language employed is surprising, as in his allusion to "other

---

[12] Barth, *CD*, I/1, pp. 339–560.

[13] Barth, *CD*, II/l, p. 16. On our knowledge of God as grounded in God's self-knowledge, see George Hunsinger, *How to Read Karl Barth: The Shape of His Theology* (New York: Oxford University Press, 1991), pp. 76–9.

[14] As in Jürgen Moltmann, *The Trinity and the Kingdom: The Doctrine of God*, Margaret Kohl tr. (San Francisco, CA: Harper & Row, 1981), pp. 139–44.

revelations,"[15] However, his argument is subtle and requires careful scrutiny. There is only one true Light, defining Revelation and sole Prophet, Jesus Christ. Yet:

> we recognize that the fact that Jesus Christ is the one Word of God does not mean that in the Bible, the Church and the world there are not other words which are quite notable in their way, other lights which are quite clear and other revelations which are quite real.[16]

With specific reference to "world":

> Nor is it impossible that words of this kind should be uttered outside this circle [of Bible and Church] if the whole world of creation and history is the realm of the lordship of God at whose right hand Jesus Christ is seated, so that He exercises authority in this outer as well as the inner sphere and is free to attest Himself or to cause Himself to be attested in it.[17]

Barth describes these "little lights" in the Night as "free communications" of the sovereign God in the events of human history, and a luminosity in the constancies of nature as well, including the natural condition of human beings. Such illuminations do not give the true Light found alone in Jesus Christ. Further, all such flickerings must be measured by that final radiance. But these truths, "revelations," are "worth something" and we must "take note of them."[18] Modest indicators are to be seen in nature:

> The creaturely world . . . the cosmos, the nature given to man in his sphere and the nature of this sphere, has also as such its own lights and truths and therefore its own speech and words. That the world was and is and will be, and what and how it was and is and will be, thanks to the faithfulness of its Creator, is declared and attested by it and may thus be perceived and heard and considered . . . Like its persistence, its self-witness and lights are not extinguished by the corruption of the relationship between God and man . . . However corrupt man may be, they illumine him, and . . . he does not cease to see and understand them.[19]

---

15 Barth, *CD*, IV/3/1, p. 97.
16 Barth, *CD*, IV/3/1, p. 97.
17 Barth, *CD*, IV/3/1, p. 97.
18 Barth, *CD*, IV/3/1, p. 155.
19 Barth, *CD*, IV/3/1, p. 139.

Barth calls these the "constants" in nature that sustain and order creation and prevent it from falling into chaos. They include the "natural laws" accessible to scientific inquiry, and also the patterns of human behavior discerned by the sociologist and psychologist, the regularities of history and the rhythms and beauties of life attested by the arts as well as by the sciences. These patterns have been adduced by others as evidence for a "natural theology". Not so for Barth:

> They do not strike him from the eternity of God, but merely as self-attestations of His creation, as part of its dialogue with itself. Nor do they strike him personally, as directed to him, but only with a universal application and in relation to qualities which he shares with men of every time and place. They enlighten him concerning himself, i.e. his possibilities, situation and environment. But they do not illumine his heart and therefore himself . . . He lives with them, but he might live equally well without them. For he does not live by them; neither by the rhythm of the creaturely world, however powerful; nor by the revelations of its regularity and freedom and certainly not by the declaration of its immanent mystery. Of what avail is it to man to know these things? He has certainly to take note of them . . . [But] they carry neither real threat nor real promise. For they speak neither of real judgment and loss nor of real grace and salvation.[20]

"Revelation" in its true sense is of a different order. There are yet other lights in the world around us, "parables of the kingdom," not the "constants" of nature but the unforeseen "free communications" of God that take place in human history. In this "wider field" we behold "the capacity of Jesus Christ to raise up of the stones, children of Abraham."[21] These

> world-occurrences . . . illumine, accentuate or explain the biblical witness in a particular time and situation, thus confirming it in the deepest sense by helping to make it sure and concretely evident and certain.[22]

Thus "Jesus Christ can raise up extraordinary witnesses to speak true words of this very different order."[23] These witnesses can

---

20 Barth, *CD*, IV/3/1, pp. 155, 156.
21 Barth, *CD*, IV/3/1, p. 118.
22 Barth, *CD*, IV/3/1, p.115.
23 Barth, *CD*, IV/3/1, p. 118.

take the form of movements that are actively hostile to Christ, for "even from the mouth of Balaam the well-known voice of the good Shepherd may sound."[24] Nothing is forbidden to God as an instrument of the divine Word.

Barth tells us he is not going to give any examples for fear of violating the event-character of free communications. However, he comes close to it now and then in descriptions that sound like the graced encounters with human "limit-situations" of Karl Rahner:

> We may think of the lack of fear in face of death which Christians to their shame often display far less readily than non-Christians near and far. We may think of the warm readiness to understand and forgive which is not so frequently encountered in the Evangelical world just because it has too good a knowledge of good and evil and in spite of its acknowledgment that justification is by faith alone. Especially we may think of a humanity which does not ask or weigh too long with whom we are dealing in others, but in which we find a simple solidarity with them and unreservedly take up their case. Are not all these phenomena which with striking frequency are found *extra muros ecclesiae* in circles where little or nothing is obviously known of from these phenomena? However alien their forms, is not their language that of true words, the language of "parables of the kingdom of heaven"?[25]

While openness to these parables of the kingdom is urged by Barth, they cannot be conjoined to Christ, as a second principle, and certainly not taken as the interpretive key to the gospel:

> As the One Word of God, He can bring Himself into the closest conjunction with such words . . . [Yet] there is no legitimate place for projects in the planning and devising of which Jesus Christ can be given a particular niche in co-ordination with those of other events, powers, forms and truths . . . As the one Word of God He wholly escapes every conceivable synthesis envisaged in them . . . [26]

In a given time and place, candidacy for the status of "free communication" must be rigorously scrutinized in the light of the one Word of God, Jesus Christ.

---

24 Barth, *CD*, IV/3/1, p. 119.
25 Barth, *CD*, IV/3/1, p. 125.
26 Barth, *CD*, IV/3/1, pp. 101, 102.

2. Scripture as primary witness to the light

How do we know this one true light, Jesus Christ? In Barth's initial dogmatic exposition of the "three forms of the Word of God" (I/1), an extended answer is given to the warrant for the first form of the Word, the witness of Scripture. He summarizes it in these words:

> The Bible constitutes itself as canon. It is the canon because it has imposed itself as such on the Church and invariably does so. The Church's recollection of God's past revelation has computed that the Bible is her object, because as a matter of fact, this and no other object is the promise of future divine revelation . . . The Bible is the canon just because it is so. But it is so because it imposes itself as such . . . The prophetic and apostolic Word is the word, the witness, the proclamation and the preaching of Jesus Christ . . . Holy Scripture is the word of men who longed for, expected, hoped for this "Immanuel," and finally saw, heard, and handled it in Jesus Christ. It declares, attests, and proclaims it . . . Thus it is in virtue of this its content that Scripture imposes itself.[27]

The Scripture is the prophetic-apostolic testimony to Jesus Christ, promised and recollected. And thus the Bible is the concrete medium by which the church recalls God's revelation in the past, is called to expect revelation in the future, and is thereby challenged, empowered and guided to proclaim it now.[28] In these earlier formulations, Barth speaks with less inhibition about "future revelation" as the actualization of the Word in its reception by the believer or the believing community through the power of the Holy Spirit (interestingly, not the "future" as the eschatological disclosure at the End). Thus we hear of the Bible "becoming" God's Word:

> It takes place as an event, when and where the word of the Bible becomes God's Word . . . when and where John's finger points not in vain but really pointedly, and when and where by means of its word we also succeed in seeing and hearing what he saw and heard.[29]

---

27 Barth, *CD*, I/1, pp. 120–21.

28 Barth, *CD*, I/1, pp. 124–5.

29 Barth, *CD*, I/1, p. 127. "John's finger" is Barth's frequent reference to John the Baptist's pointing to Christ in a famous Grünewald altarpiece.

This remains a critical aspect of Barth's doctrine of revelation in *CD*, IV/3/1, the Word spoken to you and me in the here and now. As noted, because of the misunderstanding of this as yet one more subtle captivity of the free Word to religious experience (reception), he subsequently stresses the revelatory self-sufficiency of the historic event of Jesus Christ. The Word that comes to us *now* comes through Scripture, the "'Word written." Yet, for all its unique role in the revelatory process, Scripture must not be confused with the incarnate Word.

> The Bible . . . is not itself and in itself God's past revelation . . . the biblical witnesses point beyond themselves . . . We do the Bible a poor honor, and one unwelcome to itself, when we directly identify it with this something else, with revelation itself.[30]

The words of Scripture are human words, subject to error in all about which they speak, theology and ethics as well as science and history. Its words *are* trustworthy when they witness to Jesus Christ, expected and recollected. The stress upon the humanity of Scripture is underscored in *CD*, IV/3/1 when the Bible is placed on a continuum with other human witnesses. The one Word of God, the Prophet, Jesus Christ, cannot be confused with the words of any human witness. But,

> As the one Word of God, He can bring Himself into the closest conjunction with such words . . . He has actually entered into a union of this kind with the biblical prophets and apostles, and it is the prayer and promise in and by which His community exists that He will not refuse but be willing to enter into a similar union with it. Nor can any prevent Him entering into such a union with men outside of the sphere of the Bible and the Church, and with the words of these men.[31]

2.1 The church

Basic to Barth's understanding of revelation is "the fundamental distinction of the written word of the prophets and apostles above all other human words spoken later in the church and needing to be spoken today."[32] Yet the freedom of God and the promises of God are such that we have a right to hope for "His free revelation of

---

30 Barth, *CD*, I/1, p. 126.
31 Barth, *CD*, IV/3/1, p. 101.
32 Barth, *CD*, I/1, p. 115.

grace" in the Christian community as well, albeit always expository of and accountable to "the written Word of God." Indeed, the change of the name of Barth's opus from *Christian Dogmatics* to *Church Dogmatics* witnesses to the role of the church and its tradition in his theology, and its implied revelatory underpinning. Indeed, in an earlier formulation, Barth speaks of the church as the third term in the "threefold form of the Word": the Word revealed, the Word written and the Word proclaimed. How does the church enter the revelatory trajectory?

> The Holy Spirit is simply but most distinctly the renewing power of the breath of His mouth which as such is the breath of the sovereign God and victorious truth. It is the power in which His Word, God's Word, the Word of truth, is not only in Him, but when and where He wills goes out also to us men . . . thus establishing communication between Him and us and initiating a history of mutual giving and receiving.[33]

The life of the church is the locus of this giving and receiving. Here the Word has "happened," and ever again will happen. Evidence of it includes sedimentations in "the dogmas and confessions of the Church." Respect for these deposits is a matter of "honoring our fathers and mothers." Yet the Word lives among the sisters and brothers as well. To the *present* as well as the past church comes the promise of the Spirit. In both cases, Barth stresses the role of the whole people of God, and thus the epistemological ministry of the laity, as the proper locus for hearing the Word, as against a special magisterium. But caution is in order in claiming too much for the specifics of these ecclesial happenings. As with the Bible and with the world at large, the freedom of God must be respected:

> All well-meant but capricious conjunction of Jesus Christ with something else, whether it be Mary, the Church, the fate worked out in general and individual history, or a presupposed human self-understanding, etc., all these imply a control over Him to which none of us has any right.[34]

The promise lies in the *hope for* the Word, not in confidence about its continuing presence: "Is not perhaps the surest test of genuine Christianity and Church life whether the men united in it exist wholly in this expectation and therefore not at all in the supposed

---

33 Barth, *CD*, IV/3/1, p. 42.
34 Barth, *CD*, IV/3/1, p. 101.

present possession and glorious presence of their Lord?"[35] This wariness about any claims to the "present possession" of Christ recurs at many points in Barth's thought, and has its consequences all along the trajectory we are tracing. For now, we underscore the determination to assert that all human attestations to the Word of the Prophet of God are *broken* human witnesses to truth. In Scripture there is surety of bonding, in the church there is the hope and prayer for the Spirit's illumination of the community of faith, and in the world there is the possibility of free communications with no locale to be anticipated or, in principle, excluded.

2.2 *Eschatological radiance*

The finality and clarity of God's self-disclosure awaits us at the End. What has been given to us in the darkness of human history—the Word of God as communicated through biblical, ecclesial and secular media—comes to full light at the return of Christ,

> His total presence, action and revelation which will conclude and fulfill time and history, all times and all histories . . . The theme of Christian hope, to the extent that it is not yet fulfilled nor cannot be so long as time endures, is the revelation of the fact that neither formally nor materially, theoretically nor practically, can the one Word of God be transcended . . . The inclusion of the eschatological element, then, does not imply any restriction, but the final expansion and deepening, of our statement that Jesus Christ is the one Word of God.[36]

Barth expresses the same confidence that we shall ultimately see "face to face" in a tribute to friends and colleagues who have died. Even now, there "shines on them the eternal light in which we, *adhuc peregrinantes*, shall some day need no more dogmatics."[37]

3. Affirmations

Karl Barth's understanding of the trajectory of revelation is kindred to an evangelical narrative view of the doctrine. His "christological concentration" secures the center of that story, and no chapter is lost from view.

---

[35] Barth, *CD*, IV/3/1, p. 322.
[36] Barth, *CD*, IV/3/1, p. 301.
[37] Barth, *CD*, IV/3/1, p. xiii.

As noted, a line can be traced from the inner-trinitarian life of the triune God as Revealer through a disclosive covenant with creation, through a radical fall, then the grace of "free communications" in the wider world construable as kindred to a common grace at work in the universal covenant with Noah, to the promissory covenant with Israel, to the centerpoint of disclosure in Jesus Christ, and from there to an authoritative revelatory Scripture "engendered" by the Spirit, a community and believer illumined by the same Spirit, to an end when the light of God is "all in all." We review Barth's reading of the "overarching story" with emphases proportionate to evangelical affirmations.

3.1 Jesus Christ

The twenty-first-century church, too ready to take up the proposals and premises of its surrounding culture, has a Word it needs to hear. In his own imagery, the tower rope which Barth stumbled upon rang a bell too long silent. It calls the church into a sanctuary with one center: "Jesus Christ . . . is the one Word of God whom we have to hear" (Barmen Declaration). The struggle against a demonic blood-and-soil philosophy made for a sharper hearing of that one Word. But culture has its softer voices today, no less seductive, that make listening for that bell no less necessary.[38]

In narrative terms, Barth will never let us forget the center of the story. In the historical event of Jesus Christ, an utterly new deed is done, and a defining Word spoken. Life overcomes death and an ultimate light pierces a penultimate night. "Revelation" *is* Jesus Christ and brooks no contenders. His earlier language was sometimes interpreted as a fusion of this historical event with the moment of its reception, the ever-new "becoming" of the Word of God. But his later writing seeks to avoid misunderstandings that bind the Word to the appropriation process:

---

[38] See David Wells, *No Place for Truth* (Grand Rapids, MI: Eerdmans, 1993) for an evangelical critique of evangelicalism's captivity to the narcissisms of the day, one that echoes Barth's indictment of culture-Protestantism. The writings of Donald G. Bloesch reflect the same themes in, and debt to, Karl Barth. See especially *Jesus is Victor: Karl Barth's Doctrine of Salvation* (Nashville: Abingdon Press, 1976) and throughout his seven-volume *Christian Foundations* series (Downers Grove, IL: InterVarsity Press, 1992–2004).

> There is human knowledge, and a theology of reconciliation, because reconciliation in itself is not only real but true, proving itself true in the enlightening work of the Holy Spirit, but first true as well as real in itself, as disclosure, declaration and impartation. This is the basis of certainty and clarity when it is a matter of the knowledge of Jesus Christ and His work through the work of the Holy Spirit.[39]

No understanding of Christ is possible without the trajectory of promise constituted by the special covenant with the Jewish people and the testimony to it in the Old Testament. In Israel, the first particular deed of God is done and particular disclosure given, although note must be taken that Barth's promise-fulfillment framework does not do full justice to the anti-supersessionist import of Romans 9–11.[40]

3.2 The Bible

"Jesus Christ, *attested by Holy Scripture*, is the one Word of God whom we have to hear" (Barmen Declaration). The One we hear, trust and obey is not the creature of our pious feelings, our speculative genius, our doctrinal deposits. Scripture is the sole trustworthy *source* of our knowledge of the Word of God, Jesus Christ; *sola Scriptura*, so understood, is inextricable from *solus Christus*. Christ finds us when we enter into "the strange new world of the Bible." He does so because "revelation engenders the Scripture which attests it."[41] Barth practices what he teaches by his detailed and profound theological exegesis, letting Scripture speak its own Word. So stipulated and practiced, Barth appears to reflect characteristic evangelical emphases on the authority of Scripture.

Further, the way that Barth relates Scripture and Christ coheres with an important stream of evangelical hermeneutics.[42] For Barth, Scripture is understood when it is interpreted by Christ. "Then

---

39 Barth, *CD*, IV/3/1, p. 11.

40 As argued in Fackre. "The Place of Israel in Christian Faith," *Ecumenical Faith*, pp. 152, 162–7. See also the evaluation of Katherine Sonderegger, *That Jesus Christ Was Born a Jew: Karl Barth's 'Doctrine of Israel'* (State College: Pennsylvania State University Press, 1992).

41 Barth, *CD*, I/1, p. 129.

42 See "Christocentric Infallibility" in Gabriel Fackre, *The Christian Story*, vol. 2, *Authority: Scripture in the Church for the World* (Grand Rapids, MI: Eerdmans, 1987), pp. 72–3.

beginning with Moses and the prophets, he interpreted to them all things about himself in all the Scriptures" (Luke 24:27). As with Luther, Scripture speaks its Word when it "preaches Christ." Barth's christological reading of the Bible is rich and varied.[43] Here we refer to the hermeneutical significance of Jesus Christ as the interpretive framework for understanding whatever appears in the canon and as the criterion for determining what is and is not the "pattern of teaching" for which Scripture is given to the church. In the first instance, the christological chapter itself comes into sharp profile, the Old Testament expectation and the New Testament recollection giving content to "Jesus Christ." In the second instance, the substance of Scripture, the Grand Narrative, is brought into bold relief by the deed done by God in Christ. To see Christ as the *Center* is to say that Scripture is purposed for the Story, one that leads to and away from this turning point.

3.3 The Church

The Christian community has been promised the Holy Spirit, the "renewing power of the breath of his mouth," which "where and when He wills goes out also to us."[44] As the locus of the "Word proclaimed," the church meets the Word incarnate through preaching and teaching based on the Word written, ever and again, by the gift of the Spirit. The historical moment of "illumination" in the narrative of revelation, in the ecclesial form to be discussed, is here given its due.

Barth's accent on the "becoming" of the Word is personal as well as corporate. The Word proclaimed is *pro me* as well as *pro nobis*. Within the Christian community, the believer, "where and when He wills it," is addressed and so receives the Word by the inner testimony of the Holy Spirit. This is the event of "divine-human encounter" prominent in the earlier writings of Barth, and characteristic of "neo-orthodox" views of revelation that juxtaposed "personal" to "propositional" revelation.[45] In evangelical narrative terms, the "happening" of the Word "for me" is an aspect of the soteriological chapter of revelation.

---

[43] The writer traces seven strands in *The Christian Story*, pp. 79–82.

[44] Barth, *CD*, IV/3/1, p. 421.

[45] See, for example, Emil Brunner, *Revelation and Reason*, Olive Wyon tr. (Philadelphia: Westminster Press, 1946); and John Baillie, *The Idea of Revelation* (New York: Columbia University Press, 1956).

For Barth, only in the end is the divine radiance total and God "all in all." The light given "in part," and on occasion—in Scripture and to the church corporate and personal—now shines fully and unremittingly. Here is the eschatological chapter of the evangelical narrative with the gift of illumination given as totally as it can be for eschatological eyes.

3.4 The World

In *CD*, IV/3/1, "the Bible, the church and the world" are linked as loci of "other words . . . other lights."[46] Against the long background of his battles against natural theology, Barth is yet able to speak in his later years of "free communications" and "parables of the kingdom" possible in a history outside of *Heilsgeschichte*. And he finds meaningful patterns in nature that make and keep life human and the cosmos ordered. While the latter do not have the parabolic significance of the former, both can be understood as related to the promises of the Noachic covenant and thus to yet another chapter in the evangelical narrative of revelation, albeit never understood by its own lights, always to be interpreted *christologically*. As the richness of Barth's thought unfolds, the kinship with evangelical narrative emerges.

4. Problems

Karl Barth taught a generation to be wary of theologies that take deity captive in forms of human manufacture. God is sovereign. We learn what the freedom of God means in the one place God has chosen to be free for us and among us, Jesus Christ, as this Word is given to us in the witness of Scripture. The problems with Barth's epistemology arise when he departs from his own biblical standard for understanding that freedom of God for and among us. This might be described as the influence of an "actualism" with philosophical roots in existentialist philosophy.[47] Yet actualism has

---

46 Barth, *CD*, IV/3/1, p. 97, and the section as a whole, pp. 96–103.

47 For a discussion of the role of actualism in Barth's theology—its understandings and misunderstandings—see Hunsinger, *How to Read Karl Barth*, pp. 30–2, 107–9, 112–14, 148–9, 226–8, 230–1, 271–2; Dietrich Bonhoeffer, *Act and Being*, Bernard Noble trs, Ernst Wolf intro. (New York: Harper & Brothers, 1961), pp. 78–91; Hugh Ross Mackintosh,

more to do with Barth's ecclesial tradition than his philosophical borrowings. While determinedly challenging the control of the Word by "principles" of our own making, two such refrains from the Reformed tradition have a significant impact on Barth's doctrine of revelation: the *divine sovereignty* and the *internal testimony of the Holy Spirit*. While these accents in both Reformed theology and piety are critical components of any full-orbed understanding of Christian faith and life, when functioning as arbitrating *principles* that exclude other critical accents, however, they claim more than their due.

The entrance of Reformed accents into the doctrine of revelation is related to Barth's determination to protect the decisiveness of this chapter of the story. Only here in Jesus Christ is God free *for* us and among us. Sovereignty is earthed in Christ alone. Any claim to continuity of the divine presence other than the incarnate Word imperils that particularity.

As noted in the previous section, "Bible," "church" and "world" take their place in the revelatory narrative. They do so for Barth as epistemic "articles of hope," rather than "articles of faith."[48] While the promise is there of a Word to be spoken, the actual address "happens" only "when and where He wills" it to be so, by the act of divine freedom working through the internal testimony of the Holy Spirit. The occasionalist nature of this assertion has to do with the confluence of the protective teachings of divine sovereignty and the internal testimony of the Spirit. While the high God is free to stoop low anywhere, the divine freedom is protected for no assurance can be given that the "media"—Bible, church, world—are in their respective ways always and everywhere bearers of the knowledge of God. The outworking of these principles can be seen in each of the three arenas taken up by Barth in *CD*, IV/3/1.

In epistemology as well as in ecclesiology, sacramentology etc., there can be no undialectical insistence on "the continuation of the

---

Types of Modern Theology: Schleiermacher to Barth (London: Nisbet and Co., 1937), pp. 314–16; Herbert Hartwell, *The Theology of Karl Barth: An Introduction* (Philadelphia: Westminster Press, 1964), pp. 32–7, 143–7.

48 The distinction between "hope" and "faith" is drawn from Barth's views on universalism. *Apokatastasis* is a matter of hope not doctrine because the ultimate future is in the hands of the sovereign God. Hope for universal salvation is warranted by the saving deed done for all by God in Christ, but with the eschatological reserve appropriate to the divine freedom, so articulated in *CD*, IV/3/1, pp. 477–8.

Incarnation." The once-happenedness of Jesus Christ—perfect in deity and in humanity—is not replicated in the church. However, Barth goes on to interpret this discontinuity as requiring the denial of the "present possession of the glorious presence" of Jesus Christ. At work here is the actualist premise that continues to mark Barth's thought, even after his repudiation of Kierkegaardian subjectivity and later clarifications about the objectivity of revelation in the enfleshment of the Word. Its persistence has to do with the exercise of a veto over the witness of both Scripture and the classic Christian tradition. While it is Christ who "possesses" the church, not the other way around, a sign of that ownership is the "glorious presence" of Christ in the midst of his people: "For where two or three are gathered in my name, I am there among them" (Matt. 18:20).

Christ's *promise* of solidarity calls into question undialectical views of divine sovereignty that fail to honor the Yes as well as the No of continuity between Christ and the church. The eucharistic controversies in which memorialist conceptions that distance Christ from the Lord's Supper are rightly challenged by a doctrine of the real presence are a case in point.[49] In the same vein, a doctrine of revelation in which the promise of uninterrupted *epistemic* presence is denied in order to protect the divine sovereignty must be challenged. The dialectic of presence and absence is at work in epistemology as it is in ecclesiology. Barth is right in what he affirms but wrong in what he denies.

Dietrich Bonhoeffer early identified Barth's "act" view of revelation and its consequences, connecting it to traditions that stressed the divine transcendence and the "contingency of revelation" (Duns Scotus, William of Occam), viewing such with characteristically Lutheran eyes:

> Revelation is interpreted purely in terms of act. It is something happening to receptive man, but within God's freedom to suspend the connection at any moment. How could it be otherwise, since it is "God's pleasure, majestically free" (Barth) which initiates the connection and remains its master . . . However this attempt is bound to come to grief against the

[49] The "evangelical catholic" Mercersburg theology which has influenced the writer seeks to maintain a broken but real continuity between Christ and the church and thus the real presence of Christ in the eucharist. See Charles Yrigoyen, Jr. and George H. Bricker eds., *Catholic and Reformed: Selected Theological Writings of John Williamson Nevin* (Pittsburgh: The Pickwick Press, 1978).

> fact that (according to Barth) no "historical moment" is *capax infiniti* so that the empirical action of man—"belief," "obedience"—becomes at most a pointer to God's activity and can never, in its historicality, be faith and obedience themselves . . . [For Bonhoeffer] God is *there*, which is to say, "haveable," graspable in his Word within the Church.[50]

The promise of the divine "haveability"—in this case the balancing Lutheran accent on the *finitum capax infiniti*, or divine solidarity with us—cannot be ignored by the Reformed *finitum non capax infiniti*, or divine sovereignty over us, deployed as a reductionist controlling "principle."[51] The effects of the latter show up in three areas.

4.1 The Bible

Barth bases the authority of the Bible on its "direct witness" to the Word of God, Jesus Christ. Scripture is the megaphone through which the free Word of the majestic God is spoken when and where so willed. The warrant for Scripture's authority is relocated from traditional notions that imply "possession" to occasions actualized in the freedom of God, reflecting the conjunction of the sovereignty-internal testimony partnership. The mysterious unpredictability of conviction and conversion by the internal work of the Holy Spirit is relocated from its place in the evangelical tradition and in Reformed formulations of *attesting* personally truth established on other grounds, to *testing*—that is, *establishing*—the truth of Scripture itself. Scripture is revelatory because it is revealing. Its authority rests on the dead letter coming to be, as God wills it to be, the "living" Word of God.

The motif of sovereignty functions here rightly to challenge the domestication of deity in and by a sacred book. The target that it strikes is a doctrine of verbal inspiration/inerrancy in which the perfections of the divine knowledge are attributed to the biblical "autographs."[52] Barth brings his teaching of divine sovereignty to

---

[50] Bonhoeffer, *Act and Being*, pp. 81, 83, 90–1.

[51] At work in these judgments is the learning of "mutual affirmation and mutual admonition" that emerged in the 1997 North American Lutheran–Reformed Formula of Agreement. For its exposition see Gabriel Fackre and Michael Root, *Affirmations and Admonitions* (Grand Rapids, MI: Eerdmans, 1998).

[52] For a discussion of the various views of inerrancy, see Fackre, *The Christian Story*, vol. 2, pp. 63–9.

bear to challenge this fusion. Further, the Holy Spirit does attest the truth of Scripture in mysterious and unpredictable ways, *convicting* and *convincing* by an internal testimony. Where the grace of "inspiration" is received by the grace of "illumination," Scripture's latent truth becomes patent to the believer and the believing community.

While necessary to protect Scripture from bibliolatry, the accent on divine sovereignty-cum-internal-testimony is not a sufficient warrant for the authority of Scripture. Standing alone, it precludes the promise of a trustworthy epistemic presence "in, with and under" the Word written. Barth's occasionalist understanding of biblical authority, ironically, opens him to the same charge which he mounts against the anthropocentrism of theology since Schleiermacher. Thus Carl Henry charges Barth with allowing "subjectivity" to determine the status of Scripture:

> Karl Barth's interpretation of the Bible as an instrumentality through which God sporadically communicates his paradoxical Word . . . redefines the doctrine of inspiration dynamically and connects it with the psyche of the believer.[53]

While this criticism does not do justice to Barth's assertion of the objectivity of revelation in Jesus Christ as witnessed to by Scripture, it succeeds in relating Barth's actualism to the subjectivity associated with the Reformed doctrine of the internal testimony of the Holy Spirit (and also the lingering early influence of Kierkegaard, from whom Barth later declared himself free).[54] Henry witnesses importantly here to an evangelical doctrine of revelation by drawing

---

53 Henry, *God*, p. 148.

54 Kierkegaard, rightly resisting the volatilizing of "the individual" in Hegelian speculation, Danish Christendom and the bourgeois society of the nineteenth century, formulated his protest in the starkest of terms: "Truth is subjectivity . . . Faith is the objective uncertainty, with the repulsion of the absurd, held fast in the passion of inwardness, which in the relation of inwardness intensified to its highest . . . Christianity is spirit; spirit is inwardness; inwardness is subjectivity; subjectivity is essentially passion, and at its maximum an infinite, personally interested passion for one's own happiness." Sören Kierkegaard, *Concluding Unscientific Postscript To Philosophical Fragments*, Howard V. Hong and Edna H. Hong, vol. I ed. and tr. with notes (Princeton: Princeton University Press, 1992), pp. 189, 611, 33 (in order of importance) and *passim*.

attention to the needed chapter on "inspiration," one that has not been redefined in actualist terms.

Geoffrey Bromiley, Barth's English translator, also has an evangelical ear for the absence of a defensible doctrine of biblical authority. In discussing "the problem areas" in Barth's thought, he says:

> One must also wonder whether it is not a mistake to stress the present ministry of the Spirit in the use of Scripture at the expense of the once-for-all work of the Spirit in its authorship. Barth would later resist a similar imbalance in the matter of reconciliation. Is there not also a need for rethinking in the matter of inspiration?[55]

The historic and evangelical doctrine of the inspiration of Scripture is an effort to express the divine solidarity with us vis-à-vis this medium of revelation. The Holy Spirit graced the *original* prophetic-apostolic testimony in such a manner as to render reliable its telling of the biblical story. As such, the authority of the Bible is warranted, not by a pneumatological actualism, but by a trustworthy work of the Holy Spirit in its authorial communities. This means a dialectical relation between Incarnation and inspiration, rejecting both the too-simple continuities of standard-brand theories of inerrancy, and the too-simple discontinuities of occasionalism. As has often been pointed out, Karl Barth's practice is better than his theory, for his extensive and intensive exegesis of Scripture suggests a deeper and more sustained warrant for biblical authority.[56]

4.2 The Church

As with the Bible, so with the church, for Barth the knowledge of God is given only as by divine initiative. The third form of the Word, the "Word proclaimed" in the church, "always and will always be—man's word."[57] But it can "become" something else when God so chooses.

---

[55] Geoffrey Bromiley, *Historical Theology: An Introduction* (Grand Rapids, MI: Eerdmans, 1978), pp. 420–1.

[56] For an effort to retain "the evangelical insistence on the proper relation of human to divine" in Scripture while taking into account Barth's stress on "the decision and action of the Holy Spirit," see Bolich, *Karl Barth*, pp. 195–207.

[57] Barth, *CD*, I/1, p. 79.

> It is, namely, when and where God pleases. God's own Word. Upon the promise of this divine good pleasure it makes its venture in obedience. Upon that depends the claim and the expectation.[58]

Revelation as "illumination" is promised as a gift of God's "good pleasure," always to be hoped for, but never assured as a presence within the Body of Christ.[59]

We have already alluded to the importance of the Yes and No dialectic and the sovereignty/solidarity partnership in the relation of Christ to the church. Again, Barth's warnings against idolatry are telling, especially so, when credal and confessional lore is absolutized, or divine infallibility is conferred on a corporate or personal magisterium, or the words of the preacher are thought to be coterminous with the divine Word. Of importance, as well, is the expectancy of church proclamation becoming ever and again the living Word, as in the openness to fresh and different hearings of the same in new and different contexts. But once again, as the Body of Christ is more than an unpredictable "happening," so the wisdom of the Body can be counted upon in the continuities of its teaching. Because of it, the church functions as a reliable "'resource" to understanding the biblical "source," Christ keeps his promise to be noetically, as well as soterically, among his people. "I am with you always, to the end of the age" (Matt. 28:20).

The knowledge of God given to the church, for all its fragility, development and corrigibility, is grounded in the solidarity of God with us as well as the sovereignty of God over us. Again, there are discontinuities between Christ and the illumination of the church, but also continuities, the dialectic of divine presence and distance. And again Barth's astute and detailed inquiry into the historic

---

58 Barth, *CD*, I/1, p. 79.

59 Barth's "event" ecclesiology was influential in the World Council of Churches' missiology of the 1960s, especially in its study, *The Church for Others*. One result was a sharp critique made of the local congregation for failing to hear the Word that propelled it to be a "church for others," and the judgment that the Word was active instead outside the walls of the church in secular movements for social change. For a survey of the literature of the debate between actualist ecclesiologies and those that stressed the promise of Christ's presence through Word and sacrament *in spite of the* congregation's failures, not *because of its* responsiveness, see Gabriel Fackre, "The Crisis of the Congregation," in D. B. Robertson ed., *Voluntary Associations: A Study of Groups in Free Societies* (Richmond: John Knox Press, 1966), pp. 275–98.

church teaching—its creeds, confessions and catechisms—reflects a trust in the continuing epistemic work of the Holy Spirit in the church belied by his theory. Indeed, his judgment that the biblical canon is authoritative because it represents a valid decision of the church, and the possibility of other books being added to the canon by the decision of the church catholic, suggest a "possession" of lasting truth in the church by the power of the Spirit that his theory explicitly denies.[60] An evangelical narrative doctrine of revelation will find a place in theory as well as practice for the continuing work of the Holy Spirit in the wisdom of the historic church.

4.3 The world

And what of the "free communications" in the world beyond the church, the Scripture and the events of "holy history"? Although this refrain appears to be a departure from Barth's earlier "Nein!" to Brunner, such is not the case. He is as firm as ever in his "christological concentration." But, it must be said, so are evangelical defenders of "general revelation" no less firm in their assertion of the centrality of God's disclosure in Jesus Christ. The common grace of preservation is the work of the Word, known only to be what it is by the light of Jesus Christ.

The difference between an evangelical narrative view of common epistemic grace and Barth's concept of "free communications" and "little lights" in the world lies in *how* Christ's disclosive action *extra muros ecclesiae* is understood. For Barth, once again, the actualist premise born from the principled use of divine sovereignty and inner testimony is at work. The "parables" of secular grace are unforeseen "happenings" in which a human phenomenon becomes the occasion for a "free communication."

Does this way of describing disclosures in "the outer circle" cohere with the constancies of the covenant with Noah? Barth concedes that there is a pattern of biblical teaching that promises that kind of revelatory light, albeit not the "chief line of the biblical message."[61] However, a Noachic chapter so much part of the *storyline* declaring the constancies of an epistemic grace must not be censored. The rainbow is the biblical sign of a covenant love that will not let us go forwards in the story without rudimentary knowledge of the

60 Godsey, *Table*, p. 27.
61 Barth, *CD*, II/1, pp. 109, 112.

purposes of God required for that journey. Such knowledge includes an awareness of the elemental norms of life together, and intimations of the source and goal of the world's pilgrimage.

The covenant with Noah is the assurance of modest revelatory constancies. But why not also Barth's "free communications," the unexpected and unpredictable given in unique personal and cultural moments? God is free enough to be with us in both commonalities *and* occasions, being captive to the principles of neither discontinuity nor continuity. There is a dialectic in the disclosive work of the Spirit in the world as well as in Scripture and the church.

Whether the universal *offer* of knowledge given to the world by the common grace of God is accepted or rejected depends on the presence of faith. Grace *knows* by faith, as grace *saves* by faith; thus Paul's pointed commentary in Romans about the reception of the universal disclosures of God in a fallen world. On the one hand, for all the world's inhabitants since its beginnings, "what can be known about God is plain to them, because God has shown it to them" (Rom. 1:19). On the other hand, there are those who:

> by their wickedness suppress the truth . . . because they exchanged the truth about God for a lie and worshipped and served the creature rather than the Creator . . . God gave them up to a debased mind . . . filled with every kind of wickedness, evil, covetousness, malice. Full of envy, murder, strife . . . gossips, slanderers, God-haters . . . rebellious towards parents, foolish, faithless . . . (Rom. 1:18, 25, 29, 30, 31).

Paul is not referring here to humanity as such (not all are "full of murder . . . rebellious towards parents" NRSV), but to "those who by their wickedness suppress the truth." There are others, such as "the Gentiles who do not possess the law [but] do instinctively what the law requires" (Rom. 2:14). But in this discussion of the measure of light given to all, the focus is on those who "became futile in their thinking . . . their senseless minds . . . darkened" (Rom. 1:21). From one point of view, they "know" about God and the law—a "knowledge of acquaintance." Yet in the deeper meaning of "know'" the "knowledge of friendship"—they are innocent of understanding. Paul refers to those who have obscured the light given to them as the "faithless." As gifts of grace are received only in faith, so the common grace that gives the light of the Noachic covenant requires a "common faith."

As common grace sustains the world in its journey towards salvific events yet to come, so the response of common faith commensurate with the "grace of preservation" does not save souls. It can make one responsive to the mandates of God, but not "righteous" before the majesty of God (Rom. 3:10). It does not save, but it does sustain.[62] The offer of true knowledge, sustaining knowledge, is made to all, but it reaches beyond acquaintance to friendship only by the presence of this rudimentary meaning of faith, a portent in commonality anticipating the particularities of Abrahamic faith and its heirs in Christ (Rom. 4:3–5:21). Barth's recognition of the "little lights" of God in the world *extra muros* bears testimony to the covenant with Noah in the narrative of revelation. The promise to sustain the world by a common noetic grace, however, is a promise kept always and everywhere, not only now and then.

5. Conclusion

Karl Barth, the twentieth century's "theologian of revelation" and "theologian of christological concentration," has taught a generation about the center on which the whole tale turns. He has witnessed as well to the Scripture's grand narrative of revelation.

Solus Christus as the turning point of the story does not preclude the freedom of God promising a trustworthy presence throughout, derivative and dialectical. Barth's caution that no principles of our own making should obstruct attention to that one Word, as attested by Scripture, must be applied to his own doctrine of revelation. Where deployment of the over-riding principles of divine sovereignty and inner testimony obscure the biblical witness to the length and breadth of the narrative of revelation, an evangelical No must join the evangelical Yes.

---

62 As Cruden's *Concordance* lists two meanings of' "salvation"—salvation from sin and salvation from misery—a case can be made that common grace *saves* from suffering, sickness, misery, pain, injustice. Here is salvation in "horizontal" terms, in contrast to the "vertical" relationship, salvation *coram Deo*. See the writer's discussion of the historical graces of redemption in "The Scandals of Particularity and Universality," *Mid-Stream* 22:1 (January 1983), pp. 46–51.

2

A Person of the Book? Barth on Biblical Authority and Interpretation

Kevin J. Vanhoozer

Evangelicals are a "people of the book."[1] The supreme authority of Scripture, typically cashed out in terms of verbal inspiration, inerrancy, and infallibility, is a characteristic mark of evangelical theology. Karl Barth is well known for his theology of the Word of God and for his reassertion of biblical authority in the face of its erosion in modern Protestantism.[2] Yet many evangelicals have found Barth's distinction between the Word of God (i.e. Jesus Christ) and the words of men (i.e. Scripture) disquieting, to say the least—so much so that many have questioned Barth's credentials as a "person of the book."

Given Barth's indirect identity thesis—according to which the Bible *becomes* the word of God—it is only fitting that we begin our study of Barth's doctrine of Scripture *indirectly*, through the effective history of its reception among evangelicals. The story, alas, is something of a tragicomedy of errors, complete with mistaken identities (for example, of the meaning of "is"), dramatic ironies, and outright misunderstandings. The reception of Barth's doctrine of Scripture among evangelicals also serves as a barometer of various pressures within the evangelical movement itself.[3] When hot (read:

1 See John Barton, *People of the Book? The Authority of the Bible in Christianity* (Louisville, KY: Westminster/John Knox Press, 1988).

2 According to David Mueller, reclaiming the Reformers' view of biblical authority is one of Barth's most important positive contributions (Mueller, *Karl Barth* [Waco, TX: Word, 1972], p. 144).

3 Gregory C. Bolich's book describes the story of Barth's reception in terms of two basic evangelical responses: on the one hand are those who

"reformist") air masses meet cold (read: "traditionalist") fronts, the result is invariably severe storms. One call still hear the rolling thunder occasioned by the encounter of evangelical readers who were respectively hot or cool towards Barth.

Barth thought and wrote as a "biblical dogmatician."[4] Does this qualify him as a "person of the book"? The primary goal of the present chapter is to come to a better understanding of Barth's view and use of the Bible.[5] A secondary goal is to tear down the "dividing wall of hostility" that has prevented evangelicals from appreciating Barth's accomplishment. In so doing, we may also find ourselves making progress towards the further goals of addressing tensions within contemporary evangelicalism concerning biblical authority and, *Deo volente*, of clarifying the relationship between God and Scripture.[6]

1. First contact: a hermeneutics of epistemological suspicion

The first evangelical responses to Barth were largely negative and reactionary. They were motivated by the concern that neo-orthodoxy was a modernist wolf in evangelical sheep's clothing, an uneasy yoking of biblical insights and a non-biblical philosophical

---

see him as a "foe of evangelical faith," on the other those who see him as a "potential friend" (*Karl Barth and Evangelicalism* [Downers Grove, IL: InterVarsity Press, 1980). Philip R. Thorne writes that "constructive appropriation of Barth became one source and sign of the change taking place in post-war American evangelicalism as it shed its fundamentalist pattern" (*Evangelicalism and Karl Barth: His Reception and Influence in North American Evangelical Theology* [Allison Park, PA: Pickwick Publications, 1995], p. 178). See also the way in which Barth figures in Roger E. Olson's telling of "The Story of Evangelical Theology," in *The Westminster Handbook to Evangelical Theology* (Louisville, KY: Westminster John Knox Press, 2004), esp. pp. 39–56.

[4] John Webster, *Karl Barth*, 2nd ed. (London/New York: Continuum, 2004) p. 173.

[5] Barth's doctrine of Scripture is impossible to separate from his broader understanding of God, the way in which God makes himself known, and the tie between revelation and redemption. It also depends on a correct grasp of the way Barth relates philosophy and theology.

[6] Bolich suggests that studying Barth "can aid evangelicals in effecting a workable unity, proving their validity and discovering their fundamental identity" (*Barth*, p. 27).

framework. For Cornelius Van Til, refuting Barth was a matter of preserving the integrity of the gospel, of asserting Christ's death and resurrection as space-time historical events, rather than merely events of *Geschichte*. This is a legitimate concern. Nevertheless, it is regrettable that the early evangelical reception of Barth is characterized by its (1) disproportionate concern for epistemology, (2) focus on certain statements in isolation from their "canonical" context (viz. the whole of Barth's work), and (3) lack of attention to Barth's actual exegetical practice.

1.1 Cornelius Van Til

Van Til was the first evangelical to engage Barth critically. Because he was the teacher of a number of students destined to become evangelical leaders, his interpretation of Barth wielded a disproportionate influence.[7]

In *The New Modernism*, Van Til investigates the relation between the earlier and later Barth. Though Barth himself later acknowledged that his earlier work was too indebted to modern philosophy, Van Til discerns a pervasive influence of modern critical and dialectical philosophy throughout Barth's work. Exhibit number one is Barth's consistently dialectical and activist take on revelation. If there is only one thing true of Barth's whole theology, says Van Til, it is "that it is the diametrical opposite of a theology that is based on a finished revelation of God in history."[8] The basic assumption behind all Van Til's criticisms is that Barth uses orthodox terms in a non-orthodox way: "for all its verbal similarities to historic Protestantism, Barth's theology is, in effect, a denial of it."[9] He is a dangerous enemy precisely because he comes "in the guise of a friend."

What, then, might Barth mean when he speaks of Scripture as the Word of God? Van Til is clear as to what Barth does not mean: that what there is to be known of God has been deposited in the

---

[7] It is significant, however, that the focus of his earliest treatment of Barth's doctrine of Scripture in his first book on Barth, *The New Modernism: An Appraisal of the Theology of Barth and Brunner* (Philadelphia: P&R Publishing Co., 1946), was Barth's 1927 *Die Christliche Dogmatik im Entwurf* rather than the later, more mature statement of Barth's position, the *Church Dogmatics*.

[8] Cornelius Van Til, *The Protestant Doctrine of Scripture* (Philadelphia: Dalk, 1967), p. 36.

[9] Cornelius Van Til, *Christianity and Barthianism* (Philadelphia: P&R Publishing Co., 1962), p. vii.

biblical texts once for all. Such a fixed revelation would deny God's freedom to reveal himself or not. Revelation is for Barth always indirect: always a gift-like event, never a given. It is precisely at this point that Van Til makes a fateful inference from indirect revelation (a theological notion) to *existential* event (a philosophical notion). In brief: Van Til concludes that, for Barth, the Bible becomes God's Word only in and for an existential moment (*Geschichte*) that refuses to be tied down either to history (*Historie*) or meaning. The Bible becomes revelation only when God decides to encounter its readers dialectically: if the Bible "is" the Word of God, it is only because, and when, "the 'is' is active."[10]

Van Til proceeds to measure Barth's theology by means of a single overriding conception: activism.[11] This is also why he labels Barth's theology the "New Modernism." Modernity involves the turn to the human subject (i.e. the human knower); Barth makes a turn to the divine Subject (i.e. the divine revealer). The crucial question is whether Barth's emphasis on the discontinuity of the Word of God with the words of men is an expression of modernity, or a criticism of it. Van Til leaves us in no doubt as to his own opinion: "Barth interprets the Bible in a modern activist sense just as Origen interpreted the Bible in accord with principles borrowed from Greek philosophy."[12]

Van Til is also convinced that Barth's whole approach to theology presupposes human autonomy: "It is by . . . assuming that his God is wholly revealed and wholly hidden to him that man can make sure that he has no God who has any existence prior to himself and who can make any demands on him."[13] It is difficult in the extreme, however, to construe Barth's turn away from the human knowing subject as "a projection of the would-be autonomous man"[14] or a "New Humanism."[15] Almost everybody else recognizes Barth's achievement as the rediscovery of the deity—the Wholly

---

[10] Cornelius Van Til, *Karl Barth & Evangelicalism* (Philadelphia: P&R Publishing Co., 1964), p. 14.

[11] This is in significant contrast to George Hunsinger's employment of multiple "motifs"—including "actualism"—in his *How to Read Karl Barth* (Oxford, UK: Oxford University Press, 1991).

[12] Van Til, *Protestant*, p. 36

[13] Van Til, *Christianity*, p. 412. Cf. Van Til's comment: "Barth's basic concept of a revelation as wholly revealing and wholly hiding God to man is based upon the assumption of the autonomy of man" (p. 410).

[14] Van Til, *Christianity*, p. 434.

[15] Van Til, *Evangelicalism*, p. 32.

Otherness—of God. Van Til's interpretation of Barth as a humanist is as tendentious a reading of the *Church Dogmatics* as was the Tübingen School's insistence that James had to be contradicting Paul.

Given Van Til's well-known presuppositonal apologetics, it is highly ironic that a faulty presupposition underlies, and hence undermines, his reading of Barth. Van Til reads Barth as being committed to a critical (i.e. Kantian) philosophy. Van Til seems not to have grasped the possibility that Barth may have had other, more properly theological, reasons for his dialectical approach.[16] It has also been suggested that one reason behind Van Til's "Barthian animus" is the apparent similarity between Barth's theology and Reformed orthodoxy.[17] Might it not also be because of a strong point of similarity between Barth and Van Til himself? Many would place both thinkers together on the spectrum of contemporary theology: both were biblical fideists; both were uncompromising about their respective starting-points; both made the doctrine of the Trinity their key presupposition.[18]

1.2 Carl F. H. Henry

Carl F. H. Henry followed his teacher Gordon Clark in construing Barth as an "irrationalist." Like Van Til, Clark could not conceive of how the Bible could only "become" revelation: "the Bible *is* the Word of God, but only at certain instants . . . when God lets the

---

[16] Some evangelicals have criticized Van Til for interpreting the later Barth in terms of the earlier. In this regard, at least, recent research in on Van Til's side: Bruce McCormack argues that dialectic is indeed at the heart of Barth's theology, and that Barth never shifted it from the center of his theological method and his theological concern (see McCormack, *Karl Barth's Critically Realistic Dialectical Theology: Its Genesis and Development 1909–1936* (Oxford, UK: Clarendon Press, 1995). The issue, however, is not whether Van Til was or was not right about the *presence* of dialectic in Barth's theology, but its *nature*. Van Til thought it was a residue from Barth's youthful flirtation with existentialism. McCormack (rightly in my opinion) shows that it stems from properly theological concerns.

[17] Thorne, *Evangelicalism*, p. 35.

[18] In this regard, it is regrettable that there is no book-length study comparing and contrasting these two Presbyterian and Reformed theologians. Note also that no course has been offered on the theology of Karl Barth at Westminster Theological Seminary (Philadelphia) since Van Til left the scene (personal conversation with Richard Gaffin).

Bible speak to us."[19] Barth's concept of revelation was unintelligible to the extent that Barth failed to identify the event of revelation with the verbal statements of the Bible.

For Henry, to say the Bible is the Word of God is to affirm divine revelation as verbal and conceptual. Revelation is "propositional": God makes his mind, and hence truth, known in the words of Scripture. He complains that Barth, by contrast, locates revelation (and hence truth?) in "the stratosphere of superhistory."[20] Anything that calls into question the identity of the mind of God with the words of Scripture results in skepticism. In Henry's opinion, the notion that revelation is cognitive was lost on Barth's watch: "The enigma of Barth's theory is: why should revelation—which according to Barth is not to be hardened into concepts and words—ever have become so entangled in concepts and words that it requires the disentangling he proposes?"[21]

Henry's core problem with Barth's view of Scripture is best seen in a supplementary note in *God, Revelation, and Authority* volume 4 entitled "Barth on Scriptural Errancy."[22] Barth clearly regards the prophets and apostles as "capable of error even in respect of religion and theology."[23] How then, Henry wonders, can one treat a fallible book as an authoritative norm? Henry also finds perplexing Barth's claim that what is humanly fallible may nevertheless become divinely infallible: "can even faith that moves mountains turn the writer's supposed contradictions and errors into the truth of revelation?"[24] It makes no sense to say that the Bible "becomes" true. Henry thus agrees with Clark that "the idea of sentences, propositions, verses of the Bible increasing or decreasing in truth from time to time and from individual to individual is a skeptical delusion."[25] The difficulty lies in Barth's espousing two incompatible axioms: first, that the Bible is the Word of God; second, that the Bible contains errors and contradictions. Henry's verdict is telling: "By respecting

[19] Gordon H. Clark, *Karl Barth's Theological Method* (Philadelphia: Presbyterian and Reformed, 1963), pp. 163–4.
[20] Carl Henry, *God, Revelation, and Authority* vol. 2 (Waco, TX: Word, 1979), p. 287.
[21] Henry, *God* vol. 4, p. 200.
[22] Henry, *God* vol. 4, pp. 196–200.
[23] Barth, *Church Dogmatics* (Edinburgh, UK: T&T Clark, 1956–75; hereafter *CD*), I/2, p. 510.
[24] Henry, *God* vol. 4, p. 197.
[25] Clark, *Method*, p. 172.

the law of contradiction [Barth] could and would have avoided irrationalist tendencies."[26]

Henry is aware of Barth's "analogy of grace" whereby human concepts become adequate to the knowledge of God through a divine miracle, but considers this too little, too late to save revelation as cognitive and propositional: "Where evangelicals disagree with Barth is in his explicit affirmation of the dialectical event-character of revelation that declares God to be propositionally unknowable to man in the present, and in his denial of the objectivity of the Scriptures as God's written Word that robs Scripture of any revelatory-epistemic significance as a carrier of valid information about God."[27] If revelation does not begin with words, "how can it later attach itself to one set of words rather than to another, or to any words at all?"[28]

2. Second thoughts: tentative appropriations

By the 1970s, there was a fairly widespread consensus among evangelical and non-evangelical theologians alike about the "Barthian" view of Scripture.[29] According to this consensus, Barth "is always careful to distinguish God in his revelation from the testimony to that relation which confronts us in Scripture."[30] The Bible *becomes* what it essentially is not (i.e. the Word of God) when God uses its human witness to point to Christ. This is Barth's indirect identity thesis concerning the relation of revelation and the Bible. On this reading, Barth is saying of Scripture what Arius said of the Logos, namely, "There was a time when it (the Bible) was not (the Word of God)." This way of putting it exposed the fundamental problem of Barth's position for conservative evangelicals: an *adoptionist* view

---

[26] Henry, *God* vol. 4, p. 200. Henry surely means to speak of the law of non-contradiction which stipulates that the conjunction of a proposition and its negation is a contradiction, not a dialectical truth!

[27] Henry, *God* vol. 4, p. 267.

[28] Clark, *Method*, p. 221.

[29] John Morrison has recently argued that what passed for a "Barthian" view of Scripture rests upon a misinterpretation of Barth's actual view. See his "Barth, Barthians, and evangelicals: Reassessing the Question of the Relation of Holy Scripture and the Word of God," *Trinity Journal* 25 NS (2004), pp. 187–213.

[30] David Mueller, *Karl Barth* (Waco, TX: Word, 1972), p. 56.

fares no better in describing how the Bible is the Word of God than it does in describing how Jesus is the Son of God.

Other evangelicals disagreed, insisting that Barth had raised valid points about the dangers of "biblicism" and refusing to read him as an indentured servant to existentialist philosophy. This latter group of evangelicals was more interested in appropriating Barth for the sake of constructive theology, not apologetics.[31]

2.1 Bernard Ramm

If Carl Henry was the "Dean" of post-war evangelical theologians, Bernard Ramm, author of several influential textbooks, was its Associate Dean. After years of wrestling with Barth's theology, Ramm dropped a bombshell of his own on the playground of the evangelical theologians with the publication of his *After Fundamentalism: The Future of Evangelical Theology*.[32] In it, he argued that Barth represents the most adequate theological response to the Enlightenment, and hence to the sterile confrontation between fundamentalists and modernists that had warped evangelical theology by making it defensive, suspicious, and reactionary.[33] It was during a sabbatical year in 1957–58 that Ramm learned from a personal encounter with Barth that "if we truly believed that we had the truth of God in Holy Scripture we should be fearless in opening any door or any window in the pursuit of our theological craft."[34]

Ramm gradually came to see in Barth one who was fearless in the face of modern biblical criticism, one who was able to restate the essentials of Reformed theology in the aftermath of the Enlightenment, recognizing its genuine positive gains but without

---

[31] Thorne discusses four professors from Fuller Theological Seminary—E. J. Carnell, Colin Brown, James Daane, and Ray Anderson—under the rubric of "New evangelicals" (*Evangelicalism and Karl Barth*, ch. 3). Carnell's statement—"I am convinced that Barth is an inconsistent evangelical rather than an inconsistent liberal"—captures perfectly the note of critical appropriation (Carnell, "Barth as Inconsistent Evangelical," *The Christian Century* 79 [June 6, 1962], p. 714).

[32] Carl Ramm, *After Fundamentalism: The Future of Evangelical Theology* (San Francisco, CA: Harper & Row, 1983).

[33] See Ramm's autobiographical comments in "Helps from Karl Barth," in Donald K. McKim ed., *How Karl Barth Changed My Mind* (Grand Rapids, MI: Eerdmans, 1986), p. 121.

[34] Ramm, "Helps," p. 124

capitulating to it. evangelicals, by contrast, "have not developed a theological method that enables them to be consistently evangelical in their theology and to be people of modern learning."[35] Ramm sees Barth as charting the way forward for theology, neither succumbing to the Enlightenment and becoming revisionists as the liberals did, nor ignoring the Enlightenment and becoming obscurantists, denying the validity of modern knowledge, as the fundamentalists did.

That Barth is both child and critic of the Enlightenment is evident, Ramm thinks, in Barth's view of Scripture. The critical study of Scripture is compatible with faith in its inspiration. One can study the Bible as a human and historical document and at the same time acknowledge its divine authority. In short: one can affirm both the humanity and the divinity of the Bible. But how? By recognizing an interval or *diastasis* (distance; distinction) between the Word of God on the one hand and its expression and embeddedness in a linguistically and culturally conditioned text on the other.[36] The Word of God is in some measure "refracted" because "no human language can mirror perfectly the mind of God or his Word."[37] It follows that the Word of God must be "sought" in the text through the process of interpretation: "By studying the text, the interpreter penetrates the *diastasis* to the Word of God itself."[38]

Neither Ramm nor Barth are skeptics; neither wants to say that the interval is a chasm. Nor do they employ Kant's distinction to separate the "phenomenal" text from the "noumenal" Word of God. On the contrary, Ramm says that "Barth believes that the Word of God is in Scripture as the *Sache* [subject matter] of Scripture."[39] Ramm's formula is telling: the Word is in the words.[40] Ramm therefore denies the charge that Barth has a purely subjective or existential view of the Bible becoming the Word; rather, the Word is objectively *in* the words. When Barth speaks of the Bible "becoming" the Word of God, he is speaking of its being recognized as such by particular hearers or readers who hear and read in the right spirit (i.e. in faith and obedience).[41]

---

[35] Ramm, *Fundamentalism*, p. 27.
[36] Ramm, *Fundamentalism*, p. 89.
[37] Ramm, "Helps," p. 124.
[38] Ramm, *Fundamentalism*, p. 92–3.
[39] Ramm, *Fundamentalism*, p. 92.
[40] Ramm, *Fundamentalism*, p. 94.
[41] Ramm is unequivocal on this point: "Barth does believe that Holy Scripture is the Word of God in itself" (*Fundamentalism*, p. 120).

Ramm contends that Barth treats biblical texts like Genesis 1–3 or the resurrection narratives neither as sources nor as evidence to be used for reconstructing history, but as witnesses to divine revelation.[42] To treat every part of the Bible as a source book for historical information is a violation of what Ramm considers to be the most basic principle of interpretation, namely, "a book is to be interpreted in the light of what it claims to be."[43] Ramm thinks that Barth is essentially correct in viewing Scripture as testimony to its subject matter: the revealed Word of God. Finally, Ramm agrees with Barth that the only worthwhile apologetic strategy for demonstrating the Bible to be the Word of God is to focus on its christological content rather than argue for the supposed perfection of its form.[44]

2.2 Donald Bloesch

Like Ramm, Donald Bloesch says that what he most admires about Barth is "his fresh interpretation of biblical authority."[45] Specifically, Barth meets the challenge of higher criticism by showing that it needs to be "supplemented and fulfilled by theological criticism, which is carried on only by faith seeking understanding."[46]

Bloesch counts Barth among his principal theological mentors, along with Luther and Calvin.[47] There are actually more index entries to Barth than to anyone else in Bloesch's *Holy Scripture*, the second volume of his seven-volume systematic theology. In the first volume, *A Theology of Word and Spirit*, Bloesch says that "we need to take his [Barth's] way of doing theology" over that of liberals like Tillich and conservatives like Carl Henry.[48] That means viewing God's Word as referring not to the Bible per se but to "the living Word in its inseparable unity with Scripture and church proclamation as this is brought home to us by the Spirit."[49]

---

[42] Ramm, *Fundamentalism*, p. 109.

[43] Ramm, *Fundamentalism*, p. 109.

[44] Ramm, *Fundamentalism*, p. 132.

[45] Donald Bloesch, "Karl Barth: Appreciation and Reservations," in McKim ed., *How Karl Barth Changed my Mind*, p. 126.

[46] Bloesch, "Appreciation," p. 127.

[47] Bloesch, "Appreciation," p. 126.

[48] Donald Bloesch, *A Theology of Word & Spirit* (Downers Grove, IL: InterVarsity Press, 1992), p. 271.

[49] Bloesch, *Word &* Spirit, p. 14. Elsewhere Bloesch writes: "I think Barth is biblically sound in his judgment that Christ alone is the living or

Bloesch flies Barthian colors when he distinguishes his own "biblical evangelical" stance on the doctrine of Scripture from the prevailing "evangelical rationalism" that equates revelation with Scripture and thus regards the Word of God as something that humans can grasp through exegetical procedures, and formulate through deductive reasoning: "The Bible is not in and of itself the revelation of God but the divinely appointed means and channel of this revelation."[50] For Bloesch, the particular *diastasis* between the words of men and the Word of God is a function of the Spirit's action: "the Bible . . . is not divine revelation intrinsically, for its revelatory status does not reside in its wording as such but in the Spirit of God, who fills the words with meaning and power."[51] Bloesch works a sacramental variation on a Barthian theme, comparing the Bible to a light bulb[52] and revelation—the Spirit's communicating the Word—to the light that shines through it: "The Bible is the divinely prepared medium or channel of divine revelation rather than the revelation itself."[53]

Bloesch reads Barth as distinguishing between the human form (viz. the historical and literary witness) and the divine content of the Bible (viz. Jesus Christ): "Criticism may be directed to the form but not to the content of Scripture, which lies outside the compass of historical investigation."[54] The final authority for Christian faith and theology "is not what the Bible says but what God says in the Bible."[55] At the same time, Bloesch follows Barth in affirming a conjunction between the human form and divine content brought about by the action of the Spirit and perceived only by faith. Hence the *diastasis* between the Word and the words has implications for hermeneutics as well, for Bloesch posits "a clear-cut distinction"

---

revealed Word of God, yet the Bible can become transparent to this Word by the interior action of the Holy Spirit" ("Donald Bloesch Responds," in Elmer M. Colyer ed. *Evangelical Theology in Transition: Theologians in Dialogue with Donald Bloesch* [Downers Grove, IL: InterVarsity Press, 1999], p. 192).

[50] Donald Bloesch, *Holy Scripture* (Downers Grove, IL: InterVarsity Press, 1994), p. 57. Bloesch contrasts rationalism—the attempt to arrive at truth through one's native cognitive powers—with the need to establish the claims of faith with Word and Spirit.

[51] Bloesch, *Holy Scripture*, p. 27.

[52] Bloesch, *Holy Scripture*, p. 59.

[53] Bloesch, *Holy Scripture*, p. 18.

[54] Bloesch, *Holy Scripture*, p. 177.

[55] Bloesch, *Holy Scripture*, p. 60.

between the historical meaning of the text and its "revelational" or "spiritual" meaning that the text assumes when the Spirit acts on it in bringing home its significance to people of faith in every age."[56]

3. Third wave: evangelicals meet Barth's postliberal progeny

In the 1980s and 90s Barth indeed had become, as Ramm hoped, a paradigm for a new way of doing theology. It was not associated with evangelicals, however, but with Yale Divinity School. Hans Frei's *The Eclipse of Biblical Narrative*[57] held up Barth's theological interpretation of Scripture as a model of how to make the biblical narrative itself rather than some other, extratextual framework the touchstone for biblical meaning and truth.

3.1 Why narrative?

Neither Barth nor Frei was interested in being hermeneutically fashionable. Their prime interest was rather the revelation of God in the person and history of Jesus Christ.[58] Yet form and content are inseparable, for the identity of an agent, even a divine agent, is rendered through the words, actions, occurrences, and sufferings that unfold through the story. According to Frei, Barth read the gospels as "realistic narrative" whose meaning simply is the story it depicts. This was in marked contrast to those who sought to translate the biblical story into some conceptual scheme or to view biblical meaning in terms of historical reference—the typical gestures of conservative and liberal modern theologians alike. George Lindbeck, Frei's colleague at Yale, coined the term "intratextuality" to describe this habit of redescribing reality within the framework

---

[56] Bloesch, *Holy Scripture*, p. 190. See also Millard Erickson, "Donald Bloesch's Doctrine of Scripture," in Colyer ed., *Evangelical Theology in Transition*, pp. 77–97, especially his final verdict: "Overall, Bloesch's view of Scripture, while combining elements of neo-orthodoxy and traditional evangelicalism, appears closer to the former than to the latter" (p. 91).

[57] Hans Frei, *The Eclipse of Biblical Narrative* (New Haven: Yale University Press, 1974).

[58] See also David F. Ford, *Barth and God's Story: Biblical Narrative and the Theological Method of Karl Barth in "The Church Dogmatics"* (Frankfurt: Verlag Peter Lang, 1981, 1985).

of the biblical narrative rather than translating Scripture into extrascriptural categories.[59]

3.2 The Frei-Henry encounter

The encounter between Carl Henry and Hans Frei at Yale in 1985 marked the first serious evangelical attempt to engage postliberal theology. Uncannily mirroring Van Til's critique of Barth, Henry objected to what he took to be Frei's "flight from history" and "revolt against reason" when it came to the question of the truth of biblical narrative. Frei, for his part, insisted that the narratives of Jesus' death and resurrection are referential, but he refused to subscribe to a theory of historical reference or factuality that, he feared, would displace the intratextual logic of Scripture itself: "The truth to which we refer we cannot state apart from the biblical language which we employ to do so."[60] The still-born dialogue was revived only ten years later when evangelicals and postliberals came together at one of the annual Wheaton Theology Conferences.[61]

The voice to which Henry reacted was Frei's, but the spirit was Barth's. The debate appeared to be about the nature of narrative reference, but the real issue concerned which movement—evangelicalism or postliberalism—had better claim to the title "people of the book" or, more precisely, which had the better account of the unity, authority, and interpretation of Scripture.[62] Though both men affirmed the sufficiency of Scripture with regard to its subject matter, Henry viewed the gospel narratives primarily as reports about historical facts, while Frei saw them as depictions of a particular unsubstitutable Person.[63]

---

[59] George Lindbeck, "Barth and Textuality," *Theology Today* 43 [1996]: 361–76.

[60] Hans Frei, "Response to Narrative Theology: An Evangelical Appraisal," in *Trinity Journal* 8 NS (1987): 23.

[61] Papers from the conference were later published. See Timothy R. Phillips and Dennis L. Okholm, eds., *The Nature of Confession: Evangelicals & Postliberals in Conversation* (Downers Grove, IL: InterVarsity Press, 1996).

[62] See further George Hunsinger, "What can evangelicals & Postliberals Learn from Each Other? The Carl Henry-Hans Frei Exchange Reconsidered," in Phillips and Okholm, eds., *Confession*, pp. 134–50.

[63] So Hunsinger, "Postliberals," p. 144. Cf. p. 142, where Hunsinger observes "Whereas Henry seems to think the narratives are finally about the doctrines, for Frei it is just the reverse."

3.3 *Karl* dixit*: back to the sources*

The history of the reception of Barth's texts is no substitute for an examination of the primary sources themselves.[64] It is especially important in Barth's case to listen to all that he has to say about Scripture; readers miss the true significance of Barth's statements about the Bible when they attempt to make sense of sentences apart from their "canonical" context (i.e. the whole of Barth's *Church Dogmatics*). In particular, what Barth says in the *Church Dogmatics*, I/1 about the indirect identity of Scripture with the Word of God has to be balanced by what he says in the *Church Dogmatics*, I/2 about the authority of the Bible in, and over, the church.

3.3.1 Scripture as form of and witness to God's Word. "The Word of God is God himself in Holy Scripture."[65] Barth never tired of insisting that only God can make God known. The overarching theological presupposition, without which Barth's doctrine of Scripture cannot be understood, is that revelation is a predicate of God as a free, gracious, and active subject. Jesus Christ—the Word made flesh—is the definitive Word. Yet both Jesus in his humanity and Scripture in its humanity become revelation only when God acts in and through them to make himself known: "When we speak about revelation we are confronted by the divine act itself."[66] With this thought, we are now in a position to locate where, and why, evangelicals have so often misread Barth. It all boils down to a case of mistaken identity. For evangelicals, the Word of God is an object—the deposit of revealed truth in Scripture. By contrast, for Barth the Word of God is a subject whose speaking in and through Jesus Christ creates both the canon and the church.

God's Word does not piggy-back on the writings of the prophets and apostles. On the contrary, "It is because God reveals himself

---

[64] The main sections in the *CD*, are I/1/4, pp. 88–124, "The Word of God in its Threefold Form" and I/2/19–21, pp. 457–749 "Chapter III: Holy Scripture". Other relevant sources include Barth's 1947 essay "The Authority and Significance of the Bible: Twelve Theses," in *God Here and Now* (London and New York: Routledge, 2003), pp. 55–74 and *Evangelical Theology: An Introduction* (Grand Rapids, MI: Eerdmans, 1963), ch. 3 "The witnesses," pp. 26–36.

[65] Barth, *CD*, I/2, p. 457.

[66] Barth, *CD*, I/1, p. 117.

that they are witnesses."[67] Witness is the operative concept. To bear witness means to point away from oneself. The biblical authors "do not want to offer and commend themselves to the Church, and especially not their own particular experience of God and relationship to God, but through themselves that other."[68] The biblical authors attest God's revelation in Jesus Christ: "This participation of human words in God's Word is the principal element in the Scripture principle."[69]

To affirm the Bible as a form of the Word of God, then, is to conceive of Scripture as an active rather than a standing witness. It is precisely as actual witness that the Bible in some way shares in what Jesus Christ himself is (viz. divine revelation). Hence, "The reality of revelation is indirectly identical with the reality of Scripture."[70] To be sure, there is a distance (*diastasis*) that remains: "The Bible is one thing and revelation another."[71] But Barth does not leave it at that: "Nevertheless, we have revelation not in itself but in the Bible."[72]

It is precisely as written testimony that the Bible is a form of the Word of God: "The presence and Lordship of Jesus Christ . . . has its visible form, in the time between His resurrection and His return, in the witness of His chosen and appointed prophets and apostles."[73] Nevertheless, it is thanks not to the perfection of its form but to its being elected as a human instrument of divine speech and to its christological content that the Bible is indirectly identical with revelation: "The truth, power, and validity of the witness of these men is that of their subject."[74]

While recognizing the positive value of Barth's emphasis on its witnessing function, Geoffrey Bromiley wonders whether Barth might not inadvertently undermine the role of Scripture as a form of the Word of God by differentiating the two by means of the distinction

---

67 Eberhard Busch, *The Great Passion: An Introduction to Karl Barth's Theology* (Grand Rapids, MI: Eerdmans, 2004), p. 66.

68 Barth, *CD*, I/1, p. 112.

69 Barth, *The Göttingen Dogmatics*: *Instruction in the Christian Religion* vol. 1, Geoffrey W. Bromiley tr. (Grand Rapids, MI: Eerdmans, 1991), p. 212.

70 Barth, *Göttingen Dogmatics* vol. 1, p. 216.

71 Barth, *Göttingen Dogmatics* vol. 1, p. 216.

72 Barth, *Göttingen Dogmatics* vol. 1, p. 216.

73 Barth, "The Authority and Significance of the Bible," p. 57.

74 Barth, "Authority," p. 58.

between a witness's testimony and its object.[75] Klaas Runia raises a similar objection. How, he asks, do we know when and where the Bible has become the Word of God? Does the Bible have to become the Word of God again and again? Is there no sense in which the work of the Holy Spirit is continuous? In Runia's words: "In our opinion, one of the greatest weaknesses in Barth's early works is that he has place for the reality only, and not for the continuity."[76] This complaint becomes even more pronounced with regard to our next theme.

3.3.2 Inspiration and inerrancy. The theme of God as the active subject of his revelation decisively informs Barth's view of biblical inspiration. No other topic has been singled out by more evangelicals for criticism than Barth's reformulation and rejection of the doctrines of verbal inspiration and inerrancy respectively.

As we have seen, Barth denies that the Word of God is ever "available" in a direct and straightforward and permanent way. Why not? Because the Word of God *is* God in his free and sovereign activity of making himself known. The seventeenth-century Protestant doctrine of verbal inspiration did incalculable damage, Barth thought, because it historicized or "materialized" revelation, opening it up to the possibility of becoming subject to human investigation and control: "The Bible as the Word of God surreptitiously became a part of natural knowledge of God, i.e. of that knowledge of God which man can have without the free grace of God, by his own power."[77] Note well: Barth has no qualms affirming divine supernatural communication. His reticence towards verbal inspiration is not that of the skeptic, but the prophet: while he affirms that God has spoken in Scripture and will speak again, he refuses to *presume* upon God's speaking.

---

75 Geoffrey Bromiley, "The Authority of Scripture in Karl Barth," in D. A. Carson and John Woodbridge, eds. *Hermeneutics, Authority, and Canon* (Grand Rapids, MI: Baker, 1995), p. 290. The positive merits of emphasizing the witnessing aspect of Scripture are (1) it highlights the authorizing role of God as subject and object of revelation; (2) it directs attention to Scripture's leading theme and chief content, Jesus Christ.

76 Klaas Runia, *Karl Barth's Doctrine of Holy Scripture* (Grand Rapids, MI: Eerdmans, 1962), p. 128.

77 Barth, *CD*, I/2, pp. 522–3.

Barth's gloss on 2 Timothy 3:16 ("All Scripture is inspired [breathed out] by God . . .") is telling.[78] He notes that Paul has just reminded Timothy that the Scriptures have *already* played a decisive role in his life (v. 15) and that they will once again be profitable (v. 17). Why? Because they are "of the Spirit of God," that is, because they are the Spirit's appointed instrument. It is not the instrument alone that reveals, however, but the Spirit's *speaking* in and through it.

That the human words of the Bible become the Word of God is, for Barth, ultimately a miracle: "That the lame walk, that the blind see, that the dead are raised, that sinful and erring men as such speak the Word of God: that is the miracle of which we speak when we say that the Bible is the Word of God."[79] Note that the miracle is not that the human authors spoke infallibly, but rather that God uses fallible human words to speak his infallible Word. Barth insists on this point because he cannot regard the presence of God's Word and divine truth "as an attribute inhering once for all in this book,"[80] for the simple reason that this would "materialize" the active speaking of God and consign divine freedom to being the permanent property of a creaturely entity (viz. the biblical text). God, says Barth, is not ashamed to speak through the foolishness (1 Cor. 1:21) and fallibility (1 Cor. 1:25) of men. This is the "impossible possibility" that must be accepted on faith.[81] Barth's view of biblical inspiration is one more example of his eschatological realism, that is, his belief that the event of Jesus Christ, though real and historical, does not have its condition of possibility among the resources of this world; on the contrary, it wholly depends on a miraculous and mysterious act of God.

For all his talk of miracle, Barth's denial of inerrancy has proved a stumbling block and scandal to evangelicals who cannot fathom how he can simultaneously attribute both error and authority to Scripture. Runia understands the theological reason for Barth's hesitation: the desire to preserve the sovereign freedom of God, the acting subject of his revelation. While Barth's motive for denying inerrancy is rooted not in doubt but faith, Runia nevertheless believes that in this one instance at least, Barth's faith is misdirected:

---

[78] See Barth, *CD*, I/2, p. 504.

[79] Barth, *CD*, p. 529.

[80] Barth, *CD*, p. 530.

[81] Barth is careful to add that the inspiration of the Bible "cannot be reduced to our faith in it" (*CD*, I/2, p. 534).

"The Bible knows nothing of a fundamental contrast between the dynamic and the static, between the existential and the ontological, between the personal and the conceptual."[82] And while Bromiley sympathizes with Barth's motive to protect, not undermine, the status of Scripture as God's Word by refusing to base its authority on the contingent outcome of scientific or historical corroboration, even he regrets Barth's failure to accept inerrancy as an implication of his position on the Bible's authority.[83]

3.3.3 Canon and authority. Barth's statements about the nature of Scripture in §19 need to be tempered with his statements concerning the function of Scripture in the church in sections §20 and §21, on the "authority" and "freedom" of the Word, respectively.

God's sovereign freedom remains the leading motif in Barth's discussion of the canon and biblical authority. The basic principle is simply this: God's use of Scripture is prior to and decisive for the church's use of Scripture: "The establishment of the canon is [the church's] confession of God's election and calling of His witness."[84] Scripture has supreme authority in the church because it is the testimony of commissioned witnesses.

Despite Barth's uncertain sound with regard to inspiration and inerrancy, he is unequivocal on the matter of the Bible's authority over the church. In stark contrast to contemporary postconservatives and postliberals who identify the cradle of theology with the practices of the church, Barth states that the authority of the church is the derivative authority of obedience to Scripture.[85] Barth similarly affirms the Bible's authority over theology: "Even the smallest, strangest, simplest, or obscurest among the biblical witnesses has an incomparable advantage over even the most pious, scholarly, and sagacious latter-day theologian."[86] As to church confessions, their authority too derives from their being formulations of the church's insights into the revelation attested by Scripture.[87]

In his discussion of providence and the role of God the Father Almighty in the origin of the Scriptures and the formation of the canon, Barth notes that despite their human and historical

---

82 Runia, *Doctrine*, p. 202.
83 Bromiley, "Authority," pp. 293–4.
84 Barth, "Authority," p. 60.
85 Barth, *CD*, I/2, p. 574.
86 Barth, *Evangelical Theology*, pp. 31–2.
87 Barth, *CD*, I/2, p. 620.

conditioning, "its authors were objectively true, reliable and trustworthy witnesses" because it pleased God to raise up these true witnesses.[88] Having secured the principle of God's sovereign freedom in Scripture, Barth is apparently free to treat the Bible, for all intents and purposes, as inerrant testimony to God's self-revelation. The broader "canonical context" of Barth's works, then, calls for a more nuanced evaluation of his negative view of inerrancy. His dismissal of that notion may owe less to theological consistency than to well-intentioned, though somewhat overblown, rhetoric.

4. The use of the Bible in Barth's theology: authoritative text; "free" interpretation

Evangelicals do Barth a disservice when, in analyzing his view of Scripture, they treat only his statements about the Bible and its indirect relation to the Word of God. To neglect Barth's actual use and interpretation of the Bible is to fail to examine an enormous amount of evidence that casts his more theoretical (and rhetorical) statements in a markedly different light. Such disregard explains the paradox that one whom evangelicals consider suspect with regard to Scripture is a virtual biblicist in the broader theological scheme of things.[89] Indeed, Barth considers dogmatics as secondary to exegesis: "The *Church Dogmatics* is best read as a set of conceptual variations upon scriptural texts and themes."[90]

For Barth, the church's authority and freedom is an authority and freedom "under" the Word. Barth defines "freedom under the Word" as the freedom to accept the Word and the responsibility to hear and understand it.[91] Francis Watson suggests that, "From beginning to end, Barth's *Church Dogmatics* is nothing other than

---

[88] Barth, *CD*, III/3, p. 201.

[89] Kenneth Kantzer writes: "In spite of his rejection of biblical infallibility, he always takes the biblical text with dreadful seriousness as the authoritative witness to the Word of God." ("Thank God for Karl Barth, but . . ." *Christianity Today* Oct 3 (1986), p. 15).

[90] John Webster, "Barth, Karl" in Kevin J. Vanhoozer ed. *Theological Dictionary for Theological Interpretation of the Bible* (Grand Rapids, MI: Baker, 2005), p. 83.

[91] Barth, *CD*, I/2, p. 696.

a sustained meditation on the texts of Holy Scripture."[92] In Barth's own words: "My sole aim was to interpret Scripture."[93] Hence biblical interpretation is not merely one of many doctrinal *loci* for Barth but "the foundation and principle of coherence of his entire project."[94] Evangelicals would therefore do well to consider not only Barth's theory but also his exegetical practice. Kenneth Kantzer goes even further: "evangelicals have much to learn from his constant and faithful appeal to the written text."[95]

First, the facts: Barth cites more Scripture than any other theologian in the history of theology, some fifteen thousand times in the *Church Dogmatics*, not to mention the approximately two thousand extended exegetical sections. These statistics attest Barth's conviction that the primary task of theology is to clarify what is written in Scripture. Barth uses the Bible in many different ways, including extended exegeses of individual statements, analyses of key biblical words and themes, expositions of whole books, typological interpretations, narrative analysis, and massing verses in virtual proof-text fashion.[96]

4.1 The task of exegesis: the *sachlich* text

Barth's break with the theology of his day, much like the Reformers with theirs, was as much a hermeneutical as it was a theological revolution. His 1919 *Romans* commentary was the spearhead of his revolt against the hegemony of modern biblical critical scholarship.[97]

---

[92] Francis Watson, "The Bible," in John Webster ed. *The Cambridge Companion to Karl Barth* (Cambridge, UK: Cambridge University Press, 2000), p. 57.

[93] Barth, *The Epistle to the Romans* (London: Oxford University Press, 1933), p. ix.

[94] Watson, "Bible," p. 57.

[95] Kantzer, "Thank God," p. 15.

[96] See Christina A. Baxter, "The Nature and Place of Scripture in the *Church Dogmatics*," in *Theology Beyond Christendom: Essays on the Centenary of the Birth of Karl Barth*, John Thompson ed. (Allison Park, PA: Pickwick Publications, 1986), pp. 33–62.

[97] Richard E. Burnett argues that Barth's commentary challenged the hegemony of Schleiermacher's author-oriented approach to biblical exegesis. *Karl Barth's Theological Exegesis: The Hermeneutical Principles of the Römerbrief Period* (Tübingen: Mohr Siebeck, 2001 and Grand Rapids, MI:

As a student trained by theological liberals, Barth learned to interpret the Bible as an expression of human religious experience. His hermeneutical revolution stemmed from his growing convictions that, (1) a truly critical or scientific approach is one that is appropriate to the particular subject matter being discussed and, (2) the particular subject matter or *Sache* of the Bible is neither subjective religious experience (contra theological liberals) nor the objective history of the historian (contra conservative evangelicals) but rather the revelatory and redemptive self-presentation of God in the person and history of Jesus Christ.[98]

The freedom of the Word is first and foremost the freedom of God in communicative action. Barth believed that the actuality of God's being is prior to all human attempts to inquire into its possibility. The task of biblical interpretation according to Barth is to do justice to the sovereign freedom and uniqueness of this particular subject matter. This involved not simply recovering the authors' intention (contra much evangelical biblical study) but thinking with the biblical authors about—or better, participating with them in—their subject matter. Barth's interpretative interest was less in the historical Paul than in *what* he wrote and, especially, in *about what* Paul wrote.[99] As a theological interpreter, Barth aims to understand Scripture "as articulating not simply an authorial intention but above all a single, infinitely rich theological subject-matter."[100] Historical critics who attempt to "master" the text by following methodological procedures will never penetrate the subject matter; God is not known "after the flesh." On the contrary, "in the face of this subject-matter there can be no question of our achieving, as we do in others, the confident approach which masters and subdues the matter. It is rather a question of our being gripped by the subject matter."[101] Biblical interpretation is essentially the attempt to hear and obey the subject matter of Scripture, not to observe and master it.

Eerdmans, 2004). Burnett pays special attention to the several drafts of the preface to the first edition of Barth's commentary as an important source of evidence for tracking Barth's thinking.

98 See esp. Barth's famous "Preface to the Second Edition," in *The Epistle to the Romans* 6th ed. (Oxford, UK: Oxford University Press, 1933), pp. 2–15. See also Burnett, *Barth's Theological Exegesis*, pp. 74–8 on the question of just what is the Bible's main subject matter.

99 See Burnett, *Theological Exegesis*, pp. 184–97

100 Watson, "Bible," p. 58.

101 Barth, *CD*, I/2, p. 470.

That the Bible is a witness to revelation is of the utmost exegetical significance. According to Barth, the tendency of modern readers of Scripture, whether liberal or conservative, was to treat the Bible primarily as a source. For Barth, however, the very words of the Bible are an integral part of the witness to revelation.[102] In short, to understand the Bible as a witness is to consider its verbal, literary, and canonical form as integrally related to its content. Hence Barth interprets the various parts of Scripture in light of the canonical whole and in light of the subject matter—God revealed in Jesus Christ—that unifies the whole.

Barth's decision to read all of Scripture as a unified witness to God's Word and his concomitant tendency to read the Bible as a literary whole leads him to focus on large canonical patterns and to make typological connections in a way that makes evangelical exegetes trained to read in grammatical-historical fashion uneasy.[103] By contrast, evangelicals (for example, Charles Scalise) who appreciate Brevard Childs's canonical exegesis ultimately have Barth to thank.

4.2 History, reference, truth: the empty tomb

Barth's main concern is to exegete Scripture, not to formulate hermeneutical theories. In a draft Preface to his *Romans*, Barth writes that his commentary is "an attempt to read the Bible differently . . . more in accordance with its subject-matter, content, and substance, focusing with more attention and love upon the meaning of the Bible itself."[104] As to hermeneutics, then, the main principle is to let the authors and texts have their say on behalf of their particular subject matter.[105] Evangelicals agree. The problem

---

102 Barth attributes the Bible's ability to witness to divine revelation not to a capacity of language for revelation but rather to revelation's capacity to bear witness to itself through language (so Burnett, *Theological Exegesis*, p. 228). This too is an aspect of the "freedom" of the Word.

103 Perhaps this explains why there are to date few studies of Barth's actual interpretative practice. See, however, Paul McGlasson's *Jesus and Judas: Biblical Exegesis in Barth* (Atlanta: Scholars Press, 1991) and Mary Cunningham, *What is Theological Exegesis? Interpretation and Use of Scripture in Barth's Doctrine of Election* (Valley Forge, PA: Trinity Press International, 1995).

104 Cited in Burnett, *Barth's*, p. 277.

105 Barth, *CD*, I/2, p. 725.

stems from Barth's particular construal of the Bible's subject matter, its relation to history, and hence its truth.

That the actual words of the Bible refer to the self-revelation of God is made possible only by the latter, not by the former. Scripture refers to Jesus Christ by an act of the Holy Spirit and not an inherent quality or property of the language of the Bible itself.[106] Furthermore, God's self-revelation—the event by which God uses Scripture's words to bring about an encounter of the reader with the divine subject matter—is not under human control, nor is it, strictly speaking, the kind of historical event that a historian could examine or reconstruct.

Take, for example, the Gospels' account of the empty tomb. How does this biblical narrative become the Word of God? There is no suggestion in Barth that the Holy Spirit changes the *sense* of the words on the page. No, what happens is that the *Sache*—the free God in his self-revelation—"commandeers" the biblical language, and the thoughts of the reader, so that the text actively points to the living Christ. It is ultimately the Holy Spirit who closes the gap between what is written and what the reader discovers therein.

What of truth? To what exactly does the narrative of the empty tomb *refer*?[107] Barth's position is best understood in contradistinction from both literalism (for which the empty tomb has the status of an extratextual fact) and expressivism (for which the empty tomb is a mythological expression of the faith's self-understanding and feeling).[108] The problem with literalism is its assumption that we have some access to the referent apart from its textual rendering. To assume we have independent access to God's historical self-revelation, however, is to distract us from the only norm for theology, namely, the biblical *testimony* to God's self-revelation in history.[109]

The true referent of the empty tomb narrative is, for Barth, the living Jesus Christ—a referent that is not open to either verification

---

[106] So Burnett, *Theological Exegesis*, p. 224.

[107] For Barth's exposition of this narrative, see *CD*, III/2, pp. 451–3.

[108] So George Hunsinger, "Beyond Literalism and Expressivism: Karl Barth's Hermeneutical Realism," in Hunsinger, *Disruptive Grace: Studies in the Theology of Karl Barth* (Grand Rapids, MI: Eerdmans, 2000).

[109] For an excellent discussion of the Bible as testimony and its relation to historical reference, see Mark Smith, "Testimony to Revelation: Karl Barth's Strategy of Bible Interpretation in the *Church Dogmatics*" unpub. Ph.D. dissertation, University of Sheffield, 1997.

or falsification by academic historians.[110] Barth describes the empty tomb as "the sign which obviates all possible misunderstanding."[111] Hunsinger provides a helpful paraphrase: "'Sign' is essentially an intratextual category whose extratextual force is that of analogy."[112] The point is that the empty tomb is part of the narrative identification of Jesus Christ. What counts is not the factual accuracy but the rendering of the description. The literary, intratextual, and theological point of the empty tomb is to say something about the kind of resurrection being attested: it is "real and therefore physical."[113] In sum: the witness of the narrative of the empty tomb is that of a realistic (i.e. legendary) witness that analogically depicts something utterly real.[114]

Barth's reticence to affirm the literal empty tomb had nothing to do with his having doubts about Jesus' resurrection; on the contrary, Barth had "material theological grounds" for refusing to build on the neutral ground of the historical critic. The event of Jesus' resurrection, because it involves God's acting only, is strictly speaking not part of the space-time causal network. The inaccessibility of the resurrection event to the academic historian is thus a function not of its unreality but of God's sovereign freedom. Better, then, to stay within the confines of the text in order better to understand its intratextual analogies, patterns, and connections.[115]

Despite Henry's suspicions to the contrary, Barth's reticence to specify the historical referent of the resurrection narratives stems

---

[110] Hunsinger, "Literalism," p. 201.
[111] Barth, *CD*, III/2 p. 453.
[112] Hunsinger, "Literalism," p. 212.
[113] Hunsinger, "Literalism," p. 212.
[114] Cf. Paul McGlasson's claim that "The relation between text and object consists of *analogical depiction*" (*Jesus*, p. 150). See also Bruce McCormack's argument that the relation between the historical sense of the biblical text and its revelatory significance is best understood in terms of an *analogia fidei*, a correspondence between an act of God and an act of a human subject (e.g. the human author and reader) ("Historical Criticism and Dogmatic Interest in Karl Barth's Theological Exegesis of the New Testament," in M. Burrows and P. Rorem eds. *Biblical Hermeneutics in Historical Perspective* [Grand Rapids, MI: Eerdmans, 1991], pp. 322–38).
[115] Cf. Hunsinger: "For Barth the relation between text and referent, far from being literal, was essentially a relation between a network of intratextual patterns and a real but ineffable (extratextual) subject matter, mediated by analogical predication" ("Literalism," p. 214).

not from a disregard for Scripture's truth but from an even greater regard for the integrity of God's self-revelation. Revelation is *in* history, but it is not *of* history. While the resurrection is a historical event, Barth distinguishes between the sheer occurrence of events and God's self-revelation in them. The Gospels are not historical records but testimonies to God's self-revelation in history; it follows that the referent of the resurrection narratives is discovered not by treating the Gospels as evidence but by treating them as *testimonies*: faith-based observations.[116] With this thought we return to the notion that the Bible is a witness to the Word of God.

Readers come face to face with the object of Scripture's witness only when they encounter what the prophets and apostles themselves experienced; here, too, it is a matter of the triune God, as the sovereign subject (and subject matter) of Scripture, making himself present as the referent of the words. The Spirit, as "Lord of the [reader's] hearing," is also Lord of the text's referring. With the Spirit's work in the reader, the words of the Bible work in vain inasmuch as their signification falls short of the thing (the *Sache*) itself.[117] While the sense of the Bible's words is intelligible to unaided human reason, the mystery to which they testify is not.

5. State of the Barth: the current situation

The contemporary renaissance of Barth studies affords evangelicals an opportunity to reconsider Barth's doctrine of Scripture, perhaps for the first time, as a theological proposal in its own right rather than the bastard child of modernist, existentialist, narrativist, or postmodern influences. Two recent proposals concerning the dogmatic location of Barth's view of the Bible are of particular interest.

---

[116] Mark Smith draws on C. A. J. Coady's *Testimony: A Philosophical Study* (Oxford, UK: Clarendon, 1992) to argue that testimony is a source of knowledge in its own right, a reliable cognitive mechanism for producing rational belief. Hence: the resurrection really happened, and the apostolic testimony is the evidence. See Smith, "Testimony."

[117] Without the Spirit, the Bible renders the conception (e.g. the *esse in intellectu*) but not the reality (*res*) itself. Becoming aware of the *res* is not the same as receiving more information; it is rather a matter of grasping not merely the conception of the thing but the thing itself. For further clarification of this matter, see the helpful discussion in Smith, "Testimony," ch. 5.

5.1 The ontological Scripture

In an important restatement of Barth's doctrine of Scripture, Bruce McCormack claims that American evangelicals have taken Barth's statements about the Bible's "becoming" the Word of God out of context and, furthermore, have misunderstood what it means to say that Scripture has its being in becoming.[118] McCormack's main point is that *everything*—God, the world, and especially Jesus Christ—has its being in becoming according to Barth's theological ontology.[119]

Just as important is Barth's contention that not everything becomes what it is under the same conditions. The being of God is absolutely self-determined; human being is only relatively self-determined. The being of Scripture is not self-determined at all; as discourse fixed in writing, it is rather the product of its human and divine authors. McCormack claims that, for Barth, "It is the divine will and act that make the Bible to be what it is 'essentially'."[120] So, when God chooses not to bear witness to himself to a particular reader, then the Bible does *not* become what it is to that reader: in this case, it *is not* (actually) what it *is* (essentially). By contrast, when the Bible becomes the word of God, "it is only becoming what it already is."[121]

---

[118] Bruce L. McCormack, "The Being of Holy Scripture is in Becoming: Karl Barth in Conversation with American Evangelicalism Criticism," in Vincent Bacote, Laura C. Miguélez, and Dennis L. Okholm, eds., *Evangelicals & Scripture: Tradition, Authority and Hermeneutics* (Downers Grove, IL: InterVarsity Press, 2004), pp. 55–75. McCormack also points out that Barth distinguishes the Bible from revelation only to insist that the Word of God is one-in-three (e.g. revelation, Scripture, proclamation) and three-in-one (p. 58).

[119] McCormack explains this curious notion in terms of Barth's "actualizing" understanding of the Incarnation. Significantly, the sovereign freedom revealed in God-becoming-man becomes decisive for Barth's understanding of God's (triune) being as well. To say that God's being is a being-in-act is to translate the notion of God's sovereign freedom into the realm of ontology. In short: Barth refuses to view Scripture in terms of a static divine "substance" for the same reason that he denies this category to the incarnate Christ. See the important footnote in McCormack, "Being," p. 64 n. 12.

[120] McCormack, "Being," p. 70.

[121] McCormack, "Being," p. 66. McCormack hopes also to have demonstrated that there is no contradiction between Barth's doctrine of

The key is to see the Bible's becoming as a matter of divine discretion—an actualization of *grace*, not nature.[122] McCormack's account shows how far off base is the charge that Barth espouses a subjectivism in which human faith is the condition of the Bible's becoming the word of God. McCormack's final verdict with regard to Barth's doctrine of Scripture vis-à-vis its evangelical counterpart is worth noting: "They are compatible doctrines, even if they are not identical."[123] In the final analysis, however, evangelicalism's inerrancy thesis smacks too much of nature inasmuch as it ascribes divine truthfulness as a static quality to Scripture. Barth's own notion, which McCormack dubs "dynamic infallibilism," is yet another outworking of Barth's actualistic ontology of grace.[124] Despite this ongoing tension, at least one evangelical has enthusiastically endorsed McCormack's interpretation.[125]

5.2 The economic Scripture

Whereas the first approach locates Barth's view of Scripture within his broader theological ontology, the second locates it in the economy of divine communicative action. Francis Watson captures the idea perfectly: "The theological significance of the Bible is derived not from any of its immanent characteristics—its value as a historical source, its literary qualities, its religious insights . . . but from the

---

Scripture and his actual use of the Bible as absolutely authoritative—a relation that, as we have seen, some evangelicals had seen as paradoxical (see p. 73 n. 31).

[122] Or perhaps of eschatology. Inasmuch as the Bible becomes the word of God only when there is an in-breaking of the Spirit into the world of the reader, we may say that the being of Scripture is "eschatontological," poised as it is between the "already" and the "not yet" of the Spirit's action.

[123] McCormack, "Being," p. 73.

[124] McCormack insists that Barth's ontology owes less to some philosophical scheme than it does to the properly dogmatic problem of how to reconcile the meaning of divine immutability with the historical fact of the Incarnation. In short, "being as becoming" is Barth's solution to the problem of how God could become man while remaining God (p. 74). This is yet another illustration of my own conviction that one's view of Scripture is inextricably tied up with one's view of God. See my "God's Mighty Speech Acts," in *First Theology: God, Scripture, & Hermeneutics* (Downers Grove, IL: InterVarsity Press, 2002), pp. 127–58.

[125] Morrison, "Barth, Barthians, and evangelicals."

indispensable role assigned to it in the outward movement of the divine communicative action into the world."[126] Specifically, the Bible is a continuing testimony to the history of Jesus Christ, the primary locus of God's self-communicative action. Both the event of Jesus Christ and the biblical testimony to this event are ingredients in the economy of God's self-communicative action.

The purpose of the Bible's becoming revelation to particular readers is ultimately redemption: "Revelation is a way of indicating the communicative force of God's saving, fellowship-creating presence."[127] Human readers of Scripture are drawn into the economy of this communicative action by virtue of their being addressed by Word and Spirit: "Since God's action intends communication, human beings . . . are not spectators but participants, drawn into the circle of the divine communicative action."[128]

Scripture is "holy" precisely because it has been set apart—sanctified (so Webster)—for a divine purpose: "For Barth this means that the Bible is a field of divine activity."[129] So, too, is the reading of the Bible. Gadamer spoke more than he knew when he called Barth's *Romans* a "revolutionary . . . hermeneutical manifesto":[130] to be precise, Barth affects a reverse Copernican Revolution, a turn to the *divine* Subject, in which the human act of interpreting Scripture is itself an ingredient in the economy of divine self-communication. John Webster argues that what Barth discovered in his study of Calvin was "an account of the act of the interpretative situation which sees the reading of Scripture not as a spontaneous human action performed towards a passive and mute textual object, but as an episode in the communicative history of God with us . . . God, we might say, is not only textual content but also the primary agent of the text's realization before us."[131] In sum: "*Exegesis is an aspect of sanctification.*"[132]

---

126 Watson, "Bible," p. 61.

127 John Webster, *Holy Scripture: A Dogmatic Sketch* (Cambridge, UK: Cambridge University Press, 2003), p. 16.

128 Watson, "Bible," p. 60.

129 Webster, *Barth*, p. 56.

130 Hans-Georg Gadamer, *Truth and Method*, 2nd rev. ed., Joel Weinsheimer and Donald G. Marshall tr. (New York: Continuum, 2002), p. 509.

131 John Webster, "Reading the Bible: the Example of Barth and Bonhoeffer," in *Word and Church: Essays in Christian Dogmatics* (Edinburgh, UK: T&T Clark, 2001), p. 93.

132 Webster, "Reading," p. 95 (original emphasis).

6. Beyond the impasse? divine speech acts

"God is the Lord in the wording of His Word."[133]

The present section revisits these recent proposals concerning the ontological and economic aspects of Scripture in order to resolve the long-standing dispute between evangelicals and Barth concerning the nature of biblical authority. To this end, I employ some categories drawn from speech-act philosophy, categories that help clarify where, and why, evangelicals and Barth diverge. My use of philosophy, like that of Barth's, will be ad hoc. I would therefore like to think that Barth himself would laugh at my proposal, not with derision but delight. We begin, however, by reviewing the main problem Barth's view presents to evangelicals, this time with Nicholas Wolterstorff as guide.[134]

6.1 The Wolterstorff objection: the strange silence of God in the Bible

Although God's speaking appears to be center-stage in Barth's theology, Wolterstorff says that the only thing that can truly be called divine discourse is the person and history of Jesus Christ: "God speaks by way of a human being only if God *is* that human being—Jesus Christ . . . the speech of the witness remains purely human speech."[135] In Wolterstorff's view, what happens when the Bible "becomes" the Word of God has nothing to do with divine speech. On the contrary, "God must so act on me that I am 'grabbed' by the content of what God has already said [in Jesus Christ]. I see no reason to call this action 'speech'."[136]

Wolterstorff's final verdict is that Barth's reputation as the theologian of God's Word is somewhat ironic: "God speaks in Jesus Christ, and only there; then on multiple occasions, God activates, ratifies, and fulfils in us what God says in Jesus Christ."[137] What God has to do to a person to enable the (human) biblical witness

---

[133] Barth, *CD*, I/1, p. 139.

[134] Wolterstorff is relevant for two reasons: first, as a recent critic of Barth's view of Scripture; second, for his use of speech-act philosophy.

[135] Nicholas Wolterstorff, *Divine Discourse: Philosophical Reflections on the Claim that God Speaks* (Cambridge, UK: Cambridge University Press, 1995), p. 70 (order slightly altered).

[136] Wolterstorff, *Divine Discourse*, p. 72.

[137] Wolterstorff, *Divine Discourse*, p. 73.

to become revelatory thus has nothing to do with speaking. In Wolterstorff's view, then, the connection between the Bible and God's revelation in Jesus Christ depends not upon speech acts, but upon an *act without speech*.

Wolterstorff's analysis seems to confirm evangelicals' worst fears. First, that there is a merely arbitrary relation between the Bible and God's communicative act in Jesus Christ. Second, that this *diastasis*, and Barth's emphasis on present rather than past inspiration, leads to "uncertainty about [Scripture's] objective authority."[138] Third, that Barth has confused or conflated inspiration and illumination, hence collapsing the origin (and being) of Scripture into its reception ("to be is to be received"!). Finally, Wolterstorff's analysis accentuates the concern that Barth's understanding of the Spirit's work in the lives of readers today is disconnected with the actual words, and meaning, of the text. If the Spirit's present revealing work is an act without speech, an act in which the Bible is merely an instrument the Spirit uses to present Christ, then it would appear that illumination is less a matter of communication than it is causation. The crucial question, again, is how and why the revelation of the Word of God is tied to just *these* words if their sense alone is inadequate to direct us to their referent. Any attempt to commend Barth to evangelicals must ultimately deal with Wolterstorff's objection that Barth lacks a sufficiently robust view of Scripture as a divine speech-act.

6.2 Once (and again) upon an illocution

To summarize: the Bible appears to be caught in a doctrinal standoff between Barth's emphasis on God's sovereign freedom on the one hand and evangelicalism's emphasis on a fixed and authoritative propositional revelation on the other. There is little to be gained, however, by pitting the living Word against the word written. If a house divided against itself cannot stand, how much less can the Word!

I believe that speech-act philosophy can mediate and help move the conversation beyond this theological stalemate.[139] In this regard,

---

[138] Bromiley, "Authority," p. 291.

[139] See the seminal work by J. L. Austin, *How to Do Things with Words* 2nd ed. (Cambridge, MA: Harvard University Press, 1975) and the more systematic presentation in John Searle, *Speech Acts: An Essay in the Philosophy of Language* (Cambridge, UK: Cambridge University Press, 1969).

it is significant that Barth himself comments that "the personalizing of the concept of the Word of God . . . does not mean its deverbalizing"[140] and that Barth himself describes revelation as a divine speech-act (*Rede-Tat*).[141] The notion that the Bible is caught up in divine discourse casts new light both on Scripture's ontology and its role in the economy of divine revelation.

The principal insight of speech act philosophy is that speakers do things in and by speaking. Luther had earlier said something similar: "God's works are his words . . . his doing is identical with his speaking" (*opera Dei sunt verba eius . . . idem est facere et dicere Dei*).[142] There is thus no reason to oppose persons and propositions: persons do things with words and propositions.[143] Speaking is a form of locution, a matter of making meaningful sounds (or in the case of writing, meaningful signs). An *illocution*—the essential discovery of speech act philosophers—is what one does *in* saying something (e.g. promising, commanding, stating, greeting, etc.). And a *perlocution* is what someone does *by* or *through* one's locutions and illocutions and refers to the effects of one's speech (e.g., persuading, encouraging, consoling, etc.). It goes without saying that speech acts are also *interlocutionary*: communicative interactions between persons. In this regard, it is interesting to note that J. L. Austin, the father of speech-act philosophy, lists "making a covenant" as an example of a commissive speech act.[144]

---

140 Barth, *CD*, I/1, p. 138.

141 Barth, *CD*, I/1, p. 150.

142 As cited in William Pauck's introduction to the Library of Christian Classics edition of *Luther: Lectures on Romans* (Philadelphia: Westminster Press, 1961), p. xxxiii. Note that the actual citation is from Luther's WA, vol. 3, p. 152, line 8, rather than 154, 7 as Pauck has it.

143 Every speech act has a propositional component (i.e. content), though most speech acts do more than simply convey content. The transmission of information is a necessary component of speech acts, but not the whole picture. For example, warning and promising and commanding transmit information, but the intent of these speech acts goes beyond merely informing: the speech agent in each case is *doing* something above and beyond merely informing.

144 David Gibson argues that Barth needs to recognize that the Bible is not only a witness to Christ but the document of the covenant, a witness that "binds" God to the text, and to his people, in a more intimate fashion than Barth allows. See his "The God of Promise: Christian Scripture as Covenantal Relation," *Themelios* 29 (2004), pp. 27–36.

The differences between Barth and evangelicals on the matter of the Bible being the Word of God stem from mutual misunderstandings that can be accounted for in terms of speech-act theory. Speech-act philosophy pinpoints the crucial equivocation: does "communication" (i.e. revelation) include the reader's response or not? The dictionary is no help here, for it admits both possibilities. A "communication" may be "the act of imparting propositions" or "the proposition communicated." Barth tends towards the first definition, evangelicals towards the second. Thus Barth tends to emphasize the necessity of the interlocutionary and perlocutionary dimensions of revelation (viz. the Spirit's illumination of readers in the present), whereas evangelicals tend to emphasize its locutionary and illocutionary dimensions (viz. the Spirit's inspiration of the authors in the past).

Is the Bible the word of God or is it not? Does it *communicate* Jesus Christ or does it not? We can avoid falling prey to these fateful either/ors by parsing communicative action in terms of locutions, illocutions, and perlocutions alike. The Bible *is* the word of God insofar as its inspired witnesses—which is to say the inspired locutions and illocutions—really do present Jesus Christ. Yet the Bible also *becomes* the word of God when its illumined readers receive and grasp the subject matter by grace through faith, which is to say, when the Spirit enables what we might call illocutionary uptake and perlocutionary efficacy. The full measure of Scripture as a communicative act of God, then, involves the-Spirit-testifying-about-Jesus-through-Scripture-to-the-church.[145]

We can do justice to Barth's basic concern to preserve God's sovereign freedom in revelation even while viewing the Bible as divine discourse. What may be known about God in Jesus Christ is there, in the plain sense of the biblical text plainly to be seen, yet readers need the Spirit's illumination before they can acknowledge the plain sense for what it is and follow its illocutions and perlocutions where they lead. This view also does justice to the basic concern of evangelicals to preserve the status of what is written as the word of God. God in his freedom has tied himself to the biblical texts: his word is true, trustworthy, and reliable, even when readers do not acknowledge it as such.

---

[145] I am here amending Joseph L. Mangina's description of the word of God in his *Karl Barth: Theologian of Christian Witness* (Louisville, KY: Westminster John Knox, 2004), p. 46. For further development of these points, see my "God's Mighty Speech Acts," esp. pp. 148–57.

These speech act categories do not do away with or reduce the mystery of God's word but enable a deeper appreciation of it. They also enable us to appreciate the respective contributions of Barth and evangelicals to the doctrine of Scripture. Barth helps evangelicals to avoid marginalizing (or excluding altogether) the role of the Spirit's illumination—what Ramm calls an "abbreviated Scripture principle." Evangelicals who have a healthy respect for both inspiration and illumination should have no problem parsing the economy of God's communicative action in terms of locutions, illocutions, and perlocutions. Barth serves as a reminder not to neglect the perlocutionary dimension in our doctrine of Scripture. Conversely, evangelicals serve as a reminder to Barthians that perlocutions depend on illocutions and that illocutions depend on locutions.[146] The ultimate communicative effect—understanding—cannot be had apart from the verbal (e.g. locutionary) content of the illocutionary act. Calvin acknowledges as much when he says that God "sent down the same Spirit by whose power he had dispensed the Word, to complete his work by the efficacious confirmation of the Word."[147]

Is there any textual evidence that Barth might agree with this proposed resolution? Are there grounds for hoping that, with regard to the doctrine of Scripture, the Barthian lion might one day lie down next to the evangelical lamb? I believe there are. Barth insists that the Word written "has its own divine power no matter what may be its effect on those who hear or read,"[148] thereby tacitly recognizing the distinction between what we have termed illocutions and perlocutions. He also implicitly admits that perlocutionary effects depend on the prior locutionary and illocutionary acts: "If now it is true in time, as it is true in eternity, that the Bible is the Word of God, then . . . God himself now says what the text says . . . That is the right and necessary truth in the concept of verbal inspiration."[149] Whether Barth would in fact be happy to view the Word of God as *bound* to the text is, of course, ultimately beyond our ability to say; nevertheless, I have argued that, thanks to speech-act concepts, he *could* do so consistently.

146 For a fuller development of this point, see William Alston, *Illocutionary Acts and Sentence Meaning* (Ithaca, NY: Cornell University Press, 2000), esp. p. 170.

147 John Calvin, *Institutes of the Christian Religion* (2 vols. Philadelphia: Westminster Press, 1960), I.ix.3.

148 Barth, *CD*, I/1, p. 110.

149 Barth, *CD*, I/2, p. 532.

In conclusion: evangelicals and Barth can agree, at the very least, that the Bible is a central ingredient in the economy of God's self-communication. As to ontology, Scripture is divine-human communicative action: the Bible has its *being* in its locutions and illocutions, yet the Bible *becomes* what it is when the illuminating Spirit ministers those locutions and illocutions in order to bring about the divinely intended perlocutionary effects.

Can such conceptual fine-tuning of what is involved in discourse help to overcome the stand-off between evangelicals and Barth over the Scripture principle? Should evangelicals espouse Barth's way of thinking about and interpreting Scripture? In the final analysis, it is not so much a matter of becoming Barthian but of learning whatever there is to learn about how better rightly to view and handle the Scriptures. Whatever is true in Barth's doctrine of Scripture, if there is anything worthy of praise, think on these things . . . [150]

[150] My thanks to Dan Treier and Mark Bowald for their helpful comments on an earlier draft.

3

A Bold Innovator: Barth on God and Election

Sung Wook Chung

This chapter aims to delineate critically Barth's innovations in the doctrine of God and election from a conservative evangelical perspective. Several evangelical theologians have recently attempted to incorporate Barth's theological insights into their theological construction and they have identified themselves as "postconservative" evangelical theologians.[1] Although I do agree with them that we as evangelicals can benefit from points in Barth's theology, I am not in agreement with them that Barth's theology is the hope for the future of evangelical theology. Rather, I am convinced that conservative evangelical theology should take issues with many points of Barth's theology. Let us begin with the "evangelical" aspects of Barth's theology.

1. Evangelical aspects of Barth's theology: his reformation legacy

1.1 Sola Scriptura

As I have argued in another article,[2] Karl Barth was an "evangelical" theologian primarily because of his Reformation legacy. Barth affirmed

---

[1] See John Franke, *The Character of Theology: A Postconservative Evangelical Approach* (Grand Rapids, MI: Baker, 2005).

[2] Sung Wook Chung, "Karl Barth's Evangelical Principles: Reformation Legacy in his Theology," in idem, *Alister E. McGrath and Evangelical Theology* (Grand Rapids, MI: Baker, 2003), pp. 195–212.

repeatedly that he accepted the evangelical tenets of the sixteenth-century Reformation.[3] For example, he accepted wholeheartedly the principle of *sola scriptura*. Of course, it is undeniable that his view of Scripture is different from that of the historic Reformed evangelical camp, which is represented by John Calvin, Jonathan Edwards, B. B. Warfield, James Packer, and John Stott. To be sure, he is not an "inerrantist" in his understanding of the Bible. However, it is important to appreciate that for Barth, Scripture is the only material source for believers' knowledge and experience of God. Furthermore, Scripture alone is the Word of God written and the viable instrument for our knowledge of Jesus Christ. Francis Watson agrees in commenting on the place of Scripture in Barth's theology as follows:

> Theology should never be ashamed of its own foundation in biblical interpretation. It must assert the priority of Holy Scripture over all other human and Christian discourse, both in principle and above all in practice; it must not be deterred by the accusations of "narrowness," "biblicism," "neo-conservatism," or indeed of "Barthianism" that it will inevitably incur as it strives to hold its single theme in view.[4]

1.2 Sola Gratia

Karl Barth was a theologian of grace as well. He incorporated the Reformation slogan *sola gratia* into his theological construction. He reiterated his conviction that human knowledge of God as well as human salvation is by grace alone.[5] Apart from God's grace, through which he reveals himself to us and enables us to know him, there is no other way for us to know God. In that sense, God's revelation itself is a result of his grace and God's empowerment for us to

---

[3] Kurt Anders Richardson is in agreement: "Barth recognized that, while being an evangelical in the sense of the Reformation heritage as it has come down to him in his own day . . ." in idem, *Reading Karl Barth: New Directions for North American Theology* (Grand Rapids, MI: Baker, 2004), p. 109.

[4] Francis Watson, "The Bible," in John Webster ed. *The Cambridge Companion to Karl Barth* (Cambridge, UK: Cambridge University Press, 2000), p. 58.

[5] Colin Gunton says, "It is clear that Barth's is a version of the classic Reformation theology of the gracious reorientation of the person to God by the death of Christ" in idem, 'Salvation,' in Webster, ed., *Companion*, p. 148.

know him through the work of the Holy Spirit is a consequence of his grace. Barth connected closely the idea of divine grace with that of divine sovereignty. God's gracious decision to reveal himself is totally dependent on his sovereign and free determination. God's gracious determination to redeem sinners is squarely grounded upon his free and autonomous decision. Thus, for Barth, God's grace is always a sovereign grace and God's sovereignty is always a gracious sovereignty.

1.3 Christocentrism

In addition, Barth was a christocentric theologian. He accepted, without any reservations, the Reformation conviction that Jesus Christ alone is the unique Savior of sinners from the power of darkness. Furthermore, for him Jesus Christ is the only Revealer of the triune God and even revelation itself. Jesus Christ is the very Word of God, to which the Bible witnesses. Barth says, "If in this way we ask further concerning the one point upon which, according to Scripture, our attention and thoughts should and must be concentrated, then from first to last the Bible directs us to the name of Jesus Christ."[6] Therefore, apart from Jesus Christ, there is neither revelation of God nor salvation of sinners. Apart from Jesus Christ, the Bible has no significance because it centers on the person of Jesus Christ, God the Incarnate. It is Jesus Christ that gives the Scripture its identity, life, and meaning. In sum, Jesus Christ is the heart of the Bible. The christocentric character of Barth's theology is an undeniable aspect of his evangelicalism.

1.4 Theologianhood of all believers

Finally, Barth also accepted one of the fundamental convictions of the Reformation that all Christian believers are spiritual priests before God. Whether male or female, all Christian believers can have a direct access to God through Jesus Christ, the only Mediator between God and humanity, without the need of help from human mediators including professional priests, monks, pastors, and theologians. All the believers can approach God and meet with him with confidence and boldness. Barth advanced this Reformation

---

6 Karl Barth, *Church Dogmatics*, G. W. Bromiley and T. F. Torrance ed., G. W. Bromiley tr., 2d ed., 4 vols. Plus index in 14 vols. (Edinburgh, UK: T&T Clark, 1975–81), II/2, p. 53. Hereafter, it will be *CD*.

principle of the priesthood of all believers into a creative notion of the theologianhood of all believers. According to Barth, all Christians must be theologians. Although we can have so-called professional theologians within the community of the church, it is so important to appreciate that all Christians are called to the knowledge of God. Simply speaking, Christians are those who know God! In that sense, every Christian believer must be regarded as a theologian and needs to devote his or her life to knowing God.

2. Barth's innovation in the doctrine of God

2.1 Actualistic idea of God

In spite of many "evangelical" aspects of Barth's theology, deriving mainly from its Reformation legacy, it seems undeniable that Barth deviated from the historic evangelical theology in many aspects. For example, in his theological construction he does not accept traditional theological concepts and thought patterns but rather creates his own. As G. C. Berkouwer has stated well, "It is therefore not an easy matter to expose clearly and responsibly the central thought of Barth's theology. An added complication in crystallizing its basic thrust arises from the new and strange elements upon which one comes again and again, and which are far removed from 'traditional' theological thought patterns."[7] For this reason, he has been criticized as an "innovator" in Christian theology.

One of the best examples of his theological innovations can be found in his doctrine of God. In the *Church Dogmatics*, II/1, Barth endeavored to reformulate his doctrine of God by means of the motif of actualism. As George Hunsinger has argued, "Actualism is the most distinctive and perhaps the most difficult of the motifs. It is present wherever Barth speaks, as he constantly does, in the language of occurrence, happening, event, history, decision, and act."[8] In accordance with his actualistic pattern of thought, Barth argues that "God is who He is in the act of His revelation."[9] This means that in dealing with the being of God one should not begin

---

7 G. C. Berkouwer, *The Triumph of God's Grace in the Theology of Karl Barth* (Grand Rapids, MI: Eerdmans, 1956), p. 12.

8 George Hunsinger, *How to Read Karl Barth: The Shape of His Theology* (Oxford, UK: Oxford University Press, 1992), p. 30.

9 Barth, *CD*, II/1, p. 257.

to describe God as the one who has his own unique substance or nature but rather as the one who acts in his own unique way. Barth continues to argue, "We are dealing with the being of God: but with regard to the being of God, the word 'event' or 'act' is *final*, and cannot be surpassed or compromised. To its very deepest depths God's Godhead consists in the fact that it is an event—not any event, not events in general, but the event of His action, in which we have a share in God's revelation."[10] As Hunsinger has argued, "At the most general level it means that he thinks primarily in terms of events and relationships rather than monadic or self-contained substances. So pervasive is this motif that Barth's whole theology might well be described as a theology of active relations. God and humanity are both defined in fundamentally actualistic terms."[11]

We as evangelicals may take issue with Barth's above arguments. First, how does Barth know that "with regard to the being of God, the word 'event' or 'act' is *final*?" Does he have any biblical ground for such an argument? It seems that he never provided biblical reasons for such a blunt argument. I cannot help thinking that he started his theological construction of a doctrine of God with his unique "philosophical" presuppositions that could not be verified by the Scriptural witness or any traditional theological sources. Simply speaking, he was too innovative in arguing that "To its deepest depths God's Godhead consists in the fact that it is an event . . . the event of His action."[12] Most evangelical theologians believe that the God of the Bible is a self-contained Being who has his own unique substance and nature. As the One who has his own unique substance, God acts toward humanity and in history. Most evangelical theologians do not deny that God does act in his unique way. However, most of them would deny that "God's being is always a being in act"[13] and "with regard to the being of God, the word 'event' or 'act' is *final*."[14] Barth's actualism is a pattern of thought that the Bible does not endorse explicitly or implicitly. Thus, evangelicals have problems with it.

---

10 Barth, *CD*, II/1, p. 263.
11 Hunsinger, *How to Read*, p. 30.
12 Barth, *CD*, II/1, p. 263.
13 Hunsinger, *How to Read*, p. 30.
14 Barth, *CD*, II/1, p. 263.

2.2 God as the one who loves in freedom

Another good example of Barth's actualistic mode of thought is found in his creative definition of God. His idea of God seems to fall short of the traditional evangelical understanding of God. In his *Church Dogmatics*, II/1, Barth discusses the reality of God by asking "what it is to be God, what makes God God, and what God's 'essence' is."[15] He continues to describe God as follows:

> We recognize and appreciate this blessing when we describe God's being more specifically in the statement that He is the One who loves. That He is God—the Godhead of God—consists in the fact that he loves, and it is the expression of His loving that He seeks and creates fellowship with us. It is correct and important in this connection to say emphatically His *loving*, i.e. His act as that of the One who loves.[16]

By saying this, Barth departed from the historic evangelical approach to God. First of all, in defining who God is he does not begin with an understanding of God's ontological substance or character. This means he does not begin with an affirmation that "God is spirit" or "God is good."[17] In other words, he does not identify God's essence with God's ontological nature. Rather, he identifies the essence of God with God's specific act—the act of loving. In order to validate his arguments, Barth appeals to the first letter of John:

> The tempting definition that "God is love" seems to have some possible support in 1 John 4:8, 16 . . . But it is a forced exegesis to cite this sentence apart from its context, and without the interpretation that is placed on it by its context, and to use it as the basis of a definition. We read in v. 9: "In this was manifested that love of God towards us, because the God sent his only-begotten Son into the world, that we might live through him." Again we are told in v. 10 (with a remarkable similarity of predication): "Herein is love, not that we loved God, but that he loved us, and sent his Son to be the propitiation for our sins."

---

[15] Barth, *CD*, II/1, p. 273.

[16] Barth, *CD*, II/1, p. 275.

[17] Traditional evangelical systematic theologians begin their discussion of God with an affirmation of God's goodness or God's spiritual reality. See Millard J. Erickson, *Christian Theology* (Grand Rapids, MI: Baker, 1985), pp. 263–300 and Gordon R. Lewis and Bruce A. Demarest, *Integrative Theology* (Grand Rapids, MI: Zondervan, 1996), pp. 177–212.

> And finally in v. 15: In this we have knowledge and faith in the love that God has for us, that we confess "that Jesus is the Son of God." The Love of God, or God as love, is therefore interpreted in 1 John 4 as the completed act of divine loving in sending Jesus Christ. If we want to follow M. Dibellius in describing v. 8 and v. 16 as an "equation of God," we must at least go on to say that as such (as the equating of God with an abstract content of His action) it is at once confirmed by a right understanding of John 3:16: "God so (Vulg.: *sic*) loved the world, that he gave his only-begotten Son, that whosoever believeth in him should not perish, but have everlasting life."[18]

Most evangelicals may agree with Barth that God has an attribute of love. Yes, the God of the Bible is the God of love, who manifests his compassion and mercy toward sinners. However, most evangelicals may disagree with Barth that love is God! Although we can say that God has love as one of his personal characteristics, we cannot identify love with God; God is the one who is beyond love. I cannot help thinking that Barth's identification of God with love is a reductionism.

Furthermore, Barth's idea of God as the One who loves in freedom is deficient. It is deficient because the one who loves in freedom can be evil. What if the one who loves in freedom is an evil one? An evil person may love something or someone in freedom. We cannot deny this. Human beings do love something or someone in freedom without any external coercion. Human beings do not always hate someone or something. They love their friends, colleagues, and family members. When they love their friends and family members, they love in freedom, not in coercion.

Barth may raise a question against my critique here. He may say, "How can you compare God's love with human love? God's way of loving is essentially different from human beings'." Then, I may counter his question, "What on earth makes God's loving in freedom fundamentally different from human beings' loving in freedom? I cannot see the formal difference between God's loving in freedom and human loving in freedom. I see only the formal similarity or even identity between God's way of loving in freedom and human beings' way of loving in freedom." Here we need to listen to Barth on what kind of love God does. In fact, Barth explains what God's love is like in the *Church Dogmatics*, II/1. Barth makes several statements on God's loving as follows:

---

[18] Barth, *CD*, II/1, p. 275.

> 1. God's loving is concerned with a seeking and creation of fellowship for its own sake. 2. God's loving is concerned with a seeking and creation of fellowship without any reference to an existing aptitude or worthiness on the part of the loved. 3. God's loving is an end in itself. All the purposes that are willed and achieved in Him are contained and explained in this end, and therefore in this loving in itself and as such. 4. God's loving is necessary, for it is the being, the essence and the nature of God.[19]

Still, I cannot see what makes God's loving in freedom totally different from human loving in freedom. Human beings' loving can be concerned with a seeking and creation of fellowship for its own sake. What makes this impossible to happen from the outset? Human beings' loving can also be concerned with a seeking and creation of fellowship without any reference to an existing aptitude or worthiness on the part of the loved. Why not? Many parents demonstrate their love for their children to be a fellowship without any reference to an existing aptitude or worthiness of their children. Furthermore, human beings' loving can be an end in itself and their loving can be necessary, for it is the being, the essence and the nature of them. Why not? Human beings can love something and someone in freedom! How can Barth deny that? In particular, human beings can and do love their friends and family members. Even Satan does not hate his servants, demons and evil spirits. If he hates his servants, how can his kingdom stand? In his own theological system, it seems, Barth cannot provide satisfactory answers to the questions that I raised above. This is because he started his theological reflection on God with an affirmation of God's action, not with that of God's unique nature and character.

One of the most important implications of the above discussion is that someone's action of "loving in freedom" cannot guarantee the goodness and truthfulness of his or her action. Rather, someone's good nature alone can guarantee his or her action of loving in freedom to be good. What makes God's loving in freedom fundamentally different from human beings' loving in freedom is God's goodness, truthfulness, or holiness. Because God is already good and holy before acting and loving in freedom, his loving in freedom must be essentially different from human loving in freedom. Because human nature is evil and deceitful by nature, human beings may imitate God's loving in freedom but their love can never be

---

[19] Barth, *CD*, II/1, pp. 276–9.

holy and truthful love like God's. Human beings may love their friends, husbands, wives, and children in freedom and without any external coercion but their love can never be true *agape* love.

Therefore, before saying that God is the one who loves in freedom, Barth should have said that God is good, truthful, and holy by nature! He should have begun with an affirmation of God's natural goodness or holiness rather than with an affirmation of his action of loving in freedom. The action of loving in freedom is not unique to God. Only the goodness and holiness is unique to God.

My argument can be verified by the Scripture itself. In reality, the first letter of John affirms God's truthfulness, holiness, and goodness before confirming that God is love. Barth missed this important point and it was the source of his wrong direction in his doctrine of God. Before saying God is love, John says, "God is light" (1 John 1:5) at the very beginning of his letter:

> God is light; in him there is no darkness at all. If we claim to have fellowship with him yet walk in the darkness, we lie and do not live by the truth. But if we walk in the light, as he is in the light, we have fellowship with one another, and the blood of Jesus, his Son, purifies us from all sin.[20]

Therefore, it is important to appreciate that John was affirming that God is love in the very context of affirming that God is the light. One of the implications of this point is that what makes God's loving a fundamentally different kind of loving from human loving is God's being in light, which means that God is good, truthful, and holy by nature. Apart from God's being good, even his loving in freedom is meaningless. Apart from his being holy, even his being in fellowship is useless. Apart from his being light, his giving his Son for sinners can be a lie. It is God's natural goodness, holiness, and truthfulness that make his loving in freedom good and holy and therefore genuine and authentic. We can believe in God's loving in freedom because he never lies and he is always holy, truthful, and righteous. Interestingly enough, Barth makes an argument which is the very opposite to my argument:

> It is the fellowship of the One who loves with the loved himself, and therefore that which the One who loves has to impart to the loved and the loved has to receive from the One who loves. God is not, therefore,

[20] 1 John 1:5–8 (NIV).

> the *Good* first, and then the One who loves, because He does not keep this *Good* to Himself but communicates it to others. God is the One who loves, and as such the *Good* and the sum of all good things. God is good in the fact that He is Father, Son, and Holy Spirit, that as such He is our Creator, Mediator and Redeemer, and that as such He takes us up into His fellowship, i.e. the fellowship which he has and is in Himself, and beyond which as such there is no greater *Good* which has still to be communicated to us through His fellowship with us. Loving us, God does not give us something, but Himself; and giving us Himself, giving us His only Son, He gives us everything. The love of God has only to be His love to be everything for us.[21]

According to the above passage, for Barth, God's loving in freedom guarantees God's goodness. However, for most evangelicals, God's goodness guarantees the truthfulness of God's love. Here we see a fundamental difference between evangelical theologians and Barth in their approach to the relationship between God's goodness and love. Evangelical theologians have been concerned with the moral character of God's love whereas Barth is concerned with the loving character of God's goodness. In other words, for evangelicals, at least Reformed evangelicals, God's being light is prior to and conditions God's being love whereas for Barth, God's being love conditions or determines God's being good.

2.3 Metaphysics of relationship

Another thing that the above passage demonstrates is that Barth presented metaphysics of relationship as a substitute for metaphysics of substance. He hated speculation.[22] Thus, he never defined God from a perspective of substantialist metaphysics. Rather, he began his description of God from the perspective of a specific, concrete, and active relationship within Godhead. This means that he always starts with the triune relationship of the three Persons within Godhead. So, he argued, "God is good in the fact that He is Father, Son, and Holy Spirit, that as such He is our Creator, Mediator and Redeemer, and that as such He takes us up into His fellowship, i.e. the fellowship which he has and is in himself, and beyond which as such there is no greater *Good* which has still to be communicated to us through His fellowship with us." By saying this, he demonstrates that he does not want to say God is good by

[21] Barth, *CD*, II/1, p. 276.

[22] Hunsinger, *How to Read*, pp. 51–2

nature, or God is good because he has the substance of goodness in himself. Rather, he wants to say God is good because God is in a loving relationship of Father, Son, and Holy Spirit.

It is important to note here that Barth's relational ontology is a quite innovative pattern of thought that has had no precedent in the history of Christian theology.[23] Of course, we may say that the three Cappadocian Fathers were an exception. They tended to describe God with a language of *perichoretic* communion of Father, Son, and Holy Spirit. It is patently clear, however, that the pattern of substantialist thinking has been dominant in the long tradition of Christian theology in general as well as of evangelical theology in particular for the past 2,000 years.

By redefining God on the basis of God's act and metaphysics of relationship, Barth demonstrated that he is an innovative theologian, departing from the time-honored and dominant theological tradition of historic Reformed evangelicalism. In so doing, he also constructed a God who is significantly different from the God of many Reformed evangelicals.

3. Barth's innovation in the doctrine of election

One of the by-products of Barth's innovative redefinition of God in accordance with his actualistic mode of thinking and metaphysics of relationship is his innovative approach to the doctrine of election. His idea of divine election is totally different from the traditional idea of election, which has especially been espoused by evangelical Reformed theological tradition. Bruce McCormack agrees in saying, "I am confident that the greatest contribution of Karl Barth to the development of church doctrine will be located in his doctrine of election. It was here that he provided his most valuable corrective to classical teaching."[24] Although McCormack's evaluation of

---

[23] The ontology or metaphysics of relationship was promoted by John Zizioulas' work, *Being as Communion: Studies in Personhood and Communion* (Crestwook, NY: St. Vladimir's Seminary Press, 1985) and has become increasingly popular among many theologians including both ecumenical and evangelical theologians. Among them are the late Colin Gunton, an ecumenical Reformed theologian and the late Stanley Grenz, a postconservative evangelical theologian.

[24] Bruce McCormack, "Grace and being: The role of God's gracious election in Karl Barth's theological ontology," in Webster, ed., *Companion*, p. 92.

Barth's doctrine of election is more positive than many, he agrees that Barth's doctrine of election was an innovative one.

3.1 Election as the central theme of dogmatics

First of all, it is important to appreciate that Barth understands the doctrine of election to be the central theme of dogmatics. As McCormack argues, it is "here too his dogmatics found both its ontic ground and its capstone."[25] In dealing with the doctrine of election in the *Church Dogmatics*, II/2, Barth declares God's election of grace to be "the sum of the gospel" in that it reveals divine free grace most expressly and dramatically. Barth accepted Reformed theological argument that God's election is one of the most central aspects of the gospel and it is purely grounded upon God's sovereign grace and mercy toward humanity without any consideration of human religious merit and moral state. In this sense, we may identify Barth as a Calvinian theologian.[26]

3.2 Redefinition of the idea of election

However, if we delve into Barth's doctrine of election more deeply, we can discover that his doctrine of election is absolutely innovative and without any precedent in the history of Christian theology. For example, Barth redefines the notion of "election." In the evangelical Reformed tradition, the word "election" primarily means God's "election of people" to salvation. In a stricter Calvinist context, the object of election and reprobation is people. Thus, according to the traditional Augustinian and Calvinist theological thought, the subject of election is God and the object of election is sinners. However, Barth defines "election" to be primarily about God's self-determination to be gracious toward humanity in Jesus Christ. In other words, divine election, according to Barth, is God's election of himself or more specifically, God's self-election in his Son Jesus Christ. Barth says, "It is the divine election of grace. In a free act of determination God has ordained concerning himself; He has determined himself."[27] In accordance with his actualistic motif,

[25] McCormack, "Grace," p. 92.

[26] For Barth's complex relationship with John Calvin and later Calvinism, see Sung Wook Chung, *Admiration and Challenge: Karl Barth's Theological Relationship with John Calvin* (New York: Peter Lang, 2002).

[27] Barth, *CD*, II/2, p. 101.

Barth emphasizes the decision aspect of God's election. God decides on his gracious attitude toward humanity in his Son Jesus Christ. Therefore, God's election is primarily about his self-decision or self-determination, not about his election of individuals.

One cannot deny that Barth's notion of election is innovative. No theological forebears have defined election as Barth does. Calvinistic Reformed theology has always understood God's election to be election of individuals to salvation or destruction. During the Middle Ages, Augustinian theologians understood election not as God's self-determination but as God's sovereign choice of some individuals out of the mass of sinners. Aquinas was no exception. He basically accepted and endorsed Augustine's view of election. Luther and Zwingli also defined election as election of individuals to salvation.

3.3 Jesus Christ as the elected man

For Barth, the direct object of divine election is not human beings but Jesus Christ. In his humanity, he is the elected man as the representative of all human beings. In other words, in accordance with his christocentric tendencies, Barth argues Jesus Christ is the very object of God's election in that "the attitude or relation for which God has once and for all decided, to which He has committed us and wills to be committed by us is the relation and attitude to Jesus Christ."[28] Barth is emphatic on this point:

> According to Scripture, the divine election of grace is an activity of God which has a definite goal and limit. Its direct and proper object is not individuals generally, but one individual—and only in Him the people called and united by Him, and only in that people, individuals in general in their private relationships with God. It is only in that one man that a human determination corresponds to the divine determining. In the strict sense only He can be understood and described as "elected."[29]

Therefore, according to Barth, in fact, Jesus Christ is the only One who is elected. In him, all human beings are elected indirectly. Barth is emphatic upon the universal dimension of God's election:

> But it must be said further that His election is the original and all-inclusive election; the election which is absolutely unique, but which in

---

28 Barth, *CD*, II/2, p. 8.

29 Barth, *CD*, II/2, p. 43.

> this very uniqueness is universally meaningful and efficacious, because it is the election of Him who Himself elects.[30]

Furthermore, Jesus Christ is the only One who is rejected. When Jesus Christ was rejected by God on the cross, he was rejected on behalf of all human beings and as the representative of all humanity. According to Barth, "The rejection which all men incurred, the wrath of God under which all men lie, the death which all men must die, God in His love for men transfers from all eternity to him in whom He loves and elects them, and whom He elects as their head and in their place."[31] Since Jesus Christ was rejected by God once and for all, Barth argues that no human beings are rejected by God in principle. A natural conclusion of this point is that all human beings will ultimately be saved. Although Barth never explicitly advocated the doctrine of universal salvation or *apokatastasis*, it is still undeniable that universal salvation was one of the articles of hope that he retained until his death. This means that Barth retained the double dimension of the traditional Reformed doctrine of predestination including election and rejection or reprobation, reformulating it innovatively into a double predestination of Jesus Christ alone from his christocentric perspective.

From the Reformed and Calvinist perspective, Barth's idea of Jesus as the elected man is not contrary to the Scripture because the Bible also teaches that Jesus Christ was elected by God to be the Mediator and Savior for sinners. However, his idea of God's universal election of all human beings in God's election of Jesus Christ is contrary to the explicit teachings of the Scripture. For traditional Reformed theologians, Ephesians 1:3–6 teaches that in Christ God elected some people to be adopted as his children before the foundation of the world. So, the passage teaches clearly that the primary object of God's election is not Jesus Christ but individuals.

It is important to appreciate, however, that from the traditional Arminian perspective, Barth's idea of God's decision to be universally gracious toward humanity, which is demonstrated by God's indirect election of all human beings in Jesus Christ should be appreciated and even celebrated. This is a very interesting aspect of Barth's theology. In terms of his emphasis on God's sovereign grace, Barth can be classified as a Reformed theologian. In contrast, with regard

---

30 Barth, *CD*, II/2, p. 117.
31 Barth, *CD*, II/2, p. 123.

to his emphasis on the universal dimension of God's love and grace, he can be identified as an Arminian theologian. In Barth's doctrine of election, we can find both Calvinistic and Arminian tendencies.[32]

3.4 Jesus Christ as the electing God

One of the most innovative aspects of Barth's doctrine of election lies in his argument that Jesus Christ is not only the Object of election but also the Subject of election. In other words, Jesus Christ is not only the elected man but also the electing God. Barth states, "On the contrary, Jesus Christ reveals to us our election as an election which is made by him, by His will which is also the will of God. He tells us that He himself is the One who elects us."[33] Bruce McCormack agrees that Barth's understanding of Jesus Christ as the Subject of election is quite innovative, saying, "Jesus Christ is both the Subject of election and its Object, the electing God and the elect human. That is the fundamental thesis which shapes the whole of Barth's doctrine of election. The latter half of the thesis occasions no great surprise . . . It is the first half of the thesis, however, which has proved startling to many readers of Barth."[34] In traditional Reformed evangelical theology, the subject of election has been understood to be God the Father who is in covenant with his Son Jesus Christ for the purpose of redemption of humanity. Traditional Reformed theologians called this covenant between God the Father and God the Son executed in eternity the *pactum salutis* or the covenant of redemption.

It is important to appreciate in this context that Barth was critical of the Reformed idea of the covenant of redemption between God the Father and God the Son. He made a crucial statement on the theme:

---

32 Of course, Barth would reject the accusation of Arminianism. He said, "With the Remonstrants there was the quite unmistakable introduction of a new and humanistic Pelagianism from which neo-Protestantism was later to derive" in *CD*, II/2, p. 111. However, if he believes that God's sovereign, gracious, and universal election can be inefficacious for those who "reject" God's grace by their own choice, then he cannot avoid the accusation of Arminianism. But he argues that human rejection of God's grace is void. However, he still shares with Arminians the belief that God has universal love or good will toward humanity.

33 Barth, *CD*, II/2, p. 118.

34 McCormack, "Grace," p. 94.

> The conception of this inter-trinitarian pact as a contract between the persons of the Father and the Son is . . . open to criticism. Can we really think of the first and the second persons of the triune Godhead as two divine subjects and therefore as two legal subjects who can have dealings and enter into obligations with one another? This is mythology, for which there is no place in a right understanding of the doctrine of the Trinity as the doctrine of three modes of being of the one God.[35]

Why was Barth against the traditional Reformed notion of the eternal covenant of redemption between God the Father and God the Son? Probably we may present two answers to this question. First, Barth's understanding of the Trinity was different from that of the traditional Reformed theology. For Barth, "there are not three individuals but one personality (one self-consciousness, one knowledge, one will)"[36] in God. Although we may not accuse Barth of being an overt Sabellian, it is undeniable that Barth's doctrine of the Trinity is leaning toward an inner Sabellianism in that he does not accept "real distinction or difference" between three persons of the Godhead. Of course, how to understand the term "person" has been debatable in the history of Christian theology. However, there has been an indubitable consensus among Christian theologians that God the Father can enter into a covenant relationship with God the Son. For Barth, there is only one subject of God and three self-repetitions or modes of being of one God.

Second, on the basis of his own doctrine of the Trinity, Barth believes that "the second 'person' of the Trinity is the 'one divine I' a second time, in a different form—a form which is constituted by the anticipation of union with the humanity of Christ."[37] Therefore, for Barth, Jesus Christ can be the electing Subject as God the Father was understood to be in the traditional Reformed theology. It is because there are not three centers of self-consciousness but only one center of self-consciousness in God.

4. Concluding remarks

It seems clear that conservative Reformed evangelicals cannot deny that Barth's understanding of God is innovative. It is not only

[35] Barth, *CD*, IV/1, p. 65.
[36] McCormack, "Grace," p. 103.
[37] McCormack, "Grace," p. 104.

innovative but also problematic from our perspective. His view of God was overly colored by the actualistic motif of his theological thought. His redefinition of God as the one who loves in freedom was a by-product of his innovative metaphysics of relationship which replaced the traditional metaphysics of substance. We as conservative evangelicals cannot accept Barth's idea of God as being faithful to the teachings of Scripture.

Barth's idea of divine election is also innovative and leaning toward Arminianism and universalism. It is based on Barth's somewhat unwarranted idea of the Trinity, which can be categorized as "Sabellian" not in terms of the economic Trinity but of the immanent or ontological Trinity. For Barth, strictly speaking, in God we do not have three "Persons" but rather one Person's self-repetition or three modes of being. This leads the Son of God to be the electing Subject. If we accept seriously the teachings of the Bible that God elected the church, not the whole of humanity, in Christ before the foundation of the world (Eph. 1:3–6),[38] then we cannot endorse Barth's doctrine of election as being faithful to the Word of God.[39]

[38] In fact, Barth's exegesis of Ephesians 1:3–6 has remarkable errors and problems. The discussion of the theme would need another full-length article.

[39] Special thanks go to David Buschart, Bruce Demarest, and Don Payne, my colleagues at Denver Seminary, for their helpful comments on the first draft of this article.

4

Karl Barth on Creation

Oliver D. Crisp

It is often claimed that Karl Barth is so consumed by Christology, that all other theological *loci* in his work are "christologized." They are re-forged (some might say, gerrymandered) in the shape of some aspect of his overarching christological vision. Whether this is a fair representation of Barth or not, it is true to say that, for Barth, Christ is the center of all truly Christian theology.[1] In a similar fashion, there is some truth in the idea that, under Barth's eye, the doctrine of creation is "christologized." His rendering of this doctrine involves placing Christ at the center of the theological agenda and working out from there. This is not to say that Barth's christologized doctrine of creation is just Christology under another name, although it does represent an extension of the way in which Christology has traditionally been applied to the doctrine.[2]

This chapter engages with several prominent aspects of Karl Barth's account of creation as found in the *Church Dogmatics* volume III (hereinafter, *CD*).[3] What Barth has to say on this matter, like much of

---

1 Cf. T. F. Torrance: "The evangelical heart of Barth's theology is the doctrine of Christ as the divine Reconciler . . . Barth never ceased to insist Christology gives us the determining center from which all our knowledge of God and of creation must take its shape." *Karl Barth: Biblical and Evangelical Theologian* (Edinburgh, UK: T&T Clark, 1990), pp. 20–1.

2 John Webster makes a similar point in *Barth*, 2nd ed. (London: Continuum, 2004 [2000]), p. 97.

3 All references are to the English translation of the *Church Dogmatics*, G. W. Bromiley and T. F. Torrance eds. (Edinburgh, UK: T&T Clark, 1957–69). In what follows, I shall cite this in parentheses in the body

the *Church Dogmatics*, is far too rich and theologically suggestive—not to mention prolix—to compress into one short essay. And, in any case, there are a number of very helpful accounts of *CD*, III in the recent literature, which make another short exposition of Barth's treatment of this doctrine otiose.[4] Consequently, this essay is not an exposition of, or commentary on, Barth's doctrine of creation as such, but a critical interaction with some of the more controversial issues involved in his treatment of the doctrine of creation proper, in *CD*, III/1. I say this discussion is restricted to matters pertaining to "creation proper," because there is much else in the third volume of the *Church Dogmatics* that there is not the space to enter into here, including Barth's account of providence, evil, prayer, angelology and the ethics of creation.[5] It is tempting in a treatment like this to say something about all of these important matters. I have resisted that temptation, in the belief that it would be more useful to the reader to have a critical discussion of several issues in Barth's doctrine of creation proper than a more general attempt to touch upon, and highlight, a number of important matters in a cluster of related dogmatic issues included by Barth in *CD*, III.

The focus of this essay is the relationship of Barth's doctrine of creation to that of the classical (Western) theological tradition, particularly, the Reformed strand of that tradition. We shall begin by considering some areas in which Barth's doctrine of creation overlaps with classical theological accounts of creation. We then

of the text as *CD*, followed by volume, part-volume and pagination, e.g. (*CD*, III/1, 30).

[4] See for example Eberhard Busch, *The Great Passion: An Introduction to Karl Barth's Theology*, Geoffrey W. Bromiley tr., Darrell L. Guder and Judith J. Guder eds. (Grand Rapids, MI: Eerdmans, 2004), vol. II, ch. 6; Joseph L. Mangina, *Karl Barth: Theologian of Christian Witness* (Louisville, KY: Westminster John Knox Press, 2004), ch. 4; Caroline Schroeder, " 'I See Something You Don't See': Karl Barth's Doctrine of Providence" and the response by Randall C. Zachman, both in George Hunsinger ed., *For the Sake of the World, Karl Barth and the Future of Ecclesial Theology* (Grand Rapids, MI: Eerdmans, 2004); Kathryn Tanner, "Creation and Providence" in John Webster ed., *The Cambridge Companion to Karl Barth* (Cambridge, UK: Cambridge University Press, 2000) and Webster, *Barth*, ch. 5.

[5] These are, arguably, the major themes in the first, third and fourth part-volumes of *CD*, III. I have also omitted any discussion of the theological anthropology of *CD*, III/2. This is dealt with in a separate chapter in this volume.

turn to some areas where his doctrine is at odds with the tradition, particularly that of his Reformed theological forbears. The discussion shows that, in several respects, Barth's account of creation offers some important and interesting theological insights, although not everything he has to say about the doctrine is entirely satisfactory. A concluding section offers some reflections on engaging with Barth on the doctrine of creation.

1. Four areas of overlap between Barth and the Reformed tradition on creation

The relationship of Barth's doctrine of creation to classical theology, particularly the scholastic theology of his own Reformed tradition, is complicated. There is some conceptual overlap, even agreement, such as Barth's defense of *creatio ex nihilo* (creation out of nothing).[6] But there are also key areas in which Barth departs from the tradition, particularly in his "christologizing" of the doctrine. It is important to understand this, in order to ascertain where Barth's doctrine is innovative, so that we may assess the extent to which what Barth says that is original represents a helpful contribution to this theological locus.

We begin with four areas of conceptual overlap between Barth's doctrine of creation and the Reformed tradition. First, Barth could certainly have endorsed the Reformed orthodox notion that "the triune God is the creator, but in such a way that the Father, as the 'source of the Trinity' is also the proper source of the works of creation which he has executed through the Son and the H[oly] Spirit."[7] Barth himself approves of the scholastic notion that the works of the Trinity in creation are indivisible (*opera ad extra sunt indivisa*). He says that although the Father is the Creator, to this

---

[6] See Barth, *CD*, III/1, pp. 16ff., 103. Barth is particularly keen to distance the creation narrative of Genesis 1 from any notion of God creating the world from some pre-existing chaotic matter. In this respect he stands with the tradition and against those modern theologians, such as Process thinkers like David Griffin and John Cobb, who have abandoned creation out of nothing for a more platonic doctrine of creation from existing matter.

[7] From Heinrich Heppe, *Reformed Dogmatics*, G. T. Thomson tr. (London: Wakeman Trust, 1950), p. 191. Cf. Barth, *CD*, III/1, pp. 12–14. This should not be taken to mean that this way of thinking about the relation of the Trinitarian persons to the act of creation is *peculiar* to the Reformed Orthodox.

must be added the qualification: with the Son and the Spirit. "The proposition that God the Father is the Creator and God the Creator the Father can be defended only when we mean by 'Father' the 'Father with the Son and the Holy Spirit'" (*CD*, III/1, p. 49).[8]

Secondly, like classical Reformed theologians, Barth affirms that the act of creation is a free act of God. There is, both Barth and the Reformed Orthodox declare, nothing inevitable about creation as such. God was not *bound* to create a world of some kind, nor was he bound to create this *particular* world. To affirm that God was bound to do either of these actions is to infringe divine freedom and make creation into something necessary.[9]

Thirdly, like many, though not all, of the Reformed Orthodox, Barth is supralapsarian in his doctrine of the divine decrees, although the content of Barth's supralapsarianism is different from traditional construals in important respects.[10] For one thing, he denies that

---

[8] Barth is sometimes accused of not having a robustly Trinitarian doctrine of creation. If this is un-trinitarian theology, then Barth is in the company of a great cloud of witnesses in the Christian tradition!

[9] Cf. Heppe, *Reformed Dogmatics*: "Above all it is fixed, that the creation of the world is a thoroughly free act of God, in fact an act of God free *libertate contradictionis* . . . so that God could also refrain from creating," p. 192. The Reformed Scholastics usually speak in terms of creation as necessary as a consequence of the divine decree (*ex necessitate consequentiae*), not necessary in and of itself. Barth says similar things at times. For instance, he claims that there is a genuine necessity involved in creation by the fact that God loved the world (from eternity), and gave his Son for it (cf. John 3:16)—see *CD*, III/1, p. 51. But, although Barth does not make this connection in this passage, what he does say clearly does not concern any absolute necessity. It is something like the scholastic consequential necessity, since God's love for the world is a consequence of God's free decision to create it.

[10] Supra- and infralapsarianism are the two major views in Protestant orthodoxy, concerning the logical ordering of the divine decrees. According to Barth (*CD*, II/2, p. 142) supralapsarianism has to do with God ordaining the salvation of some and damnation of others prior to (usually understood in the tradition to mean conceptually or logically prior to, not temporally prior to) his decision to create the world or redeem it—hence the "*supra*—", which refers to the fact that the *decretum absolutum* takes place "prior to" the decree concerning the fall. By contrast, infralapsarianism, according to Barth, begins with the decree to create and preserve humanity despite the fall. Only subsequent to this decree does God ordain the election of some and reprobation of others, hence *infra lapsus* (after the fall) (*CD*, II/2, pp. 143–4).

the divine decrees fork at the point where God elects some human beings and reprobates the rest. Instead, according to Barth, God elects and reprobates Christ, the Elect (and Reprobate) One, and derivatively elects all humanity "in" Christ, whose sin is expiated by Christ who stands as "the judge judged in our place."[11] This has important ramifications for Barth's doctrine of creation, as we shall see.

It is nevertheless true to say that Barth's supralapsarianism overlaps with the traditional scholastic principle that, in the matter of the divine decrees, *what is first in divine intention is last in execution*. In this regard, Kathryn Tanner observes that for Barth, "what is first in God's intention and what spurs God's relation with us from the very beginning—to be the loving Father of us all in Jesus Christ—comes last in execution. Therefore the history of God's relations with us, like the Bible, has to be read from back to front and only on that basis from the front in anticipation of the end."[12] But this does raise a question about what Barth considers the first intention of all God's works to be. If, like Tanner, we say Barth thinks that it is the redemption of all humanity in and through the work of Christ, this would appear to mean that God's end in creation is not, or is not ultimately (as has often been traditionally thought) his self-glorification. It is instead the reconciliation of humanity to Godself.[13]

However, it might be argued that it makes better theological sense to say that even if there are several ends or goals of creation including the redemption of humanity, the ultimate end of all God's works is his self-glorification—to which even the redemption of humanity is subordinate. (In which case, the redemption of humanity is one subordinate end of creation, but not its ultimate end. There is, in other words, an ordered hierarchy of "ends" of creation, in this way of thinking about God's divine decrees.) We can always ask why God has ordained the reconciliation of humanity (or some number of human beings less than the totality of humanity). It makes sense to respond to such a question, that, "God does this for his

---

[11] For an insightful discussion of Barth's doctrine of election, see Bruce McCormack's essay, "Grace and Being: The Role of God's Gracious Election in Karl Barth's Theological Ontology" in Webster ed., *Companion*, pp. 92–110. See also Sung Wook Chung's essay in this volume.

[12] Tanner, "Creation," p. 114.

[13] Barth does speak of the covenant (of grace) as the goal of creation at times. See *CD*, III/1, 231.

own glory." And this implies that divine self-glorification is a more ultimate end of creation than the redemption of human beings. But it does not make a great deal of theological sense to ask why God seeks to glorify himself, if we expect a response which points to a more ultimate goal than his self-glorification. God glorifies himself, according to a number of classical theologians (sometimes dubbed "perfect being theologians") because it would be an imperfection in God not to do so.[14] A *maximally* perfect being (that is, a being who has all possible perfections to a maximal degree) cannot, after all, seek to glorify something other than himself, for that would be to glorify something that is less than maximally perfect (assuming that God alone is maximally perfect). And giving glory to something less than maximally perfect would itself be an imperfect act. But God is maximally perfect, so he cannot glorify something less perfect than himself, the maximally perfect being. Does this offer a good reason for thinking that the ultimate end of creation is God's self-glorification? A number of classical theologians, including theologians in the Reformed tradition, have thought so. At the very least, this raises a question about the adequacy of Barth's understanding of the end or ends of creation (if Tanner is correct about Barth's views on the goal of creation).[15] (It also raises questions about his understanding of the scope of reconciliation, but that is another matter.)[16]

---

[14] This notion can be found in the work of Anselm of Canterbury, Thomas Aquinas and Jonathan Edwards, to name three. For a recent treatment of perfect being theology, see Katherin Rogers, *Perfect Being Theology* (Edinburgh, UK: Edinburgh University Press, 2000).

[15] It is sometimes difficult to pin down exactly what Barth thinks on this matter. Although he makes much of the covenant as an (the?) end of creation, he also says things that seem to conflict with this. For instance, in *CD*, III/1, p. 44, whilst commenting on Romans 11:36, he says that creation is "through God," "from God", and "for God." This sounds more like the traditional view. Perhaps the most sophisticated theological account of the ends of creation in the Reformed tradition can be found in Jonathan Edwards' dissertation, "The End of Creation," in Paul Ramsey ed., *The Works of Jonathan Edwards Volume 8: Ethical Writings* (New Haven: Yale University Press, 1989). The relationship between Edwards and Barth on this matter has been elucidated by Stephen R. Holmes in *God of Grace and God of Glory: An Account of the Theology of Jonathan Edwards* (Edinburgh, UK: T&T Clark, 2000).

[16] I have attended to this matter elsewhere. See Oliver Crisp, "On Barth's denial of universalism," in *Themelios* 29 (2003): 18–29.

Fourthly, Barth takes considerable pains to show that there is an intimate connection between the divine act of creation, and the covenant of grace whereby God graciously ordains to elect Christ as the one through whom human redemption is brought about. He speaks of creation as *the external basis of the covenant* (*CD*, III/1/41, p. 2) and of the covenant as *the internal basis of creation* (*CD*, III/1/41, p. 3). On the one hand, creation is the means by which God ordains to bring about his covenant relationship with humankind through the agency of Christ. God will redeem human beings through Christ, the Elect One, and in order to do this, God will create the world. (This offers another window onto Barth's supralapsarian understanding of the divine decrees.) But on the other hand, or looked at from another point of view, the covenant is the internal meaning or basis of the creation. It is the reason why God creates the world.

John Webster thinks that Barth's two claims about the relation between creation and covenant amount to the same thing.[17] But, without some explanation, this is not obvious. (If it were, we would have a distinction without a difference). I suggest that at least part of what Barth is getting at is this: the creation should not be treated independently of the covenant of grace. The two things are not unrelated to one another, or merely doctrines running along parallel lines in the mind of God. They are both interconnected in the divine mind. God creates the world in order to bring about his covenant (the supralapsarian element to this claim). But Barth also wants to assert that the covenant is itself somehow the "internal" basis of the creation. It is, we might say, the rationale for the creation: "The covenant is the goal of creation and creation the way to the covenant" (*CD*, III/1, p. 97). It is rather like asking which of two pillars that support a house are more fundamental to the integrity of the structure. Is it the one on the left, or the one on the right of the portico? Such reasoning is futile because both are needed for the house to remain standing. And similarly, both the creation and covenant are needed for God's purpose in creation to stand, although it is the covenant that is the goal and purpose of creation, and which gives creation its rationale.

What I am suggesting is that Barth's distinction between the "internal" and "external" in his characterization of the relationship

---

[17] Webster, *Barth*, p. 98. Barth explicitly states at one point that the relationship between creation and covenant is not reversible. See *CD*, III/1, p. 97.

between the creation and covenant in the plans of God is nothing more than a device for emphasizing different aspects of their interconnectedness in the plans of God, and the logical, or conceptual, priority of the covenant in the divine plan. But this distinction relies upon his commitment to a supralapsarian view of the ordering of the divine decrees. It is the covenant that gives meaning to creation, not the other way around. Moreover, the "internal basis" of creation can only be understood when we see that God uses creation as the means by which to redeem humanity through Christ (under the terms of the covenant in which Christ is the Elect One). So, what Barth has to say about the relationship between the covenant and creation implies a particular theological conception of the nature of creation and its rationale, or goal. And this rationale is connected in turn to his claim that creation can only be understood by faith—when we understand that Christ's work is the means by which the redemptive goal of creation is achieved.[18] It is to this matter that we now turn.

2. Four areas of disagreement between Barth and the Reformed tradition on creation

And so, via four areas of partial agreement and overlap between Barth and his theological forbears in the Reformed tradition, we come to four areas of disagreement between Barth and the Reformed tradition. And, following on from the foregoing, we begin with Barth's claim that a proper understanding of creation requires prior faith in Christ (*CD*, III/1, p. 40), without which creation cannot be understood. It is, he declares, an *articulus fidei* (article of faith), not a component of some theological prolegomenon prior to dogmatic theology proper. However, most classical theologians agree that to some extent human beings are capable of understanding that the world was created. And this can be achieved in the absence of faith, and despite the noetic effects of sin. For instance, in his *Institutes* I:i–v John Calvin maintains that the creation is a natural revelation, and that, even in a fallen state, human beings are capable of seeing

[18] Of course, it may be that the internal logic of Barth's doctrine is consistent and yet his account of creation still fails if, say, his conception of the reconciliation of humanity as the (ultimate?) end of creation is wide of the mark. I have already given one good reason from the tradition for questioning Barth's position in this regard.

in the creation the hand of a creator (though not, it should be pointed out, a saving knowledge of God in Christ).[19] But Calvin also claims that the created order can only be seen for what it truly is by those with faith. Believers should "take pious delight in the works of God open and manifest in this most beautiful theatre," that is, the theatre of God's creation. He goes on to say that although the creation "is not the chief evidence for faith, yet it is the first evidence in the order of nature." So believers should "be mindful that wherever we cast our eyes, all things they meet are works of God." Such experiences of creation should leave the Christian ready to "ponder with pious meditation to what end God created them [the world]."[20]

Barth's account of creation in *CD*, III/1 raises several issues with this sort of reasoning. The first has to do with the fact that creation is no evidence *for* faith, if this means, "evidence *in support of*" or, alternatively, "evidence *that grounds*" faith. Nature can offer no evidence for faith—no "point of contact" between the creation and human beings. For there is no *analogia entis*, or analogy of being between the created order and human beings whereby the created order may act as a conduit, or catalyst for revelation apart from the special revelation of the word of God.[21] Neither would Barth be entirely happy with discussion or reflection upon creation that did not draw attention to the fact that without a saving knowledge of Christ, one cannot truly be said to *perceive* and *understand* what it means to speak of a creation as such. Thus, at the beginning of his discussion of creation in *CD*, III/1, p. 28, he says, "Jesus Christ is the Word by which *the knowledge of creation* is mediated to us because He is the Word by which God has fulfilled creation." He goes on to say,

---

[19] Barth denied Calvin believed this in his infamous tract, *Nein!*, directed at his Swiss colleague, Emil Brunner. See *Natural Theology*, Peter Fraenkel tr. (London: Geoffrey Bles, 1946). However, most Calvin interpreters think Barth is mistaken in his reading of Calvin. See, for instance, Paul Helm, *John Calvin's Ideas* (Oxford, UK: Oxford University Press, 2004), ch. 8.

[20] John Calvin, *Institutes of the Christian Religion*, John T. McNeill ed., Ford Lewis Battles tr. (Philadelphia: Westminster Press, 1960), vol. I, xiv, p. 20.

[21] Much is made of the "analogy of being" in literature on Barth, and Barth himself says, "I regard the *analogia entis* as the invention of the Antichrist" in *CD*, I/1, xiii. But, as George Hunsinger points out, Barth never really explains precisely what he means by this term. See Hunsinger, *How to Read Karl Barth: The Shape of His Theology* (New York: Oxford

> I believe in Jesus Christ, God's Son our Lord, in order to perceive and understand that God the Almighty, the Father, is the Creator of heaven and earth. If I did not believe the former, I could not perceive and understand the latter. If I perceive and understand the latter, my perception and understanding are completely established, sustained and impelled by my believing the former (*CD*, III/1, p. 29).

In this respect, Barth goes beyond what Calvin and his successors amongst the Reformed orthodox were willing to say in his "christologizing" of creation, which he freely acknowledges:

> With . . . reference to the noetic connexion between Jesus Christ and creation we emphasize something which has been strangely overlooked and neglected, or at any rate not developed in any detail, either in more recent or even in earlier theology (*CD*, III/1, p. 29).

Whereas Calvin and the Reformed orthodox were willing to make space for natural revelation and (a limited) natural theology, such notions are anathema to Barth, for whom any concession towards natural theology of any description is tantamount to making God in our own image.[22]

According to Barth we may not presume to know what God is like from our own ratiocination, or on the basis of some putative natural revelation in the created order. We can only know what God is like where God breaks into our world in an event of revelation and makes himself known to us. Applied to his doctrine of creation, this means that human beings are incapable of knowing that this world is a creation as such (rather than, say, a cosmic accident, or a random occurrence, or a brute fact without any explanation), outside

---

University Press, 1991), p. 283, n. 2. According to Hunsinger, a rough idea of what Barth has in mind would be this: a state of affairs by which human beings are inherently open to and capable of knowing God and a procedure whereby this inherent openness is exercised such that God becomes known (in some sense). But from this it is still not clear how this involves an *analogy* of being. Cf. Emil Brunner, *The Christian Doctrine of Creation and Redemption*, *Dogmatics Vol. II*, Olive Wyon tr. (London: Lutterworth Press, 1952), ch. 1, Appendix C.

[22] Elsewhere in *CD*, III, when discussing theological anthropology, Barth argues that the *imago dei* is not some property possessed by human beings. It is Christ (cf. Col. 1:15), into whose image all the redeemed will be formed. This point is helpfully discussed by Mangina, *Barth*.

of revelation. And since the Word of God is the agent of revelation and the one who is revealed to us in Scripture, it is through the Word of God that we come to understand that God has created the world. So Barth is entirely serious in his claim that creation cannot be made sense of apart from knowledge of Christ.[23] Barth believes that the history of dogmatic theology shows how, when this insight has been ignored, the doctrine of creation has become enslaved to a general account of creation that is "naturalized." By that, he means an account of creation that is not specifically Christian, whose principal purpose is to function as a bridge to those working in the natural sciences whose sympathies lie with philosophical naturalism (roughly, the idea that all that exists is the material world), not the supernaturalism of Christian theology. Such an account of creation, according to Barth, can only end up surrendering what is distinctively Christian in the doctrine of creation, in order to make a theological account of creation palatable to a wider (and unsympathetic) audience.[24]

---

[23] At one point he offers the following argument against "all science both ancient and modern" (presumably—although he does not say as much—he means here scientific *naturalism* not natural science *per se*) in *CD*, III/1, p. 6: "If the world is not created by God it is not. If we do not recognize that it has been created by God, we do not recognize that it is. But we know that it has been created by God only on the ground of God's self-witness and therefore in faith. Therefore we know only in faith that the world is."

[24] Eberhard Busch spends some time explaining how Barth saw this declining trajectory of the theology of creation from the seventeenth century onwards. According to Busch, Barth saw the Enlightenment as the beginning of the gradual domestication of the doctrine, and its eventual assimilation to an entirely secular understanding of what "creation" means: "first the interpretation of the covenant of grace in terms of the creation, and then creation without reference to this covenant, and ultimately without reference at all to God; the understanding of 'nature' as humanity's mass of manageable things and then its negatability by humans; the understanding of the human person without reference to the fellow person and then in terms of the animal—this entire pathway began, for Barth, in a *theology* that thought of God without the human and the world, saw him in relation to creation as one not essentially connected to it." *The Great Passion*, p. 179. Cf. Thomas Torrance's comments on the "Latin heresy" of Medieval and post-Reformation theology, in *Karl Barth, Biblical and Evangelical Theologian* (Edinburgh, UK: T&T Clark, 1990), ch. 8.

Related to this is a second area of disagreement between Barth and his Reformed forbears, to do with his denial of an apologetic purpose to the doctrine of creation. At the beginning of *CD*, III/1, p. ix he declares, "there can be no scientific problems, objections or aids in relation to what Holy Scripture and the Christian Church understand by the divine work of creation." He does not pause to explain this in detail, but it seems Barth believed cosmology and theology are dealing with two very different, though perhaps complementary, accounts of the creation of the world.[25] According to Barth, once it is understood that the creation narratives of Genesis 1–3 are not to be read as a scientific textbook of what literally took place in creation, but as a story—or, as Barth puts it, a saga—which explains what went on in creation, much of the supposed conflict between cosmological and theological accounts of creation dissolve. (Compare the way in which a mechanic might offer to someone unversed in the workings of the combustion engine a story that explains why their motor car broke down, which, whilst not giving a technical account of the matter in all its facts, is nevertheless a way of explaining what the problem consisted in that is not untrue. Such a story might be a "saga" in Barth's sense. It is clearly not a "myth," which, as Barth makes clear, can have no basis in actual events). Barth maintained that the biblical account of creation is a piece of dogmatics, not apologetics, which is quite different to the way this doctrine is often treated in modern theology. Because of

[25] Cf. *Dogmatics in Outline*, G. T. Thomson tr. (London: SCM Press, 1949), p. 51 and Letter 181, to Christine Barth, where he says, "The creation story is a witness to the beginning or becoming of all reality distinct from God in the light of God's later acts and words relating to his people Israel—naturally in the form of a saga or poem. The theory of evolution is an attempt to explain the same reality in its inner nexus—naturally in the form of a scientific explanation . . . Thus one's attitude to the creation story and the theory of evolution can take the form of an either/or only if one shuts oneself off completely either from faith in God's revelation or from the mind (or opportunity) for scientific understanding." *Karl Barth, Letters 1961–1968*, Geoffrey Bromiley tr. (Edinburgh, UK: T&T Clark, 1981), p. 184. This does not mean that Barth saw no place for a more apologetic account of creation. See *CD*, III/1, p. x. Thomas Torrance, a pupil of Barth, was at pains to show how (for want of a better word) "Barthian" theology has methodological parallels with modern natural science. See, for example, Torrance, *Karl Barth*, pp. 145 ff. And his *Space, Time and Resurrection* (Edinburgh, UK: T&T Clark, 1976).

this, Barth argued that the proper form this doctrine should take is theological, not apologetic. For this reason he felt free to leave the apologetic problems associated with creation to one side in *CD*, III/1.

This approach to the creation narratives and their relation to the natural sciences have been controversial and few have followed Barth's lead. The main point of contention has to do with whether or not Barth is right about the dogmatic, rather than apologetic, purpose of the creation narratives of Genesis 1–3. There has also been some criticism, even amongst Barth's allies, of the way in which he expounds the texts of the Primeval Prologue of Genesis 1–3 in *CD*, III/1.[26] But for many evangelicals, the most serious problem with Barth's treatment of the creation narratives is his willingness to think of them as "saga," rather than as broadly historical events. Much here depends on a complex of issues surrounding the nature of the creation narratives, their place in biblical literature and their status as revelation (or their status as the vehicle for revelation, on Barth's account of revelation).

I do not propose to enter into this morass here. However, several things should be borne in mind when tackling Barth on this issue. To begin with, he is very concerned to get to grips with the text and what it says—there are literally pages of exegesis on the creation narratives in *CD*, III/1. He is also somewhat wary of tying his own exegesis too tightly to particular historical-critical theories about some putative original sources for the canonical text.[27] He does not make the mistake of thinking that because a canonical text has a literary prehistory, this *ipso facto* undermines its status as revelation, or—for Barth—its status as the vehicle for revelation. Finally, as I have already indicated, his description of the creation narratives as saga should not be misunderstood. Barth's characterization of Genesis 1–3 as saga is not a thinly veiled way of saying "Genesis 1–3 is a fairy tale," although the way he negotiates Genesis 1 and 2

---

[26] See, for example, W. A. Whitehouse's friendly criticism in his short essay, "Karl Barth on 'The Work of Creation': A Reading of Church Dogmatics III/1," in Nigel Biggar ed., *Reckoning with Barth: Essays in Commemoration of the Centenary of Karl Barth's Birth* (Oxford, UK: A. R. Mowbray and Co., 1988). Mangina also refers to Barth's rather "unusual" way of thinking about Genesis 1:2. See his *Karl Barth: Theologian of Christian Witness*.

[27] A point also noted by Mangina, see *Theologian*, p. 91.

is not always as clear as one might have hoped.[28] (However, and *ad hominem*, Barth is not alone amongst modern theologians in this regard. There is precious little theological discussion of the creation narratives in modern theology that does not treat the dogmatic implications of these passages rather like an embarrassing family secret. This, it seems to me, is a major dogmatic lacuna in modern theology, with few exceptions).

A fourth area of disagreement between Barth and traditional Reformed theology has to do with the creative act itself. Unlike classical theologians, Barth does not believe creation is a timeless act of an atemporal God, whose essence remains unaffected by the utterance of the divine fiat, and bringing into being of the created order.[29] Barth believes that the fact of the incarnation should "control" what is believed about the relation of God to time in this respect, such that creation is understood as a temporal act of God. Let us focus on two claims made by Barth in this context. The first is that God is somehow in time, although a time very different from "created time." The second is his denial of Augustine's thesis that God atemporally creates the world "with," rather than "in" time. On the question of God's relation to time, Barth says the following:

> Eternity is not merely the negation of time. It is not in any way timeless. On the contrary, as the source of time it is supreme and absolute time, i.e. the immediate unity of present, past and future . . . God Himself is temporal, precisely in so far as He is eternal, and His eternity is the prototype of time, and as the Eternal He is simultaneously before time, above time, and after time (*CD*, III/1, p. 67).

Later in the same discussion, he speaks of God's time as "absolute," as opposed to created time that is "relative time" (*CD*, III/1, p. 68). This is difficult to make sense of. It might be that Barth means God exists in some sort of exalted temporal state, where God is "in time" but without an absolute past, present or future. One could

---

[28] My concern here is just to defend Barth against certain common misunderstandings of what he is trying to say about the creation narratives, in the interests of fair play. I am not committing myself to what Barth actually says about Genesis 1–3.

[29] For expositions of the classical view, see Augustine, *Confessions*, XI–XII; Boethius, *The Consolation of Philosophy*; and Aquinas, *Summa Theologica* I.Q.10.

claim that God exists omnipresently through time and that there is no "God's eye" view from which we can say a particular moment is objectively past, present or future. Then, we could say that God is past, with reference to a particular circumstance, but that there is no past for God, objectively speaking. On such a way of thinking God does not, in one sense, have an objective past, present, or future without reference to particular circumstances, such as "God created the world some time *before* this afternoon."

But God is temporal, nevertheless. Some recent metaphysicians have discussed this sort of view of time, and it does seem to correspond to Barth's notion of God's time as "pure duration."[30] The difference between this view of an exalted, or "pure duration" view of God's time, and created time, would be that, for the creature, there is an objective past, present and future. He or she experiences the present, recalls the past and looks forward to a future in a way that, on the "pure duration" view of God's time, God does not. Perhaps this sort of distinction is what Barth means when he emphasizes the importance of history in creation: "No less than everything depends upon the truth of the statement that God's creation takes place as history in time" (*CD*, III/1, p. 69).

One of the problems with trying to make sense of Barth's understanding of God's relation to time is that what he does say on the matter is rather ambiguous at times, and difficult to get a handle on.[31] Still, this is one way in which Barth's claim that God is in time but not in "created time" could be construed. But it is still a departure from the classical view that God is timeless, and

---

[30] For more on recent metaphysical arguments in this area, see Thomas M. Crisp, "Presentism," and Michael C. Rea "Four Dimensionalism," both in Michael J. Loux and Dean W. Zimmerman eds., *The Oxford Handbook of Metaphysics* (Oxford, UK: Oxford University Press, 2003). Robert W. Jenson says, "He [Barth] describes the particular 'eternity of the triune God' as 'pure duration [*reine Dauer*].'" *Systematic Theology, Vol. 1, The Triune God* (New York: Oxford University Press, 1997), p. 217. His discussion of the way in which Barth's doctrine of divine eternity echoes elements of Gregory of Nyssa is interesting, although I have argued elsewhere that Jenson's own account of divine eternity is unworkable. See Oliver D. Crisp, "Robert Jenson on the Pre-existence of Christ," in *Modern Theology*, forthcoming.

[31] This has hampered other interpreters of Barth too. See, for example, R. H. Roberts' rather tortuous essay, "Barth's doctrine of time: Its nature and Implications," in S. W. Sykes ed., *Karl Barth: Studies of His Theological Method* (Oxford, UK: Oxford University Press, 1979).

creates the world with time. This brings us to the second aspect of his discussion of God and time that I want to mention. Barth takes issue with Augustine's account of divine atemporal creation in his *Confessions*, XI–XII.[32] There, amongst other things, Augustine says that God creates the world and time "simultaneously" (if the reader will excuse the anachronism). He denies what we might call the "container" view of time, where God creates time, and then creates the world that sits "in" time, like a ball might sit in a bowl or other container.[33]

Barth replies that God may certainly create the world in time. God is not atemporal, as Augustine believes. He has "pure duration." So the created world begins in this "pure duration" of God's eternity. Perhaps part of what he means is that, although "created time" begins with the divine fiat to create, this does not mean that it is meaningless to speak of some period of time before creation. God exists before creation in his exalted time. Nevertheless, there is a sense in which the sort of time belonging to the creation does begin at the moment God creates the world. If this is what Barth is getting at, then he is really only objecting to Augustine's idea that there is no time prior to the creation because God is time-less. Yet, although there is time before the creation, it is not "created time" but God's "pure duration," which as we have already seen, is quite different from created time.

Once again this is a departure from the classical view of God's relation to time. But if one allows that God exists in some temporally exalted state as Barth does, it is a short step from there to the view that God creates the world in time. In fact, Barth ends up "correcting" Augustine as follows: *Mundus factus cum tempore, ergo in tempore* (The world is created with time, and [therefore] in time) (*CD*, III/1, p. 71).

3. Concluding remarks

An important theme in the New Testament doctrine of creation is the fact that Christ, the Word of God, is the agent through whom all things are created and sustained. Thus, John 1:3 states, "Through him [i.e. the Word of God] all things were made; without

---

32 See the small print discussion in *CD*, III/1, pp. 69–71.

33 I owe this analogy to Paul Helm, see *Faith and Understanding* (Edinburgh, UK: Edinburgh University Press, 1997), ch. 4.

him nothing was made that was made." Colossians 1:16 says, "For by him all things were created; things in heaven and on earth, visible and invisible . . . all things were created by him and for him. He is before all things, and in him all things hold together." And Hebrews 11:3 tells us that, "by faith we understand that the worlds were framed by the Word of God." This biblical affirmation of the centrality of Christ's work in the creation and conservation of the world lies at the heart of Karl Barth's doctrine of creation in *CD* III. As T. F. Torrance points out, "The evangelical heart of Barth's theology is the doctrine of Christ as the divine Reconciler . . . Barth never ceased to insist, Christology gives us the determining center from which all our knowledge of God and of creation must take its shape.'[34]

But, as we have seen, Barth goes beyond the biblical affirmation that Christ is the agent through whom and for whom all things are created. For him the doctrine of creation can only be understood as an article of faith *in Christ*. The success of what I have called Barth's *christologizing* of the doctrine of creation can be seen in the hostility shown in some evangelical circles towards natural theology, often maligned as a way of cashing out the doctrine of creation in the absence of Christ. (Although, it should be said, not all evangelicals take this sort of view, and not all of those evangelicals sympathetic to Barth's account have taken this view as a result of reading Barth.) The influence of Barth's doctrine of creation can also be seen in the insistence by some contemporary theologians that the doctrine of creation must be connected with Christology. (See, for instance, Colin Gunton's book, *Christ and Creation*.)[35]

To my mind, discussion of the interconnections between Christian doctrines is welcome, and Barth's treatment of creation lends itself to such a way of thinking. But I am less enthusiastic about his treatment of natural theology. It seems to me that there is a right use of natural theology to which Calvin and his successors in the Reformed orthodox tradition point (*pace* Barth). This may lead back to the dreaded *analogia entis* (whatever this is exactly). But it need not. The recent development of Reformed Epistemology from philosophical theologians like Alvin Plantinga, Nicholas Wolterstorff and William Alston signals one way in which Calvin's legacy may be usefully appropriated for the theological task without ceding

[34] Torrance, *Karl Barth*, pp. 20f.

[35] Colin E. Gunton, *Christ and Creation* (Carlisle, UK: Paternoster, 1992).

ground to ways of thinking that are not profoundly shaped by the person and work of Christ.[36]

I am also not sure that Barth's attempt to tell a consistent supralapsarian story about the relationship between creation and covenant is entirely successful, because I am not convinced that Barth grasps the importance of the ultimate end of creation viz. divine self-glorification. If, as Barth's doctrine suggests, the covenant is the end of creation, is it the only end or one of several ends? And if it is one of several ends, is it the ultimate end, or a subordinate one? This question does not seem to be adequately answered in Barth's discussion.

Fewer evangelicals will be disturbed by Barth's way of thinking about God's relation to time as it bears upon the doctrine of creation, because many contemporary evangelical theologians do not believe that God is timeless.[37] But, at the very least, those who wish to reject the unanimous voice of the classical theological tradition would do well to think carefully about why they feel the greatest minds in Christian theology were so wrong on this matter. It does not seem to me that the old Harnackian thesis that classical theology was hopelessly tangled in a philosophical web of platonic presuppositions holds water on close examination. Yet a number of theologians deeply indebted to Barth continue to reiterate this thesis without sufficient regard being paid to the arguments of those who dissent from this view.[38]

Barth's account of creation is a theologically sophisticated piece of Christian dogmatics that intersects with several key concerns in his larger *corpus*, such as his polemic against natural theology and his Christology. Theologians of all stripes, evangelicals included,

---

[36] I refer to the Reformed epistemological work of Christian philosophers like Nicholas Wolterstorff and Alvin Plantinga. The *locus classicus* is Wolterstorff and Plantinga eds., *Reason and Religious Belief* (Notre Dame: University of Notre Dame Press, 1983). The most sophisticated development of this position to date is Alvin Plantinga, *Warranted Christian Belief* (New York: Oxford University Press, 2000).

[37] See, for example, the views represented in Gregory Ganssle ed., *God and Time, Four Views* (Downers Grove, IL: InterVarsity Press, 2001).

[38] See, for example, Colin E. Gunton, *Act and Being: Towards A Theology of The Divine Attributes* (Grand Rapids, MI: Eerdmans, 2002) and Robert W. Jenson, *Systematic Theology, Vol 1*. One might also compare the work of Openness theologians like Clark Pinnock, although their reasons for rejecting the traditional view of the divine nature are quite different from either Gunton or Jenson.

would benefit from availing themselves of the important insights he brings to this doctrine. I suppose that no theologian will find everything Barth says to his or her taste. But this is hardly a reason to neglect Barth: I know of no single theologian with whom I agree on every single theological matter—and I do not suppose myself to be unusual in this regard. If Barth were dismissive of the authority of Scripture or the importance of the tradition in his doctrine of creation, there might be good reason for being wary of what he says on creation.[39] But this is hardly the case. What Barth offers is a biblically informed and theologically robust doctrine of creation in which those who align themselves with classical Reformed, or, more broadly, evangelical, theology will continue to find a rich seam of ideas and careful reflection—even if, in the final analysis, one has to disagree with him in a number of important areas. And that, I suggest, is surely a reason to engage with Barth.

---

[39] Some evangelicals think that Barth's account of revelation means he does fail to take Scripture as seriously as he should and, as a consequence, we should be very wary of everything Barth has to say on every theological topic. (For Barth on revelation and Scripture, see the essays in this volume by Gabriel Fakre and Kevin Vanhoozer, respectively.) I think this is a mistake. Although Barth's doctrine of revelation is theologically innovative and could be taken in unhelpful directions, in practice, the way he uses Scripture is very conservative. It would certainly not be fair to Barth, to say that he has a low view of the status and place of Scripture in his doctrine of creation, as I hope I have already indicated.

5

Karl Barth's Anthropology

Henri A. G. Blocher

Karl Barth himself highlighted the spectacular turn (*Wendung*) in his apparent attitude towards anthropological interests: when he launched his revolution, these interests were rather suspect in his sight. He burned with a zeal in Elijah's style for God's "*deity*—a God absolutely unique in His relation to man and the world, overpoweringly lofty and distant, yes even wholly other;"[1] he would ask *Qualiter?* and answer *Totaliter aliter* (As to quality? Totally otherwise!);[2] but in 1956 (the year of his seventieth birthday), his theme had become "the Humanity of God," a combination of words which he borrowed from the social gospel thinker who influenced him in the second decade of the twentieth century, Leonhard Ragaz.[3] As a matter of fact, the thunder of the early Barth's preaching of the *krisis* falling upon everything human so deafened hearers that they missed the divine *yes* that lay hidden, dialectically, under the *no* of condemnation and exclusion: radical negation already entailed the negation of negation,[4] and Barth's theology implied a

---

[1] Karl Barth, *The Humanity of God*, John Newton Thomas tr. (Richmond, VA: John Knox, 1960), p. 37.

[2] Karl Barth, *The Word of God and the Word of Man*, Douglas Horton tr. (Grand Rapids, MI: Zondervan, 1935), p. 91.

[3] Aldo Moda, "La Dottrina barthiana dell'elezione: verso una soluzione delle aporie?," in *Barth Contemporaneo*, Sergio Rostagno ed., "Collana della Facoltà Valdese de Teologia, no. 16" (Turin: Claudiana, 1990), p. 101.

[4] Cf. Eberhard Jüngel, "La Vie et l'oeuvre de Karl Barth," Paul Corset tr.,

preliminary version of his anthropology.[5] In his whole work, Barth has bound theology and anthropology together in a more intimate way than any predecessor, even Calvin whose opening paragraphs in the *Institutes* so famously conjoin the knowledge of God and the knowledge of ourselves: he aptly coined the word *the-anthropology*, as he wrote:

> A very precise definition of the Christian endeavor in this respect would really require the more complex term "the-anthropology." For an abstract doctrine of God has no place in the Christian realm, only a "doctrine of God and of man," a doctrine of the commerce and communication between God and man.[6]

Such a place assigned to anthropology makes it difficult to keep it within bounds: if, in the work of any major thinker, "[a]nthropology provides a heuristic lens and hermeneutical horizon for other doctrines, and vice versa,"[7] it is most true with Barth. His abundance implies that thousands of pages in his writings would be relevant to the topic. Efforts to summarize them in a brief essay would bear little fruit. Hence this presentation will select salient points, focus on motives and meaning within the "quasi system" of Barth's theology.[8] Apart from a few occasional references, it will not explore the genesis of Barth's choices—as much recent research has

---

in *Karl Barth: Genèse et réception de sa théologie*, Pierre Gisel ed., "Lieux théologiques," no. 11 (Geneva: Labor et Fides, 1987), p. 37.

[5] It is the focus of Philippe Cardon-Bertalot, "Dieu comme 'réponse', l'homme comme 'question'. Anthropologie et tâche de la prédication de la théologie barthienne des années 1920," *Revue d'histoire et de philosophie religieuses* 84:3 (2004), pp. 287–310; Barth's anthropology, then, may be characterized as "correlative" (pp. 291–2, not so far from Tillich, and p. 306), under a Kierkegaardian influence from which Barth later tried to purge his thinking (pp. 297–8).

[6] Karl Barth "Evangelical Theology in the 19th Century," Thomas Wieser tr., in *The Humanity of God*, p. 11 (the paper was first read to the Goethegesellschaft in January 1957).

[7] F. LeRon Shults, *Reforming Theological Anthropology: After the Philosophical Turn to Relationality* (Grand Rapids, MI, and Cambridge, UK: Eerdmans, 2003), p. xii.

[8] Barth, *CD*, I/2, pp. 868–9: theology cannot build a system; nevertheless, it must reflect the coherence of truth, and thus, "May it not be that a 'system' which asserts itself spontaneously [*von selbst sich durchsetzendes*] (not as a system, but as a striving for definiteness and coherence) signifies obedience and is therefore a shadow of the truth?"

done—but consider the mature form of his thought: in his *magnum opus*, since "Barth has expressed the desire that he should be judged theologically by the *Church Dogmatics* rather than by earlier writings,"[9] and in shorter writings of the same period. Privilege, indeed, should go to continuity in the interpretation of all phases, following John Webster's so finely balanced assessment.[10] Continuity was probably deeper than even Barth himself could measure, as we may often observe with great minds.[11]

Since Karl Barth attempted, and to a large extent achieved, the incredible feat of reappropriating the whole biblical and Christian tradition, readers may mistakenly ascribe ordinary meanings to forms of expression he has borrowed *and* re-interpreted.[12] In order to render his innovative powers their due, in order to avoid filing the Lion's fangs, due attention should be paid to the statements that

---

[9] Geoffrey W. Bromiley, "Karl Barth," in *Creative Minds in Contemporary Theology*, Philip E. Hughes ed. (Grand Rapids MI: Eerdmans, 1966), p. 31.

[10] John Webster ed., *The Cambridge Companion to Karl Barth* (Cambridge, UK: Cambridge University Press, 2000) in his introduction, pp. 12–13: continuity "is now much more evident, however much in later work he may have retracted or modified one or other earlier position," and, especially, "'dialectic' is a permanent feature of Barth's theology, not a temporary phase left behind in the 1930s;" the apt simile is that he "changed gear." Stuart D. McLean, *Humanity in the Thought of Karl Barth* (Edinburgh, UK: T&T Clark, 1981), p. 12, to name a lesser authority, also "contend[s] that Barth continues to use dialectical thought." This is no denial of a change, and greater restraint in the use of dialectics, especially under the pressure of Erik Peterson's protests, as shown by Paul Corset, "Premières Rencontres de la théologie catholique avec l'oeuvre de Barth (1922–1932)," in P. Gisel ed., *Genèse et Réception*, pp. 171–2, and a move toward analogy. On Barthian continuity, see also Pierre Gisel ed., "Réceptions protestantes et questions ouvertes," in *Genèse et Réception*, p. 265, and Giampiero Bof, "La Ricezione di Barth in Italia," in *Barth Contemporaneo*, S. Rostagno ed., pp. 164–7.

[11] Henri Bouillard, *Karl Barth: Genèse et Evolution de la Théologie Dialectique*, "Théologie", no. 38 (Paris: Aubier-Montaigne, 1957), p. 147, recounts, how Barth could write in October 1932 of his *Römerbrief*: "This book is of another time and of another man" ("Vorwort zur englischen Ausgabe der Römerbriefauslegung," *Zwischen den Zeiten* [1932], p. 478), and he (Bouillard) brings out, p. 238, how parallel the courses of Barth's thought (on time) run in his *Dogmatics* and in the *Römerbrief*.

[12] Trutz Rendtorff, "L'Autonomie absolue de Dieu. Pour comprendre la théologie de Karl Barth et ses conséquences," Paul Corset tr., in *Genèse*

show the *difference* in his meaning and to the hermeneutical clues he has given in his comments upon his work (his "metalanguage"). Such a need is present with all powerful and provocative thinkers, who always find many admirers ready to tame their disturbing genius. Jacques Maritain shrewdly noted:

> Each time one deals with a *great* error (great not only in the sense of grievous, but great in boldness, significance and logical consistency), one naturally finds subtle, intelligent and learned commentators who *tone down* or *drain off* the meaning: they feel that simply stating what is lacks elegance—it exaggerates.[13]

Vigilance is even more required in the case of Karl Barth, who has been described and labeled as "neo-orthodox" (suggesting "updated orthodoxy" to most), despite his own comment that he found the thing ludicrous.[14] Without minimizing the break from the teaching of his liberal masters,[15] both in intention and in actual theologizing (there may be a gap between the two), if one reads

---

et Réception, P. Gisel ed., p. 236: "The *Church Dogmatics* is the most massive renovation of the Christian history of theology and dogma in recent Protestant theology. It recapitulates that history and, at the same time, revises it totally. Barth subjects it to a sharp christological critique." (Whenever I quote from a source not in English, the translation is mine.)

[13] *La Philosophie morale. Examen historique et critique des grands systèmes*, Bibliothèque des idées (Paris: Gallimard NRF, 1960), p. 219 n. 1. (Maritain uses the words *atténuateurs* and *exténuateurs*.)

[14] Karl Barth, *Final Testimonies*, Eberhard Busch ed., Geoffrey W. Bromiley tr. (Grand Rapids, MI: Eerdmans, 1977), p. 33. He added (p. 34): "I am acquainted with what is called orthodoxy. In theology it is usually equated with the theology of the 16th and 17th centuries. I respect this. But I am far from being of this school." Before this last interview (by Alfred Blatter), shortly before his death, Barth, and his life-long friend Eduard Thurneysen, had made statements of the same import throughout his career. One should note, at this point, that the German word *evangelisch* bears a quite different meaning from *evangelical* in English: nearer to "protestant," whereas Barth would use either "orthodox"or "pietist" as *grosso modo* equivalents of *evangelical* (in recent decades German evangelicals have introduced the neologistic *evangelikal*). On Barth's relation to the pietists, see the fine work by Eberhard Busch, *Karl Barth and the Pietists: The Young Barth's Critique of Pietism and its Response*, Daniel W. Bloesch tr. (Downers Grove, IL: InterVarsity Press, 2004).

[15] As is well-known, David Tracy, *Blessed Rage for Order: The New Pluralism in Theology* (Minneapolis & New York: Seabury, 1975),

Barth's statements as if they were Calvin's, one is likely to miss Barth's original sense.

One more introductory issue: this presentation will deal (though not at any length) with Karl Barth's doctrine of sin. The objection might be raised, with some appeal to Barth's statements, that the doctrine of sin should not be joined with anthropology, the study of the human being (*Sein*), essence (*Wesen*) and nature (*Natur*), since sinfulness is alien to our nature. It is alienation itself: the sum of the *unchanging* components or relationships that "persists through the antitheses of sin, reconciliation and redemption;" it constitutes "the creaturely essence and nature of man," the object of anthropology.[16] It is a strength of Barth's positions that he consistently refuses to give evil and sin a "footing" in creation as such, even under the guise of a "possibility" involved in created freedom as such.[17] Shouldn't we separate, then, anthropology from hamartiology?

Dealing with both under the same heading has been quite traditional. Karl Hase's handy compendium, *Hutterus redivivus oder Dogmatik der evangelisch-lutherischen Kirche,*[18] offers two *loci* under the title *Anthropologia*: (XI) *De Statu Integritatis;* (XII) *De Statu Corruptionis.* More familiar to many evangelicals, Augustus H. Strong and Louis Berkhof both include their treatment of sin in the part devoted to the human creature.[19] The reason, of course, is the actual sinfulness of present humankind. When one looks for human beings, s/he finds sinners!

Despite the strong statements just quoted, one could argue that there is even more warrant for yoking the doctrine of sin with anthropology in Barthian perspective than there is in more

---

pp. 27–9, located Barth in the liberal tradition, and Richard A. Muller tends to agree with this diagnosis, "The Place and Importance of Karl Barth in the Twentieth Century: A Review Essay," *Westminster Theological Journal* 50 (1988): 153, 155.

16 Barth, *CD*, III/2, p. 40; cf. pp. 42–3, "an essence which even sin does not and cannot change."

17 Barth, *CD*, IV/1, pp. 409–10.

18 . . . *Ein dogmatisches Repertorium für Studirende*, 7th ed. (Leipzig: Breitkopf & Hartel, 1848).

19 Augustus H. Strong, *Systematic Theology* (Philadelphia, PA: Judson, 1958 [1907]), under "Part V: ANTHROPOLOGY, OR THE DOCTRINE OF MAN," allocates 132 pages out of 200 to the chapter on sin; Berkhof, *Systematic Theology*, 3d ed. (Grand Rapids, MI: Eerdmans, 1946), deals with "Man in the State of Sin" as the second part under the title THE DOCTRINE OF MAN IN RELATION TO GOD.

classical systems. At times, the early Barth nearly identified sin and creatureliness.[20] In self-criticism, Barth later recognized the fact that "redemption was viewed as consisting in the abolition of the creatureliness of the creature"[21] while it should not; nevertheless, the (dialectical?) complement of the affirmation of the human being unchanged is the affirmation of human sinfulness as implying man's "whole being" now contrary to God, not just one element, and of *Unnatur*, counter-nature, as the only thing we meet in existing men. Barth even offers a lenient, almost sympathetic, evaluation of Flacius' error.[22] These expressions seem to identify sinfulness and human existence more closely and strictly than traditional reformed theology! Along the same line, Barth's rejection of a primitive state of innocence, of a time when man and woman were not sinners (as we shall see), strengthens that impression. Above all, the christological foundation of anthropology, since Christology brings the Good News of Reconciliation and victory over evil, entails that humanity cannot be considered separately from sin, for which Jesus Christ came to die.

1. Anthropology based on Christology

Barth's decision to ground his anthropology on Christology constitutes the most original feature of his treatment.[23] Even in the minority "Scotist" tradition, which asserted the eternal pre-existence of the *man* Jesus, no theologian methodically proceeded in the same way.[24] Barth can claim: ". . . we are invited to infer [*schliessen*, deduce, infer, conclude] from His [Jesus'] human nature the character of our own;"[25] for Jesus is true man, with the explanation:

---

[20] Barth, *Word of God*, pp. 89–90: "Man cannot escape his humanity, and means limitation, finitude, creaturehood, separation from God"; p. 288: the creation of the new life "consist[s] in the last end in the annulment of the creaturehood . . ."; p. 322: "The creaturehood of the sons of God and the manifestation of the sons of God are mutually exclusive."

[21] Barth, *Humanity*, p. 43.

[22] Barth, *CD*, III/2, p. 28–9; Flacius was condemned by his fellow Lutherans for teaching that original sin had become the *substance* of the human person. In *CD*, IV/1, p. 481, Barth rejects Flacius' opinion more firmly.

[23] Formally stated, e.g., *CD*, III/2, pp. 55, 59–60, and already 44.

[24] Barth, *CD*, III/2, p. 46, regrets what "has usually been the case in theological anthropology."

[25] Barth, *CD*, III/2, p. 54, "The character of" is added in the translation.

> And 'true' does not mean only that He is man as God created him, but also that He is this as we all are, and that He is therefore accessible and knowable to us as man, with no special capacities or potentialities, with no admixture of a quality alien to us, with no supernatural endowment such as must make Him a totally different being from us.[26]

At the same time, Barth warns that there is no direct identification between Jesus' human nature and ours, and that there can be no question "of a simple deduction of anthropology from Christology."[27] The notion of *indirect* derivation is supposed to solve the tension between the two kinds of statements; yet, Henri Bouillard finds a harder contradiction with the former, more wholesale, rejection of any deduction of creation from revelation (the verb is *ableiten*).[28] One must appreciate how radical Barth's choice appears to be: he does not merely claim that in Jesus, and Jesus only, is the fullness, and integrity, of manhood as God willed it, perfectly displayed—*Ecce homo!* (John 19:5); this many would hold; he avers that we know nothing of what it really means to be a human being before we look to Jesus Christ, and can tell only on the exclusive basis of what we see in him.

Barth's christological method implies that he will not receive the instructions of scientific and philosophical anthropologies.[29] He actually maintained that the only source of *theological* anthropology

---

[26] Barth, *CD*, III/2, p. 53, "Totally" is added in the translation (*zu einem andersartigen Wesen*, a being of another kind).

[27] Barth, *CD*, III/2, p. 47.

[28] Henri Bouillard *Karl Barth: Parole de Dieu et existence humaine, première partie*, "Théologie," no. 39 (Paris: Aubier-Montaigne, 1957), p. 283 n. 1, quoting from *Kirchliche Dogmatik* I/1, p. 469, i.e., in the English translation, *CD* I/1, p. 446: "Deducing creation as such from revelation and basing it on this, this is . . . an illegitimate speculation." In the same paragraph, Barth also writes: "To attribute the Church or revelation directly to creation or to the creative will of God as such is to forget or ignore the fact that the Church or revelation can be an event only as an answer to the sin of man, or it is to be forced to try to integrate the sin of man into creation. It is also to forget the free loving-kindness of God which gives the answer, or to make it a necessary member in a dialectical process." This statement sounds strangely similar to what many have said in criticism of Barth's later developments!

[29] On the topic, Konrad Stock, "Die Funktion anthropologischen Wissens in theologischem Denken—am Beispiel Karl Barths," *Evangelische Theologie* 34:6 (November/December 1974), pp. 523–38, esp. 524–6.

is the consideration of the Christ as Person and Event. However, one notes with Daniel J. Price that his attitude has grown more positive over the years, from volume I to volumes III and IV of the *Church Dogmatics*.[30] Conflict is more likely to occur with philosophy than with scientific claims, though some overlap is possible (e.g. in the case of phenomenological philosophy).[31] Barth granted there may be "material parallelism" between theology and psychology.[32] A symbolic, almost amusing, detail: in October 1968, in Darmstadt, he was awarded the Sigmund Freud prize![33] But Barth did not waver: all the contributions of scientific and philosophical enquiries only touch the *phenomena* of the *humanum*, a ghost-image, a "shadow man (*Schattenmensch*);"[34] even Karl Jaspers' transcendence is nothing more than a human property, within human existence, and can only be the *symptom* of real man.[35] Real humanity is only known in Christ.[36]

Similarly, Barth will not take into account any would-be theological knowledge based on creation and any form of revelation independently of the Incarnate Christ. One should not try first to define human nature, the "usual" procedure[37] which the orthodox also have followed, and then ascribe the same to the Word who became flesh. This decision is based on Barth's affirmation of the eternal pre-existence of the man Jesus[38]—his wording allows for a

---

30 Daniel J. Price, *Karl Barth's Anthropology in Light of Modern Thought* (Grand Rapids, MI, and Cambridge, UK: Eerdmans, 2002), p. 107.

31 Price, *Anthropology*, pp. 113–14, with 114 n. 64.

32 Price, *Anthropology*, p. 166, quoting *CD*, III/4, p. 138.

33 Quoted by G. Bof, "La Ricezione di Barth in Italia," in *Barth Contemporaneo*, S. Rostagno ed., p. 163.

34 Barth, *CD*, III/2, p. 198; cf. already pp. 121–8.

35 Barth, *CD*, III/2, pp. 114–20.

36 McLean, *Humanity*, p. 25 helpfully draws attention to Barth's vocabulary: "Real man refers to the God-man relationship, humanity to the man-man relationships, and whole man to the unity of soul and body in the individual person." Essentially, Barth, who is not perfectly consistent, uses "real" (*wirklich*) and, sometimes, "true" (*wahr*), with strong ontological overtones, for the human being in Jesus Christ (who is also the *new* man opposed to the old one, as Barth expressly declares, *CD*, III/2, p. 205).

37 *CD*, III/2, p. 44, "the traditional way" which translates *den üblichen Weg*.

38 *CD*, III/2, pp. 478–85, e.g. p. 485: "The man Jesus is in this genuine and real yesterday of God's eternity, which is anterior to all other yesterdays, including the yesterday of creation."

constant switch from and to a lighter view (pre-existent in God's design, that is fore-ordained, not yet really existing) to and from a heavier one (really pre-existent, as a matter of being)[39]—and the man Jesus' role as the "real basis of creation."[40] As such, he precedes Adam, and he must be considered theologically (despite superficial chronology) as the First Adam, whom Adam merely typified (*tupos tou mellontos*).[41] This, in turn, issues from the "christological concentration" from which the *Church Dogmatics* was born. Jesus Christ is himself the substance of God's decree of election from which everything proceeds; he is the "beginning" of *all* of God's ways.[42] Apart from Jesus Christ (incarnate), the only God one considers is an abstract God (and "abstract" for Barth is quite pejorative, opposed to "real") and the only man one considers is an abstract human being.[43] "Man never at all exists in himself"; "Man exists in Jesus Christ and in Him alone; as he also finds God in Jesus Christ and in Him alone."[44]

This conviction is of one piece with the affirmation that God's "deity *encloses humanity in itself*": "It is when we look at Jesus Christ that we know decisively that God's deity does not exclude, but includes His *humanity*."[45] This, Barth maintains in open opposition to the Reformers: "This is not the fatal Lutheran doctrine of the two natures and their properties," he says. And, had Calvin followed Barth's path on the issue, "[h]is Geneva would not have

---

39 Instances are found everywhere; a parallel duality is found in the language used for the *Logos*: the thought of the *Logos asarkos* (without the flesh, not incarnate) is vehemently rejected, but the *Logos* is still described as *incarnandus* rather than *incarnatus* before the Christmas event.

40 Barth, *CD*, III/2, p. 483: Jesus Christ "was the purpose [*Zweck*, 'goal'] and ground [*Beweggrund*, with the idea of movement, maybe 'spring'] of the divine creative action at the beginning of all times."

41 The theme distinctly appears before Barth wrote the booklet *Christus und Adam nach Römer 5* (1952), e.g. in *CD*, II/2, p. 740; *CD*, III/2, p. 205 (1 Cor. 15:47).

42 Barth, *CD*, II/2, p. 316; p. 632 and already p. 531: "If this God is He who in Jesus Christ became man, revealing Himself and reconciling the world with Himself; it follows that the relationship between Him and man consists in the event in which God accepted man out of pure, free, compassion . . ."

43 Barth, *Humanity*, p. 46.

44 Barth, *CD*, II/1, p. 149 (both quotes).

45 Barth, *Humanity*, p. 50 and p. 49.

become such a gloomy affair."[46] Several statements could suggest, in a way reminiscent of Hegel, that Jesus' deity is nothing less than his humanity as intimately united with God. Examples of this are when Jesus' *humanity* is said to be the "repetition" (*Wiederholung*, a favorite word with Barth) of God himself;[47] when Jesus Christ is said to be the Son of God *as man*;[48] and when we are told we should "discover" (*abzulesen*, literally "read from") his being as God "from the fact that as such He is very man."[49] Other strong statements, however, and often in the immediate context, show that Barth does not intend to confuse the two natures: the divine and the human remain distinct (despite what would seem to be the natural import of the words quoted). It is most likely that he means, first, that God's free, but eternal, decision to be for humankind in the man Jesus so radically involves his being that it practically belongs to his self-definition; and, second, that God's relationship with his human partner perfectly expresses what he is because it corresponds to that of the Father and the Son in the Trinity. If the Incarnation is so decisive for God, it can hardly be less so for human beings!

For anthropology, the consequence of its christological grounding is that human beings have their truest identity in their relationship to God, for who is Jesus Christ if not the Bond that binds them to God? In Christ, they are for God; they are destined for covenant (*Bund*) fellowship with him. This determination (*Bestimmung* is, again, a typical word, combining the thought of a trait conferred and of a call addressed),[50] which can be named "covenantal capacity," is what makes humans human. It entails, since it *happens* in the God-man, the historical character of the *humanum*: our being is a history, *Geschichte*. In this history, in Christ, the human partner is no inert object of grace: the human partner receives the honor of responding; he freely responds to God. *Freedom* is characteristic of the human creature in Barth's view, as it is of Barth's God, but with a sharp rebuttal of current, more or less humanistic, (mis)understandings: for freedom is not found in the fatal possibility of a foolish *No* thrown at the face of God (which is a real "impossibility," Barth

---

46 Barth, *Humanity*, p. 50 and p. 49.
47 Barth, *CD*, III/2, p. 219.
48 Barth, *CD*, IV/1, p. 115, 129, 135.
49 Barth, *CD*, IV/1, p. 177.
50 As noted by Bouillard, *Karl Barth*, p. 238.

will say), it is only the freedom of grateful obedience, "essentially not freedom *from*, but freedom *to* and *for*."[51]

This foundational interpretation, which Barth (christologically) develops in chapters on relationships with others, with one's own body, on human temporality, sounds attractive indeed. The features of humanity that are affirmed are those one can observe in the mirror of the Scriptures; Barth's firm stand on freedom agrees with Scripture's unmasking the real slavery under the guise of rebellious emancipation. As to method, one can grant that nothing may be affirmed as essentially human that would not apply to Jesus, the only man whose manhood is revealed in integrity: in him, we behold humanity for God, true humanity. A correspondence between Christ's deity and his humanity? Traditional theologians have acknowledged a wondrous harmony between the Father's eternal begetting of the Son and the Son's redemptive mission in the flesh: because the Son and human beings proceed from the same origin, from the Father (the Son as uncreated, humankind as created), it was fitting (*eprepen*) that he should take them in charge to lead them to glory, and he was not ashamed to enter their brotherhood, making their flesh and blood his own (Heb. 2:10–14b). The Son's "mediatorial" role in creation—all things were created *through* him—is part of this harmony.

These elements of happy convergence cannot hide serious difficulties, however. If we focus on the claim that anthropology should be based exclusively on Christology, three questions may be raised: *does he* (really draw his anthropological theses from that unique source)? *Could he*? *Should he*? Several scholars doubt the strict christological origin of Barth's propositions. Henri Bouillard is not convinced.[52] Gerrit C. Berkouwer, a very sympathetic critic, firmly denies that Barth be faithful to his principle.[53] Wolfhart

[51] Barth, "The Gift of Freedom. Foundation of Evangelical Ethics," in *Humanity*, p. 72; p. 75, it never ceases to be event; p. 76, it is not neutral; p. 77, it "does not allow for any vague choices between various possibilities. The reign of chance and ambiguity is excluded."

[52] Boulliard, *Karl Barth*, pp. 258, 283.

[53] Karl Barth, *Man: The Image of God*, Dirk W. Jellema tr. (Grand Rapids, MI: Eerdmans, 1961), pp. 94–5. On another point of method (not unrelated!), Henry Chavannes, *L'Analogie entre Dieu et le monde selon Thomas d'Aquin et selon Karl Barth*, "Cogitatio fidei," no. 42 (Paris: Cerf, 1969), p. 288, observes that Barth does what he denies: to deal with personality in God, he does use in fact the *viae negationis et eminentiae* which he has condemned.

Pannenberg charges him with projecting onto God a quasi-Buberian I-Thou anthropology which he has adopted beforehand.[54] Leaving aside for a moment a possible link to Buber, one must admit that Barth's procedure is hardly compelling. Barth wavers between the affirmation of the identity of Christ's humanity and ours *and* the emphatic warning that they remain different. This suggests a method rather free and elastic. Were it not for the spell of his rhetoric, how many would have been convinced?

Could he do otherwise and establish his doctrine of humanity on the sole basis of the Christ-Event (since Christology itself, as a doctrine, is drawn from the Event)? Any event as such calls for interpretation, and this requires some prior information, a frame of reference and criteria. If one denies such a need in the case of the Event of Revelation, who is Jesus Christ, and must be absolutely first, how can one escape the illuministic danger? But in the case of the Christ-Event, the difficulty is made more acute by the unique character of this event: the one we behold is confessedly God and man, in two natures! How can we discern, from the event itself and without prior knowledge, what is to be ascribed to deity and what to humanity? Peter was ready to interpret the Event, ascribing the weakness of death to the "flesh" (human nature) and the victory of life to the divine Spirit (1 Pet. 3:18b), since he had prior notions that made it possible, but Barth discounts any such notions.[55]

In Barth's approach the difficulty is still reinforced by one of his cherished *theologoumena*: in the event of Revelation, the form contradicts the contents.[56] In 1953, he has not forgotten this old paradox of his, and maintains that the form taken by Jesus' divine authority is a contradiction of it.[57] How, then, could we know from the bare Event what is distinctly true of Christ's deity and humanity? If Barth, nevertheless, is able to give the impression that his method is working, the explanation is not so hard to find. He puts to use, extensively and intensively, what he finds in Scripture—though Kathryn Tanner perceptively remarks the role of Scripture is

---

[54] According to LeRon Shults, *Reforming*, p. 118.

[55] Barth, *CD*, IV/1, p. 129, cf. 177.

[56] Barth, *CD*, I/1, p. 166 (*sie entspricht der Sache nicht, sondern sie widerspricht ihr*). *CD*, I/2, p. 499, even in the person of Jesus Christ, there is no *direct* identity of the Word and its form.

[57] Barth, *CD*, IV/1, p. 178.

not truly constitutive.[58] The teaching of the Bible does provide the guidelines and the grid needed for the interpretation of the Event. But the problem for his position is that of consistency: Barth's doctrine of Scripture, as stated (especially) in § 19 of the *Church Dogmatics*, does not allow such a decisive theological role.[59]

Should he, or anyone, presupposing an adequate bibliology, have tried to derive anthropology from Christology? In a Barthian perspective, it implies the pre-existence of the man Jesus, really the first Adam, and, beyond that, the christological concentration. Serious objections arise. As Berkouwer, who is not alone, stresses, Barth reverses the biblical order: in the New Testament, "[t]he Incarnation is described as consanguinity *with us*. Barth, however, formulates the matter in the opposite way, so that Jesus does not participate in our nature, but *we in His*."[60] The logic of Hebrews 2 (as sketched above) shows that the reversal affects theological meaning, not only superficial chronology. The use of *tupos* in Romans 5:14 is too slender a basis for the ascription of priority to the man Jesus, compared to Adam; interestingly, the apostle does not only call Christ "the *Second* Man" but insists that he does not come first (*ou prôton, epeita*; 1 Cor. 15:46–47).[61] In order to affirm Jesus' pre-existence, as distinguished from predestination (which implies no existence at all), Barth attributes the Revelation 1:8 statement to the Incarnate Christ (as such); Bouillard protests that the speaker

---

[58] Kathryn Tanner, "Creation and Providence," in Webster ed., *Companion*, p. 114: "The centrality of Christ for accounts of creation and providence is not secured, then, by their derivation from the Bible. The centrality of Christ is demonstrated primarily by how theological topics are arranged . . ."

[59] Karl Barth's doctrine of Scripture lies beyond the scope of this essay. Concerning his actual, and highly personal, handling of biblical data, see Trutz Rendtorff, "L'Autonomie absolue de Dieu. Pour comprendre la théologie de Karl Barth et ses conséquences," Paul Corset tr., in *Genèse et Réception*, P. Gisel ed., p. 244: "one should recall that Barth fought his whole life long against the obligation to submit to the criteria of official biblical interpretation, and that he developed his own interpretation of the Bible on the basis of the self-founding autonomy of theology."

[60] Barth, *Man: The Image*, p. 95. Similarly, Bouillard, *Karl Barth*, p. 266 (he notes that Barth as he goes on developing his topic no longer refers to Jesus' humanity).

[61] Paul may be responding—a firm rebuttal—to Philo's disjunction of the (heavenly) Adam of Genesis 1 and the earthly Adam of Genesis 2.

is not the man Jesus there.[62] Many would draw from Revelation 13:8 the affirmation of an eternal sacrifice of the Lamb, but Barth knows better: he perceived that the clause "since the foundation of the world" does not qualify the slaying of the Lamb but the writing of the Book; he nevertheless used the verse for his ambiguous preexistence in God's counsel.[63] According to Colin Brown, "the New Testament does not project the incarnation back into the being of God before the event took place," and "Barth's attempts to prove the contrary fall short of their goal."[64] Precisely:

> More than once Barth attempts to identify the subject of John 1:2 with the incarnate Christ (*cf. CD*, II/2, p.117; *CD*, III/1, p. 54). But this interpretation, though Barth deems it basic, seems hardly tenable. It is not warranted by the verse itself, and would seem to make John 1:14 an irrelevant tautology. Barth's exegesis of Hebrews 1:2f. and Colossians 1:15f. in *CD*, III/1, p. 53f. is equally suspect.[65]

---

[62] Bouillard, *Karl Barth*, p. 271–72. (On that verse, Barth *CD*, III/2, pp. 463, 465, 516, and elsewhere.) Though the later Barth acquired more self-restraint, Rudolf Bultmann's 1922 comments on the way of Barth's interpretation in the *Römerbrief* is worth quoting: he agrees that one must go beyond exegesis and relate with *die Sache* itself, but complains that for Barth "this ideal has become a scheme by which he does violence to the Epistle to the Romans and to Paul," "Le 'Römerbrief' de Barth," Paul Corset tr., in *Genèse et Réception*, P. Gisel ed., p. 101.

[63] The parallel passage Rev. 17:8 clearly shows that the temporal clause is attached to the writing in the Lamb's Book. Using the indexes, I checked all the passages in Barth where a reference to Rev. 13:8 is found—in none of them may Barth be charged with the current mistake; however, in *CD*, II/1, p. 123, he does speak of "the Lamb slain from the foundation of the world," yet without giving the Rev. 13 reference. In *Réalité de l'homme nouveau. Trois conférences suivies d'entretiens* [Barth spoke originally in French, in 1948, but the lectures themselves were re-translated from a German text by Lore Jeanneret] (Geneva: Labor & Fides, 1964), p. 61, Barth refers to 1 Pet. 1:19–20—but the text only tells of foreordination—and Rev. 5:6, but the symbolic vision expresses the decisive significance of the Cross for the unfolding of history, not necessarily an eternal status.

[64] Colin Brown, *Karl Barth and the Christian Message* (London: Tyndale Press, 1967), p. 110.

[65] Brown, *Christian Message*, n. 8.

Barth must feel that he stands on solid ground when he appeals to these passages:[66] they speak of Jesus Christ, the historical figure in flesh and blood, and assign him the Creator's role! His treatment, however, overlooks two important textual facts: these passages all belong to the *sapiential* vein in the New Testament, an echo of Proverbs 8:22–31 as developed in the influential book of *Wisdom* (of which 7:26 speaks of wisdom as the "image" of God's goodness, the key to Col. 1:15)—this tradition on the personified Wisdom of God, pre-existent and who shared in God's creative work, does not envisage her incarnation, and, therefore, the incarnation should not be considered an implication of the language it provides; second *datum*, these passages (at least the two most explicit ones, John 1 and Col. 1) are marked by a diptych structure—the two *prôtotokos* of Colossians 1:15 and 18, "of all creature" and "of the dead" signal the two panels, the first one devoted to the glory of the eternal Wisdom of God with the role in the first creation and the second one to the glory of Wisdom incarnate with the role in reconciliation (as Calvin well discerned); similarly, in the (more complex, and chiastic) structure of John's Prologue, the *egeneto* (became), in the midst of our days, of verse 14 answers the *èn* (was), in the radical beginning, of verse 1. What one must realize is the dependence of the "became" on the "was": if the *egeneto* is fused with the *èn* or if it is considered foundational, it "freezes" as an eternal given and *loses* its character as an *event*, a historical event—several authors have expressed their misgivings regarding that consequence of Barth's interpretation.[67] If the One whose pre-existence is affirmed is named after his incarnation name (and it is not even the case in John 1:1–5, Col. 1:19–20, Heb. 1:1–3), this does not imply that he pre-existed *as* incarnate: it fully accords

---

[66] I surmise that in his appeal to other passages, he would have granted that his theological reading could be at variance with the meaning of the human author (his doctrine of Scripture gave him permission to let the Object overrule the deficiencies of the witness); but on John 1 and Colossians 1, he probably saw no other possible meaning than the one he retained.

[67] Aldo Moda, p. 97 n. 82, cites P. Eicher, V. Subilia, P. Gisel, P. Bolognesi. It had been a complaint of Hans Urs von Balthasar, quoted by Bouillard, *Karl Barth*, p. 102 (quoting from *Karl Barth: Darstellung und Deutung seiner Theologie* [Cologne, 1951], p. 380: "in this theology of event and history, nothing seems to happen, perhaps, because everything happened in eternity"); see p. 278.

with the rules of language, especially the *communicatio idiomatum*, if one speaks of "Jesus Christ" as the Agent of creation though he was such as the Logos *before* he took on human flesh and the name "Jesus Christ"; then, the underlying truth is that of the identity of subject (the second Person of the Trinity) and of the human nature of Christ as *an[h]upostatos* and *en[h]upostatos*, which Karl Barth happily maintained.[68]

Richard Muller sees "the too facile reading of incarnation into creation" as moving "definitely into the realm of 'Christomonism'."[69] He is one of several who dare use that word,[70] undeterred by Barth's intimidating reaction: "fools (*die Toren*) would say: Christomonist."[71] While resisting the reversal of biblical order and the eternalization of the humanity of Jesus, it behooves us to avoid excessive language. Who knows? Some Colossians may have thought of such a qualification for someone who had written them a short, but weighty, epistle, long ago . . .

2. I-Thou structure and analogy of relation

If Jesus is the man for God, he is also the man for others. The very method that invites us to look to him in order to know what it means for us to be human implies that no one exists in isolation. The basic structure, *Grundform*, of humanity is, according to Barth, co-existence, exchange, interdependence, encounter (one is reminded of Heidegger's existential *Mitsein*).[72] The very effort to derive knowledge of our humanity from that of Jesus Christ implies that they are bound together as one concrete nexus. As may be, therefore, expected, Karl Barth shows himself a sharp critic of individualism: he lays down the canon, in the old conciliar style: *Si quis dixerit hominem esse solitarium, anathema sit*![73]

---

68 Barth uses the words as they were used by Protestant orthodoxy. F. LeRon Shults brilliantly demonstrates (relying especially on Aloys Cardinal Grillmeier) that their meaning was different in ancient times, even in the writings of Leontius of Byzantium, but this does not affect the doctrinal truth at stake.

69 Richard Muller, "Place and Importance of Barth: Review Essay," pp. 147–8, and he repeats the word pp. 150–51.

70 Aldo Moda, "La Dottrina barthiana," p. 89 n. 36, lists P. Althaus, Reinhold Niebuhr, Helmut Thielicke, K. Okayama, heavyweight scholars!

71 Barth, *CD*, IV/1, p. 683.

72 Barth, *CD*, III/2, p. 220.

73 Barth, *CD*, III/2, p. 319.

Daniel Price surmises that Barth's co-humanity passionate convictions might have their roots in his socialistic leanings.[74] Without following F.-X. Marquardt in making Barth's political interests the primary and decisive factor in the genesis of his thought,[75] we should take note of this first aspect of Barth's anti-individualism. The young Safenwil "red" pastor's commitment could go as far as this statement: "Jesus *is* the social movement, and the social movement *is* Jesus in the present time."[76] He never severed his ties with socialism broadly conceived, even in later years. They account for his comparative leniency, in Cold War times, for Soviet policies. At the World Council of Churches' first, founding, Assembly, in Amsterdam (1948), he successfully prevented an explicit condemnation of communism in the Declaration on Church and Society; he confronted the American Presbyterian layman John Foster Dulles (who was to become later the U.S. Secretary of State—and was the father of Avery Cardinal Dulles).[77] This deep-seated orientation may explain his constant refusal of dividing categories, categories which would cut across humankind—a trait that remained constant in him, from youth to retirement. He devised a doctrine of election that avoids positing two classes of people; when asked, in Debrecen (Hungary) in 1936, "What force does faith in predestination give when wrestling with

---

[74] Daniel Price, *Anthropology*, p. 98: "Barth cultivated a deep suspicion of Western individualism, perhaps due to his earlier interest in Christian socialism."

[75] Eberhard Jüngel replies sharply to Marquardt's *Theologie und Sozialismus* (which H. Gollwitzer, Marquardt's mentor, supported) in "La Vie et l'œuvre de Karl Barth," Paul Corset tr., in *Genèse et Réception*, P. Gisel ed., p. 49: it is "impossible to sustain historically. Politics was a predicate, a 'component' of his [Barth's] theology; his theology never was a predicate of politics" (see p. 32). With the same import, the testimony of Eduard Thurneysen, "Théologie et socialisme dans les lettres de jeunesse," Paul Corset tr., *Genèse et Réception*, pp. 140–1. One eloquent sign of the subordinate character of Barth's socialism is the fact (brought forth by Trutz Rendtorff, *Genèse et Réception*, pp. 232–3) that he was able, in the second edition of the *Römerbrief*, to call for a revolution within revolution, that would leave the *status quo* untouched (under divine judgment) and involve "the requirement of non-action."

[76] In an article "La Vie" "Jesus Christus und die soziale Bewegung," in *Der freie Aargauer* no. 153 (1911), quoted by Jüngel, F.-X. Marquardt, p. 29.

[77] Sergio Rostagno, "Karl Barth (1886–1968) dal Dio 'totalmente altro' all' 'umanità di Dio,'" Rostagno, in *Barth contemporaneo*, p. 11. See McLean, *Humanity*, pp. 62–5.

the paganized masses?" he answered: "The force that predestination gives in relation to the paganized masses can only consist in this: that we know our *solidarity* with them."[78] (Solidarity is not without political overtones!) Christology is *only* inclusive.[79] Our empirical classifications are misleading: "Thus the so-called 'outsiders' are really only 'insiders' who have not yet understood and apprehended themselves as such. On the other hand, even the most persuaded Christian, in the final analysis, must and will recognize himself ever and again as an 'outsider.'"[80] This is also why the church remains "holy" even when she plays the harlot![81] Paradox here serves the sense of human togetherness, in Christ.

A second facet of co-humanity, which Barth highlights in his dogmatic work, is the foundational relationship of each human being to her or his *neighbor*. Each *I* faces a *Thou*, and would not exist without the Thou: "I am as Thou art."[82] Regarding this I-Thou, self-neighbor, structure, Barth's connection with two other thinkers deserves some comments. Barth is sometimes contrasted with Kierkegaard, the witness of the Individual, who had such an influence on the early Barth.[83] Barth himself feels free to scold the lonely Dane's individualism:

> Where in his teaching are the people of God, the congregation, the Church; where are her diaconal and missionary charge, her political and social charge? What does it mean that, in interpreting the command

---

[78] Quoted by Sergio Rostagno, "Il Dio che ama nella libertà. La dottrina barthiana della libera scelta di Dio," in *Barth contemporaneo*, p. 153.

[79] Barth, *CD*, IV/1, p. 350.

[80] Karl Barth, *Humanity*, p. 59. Also *CD*, IV/3, p. 365: the Holy Spirit might prefer unconverted people; someone unexpected might harbor the knowledge of Jesus Christ in a way that cannot be perceived by Christians or by the person him/herself.

[81] Barth, *CD*, IV/1, p. 692 (with Luther!).

[82] Barth, *CD*, III/2, p. 250.

[83] Price, *Anthropology*, p. 89 n. 117, cites a Ph.D. dissertation by W. W. Wells, "The Influence of Kierkegaard on the Theology of Karl Barth" (Syracuse University, 1970) and, p. 94 n. 136, Alastair McKinnon's article, "Barth's Relation to Kierkegaard: Some Further Light," *Canadian Journal of Theology* 13 (1967), pp. 31–41, which criticize Barth for ignoring the continued influence of Kierkegaard on his *Dogmatics*. Price's own opinion (p. 84) sounds wise: "I believe that even in Barth's latest works, Kierkegaard's influence is perceptible, although it has been transmuted and adapted to Barth's own creative purposes."

"Thou shalt love thy neighbor as thyself," Kierkegaard could agree with St. Augustine and Scholasticism against Luther and Calvin that there must be a love of self that takes precedence over love of others?[84]

That Kierkegaard did not teach an ecclesiology can be easily granted (he claimed not to "teach" anything, anyway); in his angry love for the Church in Denmark, he tried by all means (to the sacrifice of all that he had: health, wealth and reputation) to awaken that Church to the simple meaning of the Gospel . . . Regarding the neighbor and love of self, however, Barth's memory was unfortunately selective. In his *Works of Love*, Kierkegaard does start with self-love as the divine command presupposes, "but if one must love his neighbor *as himself*, then the command, like a pick, wrenches open the lock of self-love and thereby wrests it away from a man";[85] the command presupposes self-love, but in order to explode it, to pursue the last hidden bit of it, the command "does not leave self-love the slightest excuse or the tiniest escape-hatch."[86] How far from Barth's complaint! In one of his sermons (for Friday communion, on 1 Cor. 11:23), Kierkegaard stresses that "he who encloses himself within himself and refuses to deal with others negates himself."[87] With Kierkegaard, not all preconceived ideas are warranted.

Several writers, as they come upon the I-Thou correlation, think it was borrowed from Martin Buber, or even chide Karl Barth for his failure to acknowledge the fact fully.[88] One wonders, however,

---

84 Karl Barth, *Fragments Grave and Gay*, E. Mosbacher tr. (London and Glasgow: Collins, 1971), p. 99, as quoted by Price, p. 95.

85 Søren Kierkegaard, *Works of Love: Some Reflections in the Form of Discourses*, Howard and Edna Hong tr., "Harper Torchbooks" (New York: Harper & Row, 1962, 1964), p. 34, explaining "You *shall* love."

86 *Works of Love,* p. 27; also: "Christianity presupposes that men love themselves and adds to this only the phrase about neighbors *as yourself*. And yet there is the difference of the eternal between the first and the last."

87 Søren Kierkegaard, *Discours Chrétiens*, Pierre-Henri Tisseau tr. (Neuchâtel and Paris: Delachaux & Niestlé, 1952), p. 260. I could identify the passage in a Danish edition: *Christelige Taler*, H. O. Lange ed., *Samlede Vaerker* XIII (Copenhagen: Gyldendal, 1963), 264–5.

88 Price, *Anthropology*, p. 14 n. 28: "Barth, like Brunner, borrows much of his terminology from Buber." F. LeRon Shults, *Reforming*, p. 129 n. 25: "For an analysis of Barth's unacknowledged reliance on Martin Buber's 'I-Thou' personalism, see Dieter Becker, *Karl Barth und Martin Buber*, Vandenhoeck und Ruprecht, 1982."

whether Buber's position has been accurately represented. For most people, "personalism" majors on the difference between persons and things; Buber, who thinks after Kant, is more interested in the mode of the relationship itself, in the antithesis of mediate and subject-involving immediacy. Have many noticed that, for him, a simple *thing* can become a Thou?[89] Do they know that he maintained strongly the *substantiality* of the person, and precisely as a benefit of the I-Thou relationship?[90] Perhaps, those who have not read *I and Thou* very closely beyond the title can find their ideas in Barth rather than in Buber . . . Barth's interests, however, do not lie in the opposition of persons and things, but in the rejection of individualistic isolation; he fleshes out the I-Thou scheme with a fourfold analysis of the relationship: look, talk, help, freely (consideration, dialogue, assistance, in freedom).[91] I candidly confess my admiration . . .

---

[89] Martin Buber, *I and Thou*, Ronald Gregor Smith tr. (Edinburgh: T&T Clark, 1937), p. 17: ". . . everything in the world, either before or after becoming a thing, is able to appear to an *I* as its *Thou*"; on p. 33: "The particular *Thou*, after the relational event has run its course, *is bound* to become an *It*. The particular *It*, by entering the relational event, *may* become a *Thou*." *Mana* made the Moon a Thou for primitive people, happily so for Buber, pp. 19–20.

[90] Martin Leiner, *Gottes Gegenwart. Martin Bubers Philosophie des Dialogs und der Ansatz ihrer theologischen Rezeption bei Friedrich Gogarten und Emil Brunner* (Gütersloh: Chr. Kaiser-Gütersloher Verlagshaus, 2000), p. 163, quotes from Buber's *Werke* (Munich, 1962), 1:121f: "The I of the I-Thou-Relation produces the ripening of the spiritual substance of man," whereas the I-It-Relation "cannot help him to achieve any substance." Leiner's comment is well to the point: "This passage is also of special interest because Buber, in spite of [his] relational ontology thinks the person as substance. Whatever the changes in the meaning of 'substance' that are proper to Buber's conceptual elaboration, he attaches himself basically to the tradition that does not consider person and substance as opposites, but considers substantiality (*Substanzhaftigkeit*) as a fundamental mark of the person." Leiner observes (p. 278) that, through the possibility of the I-Thou-Relation with every object that exists (*mit allem Seienden*), the Kantian-Neo-Kantian exclusion of the things of nature (*Naturdinge*) is overcome.

[91] Barth, *CD*, III/2, pp. 250–69 (looking the other in the eye, listening and speaking, helping and being helped, and with glad consent, *gerne*). On this, see Price's fine treatment, *Anthropology*, pp. 146–53.

Barth finds the foundational and supreme form of the I-Thou relation in the togetherness of man and woman.[92] This may be the most publicized feature of his anthropology! Following a hint from Wilhelm Vischer[93] and more developed suggestions by Dietrich Bonhoeffer, Karl Barth argues that the clause "male and female he created them" (Gen. 1:27c) determines the meaning of the creation of humankind (*'àdàm*) in God's image (Gen. 1:26, 27ab).[94] Just as God exists in the I-Thou relationship (hence the Trinitarian plural *let us make* in Gen. 1:26), humankind as constituted by man *and* woman is to exist in the I-Thou relationship: this is the *tertium comparationis* that warrants speaking of an *image*.[95] Sexuality (one may remember that *sexus* means a cutting, the dividing of humankind in two halves) is thus the only essential differentiation in which human beings have been created.[96] One should beware, however, of an oversimplified understanding. Barth is not simply saying (as one could think at first) that humans are the image, or in the image, of God, because the I is always bound to the Thou as it is in the Trinity, and as such it is implied and signified by the male-female difference (that would be nearer to Emil Brunner's idea). He insists that the image has no human property or quality at all.[97] Though he wavers somewhat in this, he emphatically rejects the idea that the human creature *be* the image (that the prepositions in Gen. 1, *beth* and *kaph* be so understood): the image is the divine Prototype, *after which* humankind was created.[98] Despite Genesis 5:3, there is

---

[92] Barth, *CD*, III/2, pp. 284–96 (even pp. 284–320). Bouillard, *Karl Barth*, p. 201, notes that Barth already interpreted the image as a destination of which Jesus Christ is the end in the *Kirchliche Dogmatik* II/1, p. 759 (*CD*, II/1, p. 673).

[93] Though his mother-tongue was German, W. Vischer was the professor of Old Testament at the Faculté Libre de Théologie Protestante of Montpellier, where I remember once attending a lecture of his.

[94] Barth, *CD*, III/1, pp. 184–205.

[95] Barth, *CD*, III/1, p. 185: "Thus the *tertium comparationis,* the analogy between God and man, is simply the existence of the I and the Thou in confrontation. This is first constitutive for God, and then for man created by God."

[96] Barth, *CD*, III/1, p. 186.

[97] Barth, *CD*, III/1, p. 184.

[98] Barth, *CD*, III/1, pp. 197–8. However, on p. 184, Barth stresses that man *is*, by being man, the image (his point, in that passage, is that the image is no particular quality).

no transmission of the divine image.[99] Jesus Christ only *is* the image of God (and Barth tries to interpret, against the natural reading, the "man" of 1 Cor. 11:7 as Jesus Christ![100]). But, as always with Barth's exclusive concentration in Christology, this truth unfolds itself most inclusively: Jesus Christ is the image of God *with his Church*, the "great mystery" of the man-woman relationship (Eph. 5:32), and *in him* every human being is the image.[101] We may understand these several points, in an effort to summarize, that the sexual difference is a reminder that each individual is for the other, and for the Other, a destination (*Bestimmung*) that is only fulfilled in Jesus Christ, and actually founded on him—creation being a preparation and a prefiguration, a foreshadowing, of reconciliation:[102] in this way, *'àdàm* as male and female is directed to Jesus Christ (as the God-man who is for us), the Image of God, *'àdàm* is created "after" that Image.

The christological foundation, combining Christ and the Church, of the man-woman relationship entails quite naturally the affirmation or order within it—and who says "order" says "subordination."[103] It is a symptom of the times that present-day theologians who follow Barth reverently on most issues feel obliged to criticize him here—though he develops his arguments in similar ways, and, *apparently at least*, with more biblical backing than elsewhere![104] Such is the power of conformity.

The correspondence between the divine I-Thou model and the human I-Thou structure Barth calls "analogy," and, as he maintains his hostility to the scholastic *analogia entis*, he chooses to call it *analogia relationis*.[105] The phrase is not the usual one; is it equivalent to the *analogia attributionis* he has accepted, though only *extrinseca*?[106] As a matter of fact, the way Barth has

---

99 Barth, *CD*, III/1, pp. 193, 199.

100 Barth, *CD*, III/1, p. 203.

101 Barth, *CD*, III/1, p. 205.

102 Barth, *CD*, III/1, p. 231: "Its nature is simply its equipment (*Zurustung*) for grace."

103 Barth, *CD*, III/4, pp. 169–72.

104 So Krötke, "The humanity of the human person in Karl Barth's anthropology," in Webster ed., *Companion* (pp. 159–76), p. 169. In the same volume, however, the chapter by Katherine Sonderegger, "Barth and Feminism," pp. 258–73, is thought-provoking and refreshingly independent.

105 Barth, *CD*, III/1, p. 195.

106 Barth, *CD*, II/1, pp. 238–9.

defined the analogy, the correspondence between I-Thou in the Godhead and I-Thou in humankind, rather resembles the *analogia proportionalitatis*![107] His *analogia relationis* is original,[108] mostly so in that it remains an *event*, an event that God's grace freely causes to happen (in the last analysis, the Christ-Event)—in accordance with Barth's emphasis on man's being as history, as opposed to "state" (*Zustand*).[109] Some recent commentators pour their praise on the pre-eminence achieved by the category of "relation" (sometimes with an additional degree of abstraction, "relationality"). Barth's mighty influence did promote it, and may not have avoided the deadly trap of "relationism" when it wishes to give such a priority to relation that the *relata* dwindle away: the concept of relation, being that of a linkage and connection, presupposes logically the items in relation, however contemporaneous one wishes to hold them ontologically.[110] But Barth happily escapes the quasi magical use of the word "relational," as if it were enough to render obsolete older studies and to solve older difficulties.

---

[107] Coming to his rescue, Chavannes, *L'Analogie*, p. 190 n. 185, argues that it differs from "classical analogies of proportionality" since "the relations between the two couples of two terms are not equal"; with all due respect for Chavannes's remarkable scholarship, I wonder if this produces a sufficient difference. His own account (p. 43) of Thomas Aquinas's view (*In IV Sent.*, 49/2/1 ad 6m) reads as follows: "if there cannot be any *proportio* [of God and creatures], there can be *proportionalitas*, i.e. an equality of relations; one can conceive that the finite be equal to the finite as the infinite to the infinite." Though he uses the word "equality," I surmise that Thomas would have granted that the relationship of finite to finite cannot be univocally "equal" to that of infinite to infinite; the difference with Barth on this point would not have been so significant.

[108] More than the difference discussed in the preceding note, Barth's inclusion in the analogy of the I-Thou relationship *between God and humans* implies something else than proportionality. Regarding the *analogia attributionis*, one should remember that the canonical (Aristotelian) illustration is "healthy" that can be predicated of the person, of the food, of the medicine, etc., "analogically."

[109] *CD*, III/2, pp. 157–62.

[110] See the discussion in Price, *Anthropology* (a relationist), pp. 134–7, who mentions the critique by Berkouwer, *Man: The Image*, pp. 35, 259 (Berkouwer discusses Albers's critique of H. Dooyeweerd's views). Berkouwer's wisdom, on his p. 139, is worth quoting: "And we certainly cannot play off the 'relational' against the 'ontological,' as though they were mutually exclusive." Henry Chavannes (p. 287) asks why an analogy of relation could not be an analogy of being.

Leaving aside the debate on the relational, the most vulnerable spot in his proposal seems to be the interpretation of Genesis 1:27. In an authoritative synthesis, Paul-E. Dion strongly concludes that the "male and female" clause is a stepping-stone that prepares the announcement of the blessing "Be fruitful and multiply" and that Genesis 5:1–3 implies the transmission of Godlikeness.[111] It is unlikely that "male and female" functions as an explanation of the previous statement; the common use of the title "image of God," parallel to "son of God," for kings in Egypt and Mesopotamia furnishes a more enlightening reference. No mean scholars have opted for the *beth essentiae* and the *kaph veritatis*, i.e. for the interpretation of the prepositions that makes the human being the image (in easy agreement, then, with 1 Cor. 11:7: man *is* the image of God).[112] Barth's nervousness in denying that being in God's image is in any sense a property (*Eigenschaft*) of the creature goes beyond the mark: being called and destined to covenantal fellowship is also a permanent feature of human existence. Such weaknesses, however, do not preclude theological results that illuminate and enrich the readers' understanding of human realities, and that find, beyond convergences with Freud,[113] significant support in Scripture.[114]

3. Soul and body one in the spirit

Karl Barth's doctrine of the constitution (*Beschaffenheit*) of the human individual also tries to build on Christology, but the

[111] Paul-E. Dion "Ressemblance et image de Dieu," in *Supplément au Dictionnaire de la Bible*, Henri Cazelles and André Feuillet eds., vol. X (Paris: Letouzey & Ané, 1981), cols. 391–2 (cols. 379, 384–5 on the plural in Gen. 1:26).

[112] Ceslas Spicq, *Dieu et l'homme selon le Nouveau Testament*, "Lectio divina" 29 (Paris: Cerf, 1961), p. 181, approving, n. 2, J. Jervell, *Imago Dei, Gen I/26f. im spätjudentum, in der Gnosis und in den paulinischen Briefen* (Göttingen, 1960), p. 21. David J. Clines, "The Image of God in Man," *Tyndale Bulletin* 19 (1968): 75–80. I made the same choice in my *In the Beginning*.

[113] As noted by Price, *Anthropology*, p. 161.

[114] The role of the self-neighbor and of the man-woman relationships is indeed overwhelming in the relevant data of the Bible. The theme that is lacking in Barth and would still strengthen the doctrine of human solidarity is that of the Headship of the race, in Adam first, and in Christ as Head of the New Creation (though Barth can use the title "Head," ontological inclusion dominates in his thought).

derivation is less direct and blazing. The analysis he reaches is not inserted into the "analogy of relation." The new features he brings involve a shorter distance from classical models and current views than the way he deals with many other topics. The prevailing anthropological outlook in the late modern world has been heavily monistic (against metaphysical backgrounds marked by either materialism or idealism); it is no surprise if theologians and biblical scholars, under that influence, "discovered" that the Bible (or rather "the Hebrew mind") did not endorse the traditional two-substance dichotomy, branded as a "Greek" construct (this was strong from the 1920s to the 1960s, with J. Pedersen, T. Boman and R. Bultmann as the great names).

Karl Barth, though he based the affirmation of unity on the consideration of the man Jesus Christ,[115] was hardly original in his rejection of anthropological "dualism." He was rather strikingly moderate, for he maintained the distinction, and a hierarchical subjection of the body to the soul. Daniel Price does not exaggerate: "Barth is himself a dualist and not a monist in the sense that he believes in the existence of both body and soul . . .;"[116] for him "the human being is a rational subject whose soul rules over the body;"[117] "The soul transcends the body even as it is inseparable from it. The soul is the seat of freedom; it is the center of the subject, and thus capable of exerting control over the body, which is the periphery."[118] This asymmetrical view of man as "soul of his body," Barth's central phrase, has come under attack, but Krötke valiantly defends it.[119]

The original element in Barth's doctrine of the constitution of the human individual is the role assigned to *spirit*. Barth does not espouse trichotomy, but neither does he identify soul and spirit: rather the spirit is the ground of the unity of body and soul.[120] This is strongly reminiscent of Kierkegaard,[121] though Barth does

---

[115] Bouillard, who is a very moderate critic, thinks the derivation here is not convincing, *Karl Barth*, p. 266.
[116] Price, *Anthropology*, p. 256.
[117] Price, *Anthropology*, p. 257.
[118] Price, *Anthropology*, p. 258 and *CD*, III/2, p. 397.
[119] Krökke "The Humanity of the human person," p. 169.
[120] Barth, *CD*, III/2, pp. 344–66.
[121] For Søren Kierkegaard, the human being is a synthesis of soul and body, and the synthesis is not possible without a third term, which is spirit; see *The Concept of Anxiety: A Simple Psychologically Orienting*

not name him in this context. The sensitive point is the status of this spirit: is the spirit a constituent part of human nature (as many biblical texts with *rûaḇ* and *pneuma* strongly suggest), or God's breath? And if one chooses the second alternative, should one think of a sustaining (divine) action or of the Holy Spirit? The answer is not perfectly transparent. Barth tends to move away from the view of spirit as a part of the person, but not in a very neat fashion, as if to preserve the ambiguity of several Old Testament texts.[122] He wishes, once more, to enhance or to impress in anthropology the patterns of Christology: Jesus Christ is one *in the Holy Spirit*; so must "real man" be in him. It suits Barth or his method, probably, to shape creation (since it is based on reconciliation and foreshadows reconciliation) in a way which corresponds to the Christian privilege of the indwelling, life-giving, Spirit.[123]

The appreciation of the foregoing propositions is less dependent (compared to other Barthian teachings) on theological principles than on positive biblical studies. The large amount of evidence that shows a quasi synonymous use of soul and spirit (for humans), that ascribes them interchangeably the same properties and activities and places them in poetic parallelism—while differences in connotations are enough to account for other passages—leads to the conclusion that "spirit" is a frequent anthropological designation, a designation

---

Deliberation on the Dogmatic Issue of Hereditary Sin, Reidar Thomte tr., with Albert B. Anderson (Princeton, NJ: Princeton University Press, 1980), p. 43. What Kierkegaard calls spirit seems to be close to the faculty of freedom, human transcendence or relationship to Transcendence.

[122] *CD*, III/1, p. 249: we should not identify the *spirit* or *breath of life* of the Old Testament with the Holy Spirit, but rather with the *pneuma humôn* of 1 Thess. 5:23 (without endorsing trichotomy). In several Old Testament passages it is difficult to tell whether a constituent part of the person is in view (as *rûaḇ* certainly designates in Gen. 41:8 or Ezek. 20:32, and so often) or a life-giving/sustaining of God, which may or may not be interpreted as a role of the Spirit (*rûaḇ* surely means such a sustaining in Ps. 104:29–30): one may hesitate in such a verse as Eccl. (Qo.) 12:7.

[123] To quote one more interpreter, Bruno Gherardini , "Riflettendo sulla dottrina dell'elezione in Karl Barth," in S. Rostagno ed., pp. 115–16: for Barth, "the new man by faith and baptism is no other than the old man, and the difference which Paul establishes between the one and the other is only relative. The creative act, in effect, does not distinguish itself formally from the redemptive act—as both of them coincide in the indivisible simplicity of the divine self-determination." (Reference to the *Kirchliche Dogmatik* III/2, p. 245.)

of the inner *anthrôpos* from one angle, to be clearly distinguished from the divine Spirit who sustains creation and who, in his other work, applies redemption.

Regarding the distinction of soul and body, one should focus on the truly burning issue: no one (it appears) is finding Platonic dualism, which is first metaphysical dualism, in Scripture, nor even condoning the excessive influence of Platonism on the tradition of the Church; the issue is whether a significant duality is built into the human constitution, not exclusive of unity, and substantial enough for a disembodied state to be possible (though not "normal" in a sense, and not final). Karl Barth maintained a duality, and deserves our gratitude for that stand (one can overlook an occasional lapse[124]). But he could not take into account the reversal in biblical studies—a reversal that many still ignore, or prefer to ignore. In 1961, James Barr, in his *Semantics of Biblical Language*, showed how utterly flawed and un-scientific the procedures of the Pedersens and other champions of the Hebrew mind-set were. Some scholars realized that the monistic king was barely clothed.[125] In 1976, Robert H. Gundry launched his formidable attack on the monistic reading of the Bible.[126] One may charge him with a tendency to overkill, a margin of excesses (he over-exploits his victories), but his arguments have not been refuted. Such a prestigious scholar as Anthony C. Thiselton has acknowledged their solidity.[127] Even if the

---

[124] In Barth, *CD*, III/1, p. 245, he can claim that the "heart" (the seat of thought and will) belongs to the body! The Hebrews did not ignore the metaphorical character of their language; how do they understand the "circumcision of the heart?" The meaning really intended may be what Walter A. Whitehouse summarizes in these terms: "Desiring and willing are both *seelisch* (of the soul) and *leiblich* (of the body); and both are to be understood as primarily *seelisch* and secondarily *leiblich*," "The Christian View of Man: An Examination of Karl Barth's Doctrine," in his collection *Creation, Science, and Technology: Essays in Response to Karl Barth*, Ann Loades ed. (Grand Rapids, MI: Eerdmans, 1981), p. 28; p. 25 he offers: "The term 'soul' refers to the *Dasein*, as 'body' refers to its *Sosein*."

[125] S. Laeuchli, "Monism and Dualism in Pauline Anthropology," *Biblical Research*, Papers of the Chicago Society of Biblical Research, no. 3 (1958), pp. 15–27.

[126] Robert H. Gundry, *Sôma in Biblical Theology with Emphasis on Pauline Anthropology*, Society of New Testament Studies Monographs, no. 29 (Cambridge, UK: Cambridge University Press, 1976).

[127] Anthony C. Thiselton, *The Two Horizons: New Testament Hermeneutics and Philosophical Description with Special Reference to Heidegger, Bultmann, Gadamer and Wittgenstein* (Exeter, UK: Paternoster, 1980), pp. 281–2.

Old Testament did not attest the duality (as Gundry will not grant), there is abundant proof that Judaism, between the Testaments, had incorporated an important measure of dualism into its anthropology, often with a Platonic coloring—as James Barr, again, emphasized.[128] This is obvious in the *Wisdom of Solomon* (9:15 was an important text for Augustine, which gave, for him, canonical authority to his Platonic anthropology; 8:20 also implies a strong dualism). Josephus's presentation of the three "sects" or religious parties in Judaism (in his *Jewish War* II and *Jewish Antiquities* XIII and XVIII) lays great stress on the belief of Pharisees and Essenes in the soul's disembodied survival. The doctrine of the "intermediate state," which Barth rejected, implies a strong anthropological duality, and it is very hard to ignore in the New Testament.[129] There would be some warrant for a revision of Barth's views on soul and body.[130]

4. Human existence in time

Since Karl Barth defines the being of humans as *history*, he must be interested in the temporal dimension.[131] Indeed, he devotes a major part of his anthropology to it. He again starts from Christology, "Jesus, Lord of time," but the contrast, here, between Christ and us eclipses our participation in him, at least in the description of our experience, and even of our created nature.[132] Time as the sequence

---

[128] James Barr, *Old and New in Interpretation. A Study of the Two Testaments* (London: SCM, 1966). A remarkable summary of the evidence from inter-testamental Judaism is found in Paul Hoffmann, *Die Toten in Christus, eine religionsgeschichtliche und exegetische Untersuchung zur paulinischen Eschatologie* (Münster: Aschendorff, 1966), pp. 95–174.

[129] See Hoffmann. Oscar Cullmann, though very prone to opposing Hebrew and Greek thought, acknowledged the presence of the doctrine of the intermediate state in the New Testament.

[130] For a recent synthesis of biblical arguments, John W. Cooper, *Body, Soul, and Life Everlasting: Biblical Anthropology and the Monism-Dualism Debate* (Grand Rapids, MI: Eerdmans, 2000); from a philosophical point of view, the fine article by C. Stephen Evans, "Separable Souls: Dualism, Selfhood, and the Possibility of Life after Death," *Christian Scholar's Review* 34 (2005), pp. 327–40.

[131] Barth, *CD*, III/2, p. 522: he can write: "Humanity is temporality. Temporality, as far as our observation and understanding go, is humanity."

[132] Barth, *CD*, III/2, p. 512: ". . . the man Jesus is the Lord of time, and His time is the fulfillment of time, embracing all times, the first and the

of past, present and future is the *sine qua non* of human life;[133] but the past vanishes away, the future is problematic, and the present an elusive enigma: we don't have time.[134] This frustration and hollowness of "lost" time is a sign of our fallenness and condemnation,[135] but even when Barth does not seem to consider our degenerate condition specifically, he interprets our temporality as limitation: we come from non-being, one day we did not exist and one day we shall no longer exist, we have non-being behind and before us.[136] By contrast, Jesus' time takes on the character of God's eternity: the simultaneous presence of past, present and future, that do not flee and flow;[137] its limits become doors or windows, on every side,[138] and he is the contemporary of every other time—his time is the true contents or fullness of every time. For Barth, "from the standpoint of the three dimensions of every conception of time, His time is not only the time of a man, but [*zugleich*, 'equally,' left out in the English translation] the time of God, eternal time;"[139] "the Word was made flesh, the Eternal entered time."[140]

Barth makes little effort to interpret the succession of past, present and future. He is more interested in the limits of human time, and especially the *terminus ad quem*, the ending that is called death. Though he recognizes that death as humans actually experience it is a sign of God's judgment,[141] and that death without any curse would still belong to the "shadow side" of creation (with the sea and the night), he still argues strenuously that it is a good thing in itself.[142] If our future non-being was a fall into Nothingness (*das*

---

last time . . . As there can be no repetition of the being of this man, there can be no repetition of this human being in time. It is immediately apparent how differently man in himself and in general, the man who is not Jesus Christ, is in time, has time and is temporal."

133 Barth, *CD*, III/2, p. 437.

134 Barth, *CD*, III/2, pp. 512–15.

135 Barth, *CD*, III/2, pp. 517–18.

136 Barth, *CD*, III/2, pp. 559, 574.

137 Barth, *CD*, III/2, p. 440; cf. 468.

138 Barth, *CD*, III/2, p. 439 (barriers become gateways, according to the English translation); *CD* IV/3, p. 324.

139 Barth, *CD*, III/2, p. 464.

140 Barth, *CD*, III/2, p. 512. The English translation is not very close to the original; literally: "God's eternity became time" (*Gottes Ewigkeit Zeit wurde*).

141 Barth, *CD*, III/2, pp. 588–9, 628.

142 Barth, *CD*, III/2, pp. 561–4, 630–1.

Nichtige, the hostile power), it would be evil, but God (in Jesus Christ always) is himself the limit of death, and our limit: our finitude casts us into his arms.[143] However, it remains "being not" or no longer:

> Man as such, therefore, has no beyond. Nor does he need one, for God is his "beyond" . . . He is thus finite and mortal. One day he will only have been, as once he was not . . . even as this one who has been he will share the eternal life of God Himself.[144]

Barth's propositions seem to equate the promise of life everlasting with the "eternalization" of our *past* existence. Hence his strong rejection of the "intermediate state,"[145] as already indicated. Hence his further declarations: "Future life is no continuation, in some way, of this life. The promise of eternal life does not mean that we shall survive in some heavenly garden! No! The garden is here; life is here, and here are all the glories."[146]

This thesis is valid for Jesus to some extent. For him, too, was death an "anthropological necessity."[147] W. Krötke correctly remarks: "With the thesis of the mortality of Jesus' humanity, indeed of all humanity, Barth contradicted a significant christological and anthropological tradition."[148] Of Jesus Christ's resurrection, Barth was able to write: "there can be no question of a continuation of the life of man after death . . . What is meant by this new coming of a man who is mortal and has obviously died like all others . . . [is] participation in the sovereign life of God . . . being made eternal by the omnipotent grace of God . . ."[149] It is then surprising that he should insist on the propriety of the word "coming again" (*Wiederkunft*) for the Parousia, an event that seems concretely future (in temporal succession) for Barth.[150] He valiantly wrestles

---

143 Barth, *CD*, III/2, pp. 611, 630 (throw ourselves on God).

144 Barth, *CD*, III/2, p. 632. The English translation surprisingly leaves out a clause: as the one who has been he will *not share in the nothing* but . . . (*er auch als dieser Gewesene nicht Nichts . . . teilhaftig sein werde*).

145 Barth, *CD*, III/2, p. 639.

146 Barth, *Réalité de l'homme nouveau*, p. 70. He adds: "One can define eternal life as the eternity of our finite life."

147 Barth, *CD*, III/2, p. 630.

148 Kröthe "The humanity of the human person," p. 172.

149 Barth, *CD*, IV/3, p. 311. "Made eternal" translates *verewigtes*, "eternalized."

150 Barth, *CD*, IV/3, p. 293.

with the issue. Does it imply a new act of existence? The difference between Jesus' time and ours may open that possibility. But the main problem lies with the main thesis: this time of Jesus holds all the attributes of divine eternity. How can the *atreptôs* (without change) of Chalcedon be preserved?[151] When Barth says (as quoted above) that, as the Word became flesh, eternity became time, is he not mixing the Person and the natures as orthodoxy tried to prevent?

Barth's view of eternity is implied.[152] God's "time"[153] is characterized by the co-existence of past, present and future, without succession (no real before and after).[154] "We understand things as if there were three times: what happened in the person of Jesus Christ, what is present, and what will be. But in God's eternity, these three times are only one time."[155] This notion is practically equivalent to the classical understanding of eternity as pure present, a *nunc aeternum*.[156] Classical orthodoxy, however, did not draw the logical conclusion that the diversity of our times should be relativized, that successive things so *appear to us* but are one event, *simul*, in truth (in God's eyes, the Ultimate Reference), whereas such was Barth's boldness.[157] Though Barth often writes *as if* temporal succession had some ultimate validity, clear statements show that it

---

[151] This is Bouillard's concern, *Karl Barth*, p. 271: the monophysite error is close.

[152] So Klaas Runia thinks, "Karl Barth on Man in His Time," *Reformed Theological Review* 17:1 (Feb. 1958), pp. 10–11. Runia mentions (n. 45) his doctoral thesis "De theologisch tijd bij Karl Barth," Vrije Universiteit of Amsterdam, 1955.

[153] Barth often uses the word for divine eternity: in this he merely follows biblical usage (in biblical Hebrew and Greek the same words, *'ôlàm* and *aiôn*, do service for an "age" and for "eternity").

[154] Barth, *CD*, III/2, pp. 438, 440, 536.

[155] Barth, *Réalité de l'homme nouveau*, p. 74.

[156] Barth's difference here—he still speaks about past and future, though they do not come before and after—proceeds from his christological concentration: since the only real God (non-abstract) of whom we can speak is the God of the Christ Event in time, temporal dimensions are retained. The question is: if succession or sequence is being denied, do these dimensions retain any temporal character?

[157] A stronger sense of speculative consistency probably played a part, but also, again, the christological concentration: for Barth, divine eternity and human time are bound together more closely than they are in classical theology (in the latter the remoteness of Deity works as a protection of the "firmness" of temporal dimensions).

is not the case: "If in its perfect divine actuality fulfilled time is to be the only and truly moved and moving time [and this is Barth's conviction, in context], then it does indeed mean suspension, the *total relativizing of all other time* and of its apparently moved and moving content."[158] As an illustration, Barth recalls the legendary detail in the apocryphal *Protevangel of James*, 18, that tells how Joseph, on the night Christ was born, saw everything in the world at a standstill, motionless (the water was no longer flowing, etc.).[159]

One can hardly exaggerate the strategic importance of this view for Barth's theology. In its light, the affirmation of the man Jesus' pre-existence is easily understood. The tendency to interpret creation, reconciliation and redemption as one, with a symmetrical arrangement (very much Barth's taste) of the first and the third terms, naturally flows from the same.[160] It illuminates the Barthian coalescence of history and ontology. On the one hand, history is considered in a predominantly ontological perspective (a sign of which is the fusion of Christ's Person—or the union in him of deity and humanity—and of his work for reconciliation): the all-inclusive Event is the key and ground of all reality, all being—hence the complaint that history, so ontologized, is lost as history. On the other hand, ontology is "historicized," an "actualistic" ontology of becoming, "if the eternal being of God is constituted by His eternal act of turning towards the human race—if that is what God is 'essentially'—"[161] though Barth differs from Hegel in his effort to maintain "a very strict Creator/creature distinction."[162]

---

[158] Barth, *CD*, I/1, p. 116 (italics mine). This remained Barth's position. The statement on Jesus' temporal history in *CD*, IV/4, p. 24 matches the one quoted.

[159] Barth, *CD*, I/1, p. 116. See also Barth, *Réalité de l'homme nouveau*, p. 33: "The clock has stopped . . ."

[160] See the majestic overview provided by Barth, *CD*, II/2, p. 549. He underlines that speaking of creation, reconciliation and redemption, we attest three times one thing only (as with the Trinity); this manifests what he calls "the pre-temporal, contemporaneous and post-temporal eternity of God."

[161] Bruce McCormack, "Grace and Being: The role of God's gracious election in Karl Barth's theological ontology," in Webster ed., *Companion* (pp. 92–110), p. 99; McCormack, p. 108, uses "actualistic" and "historicization."

[162] McCormack, "Grace and Being," pp. 99–100 (words quoted 100). That Barth made every effort to maintain God's freedom and his independence from the creature, even when his statements seemed to entail the opposite, is clear; see e.g. Barth, *CD*, II/1, p. 260: "God is who He is in His works.

Barth's originality cannot be doubted! The reader is left to decide whether the tensions in the doctrine are fruitful or self-destructive, and whether they find enough support in Scripture, the *norma normans*.

5. Human subjection to Nothingness

Along traditional lines, a christological foundation of the doctrine of human sinfulness would not be expected, and the idea has the ring, or clang, of violent paradox. With bold consistency, Karl Barth has done it. His achievement must not be flattened to the level of that trite (and right) understanding: in the event of the Cross, the sins of people, the sins of humankind (with Jews and Gentiles together), reached their highest point (Matt. 23:32, 35–36); the rejection of the Son of God was the supreme expression of the world's rebellion (John 16:9) and revealed the intention of sin under the guises of indifference and man-made religion. Barth *will not* accept the order: first the law; then, sin as the transgression of the law (culminating in the murderous miscarriage of law on Calvary); and, then, Atonement by the Incarnate One. Jesus Christ is theologically prior. He writes of Jesus Christ:

> He is the man whom God in His eternal counsel, giving Him the command, treated as its transgressor, thus rejecting Him in His righteous wrath, and actually threatening Him with final dereliction. That this was true of Adam, and is true of us, is the case *only because* in God's counsel, and in the event of Golgotha, it became true *first of all in Jesus Christ*.[163]

He insists that the doctrine of sin, also, must be grounded on Christology.[164] Any other procedure amounts to idolatry (after the

---

He is the same even in Himself, even before and after and over His works, and without them. They are bound to Him, but He is not bound to them." Was he able *consistently* so to do? One can often sense a tension in his own writing, e.g. *CD*, II/2, p. 509: *Indeed*, we dare not encroach on God's freedom . . . *But* (*aber*) . . .

[163] Barth, *CD*, II/2, p. 739 (italics mine). See p. 740: "It is He, and not Adam, who is the state of original innocence."

[164] Barth, *CD*, IV/1, pp. 139–44; see also IV/3, pp. 369–72.

manner of Exod. 32:4)![165] And he is able to fill hundreds of pages with an original hamartiology.

Only a brief outline will suffice here. Three affirmations constitute the core of Christology (Barth wishes to remain faithful to Chalcedon): Jesus Christ is very God; he is very man; he is one in both natures, which are united in him. Sin, *therefore*, will be seen as threefold. Christ's deity means that he humbled himself; sin, therefore, the contrary move, is *pride*. Christ's humanity means that God exalted him; sin, therefore, the contrary attitude, is *acedia*, laziness and cowardice, inertia and sluggishness (*Trägheit*), the depressive refusal to be raised by God's grace. The union of Christ's natures means that, as man, he is the true witness, or surety, of God; sin, therefore, the contrary discord, is the *lie*. Barth's commentary, together with a wealth of insights, establishes still further correlations with other triads: with the three "Christic" offices (priesthood, kingship, and prophecy), with the three "theological virtues" (the three things that abide, 1 Cor. 13:13), with justification, sanctification and vocation, with the work of the Spirit in the Church . . . His fondness for symmetry and his tremendous abilities for erecting symmetrical architecture are evident.

Sin is the human form of evil.[166] And evil is a power of cosmic magnitude: "the sowing of the enemy in the good field, the invasion of chaos, the nihilist revolution which can result only in the annihilation of all creatures."[167] This is why Barth usually calls it "Nothingness," another sign of his predominantly ontological interests. "Nothingness" was the translator's hesitant choice for *das Nichtige* (whereas "Nothingness" is usually *das Nichts* in German): suggesting the void, non-being, but also active negation, aggressive power, not far from chaos. One remembers Augustine's stress on the non-existence, non-being, of evil; Barth confesses that he "does not like [this conception] too much" and he explains: "This is Neo-Platonism, the *malum pure negativum*. Nevertheless, there is something of that."[168] What he misses in the Augustinian view is

---

165 Barth, *CD*, IV/1, p. 365.

166 Barth, *CD*, IV/1, pp. 398–401. Barth speaks in that section of *das Böse*, evil as committed by moral agents (*das Übel* would rather connote evils undergone, bad things that happen to people—etymologically *Böse* corresponds with "bad" and *Übel* with "evil," but a permutation of semantic nuances has taken place between German and English).

167 Barth, *CD*, IV/1, p. 411.

168 Barth, *Réalité de l'homme nouveau*, p. 111.

the horrendous reality, the destructive efficacy, of Nothingness—but, as soon as he highlights the Dark Power, its difference from mere (innocuous) nothing at all, he has to account for its presence! To this end Barth builds a specific theory. Evil-Nothingness is no eternal principle (no Ahriman); it does not belong to God's own being, which is fully revealed as holy goodness in Jesus Christ; it is no part of creation, which proceeds from God alone—not even, as we saw, under the guise of a natural *possibility* that would be inherent in created freedom as such; it must not be confused with the "shadow side" of creation. Evil-Nothingness is produced (not created) by God's rejection of it! By the very fact that God says "yes" to his creation (it is implied in creation as such), he says "no" to what is not his creation: and this "no," Barth claims, brings forth what it denies. Barth's explanations leave little room for ambiguity:

> Nothingness is that which God does not will. It lives only by the fact that it is that which God does not will. But it does live by that fact. For not only what God wills, but what He does not will, is potent, and must have a real correspondence.[169]

The same, basically, must be said of the Devil and the demons that should be interpreted as concrete expressions of the power of Nothingness: they were never created, have no true "being," and yet are horribly effective; "they are null and void, but they are not nothing."[170] The shadow side of creation,[171] though it belongs to the goodness of creation, is still "contiguous to Nothingness" and signifies the threat of Nothingness hovering over created being.

The use of "must" in the quotation above is significant: Karl Barth often resorts to the language of necessity when speaking of Nothingness and of its role. It was inevitable that it should arise, in strict contemporaneity with creation. It was inevitable that man, necessarily confronted with that power, stronger than he is, should be defeated and yield to it.[172] There is hardly any contingency in the fall of humankind; indeed, the word "fall" is misleading, for

---

169 Barth, *CD*, III/3, p. 352.

70 Barth, *CD*, III/3, p. 523 (p. 530, Barth rejects the fall of angels, which he does find in Jude 6, a text he discards as "peripheral").

171 Barth, *CD*, III/3, pp. 297, 352.

172 Barth, *CD*, II/2, p. 141. This passage, with its necessitarian terms, is most enlightening on the way Barth's mind was working.

there never was a superior state from which to fall: "Actually, one cannot speak of a lost righteousness or of a lost holiness; for human life started with this unfortunate snake story."[173] "There never was a golden age. There is no point in looking back to one. The first man was immediately the first sinner."[174] The shameless nudity of Genesis 2:25 was only possible because the Lord God first unveiled himself before the harlot Israel.[175] Barth does not deny the "historical" existence of early Adam (though the Genesis narrative, no myth in Barth's estimate, does not belong to the genre of history but of *Sage*, which English translators render "saga"). But he minimizes any causal role he may have played.[176] His name is the title, heading, label (*Überschrift*) the Bible gives the history of all men.[177] This, of course, corresponds to his truly *secondary* status, as a type of Jesus Christ, whose "negative side" he represents.[178] This also entails that Barth cannot accept the idea of any *inherited* or *hereditary* sin, which "has a hopelessly naturalistic, deterministic and even fatalistic ring,"[179] though he affirms "original sin" (*Ursünde*).[180] This does not mean that he wishes to water down the affirmation of natural corruption. On the contrary, since there never was a state of integrity before the "fall," sinfulness and human nature are more closely combined:

> . . . this corruption is both *radical* and *total*. That is to say, it means that the sinful reversal [*Verkehrung*, 'perversion'] of sin takes place at the basis and center of the being [*Dasein*] of man, in his heart; and that the consequent sinful perversion [*Verkehrtheit*] then extends to the whole of his being [*Sosein*, 'way of being'] without exception [none of its determinations, *Bestimmungen*, excepted].[181]

173 Barth, *Réalité de l'homme nouveau*, p. 105.
174 Barth, *CD*, IV/1, p. 508.
175 Barth, *CD*, III/1, pp. 318–19.
176 Barth, *CD*, IV/1, pp. 509–10: "No one has to be Adam. We are so freely and on our own responsibility. Although the guilt of Adam is like ours, it is just as little our excuse as our guilt is his." See p. 511: "Adam is not a fate which God has suspended over us."
177 Barth, *CD*, IV/1, p. 507.
178 Barth, *CD*, IV/1, p. 513.
179 Barth, *CD*, IV/1, p. 501.
180 The usual German word for what is called in English "original sin" (Latin *peccatum originale*) is *Erbsünde*, literally "heritage-sin."
181 Barth, *CD*, IV/1, p. 492. Comparable statements in *CD*, III/2, pp. 26, 28, 31 (with "but").

And the *corruptio boni*, even *optimi*, is *pessima* (as Shakespeare had it, lilies that fester smell far worse than reeds).

Barth sounds sterner and more pessimistic than Calvin![182] Actually, if Barth so light-heartedly proclaims the divine "No," it is because he finds the divine "Yes" of triumphant grace hidden in the most crushing condemnation. The irruption of Nothingness is "before God absolutely powerless,"[183] a mere "episode"[184] or "epiphenomenon."[185] "In the light of Jesus Christ, there is no sense in which it can be affirmed that Nothingness . . . is still to be feared, that it still . . . implies a threat and possesses destructive power."[186] This may be one of the reasons why the "me-ontological" name of Nothingness was chosen: in Christ, we may believe that Nothingness, after all (or rather from the beginning), amounts to nothing. Sin, our subjection to Nothingness, is therefore is "removed from all eternity."[187] The "old man" is obsolete (*erledigt*),[188] and this from the beginning since Jesus is Victor from all eternity. The "old man" no longer exists, he is no more than "a shadow moving on the wall . . . in reality he is absolutely nothing."[189] The man of sin "has really been displaced, overcome and put to death in Jesus Christ" and is no more than "an arbitrarily conjured shade."[190] The only *real* man is found in Christ.[191] This is why Barth can also write that the being (*Wesen*, equivalent to *Natur*) of humans never ceased to be good, as God created it.[192] This is why sin and unbelief now appear as an "ontological impossibility" or "impossible possibility"

---

182 When Calvin is read as a mere pessimist, who depreciates human nature, as by Price, *Anthropology* (p. 153 n. 203, and p. 278) he is being misunderstood (though his rhetoric induces such a misreading). Price tries not to bear the full responsibility for the judgment, and (p. 288 n. 112) introduces a better interpretation, in deference to T. F. Torrance.

183 Barth, *CD*, IV/1, p. 46.

184 Barth, *CD*, IV/1, pp. 46–7.

185 Barth, *CD*, IV/3, p. 328.

186 Barth, *CD*, III/3, p. 363.

187 Barth, *CD*, IV/1, p. 48.

188 Barth, *CD*, IV/1, p. 502. The English translation uses "set aside."

189 Barth, *CD*, IV/1, p. 89.

190 Barth, *CD*, IV/3, p. 466. "Displaced" translates *erledigt*.

191 Karl Barth is not always consistent in his choice of words. Occasionally, Barth can say, e.g., in *CD*, III/2, p. 205: "Real man can deny and obscure his reality," which is contrary to what Barth elsewhere says on *real* freedom.

192 E.g. Barth, *Réalité de l'homme nouveau*, p. 9.

(Barth never hesitates forging an oxymoron).[193] Universalism in effectual salvation (*apokastasis*) would seem to follow, and indeed Karl Barth once told Jüngel: "I don't teach it, but I don't say, either, that I don't teach it,"[194] a typical Barthian way of eluding ordinary classification. Barth's reticence corresponds to the status of all that was just said: it is true in Christ, not in ourselves—even in the believer's case, "[h]is own being contradicts his being in Jesus Christ"[195]; but, remember, the being he is in himself is but a fleeting shadow . . .

Is too much too much? Many writers feel that Barth's indulgence in paradox passes the measure. Henri Bouillard cannot take together the statements on human nature unchanged and human nature radically and totally corrupt.[196] How can Barth claim, Pierre Courthial complains, that the power of sin and Nothingness is horribly real and no longer dangerous?[197] Regarding the present efficacy of evil, and the whole "sea of suffering," Karl Barth can even write of *Jesus Christ* that "It is He the first who is surprised and startled" [this appears to be a significant under-translation for *entsetzt*, "horrified, appalled," as by an object of fear; the French version has the equivalent of "scared"][198] that it should be so. How can Barth then celebrate the total victory from the outset? The two kinds of propositions seem to cancel each other out. Hence, many feel that the evilness of evil is ultimately minimized; Pierre Gisel not only feels that Barth passes too quickly over the reality of evil,[199] but that he tends to confuse various forms of the negative that should be distinguished.[200] The ambiguity of the real man's reality is not palatable to all.[201] How can it be maintained, with words still

---

193 Barth, *Réalité de l'homme nouveau*, p. 111; and *CD*, IV/1, p. 747.

194 "La Vie et l'oeuvre" (in *Genèse et Réception*, P. Gisel ed.), p. 56. See *CD*, IV/3, pp. 477–8.

195 Barth, *CD*, IV/1, p. 97.

196 Bouillard, *Karl Barth*, p. 108.

197 Pierre Courthial, "Karl Barth et quelques points des confessions de foi réformées (suite et fin)," *Revue Réformée* 10:38 (1959/2), p. 22.

198 Barth, *CD*, IV/3, p. 328 (in the French translation, *Dogmatique*, IV/3, p. 361).

199 Pierre Gisel, "Réceptions protestantes," p. 262. Aldo Moda, "La Dottrina," p. 94, quotes V. Subilia (a Barthian or a friend of Barthianism) for a similar concern.

200 Gisel, "Réceptions protestantes," p. 272. A similar criticism strikes at the root of Hegel's dialectics.

201 E.g. "Die Funktion anthropologischen," p. 525, discerns considerable (*erhebliche*) difficulties in the concept.

retaining part of their ordinary meaning, in contradiction with the whole empirical sphere? What does "ontological impossibility" mean if sinful behavior is still the fact of experience (as Barth himself stresses)? Barth acknowledges that he resorts to queer phrases,[202] but is not the problem more serious?

Barth's concept of *das Nichtige* is a knot of difficulties. Strangely, it looks closer to the (pagan) Neoplatonic "matter," that mixture of relative non-being and evilness, than Augustine's *nihil* (though I do not deny a residue of that notion in Augustine's concept): for it is granted a kind of "thick" reality and hostile efficacy which corresponds to that "matter," whereas Augustine's *privative* emphasis tries to avoid it. To be sure, contrary to Neoplatonic dualism,[203] it is no "first principle"; but the account of its arising is even more problematic. Apart from the power (the spell!) of Barth's rhetoric, how can one accept that the implicit "No" of God should inevitably cause the irruption of the Enemy Power? The explanation of the origin of Nothingness looks like an intellectual legerdemain. And it is, as we saw, associated with a necessitarian language that apparently carries a remarkable claim: the claim to reveal the *reason* for evil, as the logic of God's will is exposed. This is Gnosticism, P. Courthial exclaims.[204]

The extraordinary difficulties of Barth's theology of sin should not blind us to the equally extraordinary consistency of his thinking. His christological concentration would not harmonize with many other options. If everything must be traced back to the all-inclusive Event, not only must creation (as it foreshadows reconciliation and depends on it) take on the character of a victory over a hostile power (Nothingness, then)—"Otherness" must be both included in the event and reduced, relativized, so that it does not destroy the supremacy of the One Event. The ontological (or me-ontological)

---

[202] Barth, *Réalité de l'homme nouveau*, p. 111. See also *CD*, IV/3, pp. 173–80, answering Berkouwer's strictures. Barth often exploits the duality of the word "godless" (*gottlos*): sinners, rebels, are not without God, indeed, ontologically, for they sin before him and depend on him for their very existence (Acts 17:28); but they are godless in the second sense of "ungodly" in their subjective apprehension and choice of behavior, and, for orthodox theology, this may not be relativized in the name of ontology.

[203] This more implicit than explicit, inasmuch as the "face" of Neoplatonism is monistic; but matter functions as a second primary principle.

[204] Courthial, "Karl Barth et quelques points," pp. 18, 20.

category of Nothingness-which-is-not-simply-nothing offers suitable service through its very ambiguity. Strongly monistic systems never managed to get rid of "otherness" entirely: they assigned to it some kind of ambiguous non-being, the *maya* of Hindu monism, "opinion" (*doxa*) opposed to truth for Parmenides. Karl Barth's christological concentration leads him to ascribe to Sin-Evil-Nothingness a much more aggressive and powerful profile. Three factors were influential: the generally Christian, and his own, sensitivity to evil in experience; the witness of Scripture, which he listened to (despite all shortcomings of his bibliology), especially on the Christ-Event as the victory over evil; and the necessity to retain the antithetical element in order to preserve the *event* character of the Event. Readers who realize how original Barth's genius proved to be (who do not tone down or drain off the meaning of what he wrote) may be drawn to the speculative feat he accomplished in spite of all the extraordinary difficulties in the way.

Decisions will be made on the basis of one's ultimate criterion, especially one's conviction on Scripture as the Word of God. Colin Brown aptly summarized one way to express the basic issue: "Despite his protests that he is not concerned with a Christ-principle but with Christ Himself, we have been obliged to conclude that it is a Christ-idea that often gives Barth his characteristic emphases."[205] Only if we let the teaching of Scripture (*sola et tota Scriptura*) control, and mold, and vivify, our ideas of Jesus the Christ shall they help us more exactly to follow Christ himself!

---

[205] Colin Brown, *Karl Barth and the Christian Message*, p. 152. Brown adds: "We cannot remain true to the New Testament, and follow Barth in his christocentric program." Barth's "protests" are referenced *CD, IV/3, p. 174.*

6

Christus Praesens: Barth's Radically Realist Christology and its Necessity for Theological Method

Kurt Anders Richardson

Barth's *Church Dogmatics* include extended exposition of the doctrine of revelation and basically identify Scripture as the concrete, certain and objective recollection of the church regarding the revelatory events of Jesus Christ. Theological method in this case hinges primarily upon the work of the Holy Spirit confirming the objective truth of God as once and for all revealed in Jesus Christ. Not content however to rest with this category of recollection as mediated in Scripture, Barth expands upon his understanding of it as the medium of the presence of the risen Christ. He goes on throughout the *Church Dogmatics* (II & IV) to develop his theological method to expound the necessity of knowing the presence of God in Christ, *Christus praesens*, in the doing of theology. This essay will concern itself primarily with this christological dimension of theological method.

1. Scripture as "anamnetic" revelation

Barth's doctrine of revelation is radical and in his initial formulation of it this appears in two primary senses: first for its break with the classic declarations of revelation as propositional and, second, for its break with natural revelation as the ground of revelation.[1]

---

[1] Cf. Barth, *CD*, I/1, pp. 111–13, 305, as discussed in the fine essay, Dennis W. Jowers, "The Reproach of Modalism: A Difficulty for Karl Barth's Doctrine of the Trinity," *Scottish Journal of Theology*. 2:56 (2003),

In the break with propositionalism in the doctrine of revelation, Barth is not rejecting the objective, or actual, or correspondent nature of the knowledge of God through God's Word, but rather that the category of proposition is not appropriate to revelation or to Scripture. Barth was also not rejecting the propositional forms of scientific knowledge of hypothesis formation and confirmation. As Jowers points out, Barth located the *principium cognoscendi* no longer in questions of "the That and the What of God"[2] but in the simple "Who is God?"[3] The problem of propositionalism in theology is that it borrows from a certain disciplinary practice and context and universalizes it as if certain knowledge is acquired on no other bases.

In this first instance, Barth is not presenting a subjectivist account of the knowledge of God in revelation but rather is making a very forceful claim that "God's revelation is a ground which has no higher or deeper ground above or below it but is an absolute ground in itself."[4] And it is certainly not the case that Barth wants to substitute revelation for all first principles in philosophy or metaphysics. If anything, Barth's intent was to show that in Christian theology a unique metaphysic would be forthcoming in revelational and scriptural terms. To assert that God's revelation is its own ground of truth is an argument that is virtually tautological: "God is God." But in that God is enunciating the truth about himself in an act of self-disclosure to creaturely subjects, the divine possibility that such an act could be incommunicable to human beings cannot be reasonably discounted.

It is not that what propositionalism is after is not what God intends in some way for human knowing of him but that propositionalism is both inadequate and inappropriate to the case. God determines the possibility and content of the knowledge of himself. Propositions are instruments of scientific theory-construction that intend a kind of "capturing" or "apprehension" of the object of knowledge. Propositions which are on the way to carefully qualified and tentative scientific narrations of interpretation are all preempted by the God who intends to be known and reveals himself in such

pp. 231–46, which opens with a helpful and succinct summary of Barth's view on the two, toward exonerating Barth's doctrine of the Trinity, with the exception that the abandonment of the word "person" creates misunderstanding.

2 Barth, *CD*, I/1, p. 301.

3 Barth, *CD*, I/1, p. 301.

4 Barth, *CD*, I/1, p. 305.

a way by Word and Spirit with the definite result that he is in fact known. At best one might say that one could sociologically propositionalize the human claim that God is known through Jesus Christ on God's terms as indicated by Barth, but this would not be part of revelation. Indeed, it would be just another way of subjecting Christian theology to the false priorities of subjectivist theology.

Another step within Barth's first move regarding the connection between revelation and Scripture can be identified in the statement: "God's revelation is God's own direct speech which is not to be distinguished from the act of speaking and therefore is not to be distinguished from God himself."[5] Barth's extensive statements about God's appropriation of human speech in Scripture find their conclusion on this point. Rather than a theory of inspiration (as perfect species of natural revelation), Barth redirects our attention to the relation God intends between his revelation and the words he commandeers to serve this intent. God's "direct speech," in the *Church Dogmatics*, I is the miraculous and continuous activity of God by his Spirit to actualize the words of Scripture as his own. This redirection of theological attention accomplishes a great deal and, at its highest point, that accomplishment is an affirmation of God's exclusive and irreversible prerogatives over the created media of revelation.

The second radical move on Barth's part is the uncoupling of the theology of revelation from notions embedded within natural theology. In his now classic removes from Thomistc and Schleiermacherian accounts, Barth is determined to establish the revelation of God as found in Scripture entirely upon the basis of God being the content of all revelation or it is actually not revelation. The possibility of the knowledge of God is a naturalized, domesticated, generalized condition which Barth most emphatically rejects. But this is not in the first instance because he finds fault with their epistemic assumptions, particularly if we are thinking in terms of the knowledge of some aspect of nature, but Barth rejects them because they do not correspond to the biblical witness to revelation where God must be both the revealer and the revealed in revelation. Indeed, the revelation is the Trinitarian knowledge of God—the perichoretic "threefoldness" of the word of God. Natural theology is rejected, not with the result that Romans 1 and other classic texts witnessing to God's self-revelation through nature are

---

[5] Barth, *CD*, I/1, p. 304.

denuded of their meaning, but because as all theology is a human project, the question is whether the particular theology corresponds to the divine intention for itself or not. Since "natural theology" as such offers a knowledge apart from the exclusive demands of the gospel—the covenantal condition pre-determined for the world through the witnesses of Scripture—natural theology cannot offer the knowledge of God on God's terms.

But what of revelation of the word of God in the *Church Dogmatics*, I? Scripture is "anamnetic" in nature. That is, Scripture serves as the one, divinely authorized agent of the church's "recollection" of revelation. This is not to say that the word of God is not heard and known afresh in all its objective content as Scripture is read and preached, but that the texts of Scripture are entirely historical according to the time of their writing and frame of reference. All well and good. Indeed, it is this perspective, already evident in the two editions of the Romans commentary, that serves well enough for a profound reorientation of Protestant theology in the twentieth century. The *Sache*, or "matter" of theology, derives entirely from the content of the Bible and yet, as we deal with revelation, we are reminded, with Vanhoozer, that the "revelation is never identical with its medium for if it were then God would be a worldly object, not God at all."[6]

God's revelation is actually an absolute miracle because revelation is his nature as we come to know it, but because when we receive his revelation we receive him. Thus, the problem of theological hermeneutics is not so much one of human understanding as of God himself.[7] Although Vanhoozer in his lengthy article is interested in a theological revision of his own philosophy of authorship in light of understanding Barth, even at the expense of exposing the incapacity of Gadamerian and Ricoeurean hermeneutics to handle the matter of theology, his exercise has achieved immense benefits. To acknowledge the incomparable claim of God in revelation in actual, realist terms is nothing short of a full recognition of Barth's positive achievement for the future of Christian theology.[8]

---

6 Kevin J. Vanhoozer, "Discourse on Matter: Hermeneutics and the 'Miracle' of Understanding," *International Journal of Systematic Theology*, 1:7 (2005), p. 9.

7 Vanhoozer, "Discourse," p. 10.

8 There is some loss again, however, when Vanhoozer moves back again to authorship and texts in general when he writes: "I believe, with Gadamer and Ricoeur, that hermeneutics is ultimately a matter of discerning the

That Scripture is appropriated by God not just once historically but repeatedly through time with the church and with God's people, testifies miraculously to the dynamic of revelation. While inseparable from the text of Scripture, revelation is not circumscribed by the physical and strictly readerly dimensions of Scripture as handled by human beings who believe in and through its words. Who God is, is answered there in the relation between them and the text, but in being answered, the living God is present and self-giving and speaking as the answer itself. In the *Church Dogmatics*, I and the history of its reception, it is easy to overlook this reality which will break forth yet further in the next volume. Suffice it to say, that for all of the qualification Barth had made about knowledge claims and claims about Scripture, the realist groundwork had been laid for going beyond the initial formulation regarding Scripture as the sole means of the church's recollection of revelation.

2. Real presence and theological method

Barth does not do theological method; he does dogmatics. In this process method is always being done along with arguing for and

---

discourse—what someone says to someone about something—in the text as work," p. 25. In his joy over the discovery as laid out on p. 12, showing Barth's reversal from the particular to the general: "It is from the word of man in the Bible that we must learn what has to be learned concerning the word of man in general" (*CD*, I/2, p. 466); and in Barth's "biblicist" method as to "consider well" the text; at the same time Barth is making the radical distinction "between the Bible and all other texts" and this is that "its subject-matter is a sovereign Subject, the living and active Word of God. No other matter speaks for itself as does God in his self-revelation: "God's revelation . . . not only wants but can make itself said and heard" (*CD*, I/2, p. 471). There is still some reorientation to do on moving from this particular to that general. By saying two things and not one: "I am assuming not that ontology is one thing for Christians and another for non-Christians, but that human being is inadequately described if we neglect the resources of Christian faith, and in particular, the creation–fall–redemption–consummation narrative framework of Scripture. If in Christ all things are indeed made new, this fact should have some kind of ontological significance," p. 32; Vanhoozer is struggling, perhaps somewhat set up by Barth in reasoning very easily from the particular to the general, with a uniformity that obviously is not there, based upon what could be characterized as a "greater" and "lesser" paradigm.

expounding the theological matter at hand. From the *Church Dogmatics*, II–IV, Barth is not finished with method, but continues with what is so integral to volume I. He does this particularly in moving beyond his initial statements on Scripture as vital recollection of historic revelation in Jesus Christ in its entirety. But as method continues to work itself out, Barth comes to assert that Scripture also conveys contemporaneous truth corresponding, by means of the work of the Holy Spirit, to the present reality of God in Christ. In this way, Barth declares, the one who proclaims the gospel, preacher or theologian, proclaims what God in person is saying presently to the church and to the world.

Borrowing here from the Pauline use of anamnesis—"remembrance" or recollection—Barth initially posited an "anamnetic" understanding of Scripture in the doing of theology. Although he says that the Holy Spirit aids the theologian and the listening church in receiving Scripture anamnetically for what it actually is, i.e. the word of God (see 1 Thess. 2:13), nonetheless Barth will come to assert that more must happen for full theological reasoning and statement to be achieved. What emerges is a new reference to the reality of *Christus preasens* and therefore of *Deus praesens* conditioning and qualifying the knowledge which theology intends to convey. Barth seems to move beyond his former limited view of Scripture as the church's form of recollection of revelation. Such a view is something uncomfortably close to "historical faith," as rejected by the Reformation theologians as inadequate for salvation. They believed in that one was only confessing a necessary truth for the apostles but not declaring personally anything about necessary, vital truth in one's own case in one's own time. Scripture as recollection, however vitally anamnetic the understanding in these terms, could not express the essential truth that Barth brings out in the *Church Dogmatics* as it develops.

Barth had become acutely aware of the distance between the times of original revelation as reported in Scripture and those of our own: "this temporal and spatial aspect,"[9] as he would later term it. But this was not out of any special regard for the so-called "Lessing's ugly ditch," the cleft between particular events—supremely the appearance of Jesus of Nazareth—and universal truths. The theologian is confronted with "Jesus Christ for us" in the incarnation and the crucifixion "in a concrete and singular then

---

[9] Barth, *CD*, IV/1, p. 288.

and there which cannot be taken away or exchanged—outside our here and now and opposed to it."[10] Barth is not at all intimidated by the historical distance of even twenty centuries, and acknowledges that "this round about way" of recollection is indirectly mediated through others' testimony to truth, their believability, "whether we are able to trust them" or not. He also acknowledges that when knowledge of God is described as only coming by this means, then it appears as if "everything does finally hang by this thread. It is obviously a very disturbing fact."[11] But Barth counters this modern move, whether by liberal or conservative interpreters, that the knowledge of God must come by direct means,

> . . . removing the distance altogether, establishing between the one remembered and our recollection a contemporaneity which has to be explained but which is real, enabling that distant event to become and to be true to us directly and therefore incontrovertibly? But what is the mediation in which recollection becomes presence, indirect speech direct, history present-day event, the *Christus pro nobis tunc* the *Christus pro nobis nunc*, the Christ who meets us, the Christ who is our Savior . . .[12]

Barth locates the knowledge of faith in the present reality of Christ. The One who was for us "then" is the One who is for us "now." This reality removes the distance and is entirely conditioned by the movement of the Holy Spirit which mediates the contemporaneous reality and the knowledge of Christ into the life of the believer (cf. Luke 12:12; John 14:26).

Barth continues in this context to further outline what he has been doing theologically since he began to grapple with the claim of Christ's contemporaneity as understood through the doctrine of the atonement. He does this in connection with the question of the presence of the crucified and risen Christ personally present to the believer, to the church and to the world. The historical "problem of distance" Barth indicates is an overarching preoccupation of nineteenth-century Protestant interpretation, and acknowledges that the issue is "methodological." And yet one must discern the real problem at the root of the methodological concern, namely, whether

---

10 Barth, *CD*, IV/1, p. 288.
11 Barth, *CD*, IV/1, p. 288.
12 Barth, *CD*, IV/1, p. 288

or not the theologian really wants to have Christ truly present in the knowing and acting fellowship of life with him. In an argument extended over a number of pages in the *Church Dogmatics*, IV/1 Barth writes:

> May it not be that the real scandal is grounded in the fact, in the Christ-occurrence, in the event of the atonement itself? . . . How can this our Judge be judged for us? . . . What can His being and activity mean in our sphere? . . . How are we going to apprehend Jesus Christ . . . how are we going to apprehend ourselves in relation to Him, ourselves as those for whom that has taken place which has taken place in Him? What does it mean to live as His fellow?
>
> Supposing our contemporaneity with the Word of God made flesh, with the Judge judged in our place, is already an event? Supposing the *Christus pro nobis nunc* is already *Christus pro nobis praesens nunc*, here and now present with us? . . . It is obvious that we do not want this, that we do not want to accept the fact that our evil case is done away with, and ourselves with it, that we do not therefore want to accept the coming of the Son of God in our place, His being and activity in contemporaneity with us, and our being in contemporaneity with Him. The assault this makes on us is too violent and incisive. If all this is true and actual, it is clear that we have good reason to close our eyes to it, to keep as far from us as we can the knowledge of this truth and actuality . . . so long as we are obviously protected against the catastrophe which the knowledge of the content, the knowledge of the *Christus pro nobis praesens*, would mean for us. We do not then have to notice that we are in exactly the same position as Peter in the boat and the women at the empty tomb and the shepherds of Bethlehem . . . We find ourselves in a relatively sheltered corner where we can dream that we are still in some way existing *ante Christum* since He is not there for us . . . and all because we think that we are excused and safeguarded by the gaping and wide chasm of temporal distance; all because of the existence of Lessing's question.[13]

Christology and methodology are intertwined with yet a third element and that is Christian living. With great depth of perception, Barth identifies how Lessing's question came to be regarded by everybody, whether in disagreement or agreement, as creating a condition of knowledge which completely removed the presence

13 Barth, *CD*, IV/1, pp. 288–92.

of Christ from us. But Christ who made atonement for us and is known as the crucified and risen Lord in our life, astonishingly has inserted himself at the level of method.

Barth wants to shift the locus of attention to what he regards as the much greater problem of our confrontation with the presence of Christ. In this methodological step theology becomes responsible for conveying what it means to faithfully receive the grace of God in fellowship with Christ. Barth's answer is a bridging of historical distance through the actuality of the living Jesus Christ whose resurrection, by the grace of God, provides the reality by which the theologian speaks with the Church in confessing "Jesus lives"—and continues, "and I with him."[14] The theologian must confess, together with all the moments of the gospel of Jesus' dying and rising and ever living that "my life too" as Christ's "younger brother" by God's revelation and grace is "hid with Christ in God" (Co 3:3).[15] This contemporaneous knowledge of God in Christ leads Barth to adopt a particularly definitive methodological stance by which God's promise achieves a "sureness and unequivocal transcendence . . . a clarity and certainty which are beyond comparison or compromise."[16] Further, this knowledge is grounded in a "free act and self-revelation of God" which "cannot be called in question." "And that gives an unsurpassable clarity and an axiomatic certainty." What is operative here, Barth claims, is nothing other than "the Yes of God, which cannot be disputed by any conceivable No," and cannot be confined to a historical moment of the past. Methodologically, theology must embrace the entire reality that "He has spoken and speaks and will speak it in his Son; and on earth with the same sovereignty in which He is God in heaven."[17] What we see here of course is Barth's description of a convictional aspect of theological knowledge that corresponds to the exclusivity and incontrovertibility of God's Word and work in Christ. But this is not an independent, let alone a corroborating or confirming principle, rather, it is a further dimension of the reality of God's active grace. The radical reality of the presence of the risen Christ in the life of the believer, of every believer, takes its place within the nexus of theological knowledge.

The grounding of these high methodological stakes already appeared much earlier in the *Church Dogmatics*. The experienced

---

[14] Barth, *CD*, IV/1, pp. 356–7.
[15] Barth, *CD*, IV/1, pp. 356–7.
[16] Barth, *CD*, IV/1, pp. 356–7.
[17] Barth, *CD*, IV/1, pp. 356–7.

reality of revelation results in an "unsurpassable clarity and axiomatic certainty" that is the fruit of the contemporaneous speaking of God through his Son. The christological/methodological import of *Christus praesens* in the *Church Dogmatics* will encompass the full range of doctrine. Indeed, what Barth considers essential to the entire work of God centered in Jesus Christ, from creation to redemption, is all based upon how "He has become one with the creature, with man."[18] Vital to any consideration of the incarnation, of God becoming human in Jesus Christ, is the coming of the living Jesus Christ to the human in the present. Everything in revelation that already accomplishes "fellowship;" the becoming and being of man as God's creature; the "befriending his fallen creature;" and finally "granting life in his perfect kingdom to his creature;" this further element must be included in the theological framework, whereby "God in his free love has granted his fellowship to what He has created." This is based upon the fact that God in Christ has become "one with the creature."[19] Thus, fellowship with the living Christ is a necessary condition for the doing of Christian theology. For Barth theology achieves the fullness of its purpose only as it is an exposition of the gospel, bearing witness to "the constancy of God."[20]

Indeed, the doctrine of *Christus praesens* is vital testimony to the integrative power of Barth's dogmatic thinking in the *Church Dogmatics*. It is one of those essential elements demonstrating the intensity of his attention to the distinctiveness, depth and richness of God's revelation in Christ. It is a little unsettling to think that one of the methodological criteria by which Barth and successive generations of theologians would judge one another's work is the degree to which the theologian in question is able to include testimony to the presence of Christ in her or his lived experience. At least, Barth seems to be indicating, the theologian must testify to the miracle of divine contemporaneity in which "God must create fellowship within us, the reality of a faith that is established by God's sovereignty over our wills."[21] This is indispensable since any other vital principle at this point produces knowledge of a different god. The matter also comes under Barth's pneumatology in which *Christus praesens* is "a recognition that can be brought about only by

[18] Barth, *CD*, IV/1, pp. 356–7.
[19] Barth, *CD*, IV/1, pp. 356–7.
[20] Barth, *CD*, II/1, pp. 514–15.
[21] Barth, *CD*, II/1, pp. 514–15.

the grace of his Holy Spirit."[22] Like the Reformation debates about a necessarily "regenerate ministry," the vital presence of Christ in the testimony of the theologian, now in Barth integral to theological method itself, suggests a rather unambiguous "evangelical" character to the entirety of the *Church Dogmatics*. Fundamentally, because God's existence in all eternity is triune means that his gracious and saving revelation is the fellowship Barth has been expounding.

> At God's end, His beginning is operative in all its power, and His present is still present. At this point, as in the doctrine of the Trinity itself, we can and must speak of a *perichoresis*, a mutual indwelling and interworking of the three forms of eternity. *God* lives eternally. It is for this reason that there are no separations or distances or privations. It is for this reason that that which is distinct must be seen in its genuine relationship . . . in this distinction and unity . . . God is eternal, and therefore the Creator and Lord of time, the free and sovereign God.[23]

The perichoretic understanding of the relations between Father, Son and Holy Spirit, mean that *Christus praesens* is also the presence of the Father and the Spirit. God as Trinity means that God in himself is distinguishable from himself in three irreversible, non-interchangeable relationships. The work of the Holy Spirit, which is actually not at all in abeyance in the *Church Dogmatics*, comes to the fore here in the context of God sharing his glory with the human creature.

> It is as well to realize at this point that the glory of God is not only the glory of the Father and the Son but the glory of the whole divine Trinity, and therefore the glory of the Holy Spirit as well. But the Holy Spirit is not only the unity of the Father and the Son in the eternal life of the Godhead. He is also, in God's activity in the world, the divine reality by which the creature has its heart opened to God and is made able and willing to receive Him. He is, then, the unity between the creature and God, the bond between eternity and time. If God is glorified through the creature, this is only because by the Holy Sprit the creature is baptized, and born again and called and gathered and enlightened and sanctified and kept close to Jesus Christ in true and genuine faith. There is no glorification of God by the creature that does not come about through this work of the Holy Spirit by which

---

22 Barth, *CD*, II/1, p. 548.
23 Barth, *CD*, II/1, pp. 639–40.

> the Church is founded and maintained, or that is not itself, even in its creatureliness, this work of the Holy Spirit. It is the Holy Spirit who begets the new man in Jesus Christ whose existence is thanksgiving.[24]

The work of the Holy Spirit is necessary for the work of the theologian since by the activity of the Spirit the theologian is "kept close to Jesus Christ in true and genuine faith," and enlivened to speak and write as an expression of gratitude to God.

All of this actually relates to the omnipresence of God in the world. Of course for Barth, the subject of the presence of God is first of all a reference to divine omnipresence "as a whole in relation to all creation as such" which "does not form any obstacle to a whole series of special presences, of concrete cases of God being here or there, which rise like mountain peaks from the plain of God's general presence with his creation."[25] Instead of divine omnipresence as limitless presence in the cosmos, Barth appeals to a biblical frame of reference with respect to the "special presence of God which always comes first and is estimated and valued as the real and decisive presence."[26] It is on the basis of God's special presence as attested in Scripture that the general presence of God is established. And Barth's Christocentrism here is close at hand. First, through the word of God by which all things are created and sustained, we must be reminded that this Word is the one who is "the essence and mystery of his revelation and so of his special presence in the world."[27] Then, in Christ the sense of God's "special presence" is termed "his proper presence," whereby God is "specially present to Israel and the Church, and as such generally present in the world as a whole and everywhere."[28]

And here we observe the critical historical and present tense distinction, between "the expectation and recollection of revelation and salvation" and "its fulfillment and presence."[29] And this distinction for Barth is utterly unique, expressed in the contrast between God's acceptance of humanity, Israel and church, in his covenant and his presence "in Jesus Christ as the Head which constitutes and controls this body."[30] The relation here is one of objective and subjective

---

[24] Barth, *CD*, II/1, pp. 669–70.
[25] Barth, *CD*, II/1, p. 477.
[26] Barth, *CD*, II/1, pp. 477–8.
[27] Barth, *CD*, II/1, p. 478.
[28] Barth, *CD*, II/1, p. 478
[29] Barth, *CD*, II/1, p. 484.
[30] Barth, *CD*, II/1, p. 485.

participation; it "is the distinction between *gratia adoptionis* and *gratia unionis*"—the latter expressing the classic final step in most Reformed accounts of the *ordo salutis*. This distinction is significant and can be regarded as the distinguishing evangelical mark of the *ordo*: "*adoptio* is different from *unio*. *Unio* is the basis of *adoptio*. *Adoptio* is based on *unio*. *Gratia unionis* is the bestowing grace of God, *gratia adoptionis* the divine grace bestowed."[31] What is significant is how this objectively and radically grounded subjective principle, the "inclusion" of the believer through union with God, will become so critical to theological method.

Barth is emphatic that this inclusion takes place only in Christ, which is the basis for distinguishing *adoptio* from *unio*. God first adopts and unites himself with humanity in Christ. Then and on that basis, everyone in Christ is adopted and united to him and the crucial element is its accomplishment by the Holy Spirit.[32] In this regard, the Holy Spirit

> is no other than the presence and action of Jesus Christ Himself . . . It is by His power that He enables men to see and hear and accept and recognize Him as the Son of Man who in obedience to God went to death for the reconciliation of the world . . . It is by His power that He enables them to live in His presence, in attentiveness to His action, in discipleship as those who belong to Him . . . When we receive Him we receive Him from Jesus Christ, as His Spirit. And we enter into the sphere of His presence and action and lordship.'[33]

Quite apart from worries about the obscurity of the Holy Spirit in the *Church Dogmatics*, we note the emphases upon the "presence" of Christ mediated to believers and their active seeing, hearing, and recognizing of him, their appropriation of him in the present. This is not only Christian possibility but actuality given the radically present "sphere" of Christ in which believers participate and in which the theologian too must dwell to accomplish theology's task.

---

[31] Barth, *CD*, II/1, p. 485.

[32] Cf. the recent contributions in pneumatology, George Hunsinger, 'The Mediator of Communion: Karl Barth's Doctrine of the Holy Spirit', in John Webster, ed., *The Cambridge Companion to Karl Barth* (Cambridge, UK: Cambridge University Press, 2000), pp. 177–94; Tom Smail, *The Giving Gift: The Holy Spirit in Person* (London: Darton, Longman & Todd, 1994).

[33] Barth, *CD*, IV/2, pp. 322–3.

7

The Spirit of God and the Spirit of Life: An Evangelical Response to Karl Barth's Pneumatology

Frank D. Macchia

> I would like to reckon with the possibility of a theology of the Holy Spirit . . . in favor of the "Enthusiasts" who were so onesidedly and badly treated by the Reformers, and still further back, in favor of all those agitated and contemplative souls, the spiritualists and the mystics of the Middle Ages.[1]

A theology of the Holy Spirit written in favor of enthusiasts and mystics? Is this Karl Barth speaking, the theologian of "revelation," of the objective word of God made flesh? The above quote from Barth can be either intriguing or frightening (or both!) to evangelicals, depending on the stream of evangelicalism in which one moves and has his or her ecclesiastical being. I am a Pentecostal, for whom the work of the Holy Spirit is highly significant for a theology that is open to all of the rich dimensions of the Christian life and to God's redemption of the world, especially through the mission of the church. I find Barth's proposed project of a theology from the vantage point of the Holy Spirit "in favor of the 'Enthusiasts'" intriguing. For those evangelicals heavily oriented toward a biblicist Christocentrism, a dogmatics from the vantage point of the outpouring and life of the Spirit can smack frighteningly of "subjectivism" or flights of theological speculation based more on

---

[1] Karl Barth, "Concluding Unscientific Postscript on Schleiermacher," in Dietrich Ritschl ed., *Karl Barth: The Theology of Schleiermacher, Lectures at Göttingen, Winter Semester of 1923/24*, Geoffrey W. Bromiley tr. (Grand Rapids, MI: Eerdmans, 1982), p. 278.

experience and religious imagination than on the inspired text of Scripture.

Some evangelicals have interpreted Barth as a "subjectivist," despite the fact that he can be quoted prolifically against this caricature. Cornelius Van Til, for example, wrote that Barth's Christ "is not the Christ of the Scriptures; it is the projection of the moral and spiritual ideals of modern man as he casts them up for himself into the void."[2] Under the influence of Kant, this void that Barth allegedly irrationally fills with experience and speculation is caused by an understanding of God and revelation as detached from reality. Recognizing that Barth can be quoted prolifically as seeking a theology of revelation based on the word of God revealed in Christ, but still clinging to Van Til's basic caricature, Edward J. Carnell called Barth an "inconsistent evangelical,"[3] who sought to base theology on both the objective word of revelation and the subjective religious experience of the believer.

Over against Carnell's judgment of inconsistency, I prefer to call Barth's pneumatology *complex*, based on the word of revelation but directed to the hearing of faith. We may not be entirely happy with the way in which Barth construes the relationship between these two poles of pneumatology, but the struggle to preserve both the Lordship of the Spirit in revelation and the presence of the Spirit in the life of faith is unavoidable. Barth's pneumatology helps us to understand the nuances of how Barth holds in tension the "objective" and the "subjective" (or, more accurate to Barth, "intersubjective"), thus getting us into the heart of this complexity and opening up for evangelicals the possibility of fruitful dialogue, both internally amongst ourselves and externally with a broader spectrum of voices. With this context of dialogue in mind, I want to explore Barth's pneumatology, starting with the vital place that the doctrine of the Holy Spirit held for Barth in his broader theological agenda.

---

[2] Cornelius Van Til, The *New Modernism: An Appraisal of the Theology of Barth and Brunner* (Philipsburg, NJ: Presbyterian and Reformed, 1953), p. 456, quoted in Gregory G. Bolich, *Karl Barth and Evangelicalism* (Downers Grove, IL: InterVarsity Press, 1980), pp. 71–2.

[3] E. J. Carnell, "Barth as Inconsistent Evangelical," *Christian Century* XXIII (6 June 1962), p. 714, quoted in Bolich, *Barth*, p. 88.

1. The place of pneumatology in Barth's theology

We will begin this section with a remarkable statement from Barth elaborating on his proposed project of a theology from the vantage point of the third article of the Apostles' Creed, namely, the Holy Spirit. Notice how he proposes reading the theologies of the Father and the Son from the lens of pneumatology:

> As to a clarification of my relationship to Schleiermacher, what I have occasionally contemplated for here and now . . . would be the possibility of a theology of the third article, in other words, a theology predominantly and decisively of the Holy Spirit. Everything which needs to be said, considered and believed about God the Father and God the Son in an understanding of the first and second articles might be shown and illuminated in its foundations through God the Holy Spirit.[4]

Barth does not oppose a theology that begins with the Spirit so long as one proceeds from this place to the objective ground of the Spirit's work in Christ and the trinitarian communion. Barth adds, therefore, that the path to follow in responding to Schleiermacher was not anthropological but rather pneumatological, not human consciousness but the outpouring of the divine Spirit.[5] Implied as decisive is what may be termed the objectivity of the Spirit's work in the context of Christology and the Trinity. The Spirit does create analogies to this work within the believing community. These analogies would have theological significance for Barth but would not play the determinative role methodologically in determining the fundamental shape and direction of pneumatology. In other words, as we will discuss in greater detail below, the Spirit plays a key role in Barth's theological agenda but most determinative to this role would be the objectivity of the Spirit's work as implied by divine revelation, reconciliation, and redemption.

Most interesting about the above quote is that Barth's plan for a determinative role for pneumatology in his theology is cast more in the form of a future proposal left unfulfilled than a finished product. The fact is that Barth died before he could write his theology from the third article. But such was his intention. As George Hunsinger has pointed out, such would have occurred in Barth's expanded

[4] Barth, "Unscientific Postscript," p. 278.

[5] Barth, "Unscientific Postscript," p. 279.

discussion of *redemption*, which would have been pneumatologically focused. Redemption as the proper work of the Spirit would represent for Barth "the final consummation of all things, the resurrection of the dead, and eternal life in communion with God."[6] This future consummation would have revealed the inexhaustible significance of Christ for all of creation. As Hunsinger remarked concerning the pneumatological fulfillment of Barth's broadly-conceived theological program, "Whereas from the standpoint of reconciliation, the work of the Spirit served the work of Christ; from the standpoint of redemption, the work of Christ served the work of the Spirit."[7] Though this prominently pneumatological portion of the *Church Dogmatics* never materialized, Barth gave programatic hints of it in the *Church Dogmatics* (e.g. *CD*, IV/2, pp. 507–11) as well as in the quote given above.

Hunsinger's insights thus help us to reconcile the divergent views of two major treatments concerning the role of pneumatology in Barth's theology: Philip J. Rosato and John Thompson. Rosato proposed that Barth was becoming "gradually more pneumatocentric than christocentric."[8] The years 1922 (when Barth wrote the famous second edition of his *Romans* commentary) to 1931 witnessed a strengthening of pneumatology in Barth's theology. In the Anselm book in particular, "tones of dialectical opposition and excessive Christocentrism give way to an understanding of the Spirit's role in creating an analogy between the existence of Christ and the faith of the believer."[9] In other words, Barth's pneumatology gradually helped him to discern more of a continuity between God's objective self-disclosure and the church's experience of this in life.

This trend according to Rosato took place in the midst of Barth's struggle with the attempt of modern Protestant theology to make sense of religious experience by positing an essential continuity between revelation and religious consciousness. Barth came to combat this "anthropocentric" (or, more accurately, "believer-centric") point of departure for theology not only with a christological center for defining revelation but increasingly from the vantage point of the

---

6 George Hunsinger, "The Mediator of Communion: Karl Barth's Doctrine of the Holy Spirit," in John Webster ed., *The Cambridge Companion to Karl Barth* (Cambridge, UK: Cambridge University Press, 2000), p. 178.

7 Hunsinger, "Mediator," p. 178.

8 Philip J. Rosato, *The Spirit as Lord: The Pneumatology of Karl Barth* (Edinburgh, UK: T&T Clark, 1981), p. 3.

9 Rosato, *Spirit*, p. 24.

implications in God's self-giving as Spirit. Pneumatology, that is, the objective divine self-giving as Spirit, increasingly became Barth's "meeting place" with modern Protestant theology.[10] Without letting go of the "dialectical opposition" between revelation and human experience, Barth struggled through a christologically-determined pneumatology to posit an analogous relationship between them. In other words, after establishing his christological center, Barth was driven more and more toward a central concern with pneumatology in his effort to find a common point of contact with his theological opponents. Rosato notes that Schleiermacher (and, by Barth's judgment, Bultmann) had in a distorted effort at a theology of the third article wrongly made human God-consciousness (or existential self-awareness) the point of departure rather than the Spirit's role in mediating between Christ and the believing community (i.e. the outpouring of the divine Spirit at Pentecost).[11] Barth eventually moved from a christologically-determined pneumatology to a full-orbed trinitarian pneumatology.[12] But Rosato makes the astounding claim that despite Barth's enduring focus on Christ in his broader theological program, he "clearly intends to write a theology of the Christian which is not christocentric but pneumatocentric."[13]

Thompson, however, takes issue with Rosato. While noting that Barth's theology is "clearly christological and pneumatic,"[14] he adds, "Rosato's view that Barth's doctrine of reconciliation is primarily pneumatological cannot be fully supported," because in reconciliation the Spirit serves the reconciling event that occurs objectively in Christ.[15] Thompson's conclusion is that, while "Jesus Christ is central, the Holy Spirit plays an indespensable role."[16] Does Barth drift toward pneumatocentrism as Rosato maintains or does Barth remain christocentric as Thompson holds?

How one answers this depends on the dimension of Barth's program of the *Church Dogmatics* to which one is referring. As Hunsinger notes, Barth's relatively undeveloped treatment of redemption helps to explain the imbalance in Barth's treatment of Christ and the

---

[10] Rosato, *Spirit*, pp. 3–5.
[11] Rosato, *Spirit*, p. 15.
[12] Rosato, *Spirit*, p. 34.
[13] Rosato, *Spirit*, p. 43.
[14] John Thompson, *The Holy Spirit in the Theology of Karl Barth* (Allison Park, PA: Pickwick, 1991), p. 8.
[15] Thompson, *Holy Spirit*, p. 81.
[16] Thompson, *Holy Spirit*, p. 35.

Spirit in favor of Christology. In other words, the basis of salvation would be in Christ's reconciling work, while the goal of salvation would accent the Spirit's representation of that work throughout creation. In this latter project of developing the eschatological goal of salvation, it is the Spirit that would occupy the central concern with Christology serving as the basis for understanding the expansive breadth of the Spirit's work throughout creation. It seems that Thompson's insights into the enduring Christocentrism of Barth's theology are justified, but not in a way incompatible with Rosato's perception of the inner *telos* of Barth's incomplete work in terms of where it was headed, namely, toward a pneumatological concentration in relation to the work of redemption throughout creation.

One place in the *Church Dogmatics* where Barth hints at his central pneumatological concern is in the final fragment in which he offers an extensive discussion of the baptism in the Holy Spirit.[17] This rich discussion of Spirit baptism by Barth attracted the attention of Pentecostals due to the fact that Spirit baptism is so rarely addressed, even within discussions on pneumatology. If treated at all outside of Holiness, Pentecostal, and charismatic churches, the topic tended to be discussed narrowly and very briefly within the strict confines of the meaning of water baptism. Even under water baptism one will usually not find an explicit discussion of Spirit baptism in its own right. Barth's extensive treatment of the doctrine signaled for many Pentecostals that his theology had aimed at being uniquely concerned with the role of the Spirit in transforming Christ's reconciling work into a historical force for the redemption of the world. This role for the Spirit could only be ascribed to God, grounding pneumatology and salvation in general in God and God's self-disclosure in Christ and not on human religiosity. We turn first, therefore, to the Lordship of the Spirit in trinitarian context.

2. The Lordship of the Spirit in trinitarian context

Barth defends the full deity and Lordship of the Spirit: "The Spirit outpoured at Pentecost is the Lord, God himself, just as the Father and just as Jesus Christ is the Lord, God himself."[18] If the

[17] Barth, *CD*, IV/4.
[18] Barth, *CD*, I/1, p. 466.

Son brings revelation objectively to history, the Spirit fulfills this revelation subjectively in creation.[19] The objective and the subjective sides of revelation are both the activity of God as Lord. This is because the creature can do nothing in the area of revelation or salvation, whether it be to bring about its objective expression or to realize it subjectively in the world. Thus, the Spirit's bringing to subjective realization the objective self-disclosure of God in Christ must also be a function of God as Lord: "Revelation in the Holy Spirit is a work that can only be ascribed to God."[20]

Our knowledge of God through the Holy Spirit has its objective source for Barth not only in God's self-disclosure historically in Christ, but ultimately in God's self-knowledge as Father, Son, and Holy Spirit. The Spirit's role in mediating the knowledge and love between the Father and the Son provides the basis for God's self-disclosure through the Son and the Spirit in history. God stands to be known, Barth writes, "only because and in the fact that God is the triune God, God the Father, God the Son, and God the Holy Spirit."[21] Our knowledge of God is grounded in God's self-knowledge as Trinity, for "in the heart of the truth in which He stands before us, God stands before himself; the Father before the Son, the Son before the Father . . . In the heart of the truth in which we know God, God knows himself."[22] Without this objectivity of God, there is no knowledge of God.

Barth does not posit a simple identification between God's self-knowledge and our knowledge of God. In the Spirit and through Christ, God's self-disclosure is a revelation of a mystery that remains hidden (a veiling in the midst of an unveiling).[23] But God is still known due to the work of Christ and the Spirit, and known by God's grace in a way analogous to God's self-knowing as Father, Son, and Spirit. Though Barth does not pursue this direction, there is potential here for a notion of the Spirit of life that leaves room for a plurality of voices with no single voice having any absolute claim on God's revelation through the Spirit.

The Spirit of interactive love is key for Barth. Barth follows the Augustinian notion of the Spirit as the bond of love between the Father and the Son.[24] Yet, Barth is careful to avoid depersonalizing

---

19 Barth, *CD*, I/1, p. 433.
20 Barth, *CD*, I/1, p. 467.
21 Barth, *CD*, II/1, p. 48.
22 Barth, *CD*, II/1, p. 48.
23 Barth, *CD*, II/1, p. 50.
24 Barth, *CD*, I/1, p. 487.

the Spirit as merely a love relation. Barth notes that the Spirit is to be glorified with the Father and the Son as the bond of love between them, but "not in a way that the Spirit is a mere attribute or relation of the Father and the Son."[25] The Spirit is involved in the divine *koinonia* between the Father and the Son as an active participant. In binding us to the Son, the Spirit creates an analogy in revelation of communion within God.

Barth's defense of the *filioque* (that the Spirit proceeds from the Father and the Son) is based on an assumed analogy between God's inner bond of love by the Spirit and the outer bond of love between God and the creation. Barth writes of the eternal communion within God,

> If the rule holds good that God in His eternity is none other than the one who discloses Himself to us in His revelation, then in the one case as in the other the Holy Spirit is the Spirit of the love of the Father and the Son, and so *procedens ex Patre Filioque*.[26]

The Spirit as the God who unites God in Godself (between the Father and the Son) also unites us to God through the Son. The Spirit does not provide any basis for a natural speculation about God from human reason divorced from God's self-disclosure in Christ.

The Spirit's work is thus bound to the elect will of the Father and the reconciliation in the Son as an inseparable act of a divine Lordship that is exercised eternally three times over as Father, Son, and Spirit. We can thus speak of the Spirit's Lordship (2 Cor. 3:17). For Barth, the Spirit is not a divine subject distinct from the subjects of the Father and the Son, but rather the one divine subject in the mode of the Spirit distinct from the modes of the Father and the Son. Of the Spirit, Barth wrote, "He is not a third spiritual subject, a third I, a third Lord side by side with two others. He is a third mode of being of the one divine subject as Lord."[27] There is no modalism here, no hidden God beyond the three, only the three modes of being in eternal relation, eternally distinct but inseparable. Lest the objective pole for the Spirit's work be seen as formalistic or abstract, it is important to focus on the way in which the Word

---

25 *CD*, I/1, p. 487.
26 *CD*, I/1, p. 483.
27 *CD*, I/1, p. 469.

disclosed historically in Christ also provides the objective basis of the Spirit's work.

3. The Spirit and Christ

Barth is clear that the Spirit "cannot be separated from the Word and his power is not a power different from that of the Word but the power that lives in and by the Word."[28] In reference to the objective Word, Barth says that the Spirit "can be only the repetition, the impress, the seeking of objective revelation upon us."[29] Another way of saying this is that "the work of the Holy Spirit is nothing other than the work of Jesus Christ."[30]

The word of Christ is not some vague mystical encounter but is rather the self-disclosure of God through Christ *in history*. The resurrection "according to the Spirit of holiness" (Rom. 1:4) and Pentecost mean that the incarnation, life, and death of Jesus were not only events significant for Jesus as a Jewish man of the first century, but also for all of humanity, past, present, and future. The resurrection for Barth shows that Jesus' history is not past or transient history but "is present to all later times and indeed to all earlier times, cosmically effective and significant history."[31] The nativity of Jesus is our nativity. As Barth noted, "Christmas day is the birthday of every Christian."[32] The history of Jesus that is made real in us by the Spirit is the concrete and real event of Jesus: "The Christian life, faithfulness to God as the free act and attitude of a man, begins with that which in the days of Augustus and Tiberius, on the way from the manger of Bethlehem to the cross of Golgotha, was actualized as that which is possible . . . with God.[33] Though Barth felt that God's actions cannot be discerned through the narrow lens of historical method, and that the Spirit causes the events of Christ to transcend Christ's time and place, he did believe that they occurred originally and significantly *in history*.[34]

---

28 Barth, *CD*, I/1, p. 150.
29 Barth, *CD*, II/1, p. 239.
30 Barth, *CD*, II/1, p. 241.
31 Barth, *CD*, IV/4, p. 24.
32 Barth, *CD*, IV/4, p. 15.
33 Barth, *CD*, IV/4, p. 17.
34 Here is where I believe Cornelius Van Til and John Warwick Montgomery have read Barth superficially and not understood him aright. See, Bolich, *Karl Barth*, pp. 87–9.

Those who accuse Barth of subordinating the Spirit to Christ should bear in mind that Barth also regarded the Spirit as active in mediating the incarnation and of anointing Jesus so that he may participate fully in the work and "majesty of the eternal Son."[35] The human existence of Jesus in its totality as a redemptive event is due to the renewing power of the Spirit that brought the worlds into existence.[36] In fact, Barth even interprets the Spirit at work in creation from the vantage point of the Spirit that mediated the incarnation and raised Jesus from the dead.[37] Likewise, the breath of God behind the resurrection of Jesus penetrated the "life, words, and acts of Jesus" during his life.[38] Christ's whole being was "filled and controlled by the Spirit."[39] Even now, Christ "lives and reigns and acts and is at work in the power of his resurrection, the force and authority of the verdict of the Spirit."[40]

This role of the Spirit in cooperating with the word in shaping Jesus' life and mission helps to protect Barth against the charge of "Christomonism." Barth defines Christomonism as the view which sees human redemption and liberation as "simply an appendage, a mere reflection, of the act of liberation accomplished by Jesus Christ in history."[41] Humanity becomes nothing more than passive participant in a work that has only Jesus as the contributing subject. Barth terms this a "subjectivism from above" in which "all anthropology and soteriology are thus swallowed up in Christology."[42] On the other hand, Barth also wishes to avoid an anthropomonism in which Jesus' history becomes the mere "stimulation, instruction, or aid, perhaps even indispensable example" of human liberation. Barth terms this a "subjectivism from below" in which the figure of Jesus is fashioned in the image of the human subject acting to define the meaning of the liberated life. In such an anthropomonism, "Christology is now swallowed up by a self-sufficient anthropology and soteriology."[43]

---

[35] Barth, *CD*, I/1, p. 486.
[36] Barth, *CD*, III/2, p. 336.
[37] Barth, *CD*, III/2, p. 360.
[38] Barth, *CD*, III/2, pp. 336–7.
[39] Barth, *CD*, IV/1, p. 309.
[40] Barth, *CD*, IV/1, p. 320.
[41] Barth, *CD*, IV/4, p. 19.
[42] Barth, *CD*, IV/4, p. 19.
[43] Barth, *CD*, IV/4, p. 20.

Barth uses pneumatology to avoid both Christomonism and anthropomonism, because the Spirit functions as the link between Jesus and the word and between Jesus Christ and the church. Due to the objective work of the Spirit creating these links, Christ cannot be dissolved into human religious imagination and the experience of the church in the Spirit cannot be collapsed into the historical Jesus, having no economy of its own in God's redemptive plan or no orientation towards an eschatological future. Though the pneumatology of the *Church Dogmatics* has a strong christological determination, greater balance would have been apparent had Barth lived long enough to develop the broader pneumatological and eschatological portions of his work. But it is Barth's strong christological determination of pneumatology and his concomitant accent on Spirit Christology that can help to mediate between evangelicals who are christocentric and those who want to give equally strong emphasis on the Spirit. It is important to say a few words at this point about the Spirit and the church, since the church is the place where the gospel of Christ is mediated to Christians through the Spirit.

4. The Spirit and the church

The Spirit for Barth is not primarily of the individual but of the Christian community born of the Spirit as the body of Christ.[44] In fact, Hunsinger notes rightly that knowledge of God is essentially a form of *koinonia* for Barth, analogous to God's self-knowledge in the communion of love in the Trinity.[45] For Barth, the Spirit that is the awakening power of the Word made flesh is also "the awakening in which the church is born of the Word."[46] The church lives from the awakening power of the Spirit and "is called to tarry for him and . . . obey him."[47] The church is that body of Christ created and continuously renewed by the Spirit.[48] Because of the Spirit, Christ is not an isolated figure but lives in communion with his church, his elect body.[49]

---

[44] Barth, *CD*, III/3, p. 255.
[45] Hunsinger, "Mediator," p. 189.
[46] Barth, *CD*, IV/1, p. 652.
[47] Barth, *CD*, IV/1, p. 660.
[48] Barth, *CD*, IV/1, p. 661.
[49] Barth, *CD*, III/3, p. 271.

The Spirit is the "Founder of the Christian community and the Guarantor of its whole action in the world."[50] The tongues of Pentecost reveal the miracle involved in a church born by the Spirit and thrust into the world to become a globally diverse body: "What the Holy Spirit is and does, the fact that he makes men capable of this authoritative and effective witness, and therefore the true mystery of Pentecost, is only revealed at this point."[51] Tongues symbolized that the Spirit opened the doorway of witness and mission to the nations: "Israel itself has not opened this door, or built this bridge, or invented this new epoch, or given itself an understanding of it."[52] It is the Spirit as the presence and operation of Jesus that did these things miraculously and by grace. As Thompson points out, Barth treats all of the theology in volume IV, part three, of the *Church Dogmatics* under the missionary aspect of the life of the church.[53]

In the power of the Spirit, people are sanctified in the context of the Word of God proclaimed in peaching and sacrament and are enlighted by God's gifts.[54] Barth was open to the extraordinary gifts of the Spirit, writing, "if all those who advocate these special manifestations want to be heard in the Church, let them show them to her and, then, I hope that the whole Church will be capable of obeying the voice of truth."[55] Of course, Barth was convinced that the scriptural witness is the fundamental voice of truth in the church. It is to the role of the Spirit in inspiring the biblical text that we now turn.

5. The Spirit and verbal inspiration

Barth defended the concept of the verbal inspiration of Scripture. He said in no uncertain terms that, "there is real inspiration . . . only in the form of verbal inspiration, the hearing of the Word of God, only in the concrete form of the biblical word."[56] For Barth,

---

[50] Barth, *CD*, III/4, p. 321.
[51] Barth, *CD*, III/4, p. 321.
[52] Barth, *CD*, III/4, p. 323.
[53] Thompson, *Holy Spirit*, p. 106.
[54] Barth, *CD*, IV/1, p. 645.
[55] Karl Barth, The *Faith of the Church*: *A Commentary on the Apostle's Creed* (London: Fontana Books, 1958), p. 112, quoted by Thompson, *Holy Spirit*, p. 99.
[56] Barth, *CD*, I/2, p. 532.

however, this verbal inspiration was not a creaturely quality of the text itself but rather the work of the Spirit in and through the words of Scripture. The function of the text as Holy Scripture is thus out of our hands and in the hands of God's Holy Spirit. "By the decision of God this text is now taken and used. And in the mystery of God it takes place here and now this text acquires this determination."[57] The problem according to Barth is that historically the verbal inspiration of the text changed "from a statement about the free grace of God into a statement about the nature of the Bible as exposed to human inquiry and brought under human control."[58] He states further that the text "was no longer a free and spiritual force, but an instrument of human power."[59]

Rather than discerning Barth's understanding of verbal inspiration in the context of his overall stress on the objective ground of revelation in the divine action rather than as a human possession under our control and manipulation, many evangelicals jumped to the conclusion that Barth based the revelation of Scripture on our experience of it, and then identified this as Barth's intention. In doing this, they ignored his many statements that revelation through Scripture is objectively God's action, regardless of what our experiences of this may or may not be. Barth's words are clear:

> The statement that the Bible is God's Word is a confession of faith, a statement of the faith that hears God speak through the biblical word of man. To be sure, it is a statement which, when venturing it in faith, we accept as true even apart from our faith and beyond all our faith and even in the face of our lack of faith. We do not accept it as a description of our experience of the Bible. We accept it as a description of God's action in the Bible, whatever may be the experiences we have or do not have in this connection.[60]

Some evangelicals further ignored Barth's clear insistence in several places that revelation or inspiration is not detached from the concrete words of Scripture but involves these words and their meanings. Barth wrote of the text, "If God speaks to man, he really speaks the language of this concrete word of man. That is the right and

---

[57] Barth, *CD*, I/2, p. 532.
[58] Barth, *CD*, I/2, p. 522.
[59] Barth, *CD*, I/2, p. 525.
[60] Barth, *CD*, I/1, p. 110; see also I/1, p. 117.

necessary truth in the concept of verbal inspiration."[61] Barth wrote in another context,

> Thus God does reveal himself in statements, through the medium of speech, and indeed of human speech. His word is always this or that word spoken by the prophets and apostles and proclaimed in the church. The personal character of God's Word is not, then, to be played off against its verbal or spiritual character.[62]

Barth's concern is not the detachment of the biblical text from revelation but rather a free text as inspired by the Spirit so that it does not come under our control as something we can master and control:

> The personal character of God's Word means, not its deverbalizing, but the posing of an absolute barrier against reducing its wording to a human system . . . This would mean his allowing us to gain control over his Word, to fit it into our own designs, and thus to shut up ourselves against him to our own ruin.[63]

Barth is clear that the Bible in its concrete verbal meaning is used by the Spirit to claim us in obedience to God: "If the biblical text in its literalness as a text does not force itself upon us, or if we have the freedom word by word to shake ourselves loose from it, what meaning is there in our protestation that the Bible is the inspired Word of God?"[64]

We cannot proceed any further in Barth's doctrine of Scripture, since that would take us too far afield of our focus on pneumatology. We will only note that many evangelicals are concerned about Barth's characterization of Scripture as fallible but functionally made to participate in divine revelation as a miracle of grace.[65] But any reaction to this point must consider the fact that Barth does not divorce the verbal expression of Scripture and the event of revelation. Furthermore, nowhere in the *Church Dogmatics* does Barth take issue with the voice of Scripture on any theme of significance to Christian doctrine. As Geoffrey Bromiley wrote, ". . .

---

61 Barth, *CD*, I/2, p. 532.
62 Barth, *CD*, I/1, p. 137.
63 Barth, *CD*, I/1, p. 139.
64 Barth, *CD*, I/2, p. 533.
65 Barth, *CD*, II/1, p. 532.

in what he has to say about the authority and freedom of Scripture as God's Word, Barth leaves little room for complaint."[66]

Barth grants us as evangelicals a way of dealing with the complexity of Scripture as a human word in witness by the Spirit to its chief subject matter, namely, the gospel of Jesus Christ. Difficult passages are not ignored but rather placed in creative tension with this witness. It is also possible to handle the text in this way, utilizing gifts of spiritual discernment in the church, a humble discernment that does not simply identify our wisdom with the Spirit's. Such a hermeneutic is not possible if one naively assumes that the entire Bible was written by the finger of God and that the literal meaning of the text is identifiable with revelation without qualification. Note must also be taken that Barth's intention in his verbal inspiration doctrine is certainly not to base the function of Scripture in revelation on human experience but rather on the objectivity of the Spirit's witness to Christ. This witness seeks to bring the good news of Jesus to the world. It is to the role of the Spirit in salvation that we turn as our last concern.

6. The Spirit and the new birth

We are saved through Christ by the Spirit, which means for Barth, as a miracle of God's grace. Barth stressed the miracle involved in the event of being "born again," a key concern for many evangelicals. Consequently, for Barth, when one discusses becoming a Christian, one is not talking fundamentally about the enhancement of a person's natural moral or religious impulses (though, for Barth, conversion will certainly involve such impulses). Neither is conversion something we do with the help of supernatural grace. Rather, becoming a Christian is fundamentally something that God does, because such a conversion represents a change from darkness to light.[67] In Barth's words, the source of our faithfulness to God "is completely missed if one does not ultimately stand before this fact with helpless astonishment."[68]

---

[66] Geoffrey Bromiley, *Introduction to the Theology of Karl Barth* (Edinburgh, UK: T&T Clark, 1979), pp. 43–4, quoted in Thompson, *Spirit*, p. 62.

[67] Barth, *CD*, IV/4, pp. 4–5.

[68] Barth, *CD*, IV/4, p. 3.

Barth highlights various metaphors used in the Bible for the utterly new life initiated miraculously at one's initiation in Christ by faith, such as Spirit baptism, putting off the old person and putting on the new, turning a heart of stone into a heart of flesh, receiving a new spirit within, awakening from sleep or death, being born again, etc.[69] This accent on human conversion or the "born again experience" is familiar to evangelicals, especially those from more pietistic streams. Yet, there is a difference. As Barth's early pietistic critics noted, Barth was hesitant to speak of the new birth primarily in terms of a subjective experience. Barth spoke of it fundamentally in terms of a divinely initiated liberating event that comes to the believing community as a promise to be embraced in obedient faith. Barth is primarily concerned in the new birth with the divine action involved than with the dynamics of human change within, for fear of collapsing pneumatology into religious consciousness. Though in need of some qualification, Jürgen Moltmann's contrast between a theology of revelation (Barth) and a theology of experience (Schleiermacher) contains a definite element of truth.[70]

The Pietists were thus dismayed that Barth did not speak strongly enough in terms of life-changing experiences of God. As Eberhard Busch noted, "We could summarize what the Pietists found crucially lacking in Barth; what they had found he basically denied, with the concept of *experience*."[71] It is important to stress, however, that, though Barth was wary of talking about experiences of God, he did not hesitate to speak of the Holy Spirit as bringing about a real change in the lives of people who come to faith in Christ. He remarks, "Whoever is given the Spirit by God becomes, as the man he is, another man—a man of God, the kind of man whom God uses, and who as he is used by God begins to live a new life."[72] Barth's understanding of experience seems more praxis-oriented than psychological or metaphysical. If one sees experience as an encounter of various dimensions that "happens" as well as welling up from within a renewed life (as Moltmann does),[73] it is

---

[69] Barth, *CD*, IV/4, pp. 6–9.

[70] Jürgen Moltmann, *The Spirit of Life: A Universal Affirmation* (Minneapolis: Fortress Press, 1992), pp. 5–8.

[71] Eberhard Busch, *Karl Barth and the Pietists: The Young Karl Barth's Critique of Pietism and Its Response* (Downers Grove, IL: InterVarsity Press, 2004), p. 181.

[72] *CD*, III/2, p. 357.

[73] Moltmann, *Spirit*, pp. 18–28.

possible to talk about different emphases within the dimensions of experience between Barth and his Pietist critics. with Barth puts emphasis on the divine transcendence of the encounter, and the Pietists emphasize the dynamics of the human response to God within the life of faith.

Though Barth recognizes genuine change in people committed to Christ, his concern was to see conversion as God's act rather than human self-improvement. Barth stressed the source of human conversion in the free act of God for humanity which then accounts for the free human response to God. In Barth's understanding, the Catholic view of Christian initiation advocates a synergism of infused grace and human cooperation, while the neo-Protestant view sees grace as the fulfillment of natural religious and moral impulses. Barth implies that both views understand the foundation on which conversion rests as both the divine and the human possibility of freedom, which to Barth is unacceptable. In dealing with this issue, Barth wished to accent the divine possibility as the sole foundation of an event of human faithfulness that is incomprehensible from a human standpoint. Our freedom comes from God's freedom.[74]

Yet, in aiming also at the dangers of the Reformation heritage, Barth wished to deny that human righteousness is a "fiction" which God assumes but which does not effect real creaturely change.[75] Barth stated his position on Christian initiation with regard to these various views as follows:

> If it is possible for a man to be faithful to God instead of unfaithful, there must be a change which comes over this man himself. Nor may this change be simply an awakening of his natural powers, nor his endowment with supernatural powers, nor his placing by God under another light and judgment in which he may stand before God. It must be an inner change in virtue of which he himself becomes a different man, so that as this different man he freely, of himself, and by his own resolve, thinks and acts and conducts himself otherwise than he did before.[76]

Though Barth accepted real change, he still considered Christians as fallen. Barth maintained that every regenerate community must also see itself as unregenerate, so that "the church is always the world

---

[74] Barth, *CD*, IV/4, pp. 4–6.
[75] Barth, *CD*, IV/4, pp. 4–6.
[76] Barth, *CD*, IV/4, p. 18.

as well."[77] Barth's accent on the liberation of faith in the life of the Spirit toward the trust and obedience of the believing community protected the church from any delusions of perfectionism. It also shifted the focus from what we possess and can do to God's possession of us and what God can do and has done to lay claim to us in Christ.

Barth's pietistic critics also disliked his lack of willingness to embrace a strong concept of the indwelling of the Spirit as possessed by believers. *Finitum capax infiniti*, the finite has the capacity to hold the infinite, was the battle cry of Pietists in response to Barth.[78] Barth actually liked to put the matter of possessing the Spirit paradoxically: "To have the Holy Spirit is to let God rather than our having God be our confidence."[79] Barth was wary of speaking of possessing God's Spirit for fear that this would play into the modernist effort to base theological judgments on human religious imagination or to place our confidence in our spiritual accomplishments rather than on God:

> To receive the Holy Spirit means an exposure of our spiritual helplessness, a recognition that we do not possess the Holy Spirit. For that reason the subjective reality of revelation has the distinctive character of a miracle, i.e. it is a reality to be grounded only in itself.[80]

When Barth states that the Holy Spirit "is the subjective side of the event of revelation" in history through Christ,[81] he refers to a work within the believing community that is grounded solely in God. The subjective side of the Spirit's work is never "possessed" by us in some unqualified sense, although it does transform us. Spirit baptism as the miracle of regeneration for Barth means that it is grounded only in the God who possesses us and lays claim to us. It is received in obedient faith as a gift of the Spirit in response to the word of promise concerning God's claim on us. The liberation to respond implies a change, but one continuously dependent only on God's Spirit. New human capacities from the Spirit arise in the believing community but these are neither the focus of our attention, nor the basis of our confidence.

---

77 Barth, *CD*, II/1, p. 144.
78 Busch, *Barth*, p. 183.
79 Barth, *CD*, I/1, p. 462.
80 Barth, *CD*, II/1, p. 244.
81 Barth, *CD*, I/1, p. 49.

Interestingly, Barth categorizes both justification and sanctification as works of the Spirit.[82] Such is suggested by Paul in 1 Corinthians 6:11. Barth views justification as the basis of salvation, and sanctification as its goal.[83] Seen from this basis, one could say that justification is stressed. Seen from this goal, sanctification is the accent. Barth wishes to see the Christian life as vocation and witness as well. His goal is ecumenical, to see the Christian life as stressing justification, sanctification, and vocation.

One is initiation in Christ by the Spirit for Barth. Though Barth referred to baptism early on as the "means of grace" that "mediates the new creation,"[84] he would later align himself more with his enduring emphasis on the freedom and sovereignty of the Holy Spirit and, under the influence of his son, Marcus', book on baptism, distinguish more sharply between water and Spirit baptism. Water baptism became the obedient response of the church to God's claim on the church by grace in Spirit baptism.[85] Since Barth believed that God laid claim to all of humanity in Christ, he referred favorably to Oscar Cullmann's idea of a "general baptism" of Jesus, which was on behalf of all of humanity.[86] Most evangelicals would feel uneasy at best with the implicit universalism of this teaching.

Barth's pneumatology does have vast implications for all of creation. Barth not only recognized soteriological functions of the Spirit, he also assumed in the light of the soteriological Spirit that all of humanity and creation itself lives from the same Spirit of God: "There could be no creature, nor any creation, if God were not also the Holy Spirit and active as such."[87] The Spirit is the "fundamental condition" of creaturely existence.[88] It can be said of humanity in general that the Holy Spirit is given to all and that all have the Spirit as having "a spiritual or intellectual nature."[89] This nature is not confused with the divine Spirit, but lives from the Spirit. In fact, this Spirit is also alien to the creature[90] but this

---

[82] Barth, *CD*, I/1, p. 189, p. 464; II/1, p. 245; III/1, p. 58.
[83] Barth, *CD*, IV/1, pp. 525–6.
[84] Barth, *Epistle to the Romans* (Oxford, UK: Oxford University Press, 6th Edition, 1968), p. 192, quoted in Thompson, *Holy Spirit*, p. 114.
[85] Barth, *CD*, IV/4, p. 32.
[86] Barth, *CD*, IV/4, p. 31.
[87] Barth, *CD*, III/1, p. 58.
[88] Barth, *CD*, III/1, p. 58.
[89] Barth, *CD*, III/2, p. 334.
[90] Barth, *CD*, III/2, p. 364.

alienation is not without relation, for God the Creator has annulled the alienation in Christ.[91]

Humanity thus lives from the Spirit as a living soul or as a "besouled body."[92] This creaturely sustenance of life is referred to by Barth as the Spirit's "special operation."[93] This is so, because this work of the Spirit in creation is "partial" and "transitory." Creatures still perish. It is the Spirit's redemptive work fulfilled in Christ that is lasting and abundant. This is the life enjoyed by those who know and love Jesus. Though Barth assumes a divine claim on all of humanity, it is not true that the Spirit for Barth merely brings to believers a "knowledge" of their salvation in Christ. Those who claim the promises of the gospel by faith enjoy an abundance of life in the Spirit not generally enjoyed in creation in general.

The fact that humanity is laid claim to by God despite their rejection would seem to evangelicals from a Wesleyan background that pneumatology as the sovereign and free work of God leaves little room for human will. Though the divine freedom and power is the all-encompassing cause of our faithfulness to God by the Spirit, the divine possibility is not the only cause. For Barth, human causality plays a role within the omnicausality of God in human faithfulness to God as well. As Barth stated concerning the faithfulness of a person to God,

> It comes upon him wholly from without, from God. Nevertheless, it is his liberation. The point is here, as in everywhere, the omnicausality of God must not be construed as His sole causality.[94]

Barth even states that the natural moral and religious self-determination of a person "is not destroyed by his conflict with God, his fellow-man, and himself" and that God sets such a person "on the path to the fulfillment of this self-determination."[95] This astounding quote contradicts the popular view that for Barth the fall abolishes any positive significance to human morality and religiosity. The fact is that humanity is not reduced in Barth's view to insignificance, destined to serve as passive puppets in the hands of a God whose omnipotence abolishes any possibility for human

---

[91] Barth, *CD*, III/2, p. 368.
[92] Barth, *CD*, III/2, p. 363.
[93] Barth, *CD*, III/2, p. 363.
[94] Barth, *CD*, IV/4, p. 22.
[95] Barth, *CD*, IV/4, p. 4.

action in our turn to God. For Barth, therefore, Spirit baptism or regeneration does not involve "the paralyzing dismissal or absence of the human spirit, mind, knowledge, and will."[96] Indeed, the Spirit consistently bears witness to *our spirits* in the human discernment and acceptance of the divine will.[97] God respects the dignity of human volition and action. Barth is quite explicit on this point, for in Spirit baptism the person "is taken seriously as the creature which is different from God, which is for all its dependence *autonomous* before him . . . [and] is empowered for his own act" (emphasis mine).[98]

Nevertheless, the human contribution to faithfulness to God, though taken seriously, is subordinated to the all-encompassing determination of the divine possibility in regeneration. Barth stated, for example, that in the shift from unfaithfulness to faithfulness through the Spirit everything one was before or apart from this change, "though not expunged, is totally relativized, bracketed, and overshadowed."[99] But, problematically, Barth so relativizes and overshadows the human element beneath the divine action that he boldly and remarkably deems the new life received in Spirit baptism to be invulnerable to the effects of human disobedience. Such a new life initiated at Spirit baptism in a person "cannot be negated or even diminished by the brokenness of his disobedience."[100] Consequently, Spirit baptism is permanent and "once and for all" as an event of renewal. evangelicals from a Wesleyan background will question whether or not Barth really gives human will adequate place in how he construes the effects of the life of the Spirit on people's lives.

I agree with Hunsinger that the "familiar alternatives of either divine 'determinism' or human 'free will' are categorically rejected" in Barth's pneumatology.[101] We cannot venture here into the different ways that Barth seeks to transcend these alternatives, except to say that there is for Barth no synergism or human cooperation with the grace of God in a way that effects salvation.

---

96 Barth, *CD*, IV/4, p. 29.
97 Barth, *CD*, IV/4, p. 28.
98 Barth, *CD*, IV/4, p. 35.
99 Barth, *CD*, IV/4, p. 3.
100 Barth, *CD*, IV/4, p. 35.
101 Hunsinger, "Mediator," p. 183.

7. Evangelical appraisal

The complexity of Barth's pneumatology offers evangelicals of different stripes substantial food for fruitful dialogue. Those who stress the objective ground of revelation in Christ will have a basis for talking to those who emphasize the work of the Spirit in life. Those who accent the sovereignty and freedom of the Spirit will need to talk to those who emphasize life-changing experiences of the Spirit. Those who center on justification can talk to those who take more of a sanctification model of salvation. Those who accent the claim of the text of Scripture on the church will be brought into conversation with those who highlight the discernment of the Spirit in the context of the biblical witness. Those who focus on the Spirit at work in the natural realm will be made to consider those who insist on the miraculous nature of the Spirit's work. Those who are comfortable with ministry gifts of teaching and administration will need to listen to those who tend to stress extraordinary gifts of the Spirit.

This is not to say that evangelicals of all sides will not find reason to question or even disagree with some of Barth's pneumatological accents. I, as a Pentecostal, find that he could have placed more stress on the experiential and contextual elements of the life of the Spirit, as well as on the human capacity ultimately and finally to reject God's claim on us. But I have found Barth's pneumatology so rich and complex that even where I take issue with him I am made to wonder whether or not I have understood him correctly or taken into consideration adequately the full significance of his challenge.

When asked how the word of God comes to us, Barth would answer that it is "on our lips and in our hearts" by the Spirit of the Lord.[102] There is no better evangelical answer than that. But in discussing its meaning, we should never so stress the "on our lips and in our hearts" that we forget the Lordship of the Spirit. But neither should we so stress the Spirit's Lordship over us that we fail to discern the Spirit permeating our graced speech and actions. Moltmann sought in critical response to both Barth and his liberal opponents an "immanent transcendence" of the Spirit's actions among us as the Spirit of life, immanent to life experience and yet having its eschatological transcendence in God.[103] Barth helps us as

---

[102] Barth, *CD*, I/1, p. 186.
[103] Moltmann, *Spirit*, p. 18.

evangelicals, however, to bear in mind that the Spirit of life is also the free and sovereign Lord of life, in our reading of Scripture, in our worship, in our personal spirituality, and in praxis. This is, in my view, Barth's enduring legacy for us.

8

Karl Barth's doctrine of Justification from an Evangelical Perspective

Alister E. McGrath

There is, I believe, little doubt that Karl Barth is an immensely significant theologian, who both deserves to be studied by evangelicals, and who amply repays the effort required to do so.[1] My own debt to Barth is immense. There are many whose love for systematic theology, and sense of its intellectual resilience and spiritual vitality, is due to an engagement with Barth. I am one of them.[2] I began the serious study of theology at Oxford University back in 1976, coming from an academically rigorous and empirically grounded scientific

---

[1] Early evangelical attitudes to Barth were shaped by a series of unfortunate misrepresentations, many of which are happily now being abandoned. Thomas F. Torrance's scathing review of Cornelius van Til's inept analysis of the theology of Barth and Brunner may be singled out for particular mention at this point, in that it identified this trend, even if it proved powerless to reverse it at this time: see T. F. Torrance, 'The New Modernism', *Evangelical Quarterly* 19 (1947), pp. 144–9. It may, of course, be noted that evangelicals are increasingly appreciating the merits of Torrance himself, both as an interpreter of Barth and a significant constructive biblical theologian in his own right: see, for example, Elmer M. Colyer, *How to Read T. F. Torrance: Understanding his Trinitarian & Scientific Theology* (Downers Grove, IL: InterVarsity Press, 2001).

[2] Readers wanting to know something about my theological development might like to dip into Alister E. McGrath, *A Scientific Theology*. 3 vols. (Grand Rapids, MI: Eerdmans, 2001–3). For a summary, see Alister E. McGrath, *The Science of God: An Introduction to Scientific Theology* (Grand Rapids, MI: Eerdmans, 2004).

discipline. At this stage, I was very much an amateur in matters of theology. My interest in theology might well have proven to be stillborn had I begun my theological studies by reading some of the works which were typical of English-language theology of this time. I continue to wonder what might have happened to me had I been introduced to theology by reading such works as Maurice Wiles's *What is Theology?*—a work which generally conveys the impression (despite, I am sure, the best intentions of its most worthy author) that theology is a dull and derivative discipline, dependent upon the social sciences and philosophy for its few insights, which has nothing distinctive, original, persuasive or—dare I say it?—*interesting* to say.[3]

However, redemption was at hand. One of those who guided my early theological development was Timothy Gorringe (now Professor of Theology at Exeter University).[4] Gorringe was working on aspects of the theology of Karl Barth, and suggested that I could do far worse than immerse myself in the *Church Dogmatics*. By the end of the first half-volume—which had just appeared in a new English translation, replacing the unsatisfactory translation originally published in 1936 I knew that I was going to be excited by the study of theology. Barth's vision of theology might well have been controversial and caused eyebrows to be raised within the English theological establishment of the time. But the vision was exciting, challenging and inspirational. Above all, I found myself impressed by the intellectual coherence of Barth's vision of "theological science," and thrilled by the vision Barth offered of a sustained theological engagement with the past:

> We cannot be in the church without taking responsibility for the theology of the past as much as for the theology of the present. Augustine, Thomas Aquinas, Luther, Schleiermacher and all the rest are not dead but living. They still speak and demand a hearing as living voices, as surely as we know that they and we belong together in the church.[5]

[3] Maurice F. Wiles, *What Is Theology?* (Oxford, UK: Oxford University Press, 1976).

[4] For Gorringe's ongoing interest in Barth, see Timothy Gorringe, *Karl Barth: Against Hegemony* (Oxford, UK: Oxford University Press, 1999).

[5] Karl Barth, *Die protestantische Theologie im 19. Jahrhundert: Ihre Vorgeschichte und ihre Geschichte* (2nd ed. Zurich: Evangelischer Verlag, 1952), p. 3.

With this in mind, I set out to ensure that I immersed myself in historical theology, as well as systematic theology, realizing that the latter could not be undertaken without the former, and that the former was incomplete without the latter. While I have misgivings about many aspects of Barth's theology, it is impossible to understate the positive impact which Barth had upon my estimate of, and enthusiasm for, theology as a serious intellectual discipline.

Barth is a theological master, who cannot be ignored or evaded by any who seek to do theology with integrity and ability. Barth's capacity to raise questions and offer answers makes him both an invaluable resource and an indefatigable sparring partner along the road as we undertake the intellectual pilgrimage that we call "theology." This does not mean that we agree with Barth. It simply means recognizing that Barth is one of those rare theologians who manages to make us *think*, sometimes through an exceptionally lucid analysis of a difficult idea, and sometimes by forcing us to clarify and justify why we disagree with him. Barth is a theologian who makes me want to preach after reading him, even if that sermon might take a direction that he might not feel entirely comfortable with.

My task in this paper is to explore Barth's thinking on the doctrine of justification. Barth's ideas in this area, as with his views on predestination, are somewhat unsettling for evangelicals, not least on account of the implicit assumption that is widespread within evangelicalism to the effect that Luther basically got things right. Barth's approach to justification challenges this view, and invites the exploration of alternatives. To appreciate Barth's importance, we must consider the historical context within which his approach is set.[6]

The doctrine of justification played a decisive role in the emergence of Protestantism during the sixteenth century.[7] Justification is one of several concepts that have been used within Scripture and the Christian tradition to articulate the reconciliation effected by God with the world through Christ. During the sixteenth century, this concept came to assume a particularly significant role in the

---

6 For a full account of the development of the doctrine of justification, see Alister E. McGrath, *Iustitia Dei: A History of the Christian Doctrine of Justification* (3rd ed. Cambridge, UK: Cambridge University Press, 2005).

7 For historical and theological reflection, see Alister E. McGrath, "The Article by which the Church stands or falls." *Evangelical Quarterly* 58 (1986), pp. 207–28.

discussion of the salvation of humanity, due largely to the enormous personal influence of Martin Luther over the evangelical movements at Wittenberg and elsewhere.

The Protestant Reformation of the sixteenth century brought about many significant changes within the life and thought of the Western churches. One of those was the reconceptualization and reformulation of the traditional Christian vocabulary of salvation using the Pauline image of justification.[8] Up to this point, the Western theological tradition had chosen to develop its thinking about how humanity is reconciled to God in terms of "salvation by grace" (Eph. 2:8). One of the defining characteristics of the Protestant Reformation is a decisive shift, both in the conceptualities and vocabulary, of the Christian theological tradition. For a relatively short yet theologically significant period, the reconciliation of humanity would be discussed within the entire Western theological tradition primarily in terms of "justification by faith" (Rom. 5:1).

The leading principle of the Reformation is generally considered to be its doctrine of justification.[9] While there is unquestionably much truth in this statement, it requires careful qualification to do justice to the historical evidence. It is certainly true that the *articulus iustificationis* is the leading feature of the theology of Martin Luther.[10] It was never, however, accepted within the more radical wing of the Reformation, which stressed the importance of obedience and discipleship, adopting doctrines of grace which stressed human responsibility and accountability towards God, rather than God's transformation of the individual.[11]

Nevertheless, the considerable personal influence of Luther over the majority of the evangelical factions within Germany and

---

[8] Vittorio Subilia, *La giustificazione per fede* (Brescia: Paideia Editrice, 1976), pp. 117–27.

[9] For some reflections on why it was so important, see Alister E. McGrath, "Justification and the Reformation: The Significance of the Doctrine of Justification by Faith to Sixteenth Century Urban Communities," *Archiv für Reformationsgeschichte* 90 (1990), pp. 5–19.

[10] See Ernst Wolf, 'Die Rechtfertigungslehre als Mitte und Grenze reformatorscher Theologie', *Evangelische Theologie* 9 (1949–50), pp. 298–308; Reinhard Schwarz, 'Luthers Rechtfertigungslehre als Eckstein der christlichen Theologie und Kirche,' *Zeitschrift für Theologie und Kirche* 10 (1998), pp. 14–46.

[11] See the important study of Alvin J. Beachy, *The Concept of Grace in the Radical Reformation* (Nieuwkoop: De Graaf, 1977).

elsewhere inevitably led to the strength of his optimism that the doctrine of justification would be adopted elsewhere,[12] and would become a determinative and distinctive mark of the mainline Reformation. Thus by the beginning of the seventeenth century the *articulus iustificationis* appears to have been generally regarded as the *articulus stantis et cadentis ecclesiae*, the "article by which the church stands or falls."[13]

As is well known, Karl Barth aligned himself with the Reformation movement in many ways, seeing his own theological undertaking as representing the continuation of this formative period in the shaping of Christian thought. Yet Barth has always made it clear that he was never to be seen as merely repeating what others had said before him. Barth's relationship with both Luther and Calvin is best described as that of "critical appropriation" rather than "uncritical assimilation."[14] Barth engages with a respectful yet critical dialogue with the past. So how does he engage with what is perhaps one of the most significant and influential aspects of the Reformation heritage? Barth's views might prove useful to contemporary evangelicalism as it continues this all-important interaction with Scripture and its own heritage. Yet evangelicals might also have points of criticism to direct against Barth, which ought to be respected and heeded.

In what follows, we shall outline the development of Barth's distinctive ideas on justification, and note their significance for evangelicalism. We begin by noting the emphasis Barth places upon the "otherness" of God in the 1910s, which is reflected in his "theology of crisis," and especially his insistence upon the chasm between God and humanity which prevents the latter from discovering or knowing God on their own terms and on their own

---

[12] There is, of course, a genuine difficulty in establishing the precise causal relationship between the origins of Luther's own theology and that of the Reformation as a whole: see Heiko A. Oberman, "Headwaters of the Reformation: *Initia Lutheri–Initia Reformationis*," in H. A. Oberman ed. *Luther and the Dawn of the Modern Era* (Leiden: Brill, 1974), pp. 40–88; Alister E. McGrath, *Luther's Theology of the Cross* (Oxford, UK: Blackwell, 1985), pp. 24 n. 45, 52–3, 142.

[13] See especially the important study of Schwarz, "Luthers Rechtfertigungslehre."

[14] On Barth's relationship to Luther, see Gerhard Ebeling, "Karl Barths Ringen mit Luther," in *Lutherstudien III* (Tübingen: Mohr, 1985), pp. 428–573. On Calvin, see Sung Wook Chung, *Admiration and Challenge: Karl Barth's Theological Relationship with John Calvin* (New York: Peter Lang, 2002).

grounds. This growing sense of the "otherness" of God from culture is reflected in many developments of the period, particularly Karl Holl's famous lecture of 31 October 1917, delivered before the University of Berlin, which inaugurated the Luther renaissance by demonstrating how radically Luther's concept of God differed from the somewhat emasculated deity of liberal Protestantism.[15] Such radical developments in the world of religious ideas could not fail to have an impact upon the doctrine of justification.

Although Barth's articulation of the "otherness" of God is primarily linked with his critique of religion and emphasis upon the total sovereignty of God in revelation, we find it being developed in an important way through the concept of the "righteousness of God." In effect, Barth redirects this notion so that in addition to its traditional Lutheran role of undermining the soteriological autonomy of humanity, it serves a new function of emphasizing the revelational sovereignty of God, and the corresponding human incapacity to achieve knowledge of God, or a relationship to God, on its own terms and through its own constructs. To illustrate this, we may turn to consider Barth's lecture of 16 January 1916 in the Aarau Stadtkirche, on the theme of "the righteousness of God."[16]

Even today, the rhetorical power of this lecture may still be felt, and the passage of time has done nothing to diminish the force of Barth's sustained critique of humanity's self-assertion in the face of God, which he links with the question of the true meaning of the "righteousness of God." For Barth, the "deepest, inmost and most certain fact of life, is that 'God is righteous'."[17] This fact is brought home to humans by their consciences, which affirm the existence of a righteous God in the midst of human unrighteousness, to be seen in the forces of capitalism as much as in the war which was raging over the face of Europe at that moment.[18] Deep within the inmost being of humans lies the desire for the righteousness of God—and yet paradoxically, just when this divine righteousness appears to be on the verge of altering their nature and conduct, humans assert their own self-righteousness. They are unable to contemplate the

[15] Karl Holl, "Was verstand Luther unter Religion?" in *Gesammelte Aufsätze zur Kirchengeschichte*, 3 vols. (Tübingen: Mohr, 1928), vol. 1, pp. 1–110.

[16] Karl Barth, "Die Gerechtigkeit Gottes," in *Das Wort Gottes und die Theologie* (Munich: Kaiser, 1925), pp. 5–17.

[17] Barth, "Gerechtigkeit," p. 5.

[18] Barth, "Gerechtigkeit," p. 7.

concept of a "righteousness" that lies beyond their own control, and are thus driven to establish a basis for their own self-justification which is independent of God.

Barth shrewdly observes that humans welcome the intervention of divine righteousness if it puts an end to wars or general strikes—but feel threatened by it when they realize that behind the *results* of human unrighteousness lies the unfathomable reality of *human righteousness* itself. The abolition of the consequences of human unrighteousness necessarily entails the abolition of human unrighteousness itself, and hence an entirely new existence. Unable to accept this, people deform the "righteousness of God" into various forms of human righteousness, of which Barth singles out three types for particular criticism.[19]

1. **Moral righteousness.** Barth rejects those spheres of human existence within which *Kulturprotestantismus* had located human morality (such as the fami1y, or the state), on the grounds that, by restricting moral action to these spheres, humans are simply ignoring the obvious fact that their action is immoral in others. For Barth, the existence of the capitalist system and the war demonstrated the invalidity of this thesis, as *both* were perpetrated in the name of morality.

2. **Legal righteousness** *(die Gerechtigkeit des Staates und der Juristen)*. Barth emphasizes (prophetically, as the Third Reich was to demonstrate)[20] that human law is essentially orientated towards the ends specified by the state itself. At best, law could be regarded as an attempt to restrict the effect of human unrighteousness; at worst, it resulted in the establishment and perpetuation of human unrighteousness by the agencies of the state itself. Once more, Barth cites the war as exemplifying the defection of human ideas of "righteousness" from those which conscience dictated should be recognized as divine.

---

[19] Barth, "Gerechtigkeit," pp. 10–12.

[20] For some useful reflections upon the impact of the *Rechtswillkürlichkeit* of the Third Reich upon Protestant understandings of the theological significance of law, see Ernst Wolf, "Zum protestantischen Rechtsdenken," in *Peregrinatio* II: *Studien zur reformatorischen Theologie, zum Kirchenrecht und zur Sozialethik* (Munich: Kaiser, 1965), pp. 191–206.

3. **Religious righteousness**. Foreshadowing his mature critique of religion,[21] Barth argues that human religion, and indeed morality, is a tower of Babel erected by humans in the face of, and in defiance of, what their conscience tells them to be right.

In these three ways, Barth argues that humans are failing to take the "righteousness of God" seriously, lest it overwhelm and transform them. They prefer to deal with shadows, and avoid the reality.[22]

For Barth, the First World War both questions and demonstrates the righteousness of God. It *questions* that righteousness, in that people are unable to understand how a "righteous" God could permit such an outrage; it *demonstrates* that same righteousness, in that it shows up human caricatures of divine righteousness for what they really are. Humans have made their own concepts of righteousness into a god, so that God is simply the "great personal or impersonal, mystical, philosophical or naive Profundity and patron saint of our human righteousness, morality, state, civilization, or religion."[23] For Barth, the war has destroyed this image of God for ever, exposing it as an idol. By asserting its own concept of righteousness in the face of God, humanity constructed a "righteous" god who was the first and least mourned casualty of the war.[24] The "death" of this god has forced people to recognize that the "righteousness of God" is qualitatively different from, and stands over and against, human concepts of righteousness.

This lecture is of considerable significance in a number of respects. Of particular importance is the dialectic between human and divine righteousness, which marks an unequivocal break with the "liberal" understanding of the nature of history, progress and civilization. "God's will is not a superior projection of our own will: it stands in opposition to our will as one that is totally distinct *(als ein gänzlich anderer)*."[25] It is this infinite qualitative distinction between human and divine righteousness which forms the basis of Barth's repeated assertion that God is, and must be recognized as, God.

The radical emphasis upon the "otherness" of God so evident in Barth's programmatic critique of concepts of the "righteousness

---

21 See J. A. Veitch, "Revelation and Religion in the Thought of Karl Barth," *Scottish Journal of Theology* 24 (1971), pp. 1–22.

22 Barth, "Gerechtigkeit," pp. 12–13.

23 Barth, "Gerechtigkeit," p. 13.

24 Barth, "Gerechtigkeit," p. 14.

25 Barth, "Gerechtigkeit," p. 15.

of God," clearly parallels the theological concerns of the young Luther.[26] It might therefore be thought that Barth's early dialectical theology, or mature "theology of the word of God," might represent a recovery of the Reformer's insights into the significance of the *articulus iustificationis*. In fact, this seems not to be the case. Barth's exploration of the leading themes of Luther's doctrine of justification does not lead him to reaffirm the centrality of the article of justification as the "article by which the church stands or falls." Rather, its themes are incorporated and reinterpreted within the parameters of a dialectical theology, with its particular concerns relating to the actuality of divine revelation.

As has often been pointed out, Barth's mature theology may be regarded as extended reflection upon the fact that God has spoken to humankind—*Deus dixit*—abrogating the epistemological chasm separating them in doing so. The actuality of divine revelation is the fundamental controlling assumption of any authentically Christian theology. God has spoken, in the fullness of time, and it is this event—or these events—which stand at the heart of Barth's theological concerns. It is the task of any authentic and responsible *Christian* theology to attempt to unfold the nature and identity of the God who had spoken to sinners in the human-ward movement envisaged in the *Deus dixit*. The structures and the inner nexus of relationships presupposed by the fact—not the *idea*—of the *Deus dixit* determine what Christian theology has to say concerning the God who thus speaks.

Barth's theological system can be regarded, in essence, as the unfolding of the inner structures and relationships which characterize the *fact* that God has spoken. The theological enterprise could thus be characterized as an exercise in *Nach-Denken*, following out the order of revelation in the human-ward movement of God in history. God has spoken to humans across the epistemological chasm which separates them, and by so speaking to them, discloses both the reality of that separation and also the possibility of its abrogation. Barth confronts us with the paradox that the inability of humans to hear the word of God is disclosed to them by that very Word. It is the reality of this divine abrogation of this epistemological

---

26 See Paul Althaus, "Gottes Gottheit als Sinn der Rechtfertigungslehre Luthers" *Luther-Jahrbuch* 13 (1931), pp. 1–28. Note especially Althaus' comment (p. 17): "Whoever wishes to make himself right before God through his own works usurps the position of the Creator."

chasm between God and humanity, and hence of the axiom *homo peccator non capax verbi Dei*, which stands at the heart of Barth's theological system—not the traditional Reformational emphasis upon the *articulus iustificationis*.

Reflection on Barth's historical context helps us appreciate this theological emphasis. Most liberal Protestant theologians were not concerned with the question of "guilt" or of "righteousness *coram Deo*," in that they had no sense of human bondage or slavery to sin. Thus Albrecht Ritschl regarded Luther's *De Servo Arbitrio* (1525), which develops the notion of human bondage to sin in some depth, as "an unfortunate botch" *(unglückliches Machwerk)*—even though it was precisely this work which Rudolf Otto singled out as the "psychological key" to understanding Luther. Similarly, Karl Holl's celebrated 1917 lecture on Luther was primarily concerned with the correct *knowledge* of God, rather than the soteriological dimension of his thought. It is significant that the Luther renaissance initially served to emphasize the Reformer's emphasis upon the deity and "otherness" of God, rather than the importance of the *articulus iustificationis* within the context of his theology.[27] Dialectical theology was initially passionately concerned with the question of the right knowledge of God, inspired by a conviction of human ignorance of God and the impossibility of any theologically significant natural knowledge of God. There is no means by which the yawning chasm (which Barth designates a "crevasse") between God and humanity may be bridged from humanity's side—hence the news that God has bridged this chasm from his side must be taken with the utmost seriousness.

Early dialectical theology thus took up one aspect of Luther's theology (the "otherness" of God) and marginalized the other (human bondage to sin). Hence for the young Barth, as we have seen, the significance of the "righteousness of God" lay in the fact that it was diametrically opposed to human concepts of righteousness. The lack of interest in human bondage to sin, so characteristic of the liberal school and nineteenth-century theology in general, thus passed into the dialectical theology of the early twentieth century. The theological drama which constitutes the Christian faith is thus held to concern humans and their knowledge of God, rather than the salvation of sinful humans, caught up in the cosmic conflict between God and sin,

---

[27] Holl, "Luther?"

the world and the devil.[28] Such a conflict is an impossibility within the context of Barth's theology, in that Barth shares with Hegel the difficulty of accommodating sin within an essentially monistic system. Barth has simply no concept of a divine engagement with the forces of sin or evil (unless these are understood in the epistemically reduced sense of "ignorance" or "misunderstanding"): instead, we find only talk about God making himself *known* to humanity. Barth even reduces the cross—traditionally the *locus* of precisely such a conflict—into a monologue between God the Father and God the Son. The impartation of knowledge is no substitute for a direct confrontation with sin, death and evil.

Whereas for Luther, the gospel was primarily concerned with the promise of the forgiveness of sins to sinful humanity, for Barth it is primarily concerned with the possibility of the right knowledge of God. Barth has thus placed the *divine revelation to sinful humanity* at the point where Luther placed the *divine justification of sinful humanity.* Although there are clearly points of contact between Luther and Barth, it is equally clear that Barth cannot share Luther's high estimation for the *articulus iustificationis*. In what follows, we propose to explore why this might be the case.

In the course of his exposition of the doctrine of justification, Barth finds himself obliged to disagree with a highly significant assessment of Luther's doctrine of justification from a respected colleague.[29] Ernst Wolf's analysis of the significance of the *articulus iustificationis* for the Reformers in general, and Luther in particular, locates the significance of the *articulus iustificationis* in terms of its function, which he conveniently finds expressed in the celebrated dictum of Luther: "articulus iustificationis est magister et princeps, dominus, rector et iudex super omnia genera doctrinarum, qui

---

28 On this theme in Luther's theology, see Gustav Aulén, "Die drei Haupttypen des christlichen Versöhnungslehre," *Zeitschrift für systematische Theologie* 7 (1930), pp. 301–38; Marc Leinhard, *Luther Témoin de Jésus Christ (*Paris: Editions du Cerf, 1968).

29 *Kirchliche Dogmatik*, IV/1 §61, 1, p. 581 (henceforth *CD*). On Barth's doctrine of justification, see Eberhard Jüngel, *Das Evangelium von der Rechtfertigung des Gottlosen als Zentrum des christlichen Glaubens* (Tübingen: Mohr, 1999). The older study of Hans Küng should also be consulted: *Rechtfertigung: Die Lehre Karl Barths und eine katholische Besinnung* (Einsiedeln: Johannes-Verlag, 1957). For a critique of this work (which is highly selective in its exposition of the Tridentine doctrine of justification), see Alister E. McGrath, "Justification: Barth, Trent and Küng," *Scottish Journal of Theology* 34 (1981), pp. 517–29.

conservat et gubernat omnem doctrinam ecclesiasticam et erigit conscientiam nostram coram Deo."[30] Wolf summarizes Luther's understanding of the function of the *articulus iustificationis* in terms of its defining the "center and limits of Reformation theology."

Wolf illustrates this interpretation of the function of the *articulus iustificationis* with reference to Luther's anthropology and ecclesiology, with convincing results, and argues for two important theses relating to its function. First, the *articulus iustificationis* is established as the leading principle of Luther's theology, as is the priority of soteriological considerations within the same context. Second, the *subjectum theologiae* is defined as God's salvific activity towards sinful humans.[31] The modesty of Barth's soteriological interests is emphasized when compared with Luther's insistence upon their dominating role in positive theological speculation. Furthermore, the secondary and derivative role of revelation within the context of Luther's theology will be evident,[32] although Barth does not seem to appreciate this point.

Barth is thus clearly obliged to dispute Wolf's analysis,[33] which he does in an important discussion of the *temporary* significance of the *articulus iustificationis*. He acknowledges the peculiar importance which Luther and his age attached to the doctrine, and further concedes that Luther did not regard the *articulus iustificationis* as the *primus et principalis articulus* merely in the polemic against Rome, but against all forms of sectarianism. However, he notes that no evangelical theologian—with the possible exception of Martin

---

[30] "The article of justification is the master and prince, the lord, ruler and judge overall categories of doctrines, which preserves and governs all church doctrine, and directs our consciences towards God."

[31] Wolf, "Die Rechtfertigungslehre", p. 14. The reference to the *subjectum theologiae* derives from WA 40 II.328.17–21: "Theologiae proprium subiectum est homo peccati reus ac perditus et Deus iustificans ac salvator hominis peccatoris. Quicquid extra hoc subiectum in theologia queritur aut disputatur, est error et venenum." For a study of this disagreement with Wolf, see A. E. McGrath, "Karl Barth and the *articulus iustificationis*: The Significance of His Critique of Ernst Wolf within the Context of His Theological Method," *Theologische Zeitschrift* 39 (1983), pp. 349–61.

[32] Thus Luther's celebrated distinction between *Deus absconditus* and *Deus revelatus* arises within the context of his soteriology: see Hellmut Bandt, *Luthers Lehre vom verborgenen Gott: Eine Untersuchung zu dem offenbarungsgeschichtlichen Ansatz seiner Theologie* (Berlin: Evangelische Verlagsanstalt, 1958). Note the reference to Barth in the preface.

[33] Barth, *CD*, IV/1 §61, I, p. 581.

Kähler—ever dared to construct a dogmatics with the doctrine of justification at its center.

This observation leads Barth to his critique of such a procedure. Conceding that the *articulus iustificationis* has been regarded as being *the* word of the gospel on several occasions in the history of the church, he points out that these occasions represented instances where the gospel, understood as the free grace of God, was under threat—such as the Pelagian controversy. Barth then argues that it is necessary to free the theological enterprise from the contingencies of such controversies.[34] Barth then asserts that the *articulus iustificationis* is not central to the Christian proclamation: "In the church of Jesus Christ, his doctrine has not always been *the* word of the gospel, and it would be an altogether restrictive and improperly exclusive act to treat it as such."[35]

In one sense, this is clearly correct: as a matter of history, it is true that the *articulus iustificationis* has not always been regarded as the center of theological speculation. However, in that the *lex orandi* continually proclaims the centrality of the soteriological dimension of Christianity to Christian prayer, adoration and worship, in that the community of faith is understood to be based upon a soteriological foundation, it is possible to argue that Barth has not represented the situation accurately. Furthermore, the fundamentally soteriological orientation of the central patristic dogmatic debates leads to the conclusion that the Trinitarian and christological dogmas are ultimately an expression of the soteriological convictions of the early church,[36] whatever reinterpretation Barth may choose to place upon them. If the *articulus iustificationis* is taken to represent an assertion of the importance of general soteriological considerations within the sphere of the church, Barth's statement is potentially somewhat misleading. However, I take the view that Barth's primary concern is to show that the "article of justification," as a matter of historical fact, has not consistently nor constantly been at the center of theological reflection.

It is, however, clear that one of Barth's chief reasons for relegating the *articulus iustificationis* to a secondary position may well be that it poses a serious and comprehensive threat to his own theological

---

[34] Barth, *CD*, IV/1 §61, I, p. 583.

[35] Barth, *CD*, IV/1 §61, I, p. 583.

[36] For this argument, see, for example, Maurice F. Wiles, *The Making of Christian Doctrine* (Cambridge, UK: Cambridge University Press, 1967).

method. Luther's emphasis upon justification as the *articulus stantis et cadentis ecclesiae* is potentially subversive to Barth's theological undertaking. It is for this reason that he singles out Wolf's study of the function of the *articulus iustificationis* within the theology of the early Reformers for particular criticism. He therefore argues that the *articulus stantis et cadentis ecclesiae*, properly understood, is not the doctrine of justification as such, but its "basis and culmination" in the "confession of Jesus Christ." This point is, however, hardly disputed, and is made by Wolf himself. The *articulus iustificationis* is merely a convenient statement of the salvific activity of God towards humanity, concentrated in Jesus Christ.

While Barth is prepared to retain the traditional designation of the *articulus iustificationis* as the *articulus stantis et cadentis ecclesiae*, it is only on account of the community of faith's need to know of the objective basis of its existence: "Without the truth of the doctrine of justification, there was and is no true Christian church.'[37] Nevertheless, so long as the essential truth of this article is not denied, Barth argues that it may withdraw into the background:

> It is precisely the justification of humanity itself, and our confidence in the objective truth of the doctrine of justification, which forbids us to postulate that its theological outworking in the true church must *semper, ubique et ab omnibus* be regarded and treated as the *unum necessarium*, as the center or pinnacle of Christian proclamation and doctrine. [38]

Barth's criticism of those who see in the *articulus iustificationis* the center of the Christian faith is thus a direct consequence of his theological method. Soteriology is necessarily secondary to the fact of revelation, *Deus dixit*. Barth's own theology may be regarded, at least in part, as a reaction against the anthropocentricity of the liberal school—a reaction particularly evident in his inversion of the liberal understanding of God and humanity as epistemic object and subject respectively. Yet Barth has essentially inverted the liberal theology, without fundamentally altering its frame of reference. As such, he may be regarded as indirectly—perhaps even

---

[37] Barth, *CD*, IV/1 §61, I, p. 583. Cf. *CD*, IV/1 §61, I, p. 578.

[38] Barth, *CD*, IV/1 §61, I, p. 584. Note also Barth's suggestion that a preoccupation with the question of how a gracious God may be found leads to a "certain narcissism": *CD*, IV/1 §61, I, p. 588.

unintentionally—perpetuating the theological interests and concerns of the liberal school, particularly the question of how God may be known.

Barth frequently emphasizes that Christ is the *locus* of human self-knowledge as a theological entity. Thus people only know themselves to be sinners, and what this implies for their theological existence and status, in the light of Jesus Christ.[39] Similarly, Barth insists that the election of humans is disclosed to them through the *speculum electionis*, Jesus Christ. In his discussion of both the positive and negative dimensions of the death and resurrection of Christ, Barth reveals an overriding concern for the *knowledge* which results:

> In the mirror of Jesus Christ, who was offered up for us, and who was obedient in this offering, it is revealed (*wird offenbar*) who we ourselves are, that is, the ones for whom he was offered up, for whom he obediently offered himself up. In the light of the humility in demonstration of which he acted as true God for us, we are exposed, made known and have to acknowledge ourselves (*durchschaut*, *erkannt und haben wir uns selbst zu erkennen*) as the proud creatures who ourselves want to be God and Lord and redeemer and helper, and have, as such, turned away from God.[40]

The frequent references to *Erkenntnis* and its cognates, where one might expect to find reference to *Heil* or *Versöhnung*, is one of the more remarkable aspects of Barth's discussion of human justification *coram Deo*. Barth's account of the justification of humanity, while not inattentive to traditional soteriological issues, appears to be redirected to focus on the epistemic situation of humanity.

Up to this point, I have presented as objective an account of Barth's doctrine of justification as possible. I have no particular concern to praise or to criticize: merely to understand him. The two important points to appreciate are Barth's decoupling of the "article of justification" from its traditional Reformational dogmatic location, and his emphasis upon the epistemic aspects of salvation. In what follows, however, I propose to be a little more speculative, reflecting on possible correlations between these observations and other aspects of Barth's thought, before turning to consider the

---

39 Barth, *CD*, IV/1 §61, I, p. 410.
40 Barth, *CD*, IV/1 §61, I, pp. 574–5.

implications of Barth's theology of justification for contemporary evangelicalism.

At a more speculative level, I would suggest that Barth's frequently observed emphasis upon salvation as *Erkenntnis* is easily understood in the light of his doctrine of election. Given that all people will be saved eventually—which is the inevitable conclusion which must be drawn from his doctrines of election, the unilateral graciousness of God, and *servum arbitrium*—the *present knowledge* of this situation is clearly of enormous importance. As all will be saved, it becomes of some importance that this salvation be actualized in the present—for such is the basic presupposition of Christian dogmatics and ethics alike. Both these disciplines are totally and absolutely dependent upon the presupposition that *humans know that they are saved*. Furthermore, in that dogmatics is a discipline which is carried out within the community of faith, it must reflect the basic presupposition upon which that community is grounded—in other words, the knowledge of its present salvation. Barth's repeated emphasis upon the cognitive character of salvation is perfectly consistent with this theology of election, in that, whatever salvation may be ultimately, it is certainly a deliverance from false thinking at present. Humankind may feel that all is lost, that there is no hope of salvation in a world permeated by sin and unbelief—and yet precisely the opposite is, in fact, the case.

With this point in mind, let us return to Martin Kähler's criticism of the soteriologies of the *Aufklärung*, Schleiermacher and the liberal school. For Kähler, a theology of the work of Christ could be classified under one of two types: the first, which corresponds to that of the *Aufklärung*, understands Christ to have communicated certain significant insights concerning an unchangeable situation; the second, which corresponds to his own view, understands Christ to be the founder of an altered situation.[41] Kähler's distinction allows two quite different approaches to the death of Christ to be identified:

1. Those which regard humanity's predicament as being *ignorance of the true situation*. Humans *are* saved, but do not realize it: upon being informed of the true situation, they are enabled to act upon the basis of this knowledge, and adjust and reorientate their

[41] Martin Kähler, *Zur Lehre van der Versöhnung* (Leipzig: Deichert, 1898), p. 337.

existence to what they now realize to be the true state of affairs. In so far as any alteration takes place in the situation, it is in the subjective awareness of humans; indeed, one could argue that the true situation is irrelevant, unless people recognize it as such—thus emphasizing the necessity of being informed of it.

2. Those which regard the predicament of humanity as being *bondage to sin or evil.* Humans are enslaved, and may not realize it: upon being informed of the true situation, they still require liberation. The knowledge of their bondage may well lead to a recognition of the possibility of liberation, and hence the search for the means of that liberation—but such liberation is not identical with, or given simultaneously with, or even a necessary consequence of, the knowledge of humanity's true situation. A victory of good over evil, of grace over sin, is required, which humans may appropriate and make their own, if they are to break free from the hegemony of sin—and precisely such a victory is to be had in the death of Christ upon the cross.

It is clear that, if such a dichotomous classification is conceded (and we must be clear that there are reasons for resisting it), Barth's understanding of the work of Christ falls into the first of these two categories. For Barth and the *Aufklärer*, Christ is supremely the revealer of the knowledge of the true situation of humankind, by which humans are liberated from false understandings of their situation. For Barth, the death of Christ does not in any sense change the soteriological situation, in that this has been determined from all eternity. Rather, he discloses the christologically determined situation to humans. The dilemma of humanity concerns their knowledge of God, rather than their bondage to sin or evil (unless these are understood in the epistemically reduced sense of "ignorance" or "confusion").[42]

It will therefore be clear that Barth does not consider his emphasis upon the theocentricity of theology, and particularly his recognition of the divinity of God, as being associated with a revival in interest in the *articulus iustificationis*. Indeed, Barth operates within much the same theological framework as the *Aufklärer*, Schleiermacher and the liberal school at this point, despite their evident differences

[42] For further discussion, see McGrath, "Karl Barth als Aufklärer?" pp. 280–3.

at others, even though he inverts some of its fundamental points of reference. Perhaps such thoughts are too speculative, too presumptive and too disturbing for some. However, I present them for consideration and reflection, believing them to merit careful consideration.

What, then, of Barth's importance for contemporary evangelicalism? A cursory survey of much evangelical writing, particularly in the field of New Testament studies, suggests that the traditional Lutheran paradigm is still seen by many evangelicals as normative. This can be seen partly in response to the debate over the "new perspective on Paul," where most evangelical scholars appear to assume that they are under an obligation to defend this sixteenth-century approach to Paul's letters.[43] Barth's dogmatic relocation of this article would pose a challenge to this assumption.

Now evangelicals ought to welcome such challenges as offering fresh opportunities to examine how important the notion of justification is to the New Testament, and what role it should play in contemporary theological reflection. Barth is asking a perfectly fair question: is it actually *biblical* to place such an emphasis upon this doctrine, when the biblical material does not appear to warrant it? After all, evangelicals are committed to being faithful to the Bible, not faithful to any particular interpreter of the Bible—even one as significant as Luther.

Furthermore, most evangelicals feel able to reject aspects of Luther's thought which they find unacceptable, arguing that these represent misreadings of Scripture, or constitute unhelpful emphases. Luther's doctrine of baptismal regeneration and his concept of the "real presence" of Christ in the Lord's Supper are excellent examples of such doctrines that many (but not all) evangelicals find troublesome. I would therefore suggest that it is entirely in order for evangelicals to rise to Barth's challenge, and demonstrate that the traditional Reformation reading of Paul at this point is merited. Even within evangelicalism, there seems to be a lack of dialogue between systematic theology and biblical studies. A full response to

[43] For a survey of some of the issues, see McGrath, *Iustitia Dei*, p. 21–32. One of the best evangelical studies, which replays close reading, is Frank Thielman, *The Law and the New Testament* (New York: Herder & Herder, 1999). For a good survey of the debate over the Lutheran interpretation of Paul, including the status of the "article of justification," see Stephen Westerholm, *Perspectives Old and New on Paul: The "Lutheran" Paul and his critics* (Grand Rapids, MI: Eerdmans, 2004).

Barth demands a reconnection of these disciplines—something that evangelicalism is well placed to achieve.

But perhaps more importantly, we need to ask a dogmatic question which arises from Barth's critique of the traditional dogmatic location of the *articulus iustificationis*: can a dogmatic system be constructed which places this notion at its center? Here, we encounter quite a serious difficulty. Virtually no systematic theologian from any Christian theological tradition has been able to construct such a system. It is clear that Albrecht Benjamin Ritschl hoped to do something along these lines back in the 1870s.[44] Martin Kähler attempted this, with very limited success, in the 1890s;[45] indeed, his difficulties in this matter may well have helped shape Barth's concerns about the doctrine. And in more recent years, the Lutheran theologian Robert Jenson has certainly signaled an interest in such a dogmatic project;[46] yet his own systematic theology does not show any such emphasis.[47] Barth's challenge would thus seem to be highly pertinent: can such a systematic theology be constructed? And if not, what are the implications for the longstanding debate over what constitutes the center and limits of the Christian faith? evangelicals have much to contribute to this debate: I believe that they should be fully engaged with it.

---

[44] See Martin Werner, *Der protestantischen Weg des Glaubens* (Bern: Haupt, 1955), pp. 799–815.

[45] Martin Kähler, *Zur Lehre von der Versöhnung* (Leipzig: Deichert, 1898). For discussion, see Rolf Schäfer, "Die Rechtfertigungslehre bei Ritschl und Kähler," *Zeitschrift für Theologie und Kirche* 62 (1965), pp. 66–85.

[46] For example, see Robert Jenson, "Rechtfertigung und Ekklesiologie," *Kerygma und Dogma* 9 (1963), pp. 41–59.

[47] Robert W. Jenson, *Systematic Theology* (2 vols. New York: Oxford University Press, 1997–99).

9

Running Like a Herald to Deliver the Message: Barth on the Church and Sacraments

Timothy George

> The Church runs like a herald to deliver the message. It is not a snail that carries its little house on its back and is so well off in it, that only now and then it sticks out its feelers, and then thinks that the "claim of publicity" has been satisfied. No, the Church lives by its commission as a herald; it is *la compagnie de Dieu*.
>
> Karl Barth, *Dogmatics in Outline*.

I was first introduced to the thought of Karl Barth in an undergraduate course on "contemporary" theology. Along with required readings by Harnack, Tillich, Bultmann, and Bonhoeffer, we were asked to read *The Word of God and the Word of Man*, a collection of Barth's early sermons and addresses. I still have that dog-eared, paperback edition, heavily underlined, with notes in the margins, and lots of question marks and exclamation points. Though I was not then, and still am not now, a Barthian with a capital "B," there was something about Barth that grabbed me right from the start. Unlike Bultmann's demythologizing and dismantling of the biblical worldview, or Tillich's abstruse philosophy of religion, here was a theology that spoke to the heart, that held high the revelation of God in Holy Scripture, and that was also presented in such a provocative, passionate, and personal way. Here was theology presented as though something eternally important was at stake. Here was a theology that mattered.

When I began formal theological studies at Harvard Divinity School, Barth was on the back burner. Neo-Kantian and liberationist paradigms prevailed and Barth, when mentioned at all, was only of antiquarian interest. But my doctoral studies propelled me back to the Reformation, especially to the connection between the doctrine of election and ecclesiology, and this in turn forced me back to Barth. I remember plowing through the *Church Dogmatics*, II/2 and discovering there "a strange new world" I had not encountered before. Although I shared many of the standard evangelical reservations about Barth, I knew that I had something to learn from him, especially about the church. Even if I could not then refer to him as "the great church father of evangelical Christendom, the one genuine doctor of the universal Church the modern era has known,"[1] as the editors of the English edition of his *Church Dogmatics* did shortly after his death in 1968, it was clear that I had encountered a titanic figure whose work, I believed, evangelicals could ill afford to ignore.

Karl Barth was a churchly theologian. What does this mean? In the first place, it refers to the fact that, unlike the majority of professional theologians, both in his day and in ours, Barth did not possess an earned doctorate. This was obviously not from any lack of scholarly ability on his part, but rather from his prior decision to pursue pastoral ministry rather than an academic career. For twelve years Barth served as a pastor, first as a pastoral assistant at a German-speaking congregation in Geneva, and then as pastor of the Swiss Reformed Church in Safenwil, a small industrial town in the Aargau. Barth's distinctive theology emerged out of his pastoral struggles. What does the preacher say to the waiting congregation every Sunday morning? How dare he say anything at all? This tension between the preacher's duty to speak for God, on behalf of God, and the enormous presumption, indeed the impossibility, of doing so is at the very root of Barth's theological discovery. He once put it like this: "We ought to speak of God. We, are human, however, and so cannot speak of God. We ought therefore to recognize both *our obligation* and *our inability* and by that very recognition give God the glory."[2]

Barth's theological training in the great liberal tradition of Schleiermacher, Ritschl, Harnack, and Hermann had not prepared him to deal with this dilemma, nor had his immersion in the Swiss version of the social gospel movement, an involvement which earned him the title "red pastor" for a while. Barth was haunted by the

---

[1] Barth, *CD*, IV/4, p. vi.

[2] Karl Barth, *Word of God and Word of Man* (London: Hodder & Stoughton, 1928), p. 186.

question King Zedekiah posed to Jeremiah long ago: "Is there any word from the Lord?" (Jer. 37:17). This question, which is every preacher's question, propelled Barth back to the Holy Scriptures where he discovered a new orientation for preaching and a new basis for theology. Out of this struggle Barth's *Epistle to the Romans* (in two editions, 1918 and 1921) was born. When speaking to his congregation at Safenwil, Barth began his sermons with the phrase, "Liebe Freunde," ("Dear friends"). However, on Reformation Sunday in 1917, Barth addressed his flock in a new way: "Liebe Gemeinde" ("Dear Church"). Although he reverted to his standard greeting in later sermons, there is no doubt that the task of preaching to his congregation week after week had a profound shaping influence on Barth's theology in those crucial years.[3]

Barth is a churchly theologian in another sense as well. He understands theology, which he defines as "the scientific self-examination of the Christian church with respect to its distinctive God-talk" (*CD*, I/1, p. 3), to be a spiritual discipline within the community of faith. The purpose of theology is to serve the integrity of preaching and thus it is part of the church's humble worship of God. Following his stint as "a young country pastor," as Barth referred to his Safenwil days, he spent the rest of his life in four university settings: in Göttingen (1921–25), in Münster (1925–30), in Bonn (1930–35), and finally in his native Basel (1935–68). There is a sense, however, in which Barth never left the pastorate, for all of his work as an academic theologian—his lectures, addresses, books, disputes, and sermons—was intended to serve and build up the church. This commitment is reflected in the title he gave to his major theological project. After publishing the first volume of his *Christian Dogmatics* in 1927, he abandoned this effort and made a fresh start under a new definitive rubric, *Church Dogmatics*. In Barth's view, theology can never be a mere branch of "religious studies," a scholarly activity pursued with presumed objectivity and lack of personal commitment. As Barth would say near the end of his career, theology is not an end in itself, but rather a service in and for the community of Jesus Christ. "Theology is committed directly to the community and especially to those members who are responsible for preaching, teaching, and counseling. The task theology has continually to fulfill is to stimulate and lead them to face squarely the question of the proper relation of their human

---

[3] Karl Barth, *Gesamtsausgabe I: Predigten 1917* (Zurich: TVZ, 1999), p. 389.

speech to the Word of God, which is the origin, object, and content of this speech."[4] Theology must be done in the service of the church or it is not a *ministerium Verbi Divini*.

Despite Barth's sturdy determination to be a theologian in the service of the church, he could be acutely critical and negative in his statements about the church. This was especially so in Barth's early writing where the gospel is depicted in stark opposition to the church. Co-existence between these two realities is not possible for "the gospel dissolves the church and the church dissolves the gospel."[5] The church, Barth seems to say, has become not a means to God but rather a substitute for God, an idol:

> In the church, the "Beyond" is transfigured into a metaphysical "something" which, because it is contrasted with this world, is no more than an extension of it. In the church, all manner of divine things are possessed and known, and are therefore not possessed and not known. In the church, the unknown beginning and end are fashioned into some known middle position, so that men do not require to remember always that, if they are to become wise they must die. In the church, faith, hope, and love are directly possessed, and the Kingdom of God directly awaited, with the result that men band themselves together to inaugurate it, as though it were a THING which men could have and await and work for.[6]

What Barth is protesting is the domestication of God in the structures and institutions of the visible church. The church understood as the repository of religious consciousness, or the apex of "Christian" civilization, or the private club of moral rectitude could no longer be the place where the thunder and lightning of God's grace breaks through to human beings. It was necessary, Barth felt, to write "Ichabod" over the door to such a church precisely so that the gates could be opened to let the King of Glory enter in. He put it like this: "Only when the end of the blind alley of ecclesiastical humanity has been reached is it possible to raise radically and seriously the problem of God."[7]

---

[4] Karl Barth, *Evangelical Theology: An Introduction* (London: Weidenfeld and Nicolson, 1963), p. 41.

[5] Karl Barth, *The Epistle to the Romans* (London; New York: Oxford University Press, 1965), p. 333.

[6] Barth, *Romans*, p. 332.

[7] Barth, *Romans*, p. 337.

Barth's critique of the church here is more like that of Luther than that of Wycliffe, Hus, Savonarola and other pre-reformers who protested vigorously against the abuses of the late medieval church. Such matters are mere trifles compared to what Barth calls "the blessed terribleness of the theme of the Church which is the very Word of God—the Word of beginning and end, of the creator and redeemer, of judgment and righteousness." In this dialectic the church is divided into two parts—the Church of Esau and the Church of Jacob. By this designation Barth does not refer to confessional differences, say, between Roman Catholics and Protestants, or to different theological camps such as conservatives and liberals. The Church of Esau is "observable, knowable and possible," whereas the Church of Jacob is where the truth of the gospel triumphs over all human deceit. This latter Church, Barth goes on to say, is "unobservable, unknowable, and impossible . . . capable neither of expansion nor of contraction; it has neither place nor name nor history; men neither communicate with it nor are excommunicated from it. It is simply the free grace of God, his calling and election; it is beginning and end."[8]

Here we are at the headwaters of Barth's dialectical ecclesiology. It is not hard to see why those with a vested interest in the church—any church—would respond to Barth's rhetoric with consternation and reproach. If the church is utterly unknowable, unobservable, so detached from history that one cannot speak of it properly, then very practical questions ensue: to whom do we pay our tithes (or church taxes in the state churches of Europe)? Who shall train the church's ministers, and how? Who shall write the church's liturgy, or lead its worship, or send out its missionaries, or do its pastoral care? It has always seemed to some of Barth's critics that his "bifurcation" of the church would lead inevitably to ecclesial nihilism.

But this is to miss the deeper point that Barth is making. It was necessary to be so decisively *against* the church, he believed, precisely in order to be so unreservedly *for* it. Even in *Romans*, where the language of *diastasis* reaches fever pitch, Barth always remains with both feet firmly planted within the physical, finite, fallen, Esau-like church.

> We must not, because we are fully aware of the eternal opposition between the Gospel and the church, hold ourselves aloof from the church or break up its solidarity; but rather, participating in its responsibility

---

8 Barth, *Romans*, p. 342.

> and sharing the guilt of its inevitable failure, we should accept it and cling to it.[9]

We must bear the tribulation of the church as participant-observers. Only through sharing its anguish are we able to pray for revival and work for reformation.

Interpreters of Barth do not agree themselves as to what extent his thought is marked by steady development or by major breaks and new trajectories. Barth himself pointed to some significant shifts in his thinking along the way, although he could also claim continuity and once boasted that, unlike Augustine, he had not found it necessary to publish a volume of retractations (*CD*, IV/2, p. xi)! In any event, Barth did recognize that some of the language he had used in *Romans* was a little over the top. In retrospect, he admitted that he had spoken "somewhat severely and brutally, and moreover—at least according to the other side—in part heretically."[10] What is clear is that he found a more constructive way to describe the church and its role in relation to the gospel and to the revelation of God in Jesus Christ.

From the 1920s onward the image that came to dominate his ecclesiology was that of herald or witness. To be sure, this image can also be found in Barth's earlier writings as well. Already he had discovered Matthias Grünewald's famous depiction of the crucifixion, originally painted for a hospice at Isenheim. Grünewald was an early Reformation painter from the Rhineland who may possibly have embraced the message of Luther near the end of his life. What drew Barth to this painting was Grünewald's portrayal of John the Baptist. He stands at the right of the cross with an open Bible in one hand while he points with the other to the torturous figure of Christ in the agony of death. In faded red letters behind John are the Latin words: *Illum oportet crescere*, *me autem minue*, "He must increase, while I must decrease" (John 3:30).

The pointing finger of Grünewald's John in this painting became the central icon of Barth's life and work. John's ministry was one of persistent negation. There is no evidence that he had the slightest interest in self-promotion. He consistently denied that he was Elijah, the messianic Prophet, or Christ. When he was asked to declare

[9] Barth, Romans, p. 334.

[10] Karl Barth, *The Humanity of God* (Atlanta: John Knox Press, 1960), p. 43. See also Barth's preface to the English translation of his Romans commentary, *The Epistle to the Romans* (London; New York: Oxford University Press, 1965).

who he was, his reply was to say, "I am the voice of one calling in the desert, make straight the way of the Lord" (John 1:23). His message was entirely referential. "Look," he said, "the Lamb of God!" (John 1:29). This image of John, of his bony finger pointing toward Christ on the cross, is precisely the perfect paradigm for every preacher, for every Christian, and consequently, for the church itself. In his famous typology of modern ecclesiologies, Avery Dulles has rightly characterized Barth's approach with the rubric, "The Church as Herald."[11]

Barth's major ecclesiological writings would only come in the 1950s as he incorporated this theme into his vast *Church Dogmatics* project. However, by that time Barth's thinking about the church had been well solidified both by his own internal theological development and by his personal involvement in some of the most significant church and political events of the twentieth century. Chief among these were his leadership in the opposition of the Confessing Church in Germany to the Nazi seizure of power on the one hand, and his serious and up-close encounter with the Roman Catholic tradition on the other.

During the early 1930s Barth found himself at the center of a political storm as he became one of the leading protagonists in the German church conflict. If Barth's distinctive theology first arose out of his struggle over how to speak seriously of God to his congregation at Safenwil, his ecclesiology was solidified amidst the struggles of the church in Germany—the struggle to witness faithfully to Jesus Christ in the face of an alien ideology that sought to undermine the integrity of the church by assimilating it to the "Führer principle." During these years Barth became, as Will Herberg would later call him, "the conscience of Christendom."[12] Barth's opposition to the "anti-Christian counter-church" of Nazism, as he put it, eventually led to his expulsion from Germany in 1935 because of his refusal to begin his lectures with the required salute and oath of allegiance to Hitler.[13]

We cannot follow here the interesting story of Barth's involvement with the Confessing Church but it is important to say that the decisive motivation for his action was his concern for the integrity

---

[11] Avery Dulles, *Models of the Church* (New York: Doubleday, 1987), pp. 76–88.

[12] Karl Barth, *Community, State and Church: Three Essays*, introd. by Will Herberg (Garden City, NY: Doubleday, 1960), p. 9.

[13] Barth, *Community*, p. 54.

of the church's witness. From his base in Basel, he declared: "The church in Volk and society has, under all circumstances, over against the state, her own task, proclamation, and order, determined by the Holy Scriptures."[14] Hitler's effort to make the German Protestant church a department of state, as it were, his usurpation of its churchly prerogatives in the interest of "national security," called forth some of Barth's strongest warnings. Against those who claimed that opposing Hitler would lead to the suffering and weakening of the church, Barth retorted, "We are called to serve this people with the Word of God . . . it is the nature of the message that it can neither be subordinated to, or co-ordinated with, any other concern, however urgent . . . I maintain that the evangelical Church ought rather to permit itself to be thinned down till it remain a tiny group in the catacombs than make a pact, even a covert pact, with this doctrine."[15] The "doctrine" Barth refers to was the widely-held belief that the Nazi revolution was another source of grace and revelation alongside Holy Scripture.

That statement was from the first issue of *Theologische Existenz heute*, a new journal founded by Barth and some of his colleagues in 1933 to remind themselves and their fellow Christians of the church's proper priorities in the crisis that engulfed them. Barth saw a direct line of continuity between the liberal, neo-Protestant theology against which he had reacted so strongly in his early theological writings and the capitulation of the church to the Nazi will to power in the 1930s. To substitute anything else—blood, soil, nation, culture, civilization, or even the visible church—for the one true and living God was sheer idolatry. The true church must maintain its freedom in the face of any and every ideology that would subvert its inner life and witness. Barth's opposition to Nazi rule was thus christologically grounded, as is clear in the first article of the Barmen Declaration, a document Barth drafted for the Confessing Church in May 1934:

> Jesus Christ, as he is attested to us in Holy Scripture, is the one Word of God whom we have to hear, and whom we have to trust and obey in life and death. We condemn the false doctrine that the church can and must recognize as God's revelation other events and powers, forms

---

[14] Barth, *How I Changed My Mind*, John Godsey ed. (Richmond: John Knox Press, 1966), p. 46.

[15] Barth, *Changed*, pp. 40–41.

> and truths, apart from and along side this one Word of God (*CD*, II/1, p. 172).

After the war, Barth continued to argue that the church should maintain a credible Christian witness in the public arena. He protested against the "atomic sin" of nuclear proliferation during the 1950s and called for opposition to the Vietnam War in the 1960s. "It is not enough," he once stated, "only to say, 'Jesus is risen,' but then to remain silent about the Vietnam War."[16] Some, however, including Reinhold Niebuhr, felt that Barth's "softer" approach to the evils of communism and his plea for Western accommodation in the face of the Soviet regime lacked the moral rigor and consistency of his earlier witness against the Nazi system.[17] But what is unmistakable is Barth's determination to weave ethics and ecclesiology into a seamless whole. Barth's doctrine of the church—here he stands in the best tradition of John Calvin—would not allow for a separatist, quietist, a-political approach to the issues of public life. To be a faithful herald of Jesus Christ means that the church must summon "the courage not to be content with the corruption and evil of the world but even within this horizon to look ahead and not back" (*CD*, IV/4, p. 270).

Barth's serious engagement with Roman Catholic theology began during his professorship at Münster when he came to know the Jesuit theologian, Erich Przywara. Throughout the early volumes of the *Church Dogmatics*, Barth wages a two-front campaign against the neo-Protestant liberalism of his youth on the one hand, and against the theology of Roman Catholicism on the other. Both of these "heresies" were linked in Barth's mind through their commitment to natural theology, their dependence on a view of God's relation to the world based upon the analogy of being. (Hence Barth's stern rebuke of his sometime collaborator, Emil Brunner, in his famous "*Nein*!" of 1934.) Increasingly, however, Barth came to regard Roman Catholicism as the more serious conversation partner, an attitude that only increased in later years through his friendship with Hans Von Balthasar, a distinguished Catholic theologian from Barth's

---

[16] George Hunsinger, "Spiritual Stars of the Millennium: Karl Barth (1886–1968)," *The Tablet*, September 30, 2000, p. 1317. See also the essays in Hunsinger's *Disruptive Grace: Studies in the Theology of Karl Barth* (Grand Rapids, MI: Eerdmans, 2000), esp. pp. 21–128.

[17] See Barth's defense of his views in his essay, "The Church Between East and West," in *Against the Stream* (New York: Philosophical Library, 1954), pp. 136f.

hometown of Basel. Thus speaking at his graveside in 1968, Hans Küng could refer to Barth, the stoutest Protestant theologian of the twentieth century, as "one of the spiritual fathers of the Catholic renewal in connection with the Second Vatican Council."[18]

In 1948 Barth traveled to Hungary to deliver an important lecture on "The Real Church" which was later published in the *Scottish Journal of Theology*.[19] In that same year Barth also addressed the first General Assembly of the World Council of Churches which met in Amsterdam. Barth's lecture reflected both his intense engagement with Roman Catholicism and his wider ecumenical involvement at this time. We can identify five major themes in this lecture which reflect Barth's thinking about the church, themes he would continue to reflect on and develop during the next two decades of his life.

1. ***The real church becomes visible only through the power of the Holy Spirit.*** Barth here sounds a note that recurs frequently in his writings about the church: the church is an object of faith as all Christians affirm in the Apostles' Creed, *credo ecclesiam*. Thus the church is not like the state, the family, or the municipality in which we live, all of which are human communities that can be defined empirically and studied sociologically and the like. Although one can also study the church as a religious community in this same way, that is, apart from a commitment of faith, this is not the church confessed by Christians in the creed. The real church is an event, a happening, that can only be seen by the eyes of faith when the Holy Spirit "enables her to step out of and shine through her hiddenness in ecclesiastical establishment, tradition, and custom." Just as a neon sign remains dark and obscure until a current of electricity floods it with color, light and movement, so too the church is a lifeless form apart from the energy and vitality given to it by the Holy Spirit.

2. ***Jesus Christ is the Lord as well as the head of the church which is his body.*** The real church is the congregation of lost sinners called together by Christ and bound to him through the miracle of divine grace. The connection between Jesus Christ and his body on earth is genuine and inviolable, so much so that Barth would

[18] Hans Küng, "Tribute to Karl Barth," *Journal of Ecumenical Studies* 6 (1969), p. 234.

[19] Karl Barth, "The Real Church," *Scottish Journal of Theology* (1950), pp. 337–53.

later refer to the church (in a very catholic-sounding phrase) as the "earthly-historical form of the existence of Jesus Christ" (*CD*, IV/1, p. 652). But the risen, ascended Christ does not surrender his lordship even to the body of which he is the head. The body is here on earth; the head is in heaven. The body functions amidst the ambiguities and temptations of a world in which the powers of darkness have not been finally vanquished; the head abides in the glory of the Father.

In an earlier writing directed against the Roman Catholic theologian, Erich Peterson, Barth refers to the fact that in some monastic communities the place of honor at every mealtime in the refectory is properly furnished with tableware, linen, and a chair which is always left unoccupied, just as at the Jewish Passover a chair is reserved for the yet-to-come Elijah.[20] Barth uses this example to underscore the "not-yet" character of churchly existence in this present age. "God has spoken in his Son, we *are* now God's children; but 'it does not yet appear what we shall be' (I John 3:2)." The empty chair at the table reminds the church, the Bride of Christ, to await the return of her Bridegroom and not to succumb to the heresy of an overly-realized eschatology.

It has seemed to some Barth critics that his talk about a Christ who is in some sense remote from the history of his community on earth—"separated from it by an abyss which cannot be bridged"—leaves him vulnerable to a semi-deist concept of Christ. But here, as elsewhere, Barth wants to say both. In the *Church Dogmatics* IV/2 (in the section "The Growth of the Community") Barth responds to such critics by emphasizing the other side of this dialectic:

> But what does it mean to speak of there and here, height and depth, near and far, when we speak of the One who is not only the true Son of Man but also the true Son of God, the man who, exalted by the self-humiliation of the divine person to being as man, exists in living fellowship with God? It certainly does not mean that these antitheses are removed and obliterated and equated in Him. But since God is not limited to be there, since He is not a prisoner of His own height and distance, it certainly means that in the man Jesus who is also the true Son of God, these antitheses, while they remain, are comprehended and controlled; that He has power over them; that He can be here as well as there, in the depth as well as in the height, near as well as remote,

[20] Karl Barth, "Church and Theology," in *Theology and Church*, T. F. Torrance ed. (London: SCM Press, 1962), p. 302.

and therefore immanent in the *communio sanctorum* on earth as well as transcendent to it (*CD*, IV/2, pp. 652–3).

3. ***The real church is the creature of the Word and always stands under the authority of Holy Scripture.*** As a Protestant theologian in the Reformed tradition, Barth understands the church to be *creatura verbi*, a "creation of the Word." Otto Weber has said of Barth that "no theologian in the history of the church has so thoroughly and painstakingly grounded his theology in Holy Scripture."[21] Barth affirms the Reformation principle of *sola scriptura* in the sense that the prophetic and apostolic witness, which constitutes the content of the Bible, as inspired and illuminated by the Holy Spirit, is the sole basis for the church's teaching and life. Barth connects Scripture and the church's proclamation early on in the *Church Dogmatics* (I/2, pp. 743–58). He insists that the church must be a hearing community as well as a reading one for as the reformers, echoing Paul, declared: "Faith comes by hearing and hearing by the word of God" (Rom. 10:17).

Barth strongly rejects the Roman Catholic understanding of tradition as a separate and equable source of authority alongside the Holy Scripture. Even after his famous visit to Rome in 1966, Barth still identified the claim of Vatican II that Scripture and tradition should be held with "equal reverence and affection" as a remaining obstacle between the two faith communities.[22] But this does not mean that the church lacks genuine teaching authority. Such authority, however, is always temporal and relative and can never be placed alongside, much less above, the voice of the living Christ speaking by his Spirit through his Word.

4. ***The real church exists under the cross and does not seek its own glory.*** Barth's writings about the church can be understood as a protest against every form of ecclesial triumphalism. The church is always *ecclesia in via*: the church on the road, the church in

---

[21] Otto Weber, *Karl Barth's Church Dogmatics*, Arthur C. Cochraine tr. (London: Lutterworth Press, 1953), p. 13.

[22] Karl Barth, "Thoughts on the Second Vatican Council," *Ad Limina Apostolorum: An Appraisal of Vatican II* (Richmond: John Knox Press, 1967). Also see the essay by Timothy George "An Evangelical Reflection on Scripture and Tradition," *Your Word is Truth: A Project of evangelicals and Catholics Together*, Charles Colson and Richard John Neuhaus eds. (Grand Rapids, MI: Eerdmans, 2002).

transit, the church under the cross. Thus the real church has no interest in vaunting itself or in acquiring the accoutrements of worldly power, prestige, or wealth. The church must not be seen, Barth says, so much as God's palace as God's shanty within the human community until the end of the world. "The splendor of the church can only consist in its hearing in poverty the Word of the eternally rich God and making that Word heard by men."[23] Such a church will be marked more by its fidelity to the gospel than its numerical success or recognition by the media. Fresh from his appearance at the first General Assembly of the World Council of Churches, Barth remarked that "the smallest village church" would be more important than the Amsterdam Assembly if its members acknowledge what is said about the church in question fifty-four of the Heidelberg Catechism:

> I believe that, from the beginning to the end of the world, and from among the whole human race, the Son of God, by his Spirit and his Word, gathers, protects, and preserves for himself, in the unity of the true faith, a congregation chosen for eternal life. Moreover, I believe that I am and forever will remain a living member of it eternally.

5. ***The real church lives for the sake of the manifestation of God's grace and glory in its mission and witness to the world.*** The church of Jesus Christ was never intended to be a *cordon sanitaire* detached from the disparities and messiness of history. In a later section of the *Church Dogmatics* (IV/3.2), Barth devotes a lengthy section to "The People of God in World-Occurrence." The church that has been called out from the world is the same church that is also sent back into it. In a sense, the church might be thought of as an advance party for the kingdom of God; in it God's purpose and plan for all humanity is foreshadowed and realized in some measure. "The community lives and grows within the world—an anticipation, a provisional representation, of the sanctification of all men as it has taken place in him, of the new humanity reconciled with God" (*CD*, IV/2, p. 654). As the divinely appointed herald of God's good news to all persons everywhere, the church is charged with communicating God's great "Yes" to the world. The church must not forget God's "No" either, but it must always lead out with the "Yes." The "No" we must speak, Barth says, will become

---

[23] Barth, *Theology and Church*, p. 282.

audible enough if we occupy ourselves with—washing of feet, care for the poor, embrace of the homeless, and other acts of service in Jesus' name.

Having outlined these major themes, it is necessary to say a word about how Barth treats ecclesiology within the overall structure of the *Church Dogmatics* before looking briefly at his view of the sacraments. Unlike Calvin, who devoted Book Four of his *Institutes* to the church which he defined as "the external means by which God invites us into the society of Christ and holds us therein," Barth does not treat the church as a separate locus of theology but weaves it into the general structure of his dogmatic project. As we have seen, the church emerges early on in the *Church Dogmatics*, I/2 in connection with the doctrine of revelation, church proclamation, and Scripture. In this context, Barth gives considerable attention to church proclamation which for him includes both preaching and the sacraments. Then, as he moves forward with the doctrine of God, and his extensive treatment of the election of Jesus Christ, Barth grounds ecclesiology within the eternal decision of God in predestination. The election of the church takes place in and with the election of Jesus Christ which is the eternal basis for the community's calling, justification, and ultimate redemption.

There are also many references to the church in Barth's doctrine of creation which he expounds in volume three of the *Church Dogmatics*, but it is in connection with volume four, the doctrine of reconciliation, that Barth describes more fully the meaning, purpose, and mission of the church. These are all treated as aspects or developments of the ministry of the Holy Spirit. The *Church Dogmatics*, IV/1 deals with "The Holy Spirit and the Gathering of the Christian Community" (paragraph 62). The *Church Dogmatics*, IV/2 takes up the theme of "The Holy Spirit and the Upbuilding of the Christian Community" (paragraph 67). And the *Church Dogmatics*, IV/3 extends this theme to "The Holy Spirit and the Sending of the Christian Community" (paragraph 72). By the time Barth reaches this focus on ecclesiology in the *Church Dogmatics*, he has nearly abandoned the word "church" in favor of "community."

The word church, he thinks, has become an "overshadowed and overburdened word." "Community" is much closer to the New Testament meaning of church as the congregation or assembly of God's people. It is this community which is confronted and created by the Word of God. It may be correctly described in three ways: (1) *communio sanctorum*, the communion of saints; (2) *congregatio fidelium*, the gathering of the faithful; and (3) *coniuratio testium*, the confederation of the witnesses—the heralds—who are called like John the Baptist in Grünewald's painting to the referential ministry pointing others to Jesus Christ and his atoning work on the cross.

Barth never lived to complete his long-awaited study of the Lord's Supper, and there is very little about this important subject in the many pages of the *Church Dogmatics*, although an impressive volume has recently been published to show what Barth would have said about the Lord's Supper had he lived long enough to address it in depth.[24] Barth actually invited such a study in the preface to the final installment of the *Church Dogmatics*, published posthumously: "Thus intelligent readers may deduce from the fragment how I would finally have presented the doctrine of the Lord's Supper" (*CD*, IV/4, p. ix.) Barth's writings on baptism, however, created quite a stir during his own lifetime and have continued to generate further discussion and controversy. In 1943 Barth published a short treatise, "The Teaching of the Church Regarding Baptism," in which he called into question the centuries-old practice of infant baptism. In the final fragment of the *Church Dogmatics* Barth returned to this theme and went even further in rejecting not only infant baptism but the last vestiges of a sacramental understanding of baptism.

Barth treats baptism in the context of ethics under the general heading, "Baptism as the Foundation of the Christian Life." Essential to his interpretation is the distinction between baptism with the Holy Spirit and baptism with water. Baptism of the Spirit refers to the divine change, effected directly by the Holy Spirit, through which Jesus Christ makes a human being a Christian. Baptism with the Spirit is "divinely effective, divinely causative, divinely creative. Here, if anywhere, one might speak of a sacramental happening in the current sense of the term. It cleanses, renews, and changes man truly and totally" (*CD*, IV/4, p. 34). Baptism with water, on the other hand, is a human act of obedience through which the believer in Christ responds in gratitude to the faithfulness of God realized in the gift of salvation and the outpouring of the Holy Spirit.

Taken together, baptism and the Lord's Supper are "eventful witnesses to God's righteous action in Jesus Christ." Through these Jesus-appointed ordinances believers receive the confirmation of their faith, and the community receives the confirmation of its origin in Jesus Christ and its life through him.[25] Barth was fond of quoting

[24] Paul D. Molnar, *Karl Barth and the Theology of the Lord's Supper* (New York: Peter Lang, 1996).

[25] Karl Barth, *Learning Jesus Christ through the Heidelberg Catechism* (Grand Rapids, MI: Eerdmans, 1964), p. 94.

a statement from the Augsburg Confession to the effect that the sacraments of the church are truly efficacious *ubi et quando visum est Deo*, "where and when God so wills it." In all of his thinking about the sacraments, Barth wanted "to avoid any suggestion that the action of the church can be substituted for the action of Christ through the Holy Spirit."[26]

One further word may be said about Barth's view of the Lord's Supper. In an interesting article on "Protestantism and Architecture" Barth suggested that at the center of an evangelical church building there should be a simple wooden table, slightly elevated, but distinctly different from an altar. Attached to this table, or placed very near it, would be the pulpit and baptismal font. This kind of arrangement, Barth thought, would demonstrate to the congregation the coinherence of Word and sacrament. In this sense, baptism and the Lord's Supper are another form of proclamation. No less than the preacher's sermon, they too herald the Word of God; indeed, as the reformers were wont to say, sacraments are "the visible words of God." Though he called himself a neo-Zwinglian with reference to baptism and the Lord's Supper, Barth could nonetheless affirm that these two "eventful witnesses" are not empty signs. "On the contrary, they are full of meaning and power. They are thus the simplest, and yet in their very simplicity the most eloquent, elements in the witness which the community owes to the world, namely, the witness of peace on earth among the men in whom God is well-pleased" (*CD*, IV/3, p. 901).

What can evangelicals learn from Karl Barth about the church? First of all, by grounding the church so completely within the Trinitarian and christological framework of his theology, Barth presents a very high ecclesiology, one that stands as a corrective to the rugged individualism and "Jesus-in-my-heart-only" piety that marks too much of evangelical life today. In the eternal election of Jesus Christ, God chose the church, the community, to be the body and bride of his Son. During his earthly ministry, Jesus summoned individuals one by one to follow him and be his disciples, but he always intended for them to do this in the company of others. "From the very outset Jesus Christ did not envisage individual followers, disciples and witnesses, but a plurality of such united by him both with himself and with one another" (*CD*, IV/3.2, p. 681). Thus Barth reminds evangelicals of the corporate character of Christian

---

[26] John Yocum, *Ecclesial Mediation in Karl Barth* (Aldershot, Hamphire: Ashgate, 2004), p. 121.

existence; he teaches us that the church is not a mere option or add-on to the Christian life, but that it is integral to the eternal purposes of God and indispensable for faithful discipleship.

Second, Barth's emphasis on the church as herald or witness resonates strongly with evangelical perceptions. Historically evangelicals have emphasized both the supreme authority of Scripture for the life of faith and the centrality of preaching in the worship of the church. Barth's doctrine of Scripture has been strongly criticized by many evangelicals, because the disjunction he presents between revelation and the biblical witness seems, despite Barth's best intentions to the contrary, to open the door to the kind of subjectivism and liberalism against which he himself reacted so vigorously. Barth's actual use of the Bible, on the other hand, is not only extensive but exemplary from an evangelical perspective. Many evangelicals will also appreciate what Barth called his "cautious and respectful de-mythologizing" of sacramentalism and some, especially those with baptistic convictions, will applaud his disavowal of infant baptism. On the Lord's Supper, Barth might have done better to follow Calvin rather than the Zwinglian trajectory of the Reformed tradition, but even here his somewhat minimalist theology can help evangelicals, many of whom have an even lower view of the Lord's table than he did! Barth did refer to the Lord's Supper as the "common nourishment" of the community of faith (*CD*, IV/2, p. 708). He also, following Calvin, called for its weekly celebration and once said: "Wherever the Supper is celebrated, there Jesus Christ himself is present. And where he is present, there the relation between God's food and drink and the earthly bread and wine is real."[27]

What ecumenism is for Roman Catholics and conciliar Protestants, mission and evangelism are for evangelicals. It was Brunner, not Barth, who said that the church exists for mission just as a fire exists for burning, but this sentiment matches Barth's understanding as well. In recent decades, the worldwide evangelical movement has carried the witness of the gospel to all corners of the globe and remains, along with Roman Catholicism, one of the two strongest impulses of Christian vitality in the twenty-first century. Barth liked to quote the Great Commission in its Johannine expression, "As the Father has sent me, so I send you" (John 20:21). He would no doubt rejoice at the deep-seated evangelical impulse to bear witness to God's grace to everyone everywhere in Jesus' name. At

[27] Barth, *Learning*, p. 109.

the same time, he would no doubt remind evangelicals that the true missionary work of the church is about more than "drawing large crowds and enjoying success," and he would perhaps chide the evangelical church for its penchant to produce "propaganda on behalf of its own spatial expansion" rather than an unadulterated witness for the gospel.

We have noted that Barth increasingly found genuine Christian fellowship and theological comradeship more easily among his Roman Catholic contemporaries than with his mainline Protestant colleagues. While I would fully expect him to be critical of various joint statements issued by evangelicals and Catholics in recent years, I also believe that he would rejoice that this conversation is taking place, and that he would encourage its continuation. He would hope, I believe, that such an engagement would—when and where God so wills it—transform both communities in the interest of the one and only gospel of Jesus Christ and for the glory of God alone.

Throughout history the church has always lived in uneasy tension between the poles of identity and adaptability. The church can, and often has, shipwrecked on either side of this divide. By emphasizing identity so strongly, the church can become a holy huddle, cut off from its environing culture and bereft of any sense of urgent mission to the world. evangelicals have sometimes succumbed to this temptation, resulting in separatism, fundamentalism, and isolation. Perhaps today the greater danger is at the other extreme, that in the valid concern for reaching out with the good news of Christ, the church will take on board too much of the world's agenda, will become too accommodated, even assimilated, to the spirit of the age and so in the process lose its very soul. If he were here today, Karl Barth might refer the evangelical church to these words from his explosive commentary on *Romans*, originally addressed to a situation perhaps not entirely different from our own:

> He who hears the Gospel and proclaims it . . . knows that the church means suffering and not triumph . . . He sees the inadequacy of the church growing apace, not because of its weakness and lack of influence, not because it is out of touch with the world; but, on the contrary, because of the pluck and force of its wholly utilitarian and hedonistic illusions, because of its very great success, and because of the skill with which it trims its sails to the changing fashions of the world.[28]

[28] Barth, *Romans*, pp. 334–5.

10

Exploring Karl Barth's Eschatology: A Salutary Exercise for Evangelicals[1]

John Bolt

Any examination of Karl Barth's eschatology must begin with a claim in the second edition of his *Römerbrief* that "If Christianity be not altogether thoroughgoing eschatology, there remains in it no relationship with Christ. Spirit which does not at every moment point from death to the new life is not the Holy Spirit."[2] How intensely Barth saw this pronouncement as the clear break with liberal, cultural Protestantism is apparent from the sentences that follow: "And this is so, be there never so much progress of social reform and never so much trumpeting of the grandeur of Christian redemption! Redemption is invisible, inaccessible, and impossible, for it meets us only in hope."[3] This section of the Romans commentary concludes with these lyrical words on hope:

---

[1] For invaluable help in locating key passages in Barth's voluminous writings that are relevant to his eschatology along with the key elements in it, I am indebted to a work of a former student, Jean de Dieu Rajaonarivony, "Transcendence and History in Karl Barth's Amillennial Eschatology," Ph.D. dissertation, Calvin Theological Seminary, 1997.

[2] Karl Barth, *The Epistle to the Romans*, Edwyn C. Hoskins tr. (Oxford, UK and New York: Oxford University Press, [1933], 1972), p. 314. Hoskins's translation is a rather tame rendering of Barth's almost violent German: "*Christentum, das nicht ganz und gar und restlos Eschatologie ist, hat mit Christus ganz und gar und restlos nicht zu tun.*"

[3] Barth, *Romans*, p. 314.

> Could we see nothing but the visible world, we should not wait; we should accept our present situation with joy or with grumbling. Our refusal to accept it and to regard our present existence as incapable of harmony, our certainty that there abides in us a secret waiting for what is not, is, however, intelligible in the unseen hope which is ours in God, in Christ, in the Spirit, in the hope by which we are existentially confronted by the things which are not. We can then, if we understand ourselves aright, be none other than they who wait. We are satisfied to know no more than the sorrow of the creation and our own sorrow. We ask nothing better or higher than the Cross, where God is manifested as God. We must, in fact, be servants who wait for the coming of their Lord.[4]

Over against all forms of humanistic optimism about transforming this world by human effort, Barth called attention to the impossibility of redemption apart from the cross, apart from dying, apart from waiting for God in hope. God's justice is made apparent in judgment upon human inadequacy, "when the world stands under the negation of judgment."[5] When Christians pray the second petition of the Lord's Prayer, "Thy kingdom come," says Barth, "they do what is qualitatively more and better than the best that all movements for the establishment of human righteousness can do, their own efforts included."[6]

Though North American evangelicalism has sought in the last half-century to distance itself from "fundamentalism," it cannot deny that it shares with fundamentalism more generally the genesis of its conflict with liberal Christianity, usually referred to as "Modernism."[7] From that fact alone Barth would appear to be an attractive co-belligerent for evangelicals and some theologians have indeed found that to be the case.[8] I do not share that judgment without significant

---

4 Barth, *Romans*, p. 315.

5 Barth, *Romans*, p. 95.

6 Karl Barth, *The Christian Life*, *Church Dogmatics*, IV/4, *Lecture Fragments*, Geoffrey W. Bromiley tr. (Grand Rapids, MI: Eerdmans, 1981), p. 261.

7 See any of the major studies of twentieth-century North American evangelicalism such as George M. Marsden, *Fundamentalism and American Culture: The Shaping of Twentieth-Century Evangelicalism, 1870–1925* (New York: Oxford University Press, 1980).

8 Among the notable public advocates for evangelical theology embracing Karl Barth is Bernard Ramm, *After Fundamentalism: The Future of Evangelical Theology* (San Francisco, CA: Harper & Row, 1983).

qualification but will argue in this essay that even for a theologian as problematic as Barth,[9] there are for evangelicals useful insights and some salutary lessons to be learned from exploring Barth's eschatology. After a brief preliminary discussion, I will develop this by considering a number of key Barthian eschatological themes: Eschatology is about Jesus Christ; Jesus is Victor; the Three Forms of the *Parousia*; *Theologia Viatorum*; Eschatology: christological or Pneumatological? These themes taken together will provide a cumulative summary of Barth's eschatology.[10]

At first glance, turning to Karl Barth for guidance in the eschatology debates bedeviling North American evangelicals would seem to be a recipe for disappointment.[11] Barth's theological interest in eschatology is utterly indifferent to the key passionate debates in the evangelical world, arguments about the millennium, conservative or progressive dispensationalism, and whether the rapture is before or after the tribulation. Instead, we must contend with some unknown entities in the conversation: time and eternity, immanence and transcendence, Christocentrism and idealism, contingency and actualism, *Historie* vs. *Geschichte*, hope in the face of nihilism (*das Nichtige*), *theologia viatorum*, as well as the *parousia* and nothingness.[12] In addition, according to a recent writer on Barth's

---

[9] See below, n. 26 and the concluding section of this essay.

[10] These themes taken together reflect a full final portrait, albeit in highly condensed and summary fashion, of Barth's eschatology, the most complete and mature statement of which can be found in *Church Dogmatics* IV/3/1 (§ 69/3) and IV/3/2 (§ 73).

[11] It will become apparent that I have in mind here the dominant dispensational premillennialism of North American evangelicals. I recognize of course that not all evangelicals share this type of eschatology. Also, some postmillennial and especially amillennial evangelicals will find Barth a friendly ally on many fronts. As Jean Rajaonarivony has shown (see n. 1) Barth can in fact be said in many respects to be amillennial. The advantage of an exercise such as the one in this essay is that it provides a fresh angle into the interminable debates among evangelicals about eschatology.

[12] See the most complete study of Barth's eschatology in recent years, John C. McDowell, *Hope in Barth's Eschatology: Interrogations and Transformations Beyond Tragedy* (Burlington, VT: Ashgate, 2000). McDowell provides an annotated bibliography on p. 5, n. 14. Key recent essay-length discussions on Barth's eschatology include Josef Smolik, "Glaube, Eschatologie, Geschichte: Zum fünften Jahrestag des Todes J. L. Hromádka," *Communio Viatorum* 17/4 (1974), pp. 177–82; John S.

eschatology, "Barth's hope, and the eschatological soil in which it is germinated and is nourished, is a little treated element."[13] What makes reflection on Barth's eschatology even more complicated is that eschatology is not a final (and uncompleted) chapter in Barth's *Church Dogmatics* but an essential ingredient in every aspect of his theology. In Barth's own words, "much about the desired sphere of eschatology may be gathered indirectly, and sometimes directly, from the earlier volumes."[14] At the same time there are elements of Barth's eschatology that have drawn serious negative attention from evangelical theologians, notably Barth's alleged universalism.[15] Much

---

Reist, Jr., "Commencement, Continuation, Consummation: Karl Barth's Theology of Hope," *The Evangelical Quarterly* 59/3 (1987), pp. 195–214; Ingolf U. Dalferth, "Karl Barth's Eschatological Realism," in S. W. Sykes, ed., *Karl Barth: Centenary Essays* (Cambridge, UK: Cambridge University Press, 1989), pp. 14–45; Gerhard Sauter, "Why is Karl Barth's Church Dogmatics not a 'Theology of Hope'? Some Observations on Barth's Understanding of Eschatology" *Scottish Journal of Theology* 53/4 (1999), pp. 407–29. F. W. Marquardt's controversial thesis about the early Barth's socialism (see George Hunsinger, ed. *Karl Barth and Radical Politics* [Philadelphia: Westminster, 1976]) makes use of eschatological themes; also see Tjarko Stadtland, *Eschatologie und Geschichte in der Theologie des Jungen Karl Bar*th (Neukirchen Verlag des Erziehungsvereins, 1966). Most major studies on Barth's theology deal in greater or lesser degree with his eschatology. Noteworthy for their attention to eschatology (transcendence and immanence; salvation in history, time and eternity) are: G. C. Berkouwer, *The Triumph of Grace in the Theology of Karl Barth*, Harry Boer tr. (Grand Rapids, MI: Eerdmans, 1956); Hans Urs von Balthasar, *The Theology of Karl Barth*, John Drury tr. (New York, Chicago, San Francisco, CA: Holt, Rinehart and Winston, 1971); Donald G. Bloesch, *Jesus is Victor! Karl Barth's Doctrine of Salvation* (Nashville: Abingdon, 1976); John Thompson, *Christ in Perspective, Christological Perspectives in the Theology of Karl Barth* (Edinburgh, UK: Saint-Andrew Press, 1978); Philip J. Rosato, *The Spirit as Lord: The Pneumatology of Karl Barth* (Edinburgh, UK: T&T Clark, 1981); Richard H. Roberts, *A Theology on its Way: Essays on Karl Barth* (Edinburgh, UK: T&T Clark, 1991); Bruce L. McCormack, *Karl Barth's Critically Realistic Dialectical Theology* (Oxford, UK: Clarendon Press, 1995).

[13] McDowell, *Hope*, p. 5; later, on the same page, McDowell speaks of "this paucity of substantial study of Barth's eschatology of hope."

[14] Barth, *Church Dogmatics*, IV/4, p. vii; cited by Mc Dowell, *Hope*, 6. McDowell refers to *CD*, I, pp. 56f., 164f.; *CD*, I/2, p.875ff.

[15] John Colwell, "The Contemporaneity of the Divine Decision: Reflections on Barth's Denial of 'Universalism,'" in Nigel M. de S. Cameron,

of this discussion is laboriously dedicated to exhausting debates about exegesis of key texts. In this essay, I will not enter that debate but look at a number of key themes in Barth's eschatology before finally exploring the link between eschatology and pneumatology as a promising way out of the interminable debates focused on exegesis alone.

1. Eschatology is about Jesus Christ

Defining the term "evangelical" most generally would be to say that an evangelical Christian is above all a "Jesus-centered" person. Not only does an evangelical hold to a high, Chalcedonian Christology affirming that the man Jesus of Nazareth is "true God and true man, one person in two natures," but an evangelical is also one who has a living faith relationship with Jesus as Savior and Lord.[16] One must be converted, born again, and make the life of discipleship, following Jesus and witnessing to his grace and power, the highest priority.[17] In a nutshell, evangelical faith is christocentric, or, so it might be better to say, Jesucentric.

Universalism and the Doctrine of Hell (Carlisle, UK and Grand Rapids, MI: Paternoster and Baker, 1992), pp. 139–60. Colwell adopts the very reasonable position that Barth should be taken seriously when he explicitly denies universal salvation as a *necessary* conclusion from the apriori of God's love, but that Barth insists it is proper for Christians to *hope* for the salvation of all people. To deny this possibility is also to limit and restrict the free grace of God.

[16] The phrase "living faith" seems to me highly preferable to the favored evangelical expression "a personal relationship with Jesus." The latter is too individualistic and ignores the reality of the church, the body of Christ apart from which no living relationship with Christ is possible according to our Lord's own words about "the vine and the branches" (John 15).

[17] The following statement from a reliable evangelical source, J. I. Packer, can serve as a useful check on the description I have provided. My purpose in this paragraph is not to suggest a comprehensive definition of "evangelical" but to show that the evangelical impulse is at bottom christocentric, or perhaps, better, Jesucentric. Note particularly the second, fourth and fifth propositions.

> What does *evangelical* mean on evangelical lips? It is an umbrella word, covering and connecting belief, spirituality, purpose, and action, both personal and corporate. The quadrilateral account of evangelicalism as biblicist, cross-centered, conversionist, and evangelistic has gained wide

However, this feature takes a decided second place when it comes to popular evangelical eschatology.[18] The dominant eschatology of North American evangelicals is dispensational premillennialism and while Jesus is not absent from this eschatology he is featured primarily as a warrior battling the forces of darkness in the last days,[19] and as a rapturing escape hatch for believers whose faith

---

acceptance in recent years. I myself profile evangelicalism in terms of six belief-and-behavior principles, thus:

1. Enthroning Holy Scripture, the written word of God, as the supreme authority and decisive guide on all matters of faith and practice;
2. Focusing on the glory, majesty, kingdom, and love of Jesus Christ, the God-man who died as a sacrifice for our sins and who rose, reigns, and will return to judge mankind, perfect the church, and renew the cosmos;
3. Acknowledging the lordship of the Holy Spirit in the entire life of grace, which is the life of salvation expressed in worship, work, and witness;
4. Insisting on the necessity of conversion (not of a particular conversion experience, but of a discernibly converted condition, regenerate, repentant, and rejoicing);
5. Prioritizing evangelism and church extension as a life-project at all times and under all circumstances; and
6. Cultivating Christian fellowship, on the basis that the church of God is essentially a living community of believers who must help each other to grow in Christ.

J.I. Packer, "A Stunted Ecclesiology? The Theory and Practice of Evangelical Churchliness," *Touchstone* 15/10 (December 2002), pp. 37–41.

[18] Adrio König judges that this phenomenon is true more generally. See his *The Eclipse of Christ in Eschatology: Toward a More Christ-Centered Approach* (Grand Rapids, MI: Eerdmans, 1989). Though König's enthusiasm gets away with him when he claims in his Preface that his approach "is so new that occasionally some readers might disbelieve their eyes" (p. vii), his point about the need to place Christ at the center of all eschatology because "Jesus Christ himself is the last and the end" (alpha and omega), is surely apropos. Interestingly enough, though his own structure borrows heavily from Barth's threefold form of the *parousia* and is hard to imagine without Barth's pioneering notion, König is equally as critical of Barth as he is of the premillennial dispensationalism, Bultmann, Cullman, and Karl Rahner (see pp. 32–7) and insists his view of Christ's "comings" differs significantly from Barth's threefold form of the parousia. That König misses the mark in attempting to distance himself from Barth is persuasively shown by Rajaonarivony, "Transcendence and History," pp. 8–11.

[19] As evidenced by the overwhelming success of the twelve-volume La

enables them to escape the trials and tribulation leading up to Armageddon.[20] Jesus the Christ, the inaugurator of the new age through his death, resurrection and sending of the Spirit is not the center of attention in the popular literature of premillennial dispensationalism; instead, tracking and tracing the movements of nations and scouring world events for "signs" as they indicate the unfolding of the prophetically foretold end-time drama receives the focus. One illustration to underscore this point, can be taken from novelist Frank Peretti's *This Present Darkness*, in many respects the forerunner and exemplar for the wildly popular *Left Behind* series.[21]

This Present Darkness describes the battle in a small town between the forces of Good, led by angels including The General, Captain of the Hosts, Tal, Guido, Strength of Many, Triskal, and others, against the demonic powers of darkness who are trying "to establish still another foothold for the coming New World Order and the New Age Christ."[22] The latter have leaders named Ba-al Rafar, the Strongman, Prince of Ashton, Lucius, and Prince of Babylon and take as their headquarters the psychology offices in the basement of a local college. Add into this mix multinational corporations, the United Nations, the forces of secular humanism and the stage is set for battle, a cultural war that sounds familiar to any North American who reads newspapers today. The outcome of this spiritual battle, with all of its earthly institutional consequences, depends on the faithfulness of "prayer warriors" providing "prayer cover" for the heavenly hosts who are engaged in battle. While this prayer battle is conducted in the name of Jesus and exorcisms

---

Haye and Jenkins *Left Behind* best-seller series (Cool Stream, IL: Tyndale House, 1995–2004). See Frank Peretti, *This Present Darkness* and *Piercing the Darkness* (Cool Stream, IL: Tyndale House), *The Oath* (Nashville, TN: Thomas Nelson), and *Prophet* (Good News Publishing, 2004).

[20] See, e.g., the artificially added-on call to conversion at the conclusion of Hal Lindsey's best-seller, *The Late Great Planet Earth* (Grand Rapids, MI: Zondervan, 1970), pp. 174ff. This appears in a chapter entitled "Polishing the Crystal Ball."

[21] For much of what follows I am indebted to a superb treatment of spiritual warfare in biblical perspective by Pentecostal New Testament scholar Robert A. Guelich, "Spiritual Warfare: Jesus, Paul and Peretti," *Pneuma* 13/1 (1991), pp. 33–64.

[22] Peretti, *This Present Darkness*, p. 257, cited by Guelich, "Spiritual Warfare," p. 52.

of demons take place in the Name, the whole drama is curiously devoid of classic christological teaching. Guelich summarizes this nicely:

> No mention is made about the work of Christ either in his coming to announce the gospel of the Kingdom or in his work on the cross and through the resurrection. [In addition], citing "in Jesus name" appears to give one power over the demon rather than reflect the person and work of Christ that underlies the use of the name. [Finally], there is no mention about Christ having already defeated the enemy, nor is there any mention of a future defeat of the enemy.[23]

It is of course true, as Guelich also observes, that we are dealing here with a work of fiction. However, as even a superficial examination of the *Left Behind* series would also demonstrate,[24] Guelich's subsequent point is also valid when he says that "this particular story, though clearly fictitious on the historical level, has been taken as 'true' or 'real' on a theological level in many circles in the church today." Guelich's summary judgment rings true: "The novel accurately depicts the nature and means of spiritual warfare as perceived by a number of Christians today."[25] The point I am making here is that much of evangelical eschatology, dominated as it is by dispensational premillennialism, fails the test of evangelicalism's own passion that it should above everything else be all about Jesus Christ. Here, whatever judgment one makes about Barth's own Christology,[26] his posture seems right: eschatology too must be about Jesus Christ.

---

23 Guelich, "Spiritual Warfare," p. 57.

24 The same is true of another volume in this same genre, Pat Robertson's *The End of the Age: A Novel* (Dallas: Word, 1995), which is dramatically boring and lacking suspense to anyone who knows a dispensational time-line. The novel is a cartoon version of the eschatological time line found in the Scofield Reference Bible.

25 Guelich, "Spiritual Warfare," p. 57.

26 For example, Ingolf U. Dalferth argues that Barth's eschatological metaphysics involves "a thoroughgoing reconstruction of the relation of God's eschatological self-presentation of Christ to our common reality in terms of the central doctrine of classical Christology, the doctrine of the *hypostatic union*." What this means is that "our world of common experience is an *enhypostatic reality* which exists only in so far as it is incorporated into the concrete reality of God's saving self-revelation in Christ. Taken by itself natural reality is an anhypostatic abstraction, unable

Barth's position could be summarized by paraphrasing and elaborating his famous *Römerbrief* quote: If it is true that the only Christianity which can be said to be truly about Christ is one that is "altogether thoroughgoing eschatological," then it is also true that the only genuinely Christian eschatology is one that is consistently and thoroughly about Christ alone. Barth does not tackle the futurist speculations of North American dispensational premillennialism directly but his careful critique of Jürgen Moltmann's "theology of hope" does give us important clues.[27] In a letter to Moltmann, responding to his *Theology of Hope*, Barth indicated his anticipation that Moltmann would have been among those "who would not just accept or reject what I intended and did in theology, but who would go beyond it positively in an independent conception, improving it at every point in a renewed form . . ." However, Barth continued, he was disappointed wondering "does your theology of hope really differ at all from the baptized principle of hope of Mr. Bloch?"[28] Barth's objection was that "this eschatology can hardly be recognized or taken seriously as *Christian* eschatology. Instead of starting out joyfully with the confession of Jesus Christ it seems

---

to exist on its own and systematically at one remove from the texture of concrete reality ("Karl Barth's Eschatological Realism," pp. 28–9; cf. p. 41). The same point is made by Roberts, *Theology on its Way*, p. 40. If this is indeed the case it not only suggests that Barth has no independent doctrine of creation apart from redemption, but that the Creator/creation distinction is also not clearly maintained. Though this represents in my view a major theological problem, I still affirm that evangelical theology needs to learn the salutary lesson that eschatology should in the first place be about Jesus Christ. This remains true even if Barth's own Christology is finally unacceptable.

[27] For a more complete treatment of this single issue see John S. Reist, Jr., "Commencement, Continuation, Consummation: Karl Barth's Theology of Hope," *The Evangelical Quarterly* 59/3 (1987), pp. 195–214; Ingolf U. Dalferth, "Karl Barth's Eschatological Realism," in S. W. Sykes ed., *Karl Barth: Centenary Essays* (Cambridge, UK: Cambridge University Press, 1989), pp. 14–45; Gerhard Sauter, "Why is Karl Barth's *Church Dogmatics* not a 'Theology of Hope'? Some Observations on Barth's Understanding of Eschatology," *Scottish Journal of Theology* 53/4 (1999), pp. 407–29. I am especially indebted here to Reist's essay.

[28] *Karl Barth: Letters 1961–1968*, Geoffrey W. Bromiley ed. (Grand Rapids, MI: Eerdmans, 1981), pp. 174–5; cited in Reist, "Commencement," p. 195.

to have painfully pasted his name on its own *futurism.*"[29] Instead, he adds, "we must concentrate strictly on the one thing by which Christian eschatology distinguishes itself from all other possible eschatologies, on the *one* person, the *new* person, in whom God 'was and is and is to come' (Rev. 4:8)."[30]

It is not difficult to transfer Barth's concerns to the preoccupations of evangelical futurism. Typically, North American evangelical eschatology, spiritually linked as it is to free market economies, is not focused on the utopian socialist or ecological dreams[31] fueled by Moltmann's hope, but on the apocalyptic movement of nations in the strategic maneuvering leading up to Armageddon. A typical Moltmann book title is *Creating a Just Future: The Politics of Peace and the Ethics of Creation in a Threatened World.*[32] The premillennial dispensational counterpart is John Walvoord's *Armageddon, Oil and the Middle East,*[33] published just as the First Gulf War was getting off the ground. What they have in common is a preoccupation with this-worldly *futurism;* what both lose sight of is the centrality of Jesus the Christ as *the* one eschatological reality that really counts. We now need to go on to consider exactly what the key eschatological dimension of Jesus Christ really is. Who is the Jesus who is the heart of Christian eschatology?

2. Jesus is Victor

Not only must Jesus Christ be at the heart of Christian eschatology, the christological-eschatological trumpet note must be triumphant—Jesus is Victor! Donald Bloesch has signaled this theme as the

---

29 In a letter to Dr. Tjarko Stadland (1967) in *Karl Barth: Letters 1961–1968*, p. 235, cited in Reist, "Commencement," p. 196; emphasis on *futurism* is also Reist's.

30 Reist, "Commencement," p. 196.

31 See here, e.g. Jürgen Moltmann's *God in Creation: A New Theology of Creation and the Spirit of God*, Margaret Kohl tr. (San Francisco, CA: Harper & Row, 1985) as the ecological replacement for his earlier socialist hope, notably in *The Crucified God.*

32 Published in London (SCM) and Philadelphia (Trinity Press International), 1989. Other titles in the same vein: *The Future of Creation*, Margaret Kohl tr. (Philadelphia: Fortress, 1979), and *God in Creation: A New Theology of Creation and the Spirit of God* (San Francisco, CA: Harper & Row, 1985).

33 Grand Rapids, MI: Zondervan, 1991.

defining note of Barth's soteriology.[34] Before we consider briefly how Barth understands the victory of Jesus Christ, we note again that it is this note of victory that is curiously missing from most popular evangelical eschatologies today. This non-reality of the kingdom *now* is a defining doctrine of dispensational premillennialism. For example, Lewis Sperry Chafer teaches that though the kingdom of God was *announced* by John the Baptist and by Jesus himself, because the offer of the kingdom was *rejected*, it was "postponed until Christ returns." To the degree that we can speak at all of the kingdom today, it must be in the form of a "mystery." In fact, "Not until the millennium will the kingdom come to realization."[35]

This postponement of the kingdom can lead to a defeatist attitude about life in the world. In the words of another popular Hal Lindsey book of a previous generation, *Satan is Alive and Well on Planet Earth*.[36] Here we run into what seems on the face of it to be a profound internal contradiction in significant segments of evangelical Christianity that is committed to dispensational premillennialism. The contradiction involves the role of spiritual gifts in the church age today. The logic of dispensational premillennialism leads to restricting the extraordinary gifts (tongue speaking, healing, exorcism) to the apostolic era and, perhaps to the consummation of the age.

Thus the Doctrinal Statement of Dallas Theological Seminary, the flagship school of dispensational premillennialism, states that "some gifts of the Holy Spirit such as speaking in tongues and miraculous healing are temporary . . . [and] that deliverance of the body from sickness or death awaits the consummation of our salvation in the resurrection."[37] Many dispensationalists, therefore, repudiate the Pentecostal and Charismatic movements of the twentieth century on grounds similar to those by which they reject post-millennial notions: There are certain expectations that are not appropriate

---

[34] Donald G. Bloesch, *Jesus is Victor! Karl Barth's Doctrine of Salvation* (Nashville: Abingdon, 1976).

[35] Lewis Sperry Chafer, *Systematic Theology* vol. V (Grand Rapids, MI: Kregel, 1993), pp. 333–58; a summary statement is provided in VII, pp. 223–4.

[36] With C. C. Carlson (Grand Rapids, MI: Zondervan, 1972).

[37] Dallas Theological Seminary, "Doctrinal Statement," Article XII, "The Holy Spirit," available online at http://www.dts.edu/aboutdts/fulldoctrinalstatement.aspx. Also see next note.

to the church age.[38] Where this becomes interesting and confusing is the fact that Pentecostal and Charismatic Christians tend to dispensational premillennial eschatology too, joining their non-charismatic brothers and sisters in a common rejection of all preterist eschatologies, eschatologies that claim that many of the prophecies of Scripture were fulfilled in Christ and the early church, and that the kingdom of God is a *present* as well as future reality.[39]

My interest in this essay is not to explore the various permutations of dispensational eschatology but to focus on the cessationist position in its more classic form. What intrigues me is that Barth's emphasis on Jesus is Victor, as part of his exposition of the work of Christ as *prophet*, was inspired by J. C. Blumhardt, who took it from what Barth himself calls "a curious source," the exorcism of a young woman, Gottliebin Dittus.[40] Barth's fascination with Blumhardt is reflected in the fact that, with some initial embarrassment about the choice, Barth included a full chapter on the preacher in his study of nineteenth-century theology.[41] And, *mirabile dictu*, Barth's affirmation of Blumhardt centers on significant *experiences* of

---

[38] See the illuminating two-volume autobiographical account of former Dallas Seminary professor Jack Deere, *Surprised by the Power of the Spirit* (Grand Rapids, MI: Zondervan, 1993), and *Surprised by the Voice of God* (Grand Rapids: Zondervan, 1996), where he rejects his former cessationist position and embraces the charismatic movement, especially in its "Third Wave."

[39] To complicate matters even more, there are also "charismatic preterists," i.e. Christians who accept the reality of current Pentecostal experience *and* hold to a covenantal/kingdom eschatology that is amillennial or postmillennial. See, e.g., the website http:www.preteristvision.org and the links provided there. Any full and balanced treatment of dispensational premillennialism would also have to take into account the shift within the tradition itself to the new progressive dispensationalism, an attempt by younger dispensational theologians to incorporate key elements of covenant theology, including a greater emphasis on the present character of the kingdom. See Craig L. Blaising and Darrell L. Bock, *Progressive Dispensationalism* (Grand Rapids, MI: Baker, 1991); Robert L. Saucy, *The Case for Progressive Dispensationalism: The Interface between Dispensational and Non-Dispensational Theology* (Grand Rapids, MI: Zondervan, 1993).

[40] Barth, *CD*, IV/3.1, p. 169.

[41] Karl Barth, *Protestant Theology in the Nineteenth Century: Its Background and History* (Valley Forge, PA: Judson Press, 1972), ch. 28, pp. 643–53. In defense of including Blumhardt, Barth appeals to the need

spiritual power. Believing the girl Gottliebin Dittus to be possessed by a demon, Blumhardt concluded that Jesus himself could directly heal, and that he as her pastor could do nothing but pray. Barth describes the matter as follows:

> The end of the struggle was the complete healing of the girl. Jesus *was* the conqueror. For Blumhardt in the midst of Pietism this breakthrough represented a quite unpietistic discovery and recognition. The contrast was not between Jesus and the unconverted heart of man, but between Jesus and the real power of darkness in which man finds himself. This was what the struggle was about, and it was here that Jesus proved victorious.[42]

This healing of Gottliebin Dittus was followed the next year by a general revival in Blumhardt's congregation and the area about, with people coming unbidden to confess their sins and ask for absolution. In Barth's words: "The healing of Gottliebin Dittus, which was followed by countless other striking events of this nature, had for both pastor and congregation the significance of a sign in the synoptic sense of the word. From it was aroused and seen once again the reality and concreteness of the power to forgive sins contained in the imminent approach of the kingdom of God."[43]

As Blumhardt, and later his son Christoph, continued the ministry of healing at Bad Boll in Southern Germany, he wrestled mightily with the profound human questions of suffering and hope, of promise and deliverance. Barth formulates the question eloquently: "Is it a tolerable theological notion that two thousand years ago the glory of God was proclaimed over the power of darkness by signs and wonders, while today patient resignation in the power of darkness is to be the last word? For Blumhardt this was intolerable. Jesus Christ the same yesterday and today. So he takes up the struggle with need in the name of Jesus."[44]

---

for "academic theology . . . to become unacademic if it is not to become immaterial . . . Theology must not be pedantically exact down to the last detail and at any price, but must also tolerate alongside itself the free, relaxed character of the knowledge and discourse of a Blumhardt. Indeed it can incorporate him within the framework of its own work" (pp. 643–4).

42 Barth, *Protestant Theology*, pp. 644–5.

43 Barth, *Protestant Theology*, p. 645.

44 Barth, *Protestant Theology*, p. 649.

Barth concludes his sketch by noting that Blumhardt's contribution was to raise "the question of theodicy, of the universality of revelation and grace, of the practical significance of the New Testament miracles, of the unity of soul and body, of the real power of reconciliation, of the character and presence of the Holy Spirit and the reality of Christian hope."[45] Though some of this came packaged in "scandalous notions," such as Blumhardt's intense belief in the imminent return of Christ[46] in his pastoral work, Barth concludes that Blumhardt's raising key questions "in a pastoral way and not academically . . . [nonetheless] brought the insight that there was something decisive to be learnt here—for academic theology."[47]

And that, it seems to me, is exactly the point to be made for evangelical eschatology. It is not necessary to validate everything claimed by the twentieth-century Pentecostal and Charismatic movements to acknowledge still that we have witnessed an outpouring of eschatological power, an outpouring that cannot be ignored as evangelical theologians reflect on the work of the Holy Spirit and the actual transformations that have taken place in individual persons and communities, changes attributed to the power of Christ's Spirit. If the exegesis of Scripture does not convince dispensationalists that the kingdom of God is a present as well as future reality, one not to be relegated to a future age beyond the present kingdom-less church age, then at least the experiences of Holy Spirit power ought to raise questions. Evangelical eschatology needs to follow Barth in taking seriously that the eschatological power of Christ has been and is being manifested in our age. *Jesus is Victor!*

3. The threefold form of the *Parousia*

The Jesus who is triumphant is also the *present* and *coming* one. The *parousia* as an important theme in Barth's writing goes back to

[45] Barth, *Protestant Theology*, p. 652.

[46] "There is a credible tradition that at Bad Boll a coach was kept ready, year in, year out, with all its equipment, ready to begin the journey to the Holy Land to meet the returning Christ, if need be" (Barth, *Protestant Theology*, p. 647).

[47] Barth, *Protestant Theology*, pp. 652–3.

the second edition of his *Römerbrief*.[48] There it functioned primarily as indicating a future reality and the absolute end of the world.

> Standing on the boundary of time men are confronted by the overhanging precipitous wall of God, by which all time and everything that is in time is dissolved. There it is that they await the Last Hour, the Parousia of Christ.[49]

For Barth, the end time, the eschatological reality, must be seen in three distinct stages or forms.

He objects to relating the notion of eschatological "merely to the final stage of the *parousia*. Eschatological denotes the last time. The last time is the time of the world and human history and all men to which a term is already set in the death of Jesus and which can only run toward this appointed end. In the Easter event as the commencement of this new coming of Jesus Christ in revelation of what took place in his life and death, it is also revealed that the time which is still left to the world and human history and all men can only be the last time, i.e., time running toward its appointed end."[50]

The Easter event is the pre-eminent *parousia*, the paradigmatic return, coming, and presence of Christ. According to Barth, "it is not merely possible but imperative that what took place in the Easter event, the fresh coming of Jesus Christ as the One who came before, should be summed up under the New Testament concept of the *parousia* of Jesus Christ."[51] By *parousia* Barth understands "in the pregnant technical sense, namely, the effective presence of Jesus Christ." This coming is, for Barth, a unified event though it comes in three distinct forms, forms that are not to be seen in ordinary time as three different dates:

> According to the New Testament, the return of Jesus Christ in the Easter event is not yet as such His return in the Holy Ghost and certainly not His return at the end of the days. Similarly his return in the Easter event and at the end of the days cannot be dissolved into His return in

---

[48] For a thorough overview of the *parousia* theme in Barth's thought see Rajaonarivony, "Transcendence and History," pp. 146–62.

[49] Barth, *Romans*, p. 500.

[50] Barth, *CD*, IV/3/1, p. 295.

[51] Barth, *CD*, IV/3/1, p. 292.

the Holy Ghost, not the Easter event and the outpouring of the Holy Spirit into His last coming. In all these we have to do with the one new coming of Him who came before.[52]

It is the Easter event that provides the basic unity of the *parousia* in all three modes:

There can be no question that in all its forms the one totality of coming again does really have the character, colors and accents of the Easter event. There can be no question that this is only the first if also the original form of this one totality.[53]

We do not have the space in this essay to explore all the details of Barth's *parousia* understanding in its three forms of Easter, Pentecost, and Consummation.[54] For Barth, its unity is finally found in the perichoretic unity of the triune God himself. God's essence is to be found in his act of reconciling the world in Christ, a reconciling work that takes place during the *parousia*, a work that is also intimately tied to the characteristic work of each person in the trinity as Creator, Reconciler, and Redeemer.[55] The distinctions within the Godhead in terms of function must be maintained as well as their unity. Barth speaks of

. . . the threeness of the revealer, revelation, and being revealed, the threeness of God's holiness, mercy and love, the threeness of Good Friday, Easter, and Whitsunday, the threeness of God the Creator, the Reconciler, and God the Redeemer.[56]

In the same way that the works of the one triune God, though attributed to each person, are still unified thanks to the perichoretic mutuality of Father, Son and Holy Spirit, so too, according to Barth,

when we treat of the unity of the three forms or stages of the one event of the return of Jesus Christ, it is perhaps worth considering and

---

52 Barth, *CD*, IV/3/1, p. 294.
53 Barth, *CD*, IV/3/1, p. 294.
54 For a thorough treatment see Rajaonarivony, "Transcendence and History," ch. IV.
55 Rajaonarivony, "Transcendence and History," pp. 175–7.
56 Barth, *CD*, I/1, pp. 361–2.

exegetically helpful, again in the analogy of the doctrine of the Trinity, to think of their mutual relationship as a kind of "perichoresis."[57]

Again, we do not need to join Barth in the full measure of his trinitarian speculation to appreciate that the notion of a threefold *parousia*, the effective coming and presence of Christ as a past and present reality as well as a future reality, provides us with a solid biblically based, kingdom-oriented perspective that is far superior to the futuristic speculation of dispensational premillennialism. By directing us to the presence of the victorious Christ *now*, this emphasis helps us to stay way from the kind of escapism that often accompanies evangelical futurism. The one question that might be raised at this point, after we have now struck a threefold blow at eschatological futurism is, how does the future then function in Barth's eschatology?[58] This is an all the more pressing question since a number of critics, notably Richard Roberts,[59] contend that Barth's eschatology is purely transcendental because the Eternal is so pervasive that contingent temporality is obliterated.[60] So, then what about the future?

---

[57] Barth, *CD*, IV/3/1, p. 296.

[58] This question receives a heightened urgency if the thesis of Jean Rajaonaravony, namely, that Barth's eschatology is a sophisticated version of amillennial transcendentalism, is correct. See especially chapter 2 of "Transcendence and History."

[59] Roberts's *A Theology on its Way*, includes two essays published earlier as "Karl Barth's Doctrine of Time: Its Nature and Implications," in *Karl Barth: Studies of his Theological Method*, S. W. Sykes ed. (Oxford, UK: Clarendon Press, 1979), pp. 88–146; and "The Ideal and the Real in the Theology of Karl Barth," in *New Studies in Theology*, I, Stephen Sykes and Derek Holmes eds. (London: Duckworth, 1980), pp. 163–80.

[60] This is also the contention of Jürgen Moltmann, *The Coming of God: Christian Eschatology*, Margaret Kohl tr. (Minneapolis: Fortress, 1996). Moltmann contends that in Barth's eschatology of the "eternal moment now"—*nunc aeternum*—the tension between already and not yet is gone and is replaced by the tension between eternity and time. In conclusion: "If eschaton means eternity and not End-time, then eschatology has no longer anything to do with the future either" (pp. 14–15). It should be noted that G. C. Berkouwer (*The Triumph of Grace*) and Philip Rosato (*The Spirit as Lord*) also judge that the future is a problematic matter in Barth's thinking but they consider the problem to be more of an epistemological one: because the Future's outcome is already an ontological reality in Jesus Christ, the only truly temporally future thing is noetic; we shall come to know what is already the case. As John C. McDowell notes, "The

4. *Theologia Viatorum*

The best explicit answer can be found in a key Barthian theme, *theologia viatorum*. Barth's theology of the Word is radically actual; God's Word can never be possessed or restricted; one can never say, "lo here" or "lo there" about the Word of God, not even about the Bible. God's Word, as Barth already contended in his *Göttingen Dogmatics* "is to be regarded as a living, actual, and present factor, the Word of God which now both is and should be proclaimed and heard . . . The Word of God is God speaking. It is ongoing as Christian preaching. It is not ongoing as revelation in the strict sense. It never took place as such. Nor is God's Word ongoing as Holy Scripture. It is in time as such . . . But as Christian preaching, which proceeds from revelation and Scripture (as the Holy Spirit proceeds from the Father and the Son), the Word of God is ongoing. It is present."[61] Furthermore, this Word, too, comes in three forms, as revelation, Scripture, and preaching—"it is one in three and three in one."[62] All proclamation is given guidance and direction by the church's dogmas "which set up border-posts and anchor buoys. They tell us what will do and what will not do, what we may say and what we may not say if what we say is to be Christian preaching."[63]

From this it can be seen that both preaching and dogma itself are eschatological realities.[64] Dogmatic theology, must, like the proclamation it serves, be provisional, on the way. Gerhard Sauter contends, "even to this day," that with the notion of dogma as eschatological, "the uniqueness of [Barth's] theological work is best expressed, namely that dogmatics can only be an approximation of the truth of theology *by God*. Theology is and remains *theologia*

---

theme that pervades all of these studies is that Barth tends to subsume all reality and contingency within a christological matrix, so that they lose their existence" (*Hope in Barth's Eschatology*, p. 41). We do not have space here to enter into all these objections but, after summarizing Barth's position, will return briefly to Roberts' critique.

[61] Karl Barth, *The Göttingen Dogmatics: Instruction in the Christian Religion*, vol. 1 (Grand Rapids, MI: Eerdmans, 1991), pp. 15–16.

[62] Barth, *Göttingen Dogmatics*, p. 14ff.

[63] Barth, *Göttingen Dogmatics*, pp. 17–18.

[64] For an extended treatment of Barth's eschatological view of dogma, see Gerhard Sauter, "Dogma—ein eschatologischer Begriff," in *Parrhesia: Karl Barth zum Actzigsten Geburtstag* (Zürich: EVZ, 1966), pp. 173–91.

viatorum: it must always be present, if God is to come to word in its speaking."[65] God's coming is thus always in the form of promise, promise proclaimed in preaching.

Does this actualism have a real future *in time*? Barth addresses this question directly in an early essay, "The Problem of Ethics," delivered to a conference of ministers in Wiesbaden in September 1922.[66] Barth begins by posing the riddle of human existence as one in which we have no choice but to live and make ethical choices. "We live from moment to moment. And living means *doing*, even when doing means doing nothing." As we strive for a goal that will help order our life's choices, we come face to face with the question of the ultimate goal. Barth describes this with wondrous prose: "Every random and temporal 'What shall we do?' contains a 'What' to which no random and temporal 'That' can give a satisfying answer, because it is a last and eternal 'What.' And with the question, the crisis in our lives continues, and with the crisis, our relationship to God. We *live* in this relationship."[67] After then traveling lightly through the post-Kant years of liberal protestantism which "invested [human] effort" with a heavenly light, Barth startles the reader: "but to us that light is darkness," and cites the Letter to the Hebrews: "it is a fearful thing to fall into the hands of the living God."[68]

We are, says Barth (in 1922!), in a new situation and "it is foolish to go on talking with glibness and certainty as if nothing had happened. The era of the *old* ethics is *gone* forever. Whoever now desires certainty must first of all become *uncertain*. And whoever desires to speak must first of all be *silent*. For something *has* happened . . . over against man's confidence and belief in himself, there has been written, in huge proportions and with utmost clearness, a *mene mene tekel*."[69] Where does Barth then go? To millenarian thinking.[70]

---

65 Sauter, "Not a Theology of Hope," p. 412.

66 Karl Barth, "The Problem of Ethics Today," in *The Word of God and the Word of Man* (New York: Harper Torchbook, 1957 [1928]), pp. 136–82. Page references that follow in the text are to the Torchbook edition.

67 Barth, "Ethics," p. 141. It is hard not to ask the mischievous question whether this little catechism is not in fact a piece of natural theology; a correlational introduction of human questions to which only a divine answer can be given.

68 Barth, "Ethics," p. 149.

69 Barth, "Ethics," p. 149.

70 Barth, "Ethics," p. 157.

This is surprising, as Barth himself acknowledges, for millennialism is profoundly this-worldly, appealing to socialists (among whom Barth counts himself) as well as Kantians, as a salvation *in time*. How can this apparent contradiction be reconciled; why does Barth, even while responding to liberal Protestantism, react so strongly to the Lutheran repudiation[71] of Anabaptist millenarianism? Barth attempts to bring this all together by turning millennial hope into a promise of God's acting that sustains and motivates believers to action in the world today. We do not grasp what does not belong to us,[72] and though resting on this promise may appear to be "a mere play on words"[73] our only avenue is to accept the *judgment* of God and rely on his *grace*.[74] Above all, it means accepting the provisionality of our knowledge, our ability to understand God and his ways. "We shall have to reckon with the possibility that our thought may fall short of what we mean it to be. We have no way, of ourselves, of capturing *truth*. We are not capable of making *reality* correspond to what we say when we repeat the Pauline paradoxes. *God* alone can do that."[75]

In his discussion of preaching the Word of God in the *Church Dogmatics*, I/2, the provisional, anticipatory, promissory—and therefore eschatological—character of Barth's thought receives among its most eloquent articulations.[76] Preaching is a "human impossibility, the impossibility of the attempt to speak of God" (p. 750). But the church and the preacher live in hope. "If there is proclamation, if the attempt does not fail, it is just at the point where success is achieved that it can and will be understood, not as a human success, but as a divine victory concealed in human failure, sovereignly availing itself of human failure." This is never a necessity, it cannot be self-explanatory, "it can only be hoped by faith in the foundation which God himself has laid for the Church, that is, by faith in Jesus Christ" (p. 751).

The preaching task, rooted in dogmatics, must also be cognizant of the need for "pure doctrine;" pure doctrine is "a duty laid upon the church" to ensure the faithfulness of its proclamation (p. 768).

---

71 Barth, "Ethics," pp. 147, 160.
72 Barth, "Ethics," p. 177.
73 Barth, "Ethics," pp. 175–6.
74 Barth, "Ethics," p. 178.
75 Barth, "Ethics," pp. 176–7.
76 The page references which follow in the text are to *CD*, I/2, "The Doctrine of the Word of God."

This does not happen through the church's codification of doctrine and maintaining legal subscription to it—which would be to attempt to nail down the living Word of God—but it happens as an act, as an event. "If by the grace of the Word of God it happens that the human word of Christian proclamation is pure doctrine, it does not happen in a static situation, but as an action of faith and obedience, an action of the Holy Ghost in the church. Pure doctrine is a deed, not a thing—not even a matter of thoughts and words. Therefore pure doctrine is not identical with any existing text—whether it is that of specific theological formulae, or that of a separate theological system; or that of the Church's creed, or even the text of the Bible. Pure doctrine is an event—a fulfillment of the promise given to the Church" (p. 768).

Finally, when Barth then moves on to speak of the relation between dogmatics and ethics, he sets aside all formulations which make the link a human responsibility. The only ethical task of the church is to listen to the Word of God, to be freshly renewed by the "promise which is the basis of the Church and its message" (p. 806). The church has the promise "that Jesus Christ wills to be present in its midst and to speak through it" and that is the only way the church can and should attempt to be "a light unto the world." "To give effect to this promise and to be this church is its only duty, as well as the only necessity of its life. It is, then, the only law by which it must judge itself" (p. 806). Methodologically, this means that dogmatics resists neat and full systematization (p. 872). When push comes to shove "dogmatics must actually be Christology and only Christology" but not in any narrow sense. "Jesus Christ is given to us as the Word spoken by the Father." Dogmatics is "the call to the Church to venture what must be ventured, what in view of the promise given to the Church ought not to remain unventured" (p. 884). This "human impossibility" nonetheless becomes a possibility when ventured modestly (p. 868) with full awareness "of the necessary limits of human creaturely knowledge" (p. 878).

From this summary description, it is not surprising that Richard Roberts finds the Barth of the *Church Dogmatics* inadequately pursuing a *theologia viatorum*. An Eternal Now is not the most promising guide for a pilgrimage *in time*. At the same time it is also important to note what Roberts himself means by such a theology "on the way." Roberts situates the theology of the early Barth in the Weimar Republic, in the "intoxicating combination of nihilism and eschatological consciousness . . . This was the age under the sign of Nietzsche."[77] At issue during this time was a twofold crisis: the dissolution of the subject and the crisis of language itself. Roberts contends that the early Barth—the Barth of the two *Römerbrief*—prophetically engaged the cultural crisis represented by Weimar and "taken together as a single intertextual whole constitute the richest and most important theological work of the twentieth century."[78] The God we encounter in these texts is "a God whom we cannot predefine; He is to us from the future; he stands in judgment upon the *theological* articulations that we inherit from the past."[79] In short, the Barth of the *Römerbrief* is a postmodern theologian, the theology articulated "is first and foremost an atheology . . . the deconstruction they propound is no mere criticism of religion as such . . . but a deconstruction of both 'God' and 'subjectivity.'"[80] In other words, the Barth of the *Römerbrief* is more like Thomas Altizer of the radical "Death of God" theology than say Luther or Calvin. *Theologia viatorum* here becomes nothing less that the celebration of a-theism in the name of modesty and epistemological humility.

This attempt to capture Barth for postmodern atheology will not fly. While there is plenty of room for a critique of Barth's understanding of time and eternity, it must not be overlooked that Barth himself was quite aware that some eschatological visions produce passivity in believers. He judged that to be the case for excessively futurist eschatologies. "Now there have been many and varied attempts to fix Christian expectation so exclusively on the ultimate dénouement that a hopeless view is taken of penultimate developments."[81] While penultimate goals are just that—penultimate—and to be set aside, this does not mean passivity or indifference to them. "Yet no one should imagine, or proclaim to the world as the way of Christian hope, that prior to the goal and end regard should be had only to the ultimate dénouement and not to penultimate developments."[82] Barth is even quite eloquent about the importance of penultimate, provisional and temporal human action, in words that evangelical dispensationalists should heed:

---

77 Roberts, *A Theology on its Way?*, p. 171.
78 Roberts, *A Theology on its Way?*, p. 197.
79 Roberts, *A Theology on its Way?*, p. 197.
80 Roberts, *A Theology on its Way?*, p. 197.
81 Barth, *CD*, IV/3/2, p. 936.
82 Barth, *CD*, IV/3/2, p. 936.

> The Christian hopes as he serves, and as he thus expects provisional and temporal encouragement, equipment and direction for his service. He expects those feeble lights as lights on his temporal way. And because he expects them in intimation of the great light, he will not sit down waiting for something to come and snatch him away, but will manfully go forward hoping for the concrete help needed to enable him to do so. In this respect, too, Christian existence is existence in movement. Hope takes place in the act of taking the next step.[83]

When we keep in mind that Barth also has a strong divine command ethics, focused on Jesus Christ,[84] it does not seem fair to dismiss Barth's ethics as utterly transcendent and otherworldly. John Webster's judgment is more balanced and to the point:

> To hope is not simply to wait, but to be impelled in a very definite direction, stemming from and looking towards the great consummation of Jesus' perfect work. Thus language about Christian hope does not mean some eschatological suppression of the ethical; rather it involves a description of the world as a reality whose situation has been so transfigured by God's act in Jesus Christ that hopeful human action is both possible and necessary.[85]

Similarly, appealing to Barth's own political involvement, George Hunsinger makes this observation about Barth's social ethics and politics:

> This thoroughgoing political involvement means that it is fundamentally false to portray Barth as a theologian who did his thinking in monkish isolation from the world . . . He took the world as seriously as he took the Bible. His thinking moved from praxis to theology as well as from theology to praxis. [In addition] it is as fundamentally false to suppose that there is no conceptual link between Barth's theology and his politics

---

[83] Barth, *CD*, IV/3/2, pp. 938–9.

[84] "Who the commanding God is and who responsible man is . . . is not hidden from us but is revealed and may be known in the one Jesus Christ: God and man . . ." *The Christian Life* (*Church Dogmatics* IV/4 – *Lecture Fragments*), Geoffrey W. Bromiley tr. (Grand Rapids, MI: Eerdmans, 1981), p. 5.

[85] John W. Webster, *Barth's Moral Theology* (Edinburgh, UK: T&T Clark, 1998), p. 81.

[86] George Hunsinger ed. and tr., *Karl Barth and Radical Politics* (Philadelphia: Westminster, 1976), p. 224.

> as it is to suppose that his theology leads to political complacency. The relationship between theology and politics in Barth's mature thought is formally analogical, materially socialist, and existentially actualist.[86]

In conclusion, once again, it is not necessary to adopt all of Barth's theological grounding for his theology of proclamation—e.g. the trinitarian basis of the threefold form of the Word of God—to still appreciate the emphasis on pilgrimage, on modesty of theological claims, on the church being more circumspect in its ethical pronouncements to the world. His insistence on a more transcendent notion of the millennium as a judge of all earthly pretensions to utopia sounds much like classic amillennialism.[87] Above all, evangelical eschatology could use a healthy dose of both modesty in its futuristic claims and in emphasizing pilgrimage *now* rather than only as a *telos* in a dispensational time line. This would be in keeping with the position of the Early Church, reflected in such writings as the *Epistle to Diognetus*.

5. Eschatology and pneumatology: an alternative model of human agency

My portrait of Barth's eschatology has, up to this point, been sympathetic and relatively free from critique. This is not because I judge Barth's theology to be without problems for evangelicals. On the contrary. In addition to the problem of universalism noted in the opening section of this essay, it should also be clear to a discerning reader that there are major issues for evangelicals with Barth's doctrine of Scripture. For the purposes of this essay, however, I will only take significant distance from Barth in his christological understanding of human agency. I grant that some of the critique, namely, that human agency disappears in Barth's christomonist vision,[88] is excessive. Nonetheless, it seems to me that it is a serious theological mistake to attempt to understand human agency in christological categories; rather, pneumatology is the proper arena.

I take my cue here from Dutch Reformed theologian Arnold van Ruler (1908–1970), who has pointed out as clearly as anyone

[87] This is the basic thesis of the Ph.D. dissertation by Rajaonarivony, "Transcendence and History."

[88] See the useful Introduction to Webster's *Barth's Moral Theology*.

the key differences between a christological and a pneumatological perspective on salvation.[89] In Christology the focus is on the incarnation and atonement; the *Logos* assumes a human nature and the Mediator's sacrificial death is substitutionary—Christ dies on our behalf (*huper*) and in our place (*anti*). The work of Christ is outside of us (*extra nos*) and has a once-for-all (*eph hapax*) character. The atoning death of the Savior, as the book of Hebrews makes clear, is all-sufficient. However, these christological categories are wholly inapplicable to pneumatology. The Holy Spirit obviously does not become incarnate; the category of *adoption* rather than *assumption* is appropriate here. Furthermore, while the incarnation is specific to the person of Jesus Christ, the work of the Holy Spirit is directed to many human persons, all of whom retain their creaturely identity and personhood. While in the incarnation the *Logos* took on the human nature; in pneumatology by contrast "the focus is not on the human nature but rather on the human person, on me and on you, on the many human persons and on their fellowship, in which the Spirit dwells. *He* dwells within *me* and within *us*. He and I are in no way one and the same but two distinct realities. The person in whom the Spirit comes to dwell does not first of all have to be created but already exists by virtue of creation and birth."[90]

Similarly the category of "substitution" has no place in pneumatology. Though crucial in Christology (underscoring the full reality of God's initiative in grace) so that we can and must say "Christ died for us," we cannot and must not say "Christ believes for us." On the contrary, "It is *we* who believe . . . Faith is a gift and work of the Holy Spirit."[91] Yet, it is *our faith*. For this reason Van Ruler suggests that we must think of a category or categories that underscore the work of God the Holy Spirit *in* us and *together with* us. "One surely cannot say that the Spirit in us prays in our place, or believes in our place, or confesses in our place, or does good works in our place? He converts us, but in such a way that we ourselves are converted."[92] Instead of assumption we must use categories of indwelling and adoption and instead of substitution

[89] Arnold A. Van Ruler, "Structural Differences Between the Christological and Pneumatological Perspectives," in *Calvinist Trinitarianism and Theocentric Politics*, John Bolt tr. (Lewiston, NY: Edwin Mellen, 1989), pp. 27–46. Cf. "Grammar of a Pneumatology," ibid., pp. 47–87.

[90] Ruler, "Structural Differences," p. 32.

[91] Ruler, "Structural Differences," p. 27.

[92] Ruler, "Structural Differences," p. 34.

we must use *reciprocity* according to Van Ruler. In an attempt to do justice to the divine initiative as well as honoring the full involvement of the human person, Van Ruler suggests the term *theonomous reciprocity* concluding: "It is the Spirit that does and gives everything. It is the Spirit, for example who sets our will free so that we obtain a truly free will. Nevertheless, a theonomous reciprocity is still a genuine *reciprocity*. The chief characteristic of the Holy Spirit's work is that it sets us to work."[93] In other words, "In the application of salvation, it is I who have salvation applied to me by the Spirit and in the Spirit, in order that it fully becomes my salvation. Everything hinges on this happening. God's cause must truly become my cause; I repeat God's words as truly mine. That this result takes place is the essence, or, at any rate, the goal of the Spirit's activity."[94] The most explicit scriptural evidence for Van Ruler's notion of theonomous reciprocity may be Romans 8:16: αὐτὸ τὸ πνεῦμα συμμαρτυρεῖ τῷ πνεύματι ἡμῶν ὅτι ἐσμὲν τέκνα θεοῦ. "The Spirit himself testifies that we are God's children."

This perspective is quite different than Barth's. Even as Barth transitions in the *Church Dogmatics* IV/3/1 from Christology ("Jesus is Victor", §69/3) to anthropology/soteriology ("The Promise of the Spirit", §69/4),[95] he remains centered on the christological reality of the atonement. The answer to the human question "is already given in the being and action of Jesus Christ, in the fulfillment of his atoning work, so that we have only to emphasize this afresh, understand it as the answer to our present question. In other words, to find our answer we must turn again to His being and action as such."[96]

My suggestion here is that many of the conundrums that arise from Barth's theology—especially the tension between eternity and time, divine and human action—could be better handled by acknowledging and seriously working with the careful distinction between a christological and pneumatological perspective, and not being restricted to Barth's Christocentrism. The eschatological future is the province of the Holy Spirit who does not exclude our human involvement and work in the coming of the kingdom.

---

[93] Ruler, "Structural Differences," p. 35.

[94] Ruler, "Structural Differences," p. 78.

[95] Barth himself speaks of transitioning from "the christological sphere in the narrower sense" to "the anthropological," which he also describes as "the sphere of our own life and the life of man generally." (*CD*, IV/3/1, pp. 275–6).

[96] Barth, *CD*, IV/3/1, p. 278.

6. Conclusion

It is my contention in this essay that an engagement with Karl Barth's eschatological theology is a useful exercise for evangelicals. Barth helps us focus our own eschatology on Jesus Christ instead of Middle East politics and conspiracy theories involving secular humanism. In addition, he reminds us to consider the present victorious reign of Christ as an encouragement for our own life of pilgrimage on the way. In addition, his threefold form of the *parousia* is a constructive, biblically-based model for thinking about the coming and presence of Christ. Where Barth needs modification on this score, namely, in thinking more pneumatologically about the eschatology, evangelicals also have much to learn, for example in how to take better cognizance of the way in which the Holy Spirit puts us to work. That last point has a great deal to do with evangelicals being able to develop a better theology of Christian vocation.[97]

[97] One good example is Miroslav Volf. Commonalities with respect to a doctrine of vocation also exist between John Calvin (see *Commentary* on Psalm 127; *Institutes;* and John Paul II's encyclical *Laborem Exercens*).

11

Karl Barth and the Theology of Religions

Veli-Matti Kärkkäinen

1. Various interpretations of Barth's view of religions

Interpretations of Karl Barth's attitude toward other religions radically differ from one another, to the point that it is very difficult to determine to which theology of religions camp he belongs.[1] The Korean-American theologian Paul S. Chung, who has studied Barth

1 For basic concepts and issues in the contemporary theology of religions, see Veli-Matti Kärkkäinen, *An Introduction to the Theology of Religions: Biblical, Historical & Contemporary Perspectives* (Downers Grove, IL: InterVarsity Press, 2003). Typologies are still in the making; the most widely used is that of exclusivism (to be saved, one needs to respond to the gospel offered by Christian proclamation), inclusivism (while Christ is the only Savior, in order to be saved one does not necessarily need to have a faith response when that is not possible); and pluralism (all religions are basically equal ways of salvation). With all the critique against its limitations, for a general survey like this one, this typology is still useful at least heuristically and pedagogically. In my own book (following the Catholic Jacques Dupuis), I name these ecclesiocentrism, Christocentrism, and Theocentrism. Instead of using the term *exclusivism*, which easily becomes a pejorative term, here I prefer the term *particularism*, denoting the traditional Christian view according to which salvation entails a (personal) response of faith to the gospel offered by the proclamation of the church. For an interesting and promising new typology, see Paul F. Knitter, *Introducing Theologies of Religions* (Maryknoll, NY: Orbis, 2002).

extensively from the perspective of Asian Buddhism and religions,[2] puts it succinctly:

> Karl Barth has long been regarded as a staunch evangelical-conservative theologian in his attitude toward non-Christian religions . . . According to Paul Knitter, Barth's view of other religions is exclusivistic because he does not believe a common ground can be found and also because he emphasizes revelation in Christ over against religions. In fact, Barth's theology is often regarded as outmoded and inappropriate with respect to the reality of religious pluralism.[3]

Chung's own assessment of Barth, however, differs radically from this standard exclusivistic view: "To the contrary, Barth's theology presents within itself a structure or radical openness toward the world. These aspects have been overlooked and his so-called Christocentrism has been unilaterally misunderstood as an antireligious and anticultural stronghold. Therefore . . . I attempt to rehabilitate Barth's world-open theology in view of the reality of religious pluralism."[4]

So, obviously, there are at least two schools when it comes to assessing Karl Barth's views regarding other religions: the traditional view which labels him more or less exclusivistic and the newer view which attempts to see him as a sort of pluralist. An evangelical assessment of Barth's significance to the theology of religions requires

---

[2] See further Paul S. Chung, "Karl Barth and Religious Pluralism: A Conflict?" in *Theology between East and West: A Radical Heritage: Essays in Honor of Jan Milic Lochman*, Frank D. Macchia and Paul S. Chung eds. (Eugene, OR: Wipf & Stock, 2002), pp. 35–58; Chung, *Martin Luther and Buddhism: Aesthetics of Suffering* (Eugene, OR: Wipf & Stock, 2002), which includes extensive discussion of Barth's theology, too, in relation to Asian religions and spiritualities. For a somewhat different reading of Barth through an Asian lens, see Pan-chiu Lai, "Barth's Theology of Religion and the Asian Context of Religious Pluralism," *Asia Journal of Theology* 15: 2 (2001), pp. 247–67.

[3] Paul S. Chung, "Karl Barth and Religious Pluralism—Reading Barth through the Lens of Asian Religions," *Theology News and Notes* 52: 1 (Winter 2005), p. 10; see also his "Karl Barth and Religious Pluralism: A Conflict?" p. 36; on p. 44 he complains: "Karl Barth has been deeply misunderstood because of his early overemphasis on the revelation in Jesus Christ (so-called *Offenbarungspositivismus*) on the one hand, and his attachment to the theology of the Word of God on the other."

[4] Chung, "Asian Religions": 10.

a careful look at these two schools of interpretation followed by a return to Barth's own writings to look at the evidence.

As mentioned above, the view of Barth as a "staunch evangelical" exclusivist has been the commonplace.[5] Knitter summarizes the exclusivistic attitude of Barth toward other religions with the help of four famous Protestant "alones." First, we are saved by grace alone, which Barth simply picked up from the New Testament. According to Knitter, for Barth "human beings are in a mess, and they can't get out of this mess by themselves. They're stuck. Biblical or theological terms to describe this state are 'original sin' or 'fallen nature.'"[6] Second, we are saved by faith alone, which is the negative flip-side of "not by works." To put one's trust anywhere else than God who justifies the sinner, Barth would say, leads nowhere. Third, we are saved by Christ alone: "It is in Jesus Christ, and only in him that God has acted and revealed the true nature of things—that God is ready to love us, affirm us, and rescue us purely out of divine love, not because we deserve it or have merited it."[7] It is about God's grace. Fourth, according to Knitter's interpretation, Barth contends we are saved by Scripture alone since Christ "is *revelation* in the truest sense of the word . . ."[8] Furthermore, Knitter points to the fact that Barth speaks of religion as "unbelief."[9] Moreover, while Barth included Christian *religion* under the critique of religions in general, he still believed that Christian faith is the true religion—but only because of Christ; it has nothing whatsoever to do with either Christians or their religions per se.[10]

---

[5] Paul F. Knitter has discussed Barth's theology of religions in many places beginning from his doctoral work at Marburg University in the early 1970s; see Knitter, *Towards a Protestant Theology of Religions: A Case Study of Paul Althaus and Contemporary Attitudes*, Marburger Theologische Studien (Marburg: N. G. Elwert, 1974), pp. 20–36. A more accessible discussion of Barth can be found in Knitter, *No Other Name? A Critical Survey of Christian Attitudes Toward the World Religions* (Maryknoll, NY: Orbis, 1985), pp. 80–7. Knitter's newest book, *Theologies* (pp. 23–31) is a good place to start with this standard view of Barth.

[6] Knitter, *Theologies*, p. 24.

[7] Knitter, *Theologies*, p. 24.

[8] Knitter, *Theologies*, p. 25 (italics his).

[9] Knitter, *Theologies*, p. 25, with reference to Barth, *CD*, I/2, pp. 299–300.

[10] Knitter, *Theologies*, p. 26.

This interpretation of Barth's view of religions offered by the leading American Catholic theologian of religions is the standard view of Barth among evangelicals. A quick look at even the newest works by evangelicals affirms it.[11] It is not only evangelicals who have taken Barth as a major advocate of an exclusivistic view; this used to be the hallmark of interpretations also among mainline Protestant and Catholic writers.[12]

Knitter is of course aware of the fact that recently the exclusivistic view has been challenged. Yet even in his newest book, from 2002, he just mentions (in a footnote!) the fact that this view is based on Barth's early views and that later Barth came to speak of "other lights" outside of the Light. However, two reasons push Knitter to continue presenting Barth as an exclusivist: first, it is the early views

---

[11] Winfried Corduan, *A Tapestry of Faiths: The Common Threads Between Christianity & World Religions* (Downers Grove, IL: InterVarsity Press, 2002), p. 27 (see also p. 31, n. 1); Gerald R. McDermott, *Can Evangelicals Learn from World Religions? Jesus, Revelation & Religious Traditions* (Downers Grove, IL: InterVarsity Press, 2000), pp. 28, 49–50, 53–4. McDermott acknowledges Barth's references to "other lights," but similar to Knitter, does not regard them as implying any kind of pluralism (pp. 108–9). Amos Yong, *Beyond the Impasse: Toward a Pneumatological Theology of Religions* (Grand Rapids, MI: Baker Academic, 2003), mentions Barth as a key influence on evangelical views of religions, yet he makes two important comments to qualify: first, he reminds us of Barth's critique of all religions, including Christianity (p. 23) and, second, he refers to Barth's desire at an older age to develop a pneumatological approach to religions (p. 92). Interestingly enough, two recent major works by evangelical scholars on religions ignore Barth totally even though the subject matter of both is such that Barth could have been an important interlocutor, namely, revelation and salvation, respectively: Timothy C. Tennent, *Christianity at the Religious Roundtable: Evangelicalism in Conversation with Hinduism, Buddhism, and Islam* (Grand Rapids, MI: Baker Academic, 2002) (the two references to the Swiss theologian in the whole book are but illustrations); Terrance L. Tiessen, *Who Can Be Saved? Reassessing Salvation in Christ and World Religions* (Downers Grove, IL/Leicester, England: InterVarsity Press, 2004). (This book of five hundred pages only mentions Barth a couple of times, both from secondary sources, even though it purports to advance a Reformed understanding of the doctrine of salvation in the context of religious pluralism).

[12] For a careful exposition with ample references to original sources as well as balanced critique, see the important article by Peter Harrison, "Karl Barth and the Non-Christian Religions," *Journal of Ecumenical Studies* 23: 2 (Spring 1986), pp. 207–24.

that have had a determinative influence on Protestant attitudes (and one could add, evangelical in particular). Hendrik Kraemer's now classic *The Christian Message in a Non-Christian World* (1938),[13] a staunch defense of a traditional Protestant attitude towards other religions prepared for the famous International Missionary Council's[14] World Conference in Tambara, India, in 1938 is a prime example. Second, according to Knitter, Barth insisted that "'the other words and other lights' could be not heard and seen without Christ."[15]

The newer interpretation of Barth works hard to make his theology of religions appear (more) pluralistic. What are the reasons for this kind of evaluation? There are several. One has to do with changing the focus from early Barth to later Barth, which in fact means reading the earlier parts of the *Church Dogmatics* that seem obviously more exclusivistic in light of some statements in the later parts that seem to qualify the earlier standpoint. The later parts of Barth's magnum opus include references to "secular parables" as well as "lights outside the church." Another resource for opening up Barth's exclusivism is a focus, rather than on revelation, on his Christology, concentrating on election and reconciliation which, again especially in the later parts of the *Church Dogmatics* (especially in volume 4 on Reconciliation), can be seen as speaking for the inclusion of the whole of humanity into the saving work of Christ, thus advocating a kind of soteriological universalism. Furthermore, some students of Barth, including Chung, have made references to his pneumatology as a way to further interfaith dialogue in an unprecedented way. It is well known among the interpreters of Barth that towards the end of his life the Swiss theologian entertained the idea of developing a more fully pneumatological approach to theology in general and to other religions in particular.[16]

---

[13] New York: Harper & Brothers, 1938. For a brief exposition, see Kärkkäinen, *Introduction*, pp. 181–6.

[14] Later: Commission on World Mission and Evangelization of World Council of Churches.

[15] Knitter, *Theologies*, pp. 26–7 n. 11.

[16] Interestingly, Paul Tillich, a contemporary of Barth, also became interested in the pneumatological approach to religions; yet Tillich had already done groundwork for a pneumatological approach in his overall systematic work. For an important discussion by an evangelical/Pentecostal scholar of Tillich's pneumatology in the theology of religions, see Amos Yong, *Discerning the Spirit(s): A Pentecostal–Charismatic Contribution to Christian Theology of Religions* (Sheffield: Sheffield Academic Press, 2000), ch. 3.

Yet another way of negotiating is to refer to the few contacts that Barth had with other religions, mainly with Buddhist traditions. In the *Church Dogmatics* I/2 Barth enters into a brief dialogue with Pure Land Buddhism.[17] The work of the Japanese Katzumi Takizawa has been groundbreaking, and Chung builds on his contributions.[18] I will take up these issues when scrutinizing the relevant portions of Barth's own texts.

So far I have presented two schools of interpretation concerning Barth's theology of religions. These two are extremes. Not all are content with either choice. Trevor Hart has recently suggested a very peculiar kind of reading of Barth's theology of religions, calling it "committed pluralism," a term owing to the late Lesslie Newbigin.[19] Suffice to say that this reading of Barth makes him neither an exclusivist nor a pluralist in the conventional sense of the term, but rather a christocentric theologian who still is open to the possibility of salvation outside of the Christian church but not unrelated to Christ.

In light of this lack of unanimity, what would be the most fruitful way for evangelicals to approach the question of the theology of religions in Barth's theology? In my recent monograph *Trinity and Religious Pluralism* (2004),[20] which took a critical look at the latest "turn" in the theology of religions, namely, the turn to the Trinity, I concluded that Barth is neither exclusivist nor pluralist but rather inconclusive. My conclusion was simply that Barth never resolved the tension between what I call "revelational restrictivism" and "soteriological universalism."[21] My leading observation was that there is a clear bifurcation in the Barthian view of religions:

---

[17] For a helpful exposition and balanced assessment, see Charles T. Waldrop, "Karl Barth and Pure Land Buddhism," *Journal of Ecumenical Studies* 24:4 (Fall 1987), pp. 574–97.

[18] See especially Katzumi Takizawa, "Was hindert mich noch getauft zu warden," in *Das Heil in Heute: Texte einer japanischen Theologie*, Von Theo Sundermeier hrsg. (Göttingen: Vandenhoeck & Ruprecht, 1987). For another Asian engagement with Barth, see Heup Young Kim, *Wang Yang-ming and Karl Barth: A Confucian-Christian Dialogue* (Lanham, MD: University Press of America, 1996).

[19] Trevor Hart, "Karl Barth, the Trinity, and Pluralism," in *The Trinity in a Pluralistic Age: Theological Essays on Culture and Religion*, Kevin Vanhoozer ed. (Grand Rapids, MI: Eerdmans, 1997), p. 139.

[20] Veli-Matti Kärkkäinen, *Trinity and Religious Pluralism: The Doctrine of the Trinity in Christian Theology of Religions* (Aldershot, UK: Ashgate, 2004).

[21] Kärkkäinen, *Trinity*, pp. 13–27.

> There is no denying the fact that Barth represents an unabashed restrictivism toward other religions. But what seriously complicates the picture is that, on the other hand, his Christology and thus soteriology seem to lead him eventually to universalism, the idea that (hardly) anybody will perish at the end. There are also other qualifying perspectives, such as Barth's criticism of Christianity among religions questioning the typical textbook view, according to which for Barth Christianity without qualification is the norm.[22]

What makes the interpretation of Barth's views of religions even more complicated than that of some other topics has to do with the obvious fact that Barth never produced a distinctive theology of religions. The concept of religions per se is not a foreign topic to him; yet he operates with a general concept of religion—which, of course, is a highly debated issue in religious studies—and it is often hard to say how much of that is general critique of religion and how much deals with either specifically Christian religion or other particular religions. The fact that much of his theology, especially in the first part of his career, gets its energy from a vehement reaction to Classical Liberalism could have led him to develop a more nuanced view of religions. The attempt to work towards a more nuanced understanding of religions would have made sense for many reasons, not least because the seeds of contemporary pluralism can be found not only in the Enlightenment in general but in Classical Liberalism in particular.

Without the dramatic change of intellectual and theological climate with the advent of the Quest of the Historical Jesus and the this-worldly orientation of much of Liberalism, pluralistic theologies would never have been able to find their way to the center of Christian theology. Interpretations of Barth are also complicated by what the evangelical interpreter of Barth's theology of religions, Donald Dayton, so succinctly describes: "What Barth takes away with one hand he gives back with the other."[23] Add to the equation the ever-present question of whether—or in what way(s)—Barth's theology changed over the long period of constructive theological work, and you face the major complications of the task of outlining Barthian theology of religions for evangelicals.

---

[22] Kärkkäinen, *Trinity*, pp. 13–14.

[23] Donald W. Dayton, "Karl Barth and Wider Ecumenism," in *Christianity and Wider Ecumenism*, Peter C. Phan ed. (New York: Paragon House, 1990), p. 184.

In what follows, I will discuss critically Barth's theology of religions, trying first to discern the resources that speak for particularist tendencies and, after that, what kind of resources seem to advocate a more open-minded attitude toward religions. Following that investigation—which represents yet another reconstruction of Barth's theology of religions since he never attempted one himself—I will come to the question of Barth's relevance to evangelical theology of religions. I hope my reading of Barth can be described as one that both wants to listen carefully to the dynamic and often tension-filled theological reflection on religions by this great Swiss theologian, and to offer a critical yet appreciative assessment from the vantage point of evangelical theology.

2. Particularist orientations in the Barthian theology of religions

In my reading of Barth's own theology, I see three main motifs that all speak strongly for a particularist tendency. To simplify some very complex issues, let me identify these three in the following way:

1. Trinity as the way to identify the God of the Bible.
2. Christ as the "hourglass" of Christian theology.
3. Revelation in Christ as the only "Christian" concept of revelation.

These motifs, especially 2 and 3, have been extensively referred to by evangelical writers to the point that Barth has been hailed as the hallmark of a particularist view. Let me take up each of these key motifs and look at them in relation to the question of the theology of religions.

2.1 Trinity as the way to identify the God of the Bible

While Barth himself was never able to work out the implications of his Trinitarian "rule" for the theology of religions, in my reading of the Swiss theologian's corpus its significance for our theme is immense: "The doctrine of the Trinity is what basically distinguishes the Christian doctrine of God as Christian, and therefore what already distinguishes the Christian concept of revelation as Christian, in contrast to all other possible doctrines of God or concepts of revelation" (*CD*, I/1, p. 301). In other words, the doctrine of the

Trinity is the only possible Christian answer to the question of who the self-revealing God of the Bible talks about.

As is now well known, one of Barth's lasting contributions was the inauguration (with the Catholic Karl Rahner) of the contemporary renaissance of the doctrine of the Trinity. Trinity for Barth was not only a chapter in theology but also its structuring principle and prolegomenon.[24] By rehabilitating the doctrine of the Trinity from its neglect and making the doctrine of God central to Christian faith, he not only combated what he saw as the main fallacy of Classical Liberalism's immanentist leanings,[25] but also gave guidance on how to approach other religions. For Barth, the doctrine of the Trinity is not only the structuring principle of Christian doctrine but also the means of identifying the God of the Bible.

It is from the Trinitarian structure of his theology that his other key topic flows, namely, the doctrine of revelation: the first topic to be developed in *Church Dogmatics*, the Trinitarian basis having been laid out, is of course the doctrine of revelation, the Word of God. Revelation is Trinitarian in its structure: his starting point is the famous formula in the beginning of the *Church Dogmatics*: "God reveals himself. He reveals himself through himself. He reveals himself" (I/1, p. 296). In other words, for Barth, God's revelation and God's being are identical. God is who God is revealed to be (I/1, p. 299).

Not only is revelation Trinitarian in its structure, God *ad extra* in relation to the world and us can only be known as Trinitarian; this is the meaning of the biblical idea of God as love. The trinitarian God revealed in Jesus Christ is a God who desires to enter into communion with human beings in his love. God is seen to be trinitarian as he is revealed in the self-giving love of the Father for the Son, which itself corresponds to the self-giving love of God for his creation. The trinitarian love relationships are fundamental to the loving relationship between God and the world (II/1, pp. 48–49).

---

[24] See further, Kärkkäinen, *Trinity*, pp. 14–15.

[25] For the classic locus, see Karl Barth, "The Humanity of God," in *Karl Barth: Theologian of Freedom*, Clifford Green ed. (London: Collins, 1979), p. 48: for Classical Liberalism, "to speak about God meant to speak about humanity, no doubt in elevated tone, but . . . 'about human faith and works.' Thus, in Liberalism 'human beings were magnified at the expense of God—the God who is sovereign Other standing over against humanity,' the 'free partner in history.'"

Enough has been said here to make the claim that, unlike some pluralists of the day such as John Hick,[26] Barth would not facilitate interfaith dialogue by bracketing out the doctrine of the Trinity. Trinity was for him what made the Christian conception of God "Christian." Deny Trinity, and you deny the uniqueness of the biblical God. This leads Barth of course to the second main tenet, namely, his Christocentrism, sometimes pejoratively labeled as "Christomonism."

2.2 Christ as the "hourglass" of Christian theology

Not inappropriately, the Catholic interpreter Hans Urs von Balthasar described Barth's theology as an hourglass "where God and man meet in the center through Jesus Christ."[27] Because Christian theology has a Trinitarian structure, for Barth it is christocentric. The way the Trinitarian God reveals God's self is through and in Christ:

> When Holy Scripture speaks of God, it concentrates our attention and thoughts upon one single point . . . We may look closer and ask: Who and what is the God who is to be known at the point upon which Holy Scripture concentrates our attention and thoughts? . . . then from first to last the Bible directs us to the name of Jesus Christ (*CD*, II/2, pp. 52–3).

Consequently, because the Trinitarian God is revealed in Christ and only in Christ, the world and humanity, including religions as mediators of the human search for God, are channeled through Christ. There is a christological origin to the world and to humanity.[28]

How Christocentrism, on the one hand, seems to restrict the idea of revelation and, on the other hand, to open the way for a sort of soteriological universalism, is one of the key dynamics of Barth's theology. While all commentators recognize this dynamic, no unanimity yet exists as to how it really shapes Barth's view of religions. Evangelicals have quite one-sidedly focused on the christological revelational restrictivism. More pluralistically oriented

---

[26] See further, Kärkkäinen, *Trinity*, p. 113.

[27] Hans Urs von Balthasar, *The Theology of Karl Barth* (New York: Holt, Rinehart & Winston, 1979), p. 170.

[28] See, e.g. Barth, *CD*, II/1, pp. 94–100.

commentators have tried to draw from the emerging universalism materials for a more open-minded reading of Barth. Let me take one topic at a time.

2.3 Revelation in Christ as the only "Christian" concept of revelation

When Barth, as is well known, insists on the christocentric approach to revelation—meaning that only revelation given in Christ "from above" can be counted as "revelation" in the Christian sense—he is of course not naively dismissing "revelations" outside of Christ. Theologically, he just doesn't consider these as "revelation." Depending on the viewpoint, at their best they can be either acknowledged as something valuable—as the grace-orientation in Pure Land Buddhism—or, at their worst, not only not good but outright dangerous, being another illustration of the twisted nature of fallen humanity in its desire to replace God-given truth with human-made substitutions.

Revelation in the Christian sense means that God "reveals" to the world something human beings could not possibly find on their own. Religions cannot find God. Even Christian religion cannot do it. Only God can, since "Revelation is God's self-offering and self-manifestation . . . In revelation God tells man that he is God." Totally different from Classical Liberalism or typical expectations among religions, this revelation, rather than being an elevation of already existing knowledge of God, provides humanity with "something utterly new, something which apart from revelation he does not know and cannot tell either himself or others" (*CD*, I/2, p. 301). This "new" can only be found in Christ as the Trinitarian God reveals God's very own self to humanity (*CD*, II/2, pp. 52–3, quoted above).

If so, what, if any, is then the value of religions in general and of specific religions such as Christianity, Judaism, or Hinduism, in general? It is here that we come to the built-in tension that characterizes the theology of this "twentieth-century church father" and which, as I have argued, Barth never resolved. To begin with, let us listen carefully to the younger Barth in the first part of his magnum opus. Here is the *locus classicus*, routinely cited by all commentators of Barth: the famous "paragraph 17 (over 80 pages!), titled "The Revelation of God as the Abolition of Religions" in volume one, entitled "The Doctrine of the Word of God":

> From the standpoint of revelation religion is clearly seen to be a human attempt to anticipate what God in His revelation wills to do and does do. It is the attempted replacement of the divine work by a human manufacture. The divine reality offered and manifested to us in revelation is replaced by a concept of God arbitrarily and willfully evolved by man. "Arbitrarily and willfully" means here by his own means, by his own human insight and constructiveness and energy (*CD*, I/2, p. 302).

If this passage is routinely cited as the key affirmation of the "restrictivist" theology of revelation of Barth, it is also commonplace to add the important linguistic note concerning the German word *Aufhebung*. It does not take too much mastery of German to note that the English rendering "abolition" certainly does not retain the ambiguity of the original meaning of "lifting up"!

While "abolition" is the contemporary meaning of the term, *Aufhebung* can also mean something like "purification" or "cleansing" of something "lifted up." (Students new to Hegel are warned to be alert to each occurrence of *Aufhebung* in his writings.) Having acknowledged this ambiguity of the term, however, one has to keep in mind the fact that words change meaning over the course of time. Etymology, while an interesting and often exciting exercise into the mysteries of word meanings, can also be used to explain away the force of the current meaning. While it is impossible for us to see into the mind of Barth when penning these famous lines of paragraph 17, everything about the immediate context seems to favor the contemporary face-value meaning of the term, namely, "abolition." Indeed, that is the meaning of the term for this passage. For Barth, religions are not helpful ways to reach out to the knowledge of God. Indeed, not only are they not helpful, but they can easily become perversions of will, obstacles to the knowledge of God.

Another way of qualifying the seemingly one-sided—and certainly very limited—view of revelation among religions even in the younger Barth is to resort to the other standard note, namely, the fact that Barth is said to include not only other religions but also Christian religion under the condemnation of religions as forms of a futile human search for God apart from Christ. Before approving this qualification, one needs to note the important observation that this only happens in the later part of the *Church Dogmatics*, in the context where Barth—as will be seen momentarily—seems to open windows into some kind of limited embrace of "lights" outside the

"Light" in Christ. What I mean is this: methodologically, one does not have the right to jump from volume one to volume four and read the former in light of the latter.

Not only is there a wide time gap, but it also hinders our appreciating the radical tension-filled nature of Barth's theology. It would be much more appropriate to find qualifying statements, if any, in the first part of the *Church Dogmatics* such as the above mentioned Pure Land discussion in the very same place as paragraph 17 (*CD*, I/2). Chung, who otherwise advocates a more open-ended reading of Barth, gives a very accurate portrait of that discussion. Pure Land Buddhism for Barth "stands close to the grace religions of the Reformation . . . there is a holy, providential disposition in the faith of Amida Buddha." Yet, as Chung adds, Barth "does not discern the name of Jesus Christ in this Buddhism . . ."[29] We come back to where we began in this subsection: for the younger Barth, only revelation in Christ can be called "revelation" in the Christian sense of the word. Later Barth came to qualify this statement, yet never leaving behind Christocentrism.

3. Universalist orientations in Barthian theology of religions

Having discussed three interrelated key motifs that speak for a particularist orientation to religions in Barth, I will now take up themes that make it a very problematic issue to label Barth a typical evangelical or Protestant particularist:

1. Acknowledging "lights" outside the Christian revelation in Christ.
2. Universal reconciliation in Christ does not leave anybody or anything outside.
3. Christian religion as the "Justified Sinner."

Other motifs that distance Barth from traditional evangelicalism could probably be mentioned as well. Barth's radically different view of Scripture, based on his idea of revelation as "encounter" with Christ rather than a way of conveying information (such as the traditional propositional view of revelation), comes first to mind. Barth, as is well known, is not only ready to acknowledge some "errors" in the Bible; he indeed affirms that as human witnesses to

---

[29] Chung, "Asian Religions," p. 10.

the divine act, biblical authors could have erred—and did err—in all they wrote.[30] The value of the Bible is not in the quality of the witnesses' report but in the miracle brought about by the Spirit of God: even though the human testimonies found in the Bible are just that, human reports, they can be used—and are being used—by the Spirit to bring about faith. While there is much to commend in Barth's theology of religions for evangelicals, especially the anti-liberal condemnation of one-sided immanentism, the differences between Barth and typical evangelicalism are huge.[31]

3.1 Other Lights

There is no denying, in the last volume of the *Church Dogmatics*, that there are some passages which reflect a change of tone, if not of opinion, in the mature Barth's assessment of other religions. The often quoted passage to that effect can be found in paragraph 69 in volume four (part three) speaking of "secular parables" in the context of the discussion of the prophetic office of Christ:

> We recognize that the fact that Jesus Christ is the one Word of God does not mean that in the Bible, the Church and the world there are not other words which are quite notable in their way, other lights which are quite clear and other revelations which are quite real . . . Nor does it follow from our statement that every word spoken outside the circle of the Bible and the Church is a word of false prophecy and therefore valueless, empty and corrupt, that all the lights which rise and shine in this outer sphere are misleading and all the revelations are necessarily untrue. (*CD*, IV/3, p. 97)

"Even from the mouth of Balaam," asserts Barth, "the well-known voice of the Good Shepherd may sound, and it is not to be ignored in spite of its sinister origin" (*CD*, IV/3, p. 119). Chung notes that here Barth combines dialectically the Word of Jesus Christ with

---

[30] It is of course ironic that when Barth is doing theology and inserting those endlessly long exegetical discussions into the *Church Dogmatics*, his treatment of Scripture does not seem to differ much from that of the more conservative Protestants or evangelicals!

[31] I am of course aware of the fact that in contemporary evangelicalism some evangelical theologians often perceived by their more conservative counterparts as "liberals," such as Donald Bloesch and Clark Pinnock, find in Barth's "model" of revelation much to commend. I am speaking more in terms of the majority of evangelicalism's view of Scripture.

various truth claims in a pluralistic society. It means that for Barth, "God cannot abandon any secular sphere in the world reconciled with God in Jesus Christ . . . Given this fact, Barth's position implies an inclusive-universalist tone with a radical openness to forms of secularism or pluralistic truth claims, even in spite of sinful origins."[32]

Earlier I warned against reading earlier parts of the *Church Dogmatics* in light of the later ones in an attempt to reconcile the tension that I believe belongs to Barth's own dynamic, dialectical theology. With this in mind, it is important to note that not only in later parts but already in the first, programmatic volume of the *Church Dogmatics*, the one on the Word of God, Barth acknowledges that God can indeed speak to us in surprising ways, be it through Russian communism, through a flute concert, or even through a dead dog. When God speaks—no matter what way—we had better listen, Barth is urging. Humility and openness should be the proper attitudes of the listeners, Christians (*CD*, IV/3, pp. 55–60). Chung summarizes:

> Barth's view does not imply an exclusivist position, but an inclusivist one, with radical openness to the strange voices outside the walls of Christianity. Profane words and lights are regarded to be as true as the one Word, because God is active also in other religions and cultures. The reconciliation of God is not only for the church but for the world. Therefore, the church has the task of examining closely whether these profane words and lights are in agreement with Scripture or church tradition or dogma, whether the fruits of these words outside Christianity are good and their effect in the community is positive.[33]

3.2 Universal reconciliation

The occasional openness to acknowledge the value of "revelations" outside the Christian revelation may not sound too strange in Barth's theology when compared against his two interrelated ideas in his Christology and soteriology, namely, his view of election as encompassing all of humanity and the idea of reconciliation encompassing all of the created order. If God had implicitly assumed the humanity of all human beings in the incarnation of the Son of God, then it means that the whole of humanity exists in

---

[32] Chung, "Asian Religions," p. 10.
[33] Chung, "Conflict," p. 43.

Jesus. This is indeed what Barth explicitly states: "In Jesus Christ it is not merely one human but the *humanum* of all men, which is posited and exalted as such to unity with God" (*CD*, IV/2, p. 49). Technically put, this means that all human beings are related to the humanity and divinity of Jesus Christ *anhypostatically* and *enhypostatically* (*CD*, IV/2, p. 59).

This means that for Barth creation and redemption form one divine economy, as the evangelical Dayton aptly puts it: "Creation is the arena of redemption from the beginning."[34] Redemption is not an afterthought, a kind of emergency plan. In Jesus Christ, the "first creature" and the goal of creation, God has obligated himself to an eternal covenant. The covenant is not only a "covenant of grace" in the limited sense of making the incarnation a contingent response to human sin (in the classical terminology, the infralapsarian view), but also the proper goal of and—we may say—"reason" for creation (the supralapsarian view).

Chung rightly points out that this "leads to radical openness to the truth claims of other cultures and religions." And he adds: "In the light of universal reconciliation, there is no such thing as something human as ultimately alien to God. It seems to me that with respect to reconciliation there is an essential 'theanthropological' unity between God, human beings and the cosmos."[35]

Here we come to the affirmation I already hinted at when speaking of "other lights." If reconciliation is universal, it means there is no sphere in the created order alien to the Creator. Says Barth, "In the world reconciled by God in Jesus Christ there is no secular sphere abandoned by him . . . even where from the human standpoint, it seems to approximate dangerously to the pure and absolute form of utter godlessness." Now that Christ has risen from the dead, we must "be prepared at any time for true words even from what seems to be the darkest places" (*CD*, IV/3, p. 119).

Against this background what Barth says in the context of discussing the Adam-Christ typology of Romans 5 becomes understandable: "Not only Christians, but all persons are included in the realm of Christ's effectiveness. Dogmatically reversed, this means that the reality of Christ is the framework and realm in which human beings as such are included."[36]

---

34 Dayton, "Karl Barth," p. 185.

35 Chung, "Conflict?" p. 47.

36 Karl Barth, *Christus und Adam; nach Röm. 5* (Zollikon-Zürich: Evangelischer Verlag, 1952), p. 50, quoted in Chung, "Conflict?" p. 42.

Summa summarum: In dogmatic discussions it is a commonplace to note that Barth recasts the Reformed doctrine of election upside down. He insists that all God's elective actions are centered on Christ and Christ only (in his dual agency of the "Electing God" and the "Elected Man." He thus sharply critiques the idea of "double predestination" according to which God has chosen some for salvation and others for perdition.) The implications of this for the theology of religions have not been extensively discussed, however.[37] What are the implications for the theology of religions of Barth's conclusion that as the representative of the whole human race, Christ has freely chosen, not only to become a man, but to become a man *for us?* He chose the "reprobation, perdition, and death" that was ours (*CD*, II/2, p. 163).

Voluntarily, he chose to be rejected by humanity and be crucified on the cross. On the other hand, we can also investigate the implications for the church's mission of the corollary idea of Barth: that all human beings are included in the election of Jesus Christ. Since Christ has been condemned, no other condemnation follows. Since not all are living as elected, it is the task of the elect community to proclaim that even such a person "belongs eternally to Jesus Christ and therefore is not rejected, but elected by God in Jesus Christ" and "that the rejection which he deserves on account of his perverse choice is borne and cancelled by Jesus Christ; and that he is appointed to eternal life with God on the basis of the righteous, divine decision" (*CD*, II/2, p. 306). The triune God has bound himself to humankind in an everlasting covenant. This binds humankind into a solidarity rather than into an arrogant "sheep" and "goats" divide. Thus, Barth always annoyed conservative circles by refusing to categorize people into two camps, "saved" and "lost."

No wonder the neo-orthodox colleague of Barth, Emil Brunner, asked this pointed question:

> What does this statement, "that Jesus is the only really rejected person," mean for the situation of humanity? Evidently this: that there is no possibility of condemnation . . . The decision has already been made in Jesus Christ—for all of humanity. Whether they know it or not, believe it or not, is not so important. They are like people who seem to be

[37] Again, I register my amazement at the virtual neglect of Barth by evangelical scholars on the discussion of salvation among world religions, even by Reformed scholars such as Tiessen, *Who Can Be Saved.*

> perishing in a stormy sea. But in reality they are not in a sea in which one can drown, but in shallow waters, in which it is impossible to drown. Only they do not know it.[38]

3.3 Christian religion as the "justified sinner"

When speaking of "other lights" Barth makes two significant moves that are important when painting a more balanced picture of his complicated theology of religions. The first one has to do with his willingness to let other religions or secular ideologies serve as correctives to Christianity. The second one has to do with his inclusion of Christianity under the critique of religions.

Barth also reminds the church of the fact that occasionally non-Christians behave in a way nobler than Christians. At times true words can be heard from "openly pagan" worldliness:

> We may think of the mystery of God, which we Christians so easily talk away in a proper concern for God's own cause . . . We may think of the lack of fear in the face of death which Christians to their shame often display far less readily than non-Christians far and near . . . especially we may think of a humanity which does not ask or weigh too long with whom we are dealing in others, but in which we find a simple solidarity with them and unreservedly take up their case (*CD*, IV/3, p. 125).

When speaking of the futility of religions as the human search for God, Barth also maintains that "the criticism expressed in the exclusiveness of the statement affects, limits, and relativizes the prophesy of Christians and the Church no less than the many other prophecies, lights, and words relativized and replaced by it" (*CD*, IV/3, p. 91). This simply means that Christianity is not immune from criticism of religion any more than acknowledgment of its relative value—and here the term *relative* has to be taken in its literal sense: "in relation to" Jesus Christ.

Even when at the end of the day Barth finally elevates Christianity as the "true religion," it can only be so after the "justification" of

---

[38] Emil Brunner, *The Christian Doctrine of God* (New York: Continuum, 1949), pp. 348–9. My own characterization of Barth's "universalism" is the following: "In my reading of Barth . . . there is no doubt about the fact that his Christology makes him first an 'anonymous universalist' and later, when the implications are spelled out by Barth himself, a 'reluctant universalist.'" Kärkkäinen, *Trinity*, p. 25.

that religion, something like resurrection after death. The reason for regarding Christianity as the true religion is based on the central Reformation doctrine, namely, justification by faith: "We can speak of 'true' religion only in the sense in which we speak of a 'justified sinner'" (*CD*, I/2, p. 325). In religion itself, including Christian religion, there is nothing valuable; only insofar as the religion allows itself to be taken over by God's judgment and grace can it be true. But that is not the whole picture: eventually there will also be some kind of "justification" of "other lights" too, when "they are taken, lifted, assumed, and integrated into the action of God's self-giving and self-declaring to man and therefore to the world made by him. And in the power of this integration they are instituted, installed, and ordained to the *ministerium Verbi Divini*" (*CD*, IV/3, p. 164). Here the other meaning of the term *Aufhebung* comes to focus: there will not only be "abolition"—"no" to religions, including Christianity—but also "lifting up," a qualified "yes" and that by virtue of the revelation in Christ. This is made explicit in the same context:

> This . . . is the critical, but also, since it is genuinely critical, the positive relationship of the light of life to the lights which the God whose saving action is revealed by the one light does not withhold from his creatures as such but gives them in His eternal goodness (*CD*, IV/3, p. 164–5).

The idea of Christian religion as a justified sinner has profound implications for interfaith dialogue. Trevor Hart puts it succinctly when he says that a Barthian at the dialogue table is "a sinner among sinners, who feels that his own glass home is rather too fragile for him to be throwing any stones."[39] The Christian knows that his or her own religion is under the judgment of religions and apart from the "justification" does not have a grasp of revelation. It is only when the triune God reveals himself and thus draws human beings into his own self-knowledge that human persons can know God.

Here I would like to qualify the statement by Chung according to which the "profane words and lights are regarded to be as true as the one Word" by saying something like this: Barth has qualified his exclusiveness by opening up to revelationary words outside the

---

[39] Trevor Hart, "Karl Barth, the Trinity, and Pluralism," in *The Trinity in a Pluralistic Age: Theological Essays on Culture and Religion*, Kevin Vanhoozer ed. (Grand Rapids, MI: Eerdmans, 1997), p. 139.

church as long as they are measured against the revelation given through Christ. Indeed, this is what Chung is saying later—gleaning from George Hunsinger:

> Other lights are neither self-contained nor self-sufficient in enjoying a simple autonomy in relation to the one great light. Other lights, however, are not conceived to be outside the one great light by remaining an external or alien heteronomy. True religious words or secular parables are conceived as coexistent with Jesus Christ as the one Word of God that might be regarded as the theonomous principle.[40]

So, whatever lights are out there, they cannot be totally unrelated to the Absolute Light; nor should they necessarily be exhausted by it since in the final analysis all belongs to Christ.

4. Barth's theology of religions and evangelicals

The theology of religions of Barth, which is necessarily a theological construction, emerges as complex, tension-filled and—in my reading of his theology—somewhat self-contradictory. Evangelicals[41] have one-sidedly referred to Barth as a major supporter of their particularist view. To that tendency Chung brings a pointed critique when he says that the major defect of this[42] "interpretation of Barth is linked to . . . [the] neglect of Barth's universal Christology in relation to

[40] Chung, "Conflict," p. 49, with reference to George Hunsinger, *How to Read Karl Barth: The Shape of His Theology* (New York: Oxford University Press, 1991), p. 263.

[41] For orientation to key issues in contemporary evangelical theology of religions, see further Kärkkäinen, *An Introduction to the Theology of Religions*, ch. 15; "Evangelical Theology and Religions," in *Cambridge Companion to Evangelical Theology*, Timothy Larsen and Daniel J. Treier ed. (Cambridge, UK: Cambridge University Press, 2006); "Evangelicals, Pluralism, and Religions: Evangelicals Enter the Theology of Religions," *Theology News and Notes* 52:1 (Winter 2005), pp. 19–22; "Trinity and Religions: On the Way to a Trinitarian Theology of Religions for evangelicals," *Missiology* (Winter/Spring 2005), pp. 159–74; and "The Uniqueness of Christ and Trinitarian Faith," in *Christ the One and Only: A Global Affirmation of the Uniqueness of Jesus Christ*, Sung Wook Chung ed. (Milton Keynes, UK: Paternoster/Grand Rapids, MI: Baker, 2005).

[42] Chung mentions here Knitter. I am applying that statement to encompass all interpretations in this perspective.

such themes as universal reconciliation and God's speaking through strange voices and secular parables of the reign of God."[43]

In this essay I have laid out various approaches to the interpretation of Barth's view of religions as well as looked at two kinds of orientations to the theology of religions in his own theology, those that clearly speak to particularist leanings and those that argue for a more open-minded and inclusive attitude. "Softening" Barth's alleged exclusivism provides a needed balance to the standard one-sided hermeneutic of his theology; yet at the same time one needs to be clear about the fact that it does not make him a pluralist. Barth is difficult to classify. In my earlier study, I concluded that,

> respect and honor rather than outright denial is the attitude that best describes Barth's opinion of Christianity's relation to other religions, and that attitude grows out of his trinitarian doctrine, especially of self-revelation. Also, it is significant in my mind that for Barth a respectful and humble attitude is coupled with the insistence on the church's mandate to witness to all people about the triune God and what God has done in Jesus Christ. Even if that kind of attitude may not foster the open-ended dialogue that is vogue in our age, it does not totally close the doors for a dialogue.[44]

At this point, it is difficult to assess the implications this opening up of Barth's views may have for the evangelical theology of religions. On the one hand, it makes the evangelical claims to Barth as their conservative godfather appear quite problematic. On the other hand, continuing study of Barth's dynamic view of religions

---

[43] Chung, "Conflict," p. 45.

[44] Kärkkäinen, *Trinity*, p. 25. Dayton ("Karl Barth and Wider Ecumenism," p. 188) has come to the same kind of conclusion concerning Barth's theology of religions: I find Dayton's final conclusion to his study on potential resources to open up Barth's exclusivism compelling in light of Barth's overall theology: "The results of this study are modest. We have not challenged directly Barth's own exclusivism. We have merely argued that he is often misunderstood—that his thought is more subtle and dialectical than is often assumed. I am not sure that Barth himself would have developed his own thought in the direction of dialogue with other religions (indeed, there are signs and incidents that indicate that he did not have much personal interest in these questions), but I do think that it is possible on Barthian premises to have more engagement with other religions than is usually assumed. This is to be sure a modest place, but I believe it to be a valuable place nonetheless."

may help evangelicals negotiate some of the built-in knots in their own theology, namely, the insistence on Christ as the fullness of revelation, yet Christ as the agent of creation and reconciliation. That Barth was not able to put these themes together in a theologically satisfactory way does not mean anyone else could either. Barth produced his magnum opus prior to the advent of multireligiosity as the everyday life experience in the new global village. Similar to Paul Tillich, it was only towards the end of Barth's long career that the theology of religions quest became a more urgent one. Then, however, it was too late for him. It is left to the later generation of evangelicals and others, in a critical dialogue, to continue assessing his heritage.

12

Karl Barth, the Postmodern Turn, and Evangelical Theology

John R. Franke

In recent years a number of the interpreters of Karl Barth's thought have suggested that his work may yet have its greatest influence in the coming century rather than in the one in which he lived.[1] In one sense this may seem surprising, given that Barth would undoubtedly be named on any shortlist of the most significant theologians of the twentieth century. Yet, at the beginning of the past decade, George Hunsinger was able to write with justification that although Barth is often acknowledged as the greatest theologian of the century, he has also "achieved the dubious distinction of being habitually honored but not much read."[2]

This has perhaps been particularly true in the English-speaking world. Further, where he has been read a good case can be made that he still has not been *heard*.[3] However, at the beginning of the twenty-first century the Anglo-American situation has changed considerably and there is now ample evidence of a revival of interest in the study of Barth. In recent years a steady stream of books, articles, and dissertations have been produced which provide

---

1 Portions of this essay are drawn from John R. Franke, "God Hidden & Wholly Revealed: Karl Barth, Postmodernity, and Evangelical Theology," *Books & Culture* 9:5 (2003), pp. 16–17, 40–2. I extend thanks to *Books & Culture* for permission to use previously published material here.

2 George Hunsinger, *How to Read Karl Barth: The Shape of His Theology* (New York: Oxford University Press, 1991), p. 27.

3 Bruce L. McCormack, "The Unheard Message of Karl Barth," *Word & World* 14:1 (1994), pp. 59–66.

commentary on Barth's theology; the Karl Barth Society of North America is flourishing; and the newly established Center for Barth Studies at Princeton Theological Seminary is promoting scholarly and ecclesial engagement with his thought. John Webster notes that in the midst of all this activity, the most important development has been that "Barth is read, and read *in extenso*."[4]

At least two reasons can be identified as accounting for this resurgence of interest in Barth's thought. The first is simply the concern of historical scholarship to gain purchase on a more accurate conception of what Barth was in fact attempting to say in his work. Over the past twenty-five years the Swiss edition of Barth's collected writings has made generally available a large quantity of important and previously unpublished material such as lectures, sermons, and letters. Of particular importance are the lecture cycles from the early years of Barth's career as a theology professor. The availability of these writings has provided the opportunity to examine carefully the development of Barth's thought. This critical scrutiny has led to significant revisions in the standard profile of that development, particularly the notion that Barth abandoned the dialectical thinking characteristic of his early theology. This has, in turn, led to important alterations concerning the precise contours of his mature theology contained in the *Church Dogmatics*.

The second reason for this renewed interest in Barth may be found in the new opportunities for theology arising out of the shifting cultural climate. As we venture into the twenty-first century the discipline of theology is in a state of transition and ferment brought about by the breakdown of the assumptions of the modern world spawned by the Enlightenment. This breakdown has been precipitated by the emergence of postmodernity with its withering critique of the modern, scientific quest for certain, objective, and universal knowledge and its attempt to engage in new forms of discourse in the aftermath of modernity's demise. This postmodern attempt to construct new paradigms for knowledge and intellectual pursuit has significantly shaped the discipline of theology in the past decade as theologians from various contexts and traditions have sought to "fill the void" left by the perceived failure of modernity.

Surprisingly and somewhat ironically, the thought of Karl Barth has come to be closely associated with several of these recent attempts to rethink theology after modernity. The perceived affinity of Barth's

---

[4] John Webster, "Editorial," *International Journal of Systematic Theology* 2:2 (July 2000), pp. 126.

theology with some of the intellectual tendencies of postmodernism has led to a number of recent attempts to relate Barth to the concerns of a postmodern theology. In this chapter we will briefly survey some of the most significant recent English-language Barth scholarship, after which we will suggest some implications of this for evangelical theology as it seeks to engage the challenges of the postmodern turn. In order to situate the discussion to follow, let us briefly describe the postmodern turn.

1. The postmodern turn

The current cultural context in North America, as well as in much of the world, can be generally and felicitously labeled and described as "postmodern." At the beginning of the twenty-first century the intellectual milieu of Western thought and culture is in a state of transition precipitated by the perceived failure of the philosophical, societal, and ethical assumptions of the modern world spawned by the Enlightenment. This transition has led to an attempt in various fields of inquiry to critique old paradigms and establish new ones to take their place. This discussion of a paradigm change has led to a wide variety of construals concerning the nature of the postmodern turn.

Yet, in spite of the numerous manifestations of the postmodern condition and the divergent opinions and struggles concerning the portrayal of postmodernity in various domains and situations, Steven Best and Douglas Kellner maintain that "there is a shared discourse of the postmodern, common perspectives, and defining features that coalesce into an emergent postmodern paradigm."[5] However, since this new postmodern paradigm is emerging, but neither mature nor regnant, it continues to be hotly contested by both those who desire to embrace it for particular purposes as well as those who find reason to oppose it. Best and Kellner suggest that the representations of this emerging paradigm that take shape in the context of intellectual, social, and cultural activity constitute "a borderland between the modern and something new for which the term 'postmodern' has been coined."[6]

---

[5] Steven Best and Douglas Kellner, *The Postmodern Turn* (New York: Guilford Press, 1997), p. xi.

[6] Best and Kellner, *Turn*, p. xiii.

Two key aspects of the shared discourse of postmodern thought concern the linguistic turn and the nonfoundationalist turn. Let us briefly describe each of these beginning with the linguistic turn. Postmodern thinkers maintain that humans do not view the world from an objective or neutral vantage point, but instead structure their world through the concepts they bring to it, particularly language. Human languages function as social conventions and symbol systems that attempt to engage and describe the world in a variety of ways that are shaped by the social and historical contexts and perceptions of various communities of discourse. No simple, one-to-one relationship exists between language and the world and thus no single linguistic description can serve to provide an objective conception of the "real" world. Language structures our perceptions of reality and, as such, constitutes the world in which we live.

The work of Ludwig Wittgenstein is of central importance in the development of the linguistic turn. Wittgenstein came to realize that rather than having only a single purpose—to make assertions or state facts—language has many functions. This conclusion led to Wittgenstein's important concept of "language games." According to Wittgenstein, each use of language occurs within a separate and seemingly self-contained system complete with its own rules. Similar to playing a game, we require an awareness of the operative rules and significance of the terms within the context of the purpose for which we are using language. Each use of language, therefore, comprises a separate "language game." And each "game" may have little to do with the other "language games."[7] For Wittgenstein meaning is not related, at least not directly or primarily, to an external world of "facts" waiting to be apprehended. Instead, meaning is an internal function of language. Because the meaning of any statement is dependent on the context or the "language game" in which it appears, any sentence has as many meanings as contexts in which it is used.

Another key figure in the linguistic turn is the Swiss linguist, Ferdinand de Saussure. In contrast to his predecessors who viewed language as a natural phenomenon that develops according to fixed and discoverable laws, Saussure proposed that a language is a social phenomenon and that a linguistic system is a product of social

---

[7] Ludwig Wittgenstein, *Philosophical Investigations*, G. E. M. Anscombe tr. (New York: Macmillan, 1953).

convention.[8] Others such as anthropologist Claude Levi-Strauss and the proponents of what has come to be known as "the sociology of knowledge," generated an awareness of the connection between language and culture and both personal identity formation and social cohesion.[9] Viewing language in this fashion presumes that it does not have its genesis in the individual mind grasping a truth or fact about the world and then expressing it in statements. Rather, language is a social phenomenon, and any statement acquires its meaning within the process of social interaction.

From this perspective, language and culture generate a shared context in which a people engage in the construction of meaning and in the task of making sense out of the world. In the words of Raymond Williams, culture functions as a "signifying system through which necessarily (though among other means) a social order is communicated, reproduced, experienced and explored."[10] In this process, language plays a crucial role. The language that we inherit from our social community, together with non-linguistic modalities such as metaphorical images and symbols, provide the conceptual tools through which we construct the world we inhabit as well as the vehicles through which we communicate and thereby share meaning with others. In the words of Peter Berger and Thomas Luckmann, "Language objectivates the shared experiences and makes them available to all within the linguistic community, thus becoming both the basis and the instrument of the collective stock of knowledge."[11]

In this social process of world construction and identity formation, language provides the structure of our particular and collective experience, perspective, and understanding. Our conceptions of

---

[8] David Holdcroft, *Saussure: Signs, System and Arbitrariness* (Cambridge, UK: Cambridge University Press, 1991), pp. 7–10.

[9] See, for example, Peter L. Berger and Thomas Luckmann, *The Social Construction of Reality: A Treatise in the Sociology of Knowledge* (New York: Anchor Books, 1967), pp. 99–104. For a fuller statement of Berger's views, see Peter L. Berger, *The Sacred Canopy: Elements of a Sociological Theory of Religion*, (Garden City, NY: Doubleday, 1969), pp. 3–51. For a summary and appraisal of Berger's contribution, see Robert Wuthnow, *Rediscovering the Sacred: Perspectives on Religion in Contemporary Society* (Grand Rapids, MI: Eerdmans, 1992), pp. 9–35.

[10] Raymond Williams, *The Sociology of Culture* (New York: Schocken Books, 1982), p. 13.

[11] Berger and Luckmann, *Construction*, p. 68.

what it means to be human, the formation and development of our moral, ethical, religious, and ideological convictions, and our understanding of our place and responsibilities in the world are shaped by our language and the discourse and practices of the particular communities in which we participate. We learn to use language and make sense of it in the context of our participation in a community of users that are bound together through common social conventions and rules of practice. Hence, the world we experience is mediated in and through our use of language, meaning that to some extent the limits of our language constitute the limits of our understanding of the world. Further, since language is a socially construed product of human construction, forged in the context of ongoing interactions, conversations, and engagements, our words and linguistic conventions do not have timeless and fixed meanings that are independent from their particular usages in human communities and traditions. In this sense, language does not represent reality so much as it constitutes reality.

Postmodern thought is also characterized by a nonfoundationalist turn. The chastened rationality of postmodernity entails the rejection of epistemological foundationalism and the adoption of a nonfoundationalist and contextual conception of epistemology. In the modern era, the pursuit of knowledge was deeply influenced by Enlightenment foundationalism. In its broadest sense, foundationalism is merely the acknowledgment that not all beliefs are of equal significance in the structure of knowledge. Some beliefs are more "basic" or "foundational" and serve to give support to other beliefs that are derived from them. Understood in this way, nearly every thinker is in some sense a foundationalist, rendering such a description unhelpful in grasping the range of opinion in epistemological theory found among contemporary thinkers. However, in philosophical circles, foundationalism refers to a much stronger epistemological stance than is entailed in this general observation about how beliefs intersect. At the heart of the foundationalist agenda is the desire to overcome the uncertainty generated by the tendency of fallible human beings to error, and the inevitable disagreements and controversies that follow. Foundationalists are convinced that the only way to solve this problem is to find some universal and indubitable means of grounding the entire edifice of human knowledge.

The modern quest for epistemological certitude, often termed "strong" or "classical" foundationalism, has its philosophical beginnings in the thought of the philosopher René Descartes. Descartes sought to reconstruct the nature of knowledge by rejecting traditional medieval or "premodern" notions of authority and replacing them with the modern conception of indubitable beliefs that are accessible to all individuals. The goal to be attained through the identification of indubitable foundations is a universal knowledge that transcends time and context. In keeping with this pursuit, the ideals of human knowledge since Descartes have tended to focus on the universal, the general, and the theoretical rather than on the local, the particular, and the practical. This conception of knowledge became one of the dominant assumptions of intellectual pursuit in the modern era and decisively shaped its cultural discourse and practices.

In the postmodern context, however, this classical variety of foundationalism is in dramatic retreat, as its assertions about the objectivity, certainty, and universality of knowledge have come under fierce criticism.[12] Merold Westphal observes, "That it is philosophically indefensible is so widely agreed that its demise is the closest thing to a philosophical consensus in decades."[13] J. Wentzel van Huyssteen agrees: "Whatever notion of postmodernity we eventually opt for, all postmodern thinkers see the modernist quest for certainty, and the accompanying program of laying foundations for our knowledge, as a dream for the impossible, a contemporary version of the quest for the Holy Grail."[14] And Nicholas Wolterstorff offers this stark conclusion: "On all fronts foundationalism is in bad shape. It seems to me there is nothing to do but give it up for mortally ill and learn to live in its absence."[15] The heart of the postmodern quest for a situated and contextual rationality lies in the rejection of the foundationalist approach to knowledge along with its intellectual tendencies.

Postmodern thought raises two related but distinct questions to the modern foundationalist enterprise. First, is such an approach to knowledge *possible*? And second, is it *desirable*? These questions are connected with what may be viewed as the two major branches of postmodern hermeneutical philosophy: the hermeneutics of finitude

---

[12] John E. Thiel, *Nonfoundationalism* (Minneapolis: Fortress Press, 1994), p. 37.

[13] Merold Westphal, "A Reader's Guide to 'Reformed Epistemology,'" *Perspectives* 7:9 (November 1992), pp. 10–11.

[14] J. Wentzel van Huyssteen, "Tradition and the Task of Theology," *Theology Today* 55:2 (July 1998), p. 216.

[15] Nicholas Wolterstorff, *Reason Within the Bounds of Religion* (Grand Rapids, MI: Eerdmans, 1976), p. 52.

and the hermeneutics of suspicion. However, the challenges to foundationalism are not only philosophical, but also emerge from the material content of Christian theology. Merold Westphal suggests that postmodern theory, with respect to hermeneutical philosophy, may be properly appropriated for the task of explicitly Christian thought on theological grounds: "The hermeneutics of finitude is a meditation on the meaning of human createdness, and the hermeneutics of suspicion is a meditation on the meaning of human fallenness."[16] In other words, many of the concerns of postmodern theory can be appropriated and fruitfully developed in the context of the Christian doctrines of creation and sin.

Viewed from this perspective, the questions that are raised by postmodern thought concerning the possibility and desirability of foundationalism are also questions that emerge from the material content of Christian theology. They both lead to similar conclusions. First, modern foundationalism, with its emphasis on the objectivity, universality, and certainty of knowledge, is an impossible dream for finite human beings whose outlooks are always limited and shaped by the particular circumstances in which they emerge. Second, the modern foundationalist emphasis on the inherent goodness of knowledge is shattered by the fallen and sinful nature of human beings who desire to seize control of the epistemic process in order to empower themselves and further their own ends, often at the expense of others.

The limitations of finitude and the flawed condition of human nature mean that epistemic foundationalism is neither possible nor desirable for created and sinful persons. This double critique of foundationalism, emerging as it does from the perspectives of both postmodern philosophy and Christian theology, suggests the appropriateness and suitability, given the current intellectual situation, of the language of nonfoundationalism as descriptive of an approach to the task of theology that is both postmodern and faithful to the Christian tradition. These aspects of the postmodern turn have played a significant role in the development and practice of theology over the course of the past twenty-five years and have contributed substantially to the current situation. We now turn our attention to recent interpretations of Barth's theology, and their relationship to postmodern thought.

---

[16] Merold Westphal, *Overcoming Onto-theology: Toward a Postmodern Christian Faith* (New York: Fordham University Press, 2001), p. xx.

2. Postmodern readings of Barth

With respect to the use of Barth's work to fund theological proposals that may be broadly construed as postmodern, we can identify two recent approaches: the nonfoundational "postliberalism" advocated by Yale theologians Hans Frei and George Lindbeck, and the emphasis on "otherness" and "non-givenness" that result from the limitations of human language espoused by Walter Lowe, Graham Ward, and William Stacy Johnson. The importance of Barth's theology for these proposals points to the ongoing significance of his thought in the construction of contemporary theology and to the variety of ways in which aspects of his thought may be developed.

Postliberal theology is marked by two distinctive tendencies. The first is the rejection of philosophical foundationalism in a tendency to resist any attempt to find a neutral and ultimate vantage point from which to assess the truth and coherence of theological statements. This nonfoundational approach to theology leads to a second tendency, that of understanding Christian theology primarily as an act of communal self-description. The most significant figure in the development of the nonfoundational perspective in theology is Hans Frei, who was also, not coincidentally, one of the premier Barth scholars in America. His book *The Eclipse of Biblical Narrative*, established him as one of the leading defenders of the movement commonly associated with Barth's theology known as "neo-orthodoxy" during a period when its influence was at low ebb in America. In *Types of Christian Theology*, an edited and fragmentary book based on his lectures and published after his untimely death, we are able to glimpse Frei's understanding of Barth and his relationship to the developments in theology during the twentieth century.[17]

In this work Frei attempts to sort out the approaches of various modern theological alternatives to the perennial question of the relationship of theology to philosophy. He achieves this by posing a spectrum of opinion ranging from strong foundationalism (the belief that Christian theology is subordinate to the discipline of philosophy which sets forth the rules of correct discourse for

---

[17] Hans W. Frei, *The Eclipse of Biblical Narrative: a Study in Eighteenth and Nineteenth Century Hermeneutics* (New Haven: Yale University Press, 1974); *Types of Christian Theology*, George Hunsinger and William C. Placher eds. (New Haven: Yale University Press, 1992).

all fields of knowledge) to strong nonfoundationalism (the belief that Christian theology is an internal, contextual exercise in self-description that rejects in principle the notion of general, universally valid theories of knowledge that apply to all intellectual disciplines). The question that Frei seeks to address concerns the very nature of the discipline: Is Christian theology primarily a philosophical discipline that is open to *external* description (that is, explication from outside the believing community) or is it primarily an *internal* act of Christian self-description (i.e. faith seeking understanding)? In the former, theology is subject to the current canons of reason in philosophy and is therefore best done in the context of the academy, while the latter account suggests that theology is subject only to explicitly Christian discourse and is thus best pursued in the context of the church.

Frei identifies three representatives of positions that seek to navigate between these extremes: revisionist (or liberal) David Tracy, nineteenth-century liberal Friedrich Schleiermacher, and Barth. Tracy is on the foundationalist end of the spectrum but allows, at least in theory, for a serious accounting of the explicitly Christian religion that is to be correlated with common human experience. However, the result of his procedure, given his assumptions concerning the nature of human experience as universal and therefore its priority in the task of correlation, leads inevitably to the eclipse of *distinctively* Christian theology. This is because the specifically Christian content of theology is thoroughly subsumed by philosophy on the basis of a general and supposedly universal theory of integration, in this case that of philosophical anthropology.

The main difference between Schleiermacher and Tracy, in Frei's reckoning, is that Schleiermacher attempts to correlate the external, philosophical description of theology, which is subject to accepted criteria of universal validity, with Christian self-description apart from any general theory that would predetermine the outcome of the process. The two are seen as bearing equal weight in the task of theological correlation. In this sense Schleiermacher is technically not, contrary to the standard portrait, a foundationalist. However, in his definitive theological work, *The Christian Faith*, his application of the formal principles of his theological method gives the appearance of foundationalism. This is due to the significant alterations he makes to the historical content of Christian theology on the basis of his conception of the "essence" of Christianity as a particular communal expression of the universal human condition (the feeling of absolute dependence). Given the material content of his teaching it is hardly surprising that Schleiermacher has been viewed as being at the headwaters of foundationalist theology.

In his presentation, Frei maintains that Barth agrees with Schleiermacher's conception of Christian theology as a nonsystematic correlation of Christian self-description and general philosophical method, but does not regard them as equals. Barth places greater priority on Christian self-description than Schleiermacher and reverses the procedure of Tracy by arguing that self-description governs and limits the use of philosophy in theology rather than vice versa. According to Frei, Barth affirmed that "absolute priority be given to Christian theology as Christian self-description within the religious community called the Church, or the Christian community"[18] and thus conceived of theology as "normed Christian self-description or critical self-examination by the Church of her language concerning God, in God's presence."[19] In this understanding, Christian theology can be viewed as being primarily concerned with teaching the particular language and concepts that shape the beliefs and practices of the community.

In locating Barth on the more nonfoundational side of his typology with the emphasis on self-description as the principle task of theology, Frei implied a reading of Barth that concentrates attention on the internal logic of theological assertions within the Christian community at the expense of questions concerning reality-reference. Frei's Yale colleague, George Lindbeck, extended and developed the approach to theology suggested by this reading of Barth in his highly influential book *The Nature of Doctrine* (1984). While Lindbeck did not attempt to offer a critical reading of Barth's theology his use of Barth, based on the interpretation offered by Frei, and his significance in the development of postliberalism has provided the basis for an increasingly common postmodern, nonfoundationalist reading of Barth's theology.

A second postmodern interpretation of Barth develops the theme of God as "wholly other" found in his early writings. The basic thrust of this approach suggests that finite human beings are simply incapable of describing the infinite God within the context of a single linguistic context, much less a particular theological system within

---

[18] Frei, *Types*, p. 41.
[19] Frei, *Types*, p. 42.

a particular linguistic context. Both Walter Lowe[20] and Graham Ward[21] bring Barth into conversation with the French postmodern linguistic and literary theorist Jacques Derrida and attempt to draw out affinities between the two, while William Stacy Johnson develops this theme more generally.[22] The picture of Barth's theology that emerges in these books is one that calls into question not only the standard interpretations of his work, but also the very notion of theology as traditionally conceived.

Lowe focuses his attention on the second edition of Barth's Romans commentary, published in 1922, in which Barth calls into question all human theological complacency that assumes to have definitively settled the question of God and his relationship to the world. Lowe extends this early Barthian theme in tandem with Derrida in order to develop a revised metaphysics and ontology that effectively renders the historical reality of the church's conception of God as fundamentally ambiguous. However, in developing his thesis, Lowe departs from standard interpretations of Derrida as a deconstructive nihilist with little interest in the question of truth. He devotes a chapter to Derrida's understanding of the truth-question in an attempt to demonstrate that Derrida is not a relativistic nihilist and that his thought cannot properly be employed in support of such purposes.

Lowe suggests that the mistaken turn in much postmodern thought is that in its realization that truth could not be finally and completely grasped, it concluded that the very question of truth must be abandoned. He maintains that the question of truth is a reality that should not, and cannot be disposed of, but rather needs to be recast in light of the contextual nature of the finite human condition. Thus, for Lowe the purpose of his interpretation of Barth and Derrida and the radical otherness of God is not simply deconstructive, but rather to open up new critical and constructive possibilities for theology on the basis of a metaphysically chastened view of God that thoroughly contextualizes all human thought.

While Lowe looks to the early Barth of *Romans* II to develop his thesis, Graham Ward engages with the later Barth of the

---

[20] Walter Lowe, *Theology and Difference: The Wound of Reason* (Bloomington, IN: Indiana University Press, 1993).

[21] Graham Ward, *Barth, Derrida, and the Language of Theology* (Cambridge, UK: Cambridge University Press, 1995).

[22] William Stacy Johnson, *The Mystery of God: Karl Barth and the Postmodern Foundations of Theology* (Loiusville, KY: Westminster John Knox, 1997).

Church Dogmatics to discuss the challenges for theology created by an awareness of the inadequacy of human language to provide immediate access to reality. It is this "crisis of representation" that raises the question of God and the possibility of theology for Ward and provides the context from which he views the emergence of Barth's thought. He argues that the central challenge for Barth was to provide a theological account of the meaningfulness of language in general and to address specifically the question concerning the way in which the Word of God comes to expression in human words. However, according to Ward, Barth's attempt to resolve the problem of theological language, while suggestive of a way forward, finally ends in incoherence.

Ward appeals to Derrida as the thinker who supplies a "philosophical supplement" that may be added to Barth in order to give greater coherence to his conception of theological language. This linking of Derrida to Barth results in the construction of the conditions necessary for the development of a postmodern theology of the Word and human language. The result of this for Ward is a postmodern Barthianism in which the presence of God in human language is that of absence. In other words, what finite human beings are really able to "know" about God is his fundamental hiddenness and incomprehensibility. Ward situates his interpretation of Barth as leading to a conservative postmodern theology, albeit one in which the emphasis on the radical otherness of God suggests significant alterations to traditional conservative accounts of the theological task.[23]

William Stacy Johnson offers another attempt at bringing Barth into conversation with postmodern themes and provides a fresh rethinking of Barth's theology as a whole. Johnson also develops the notion of the hiddenness and mystery of God, but with a different nuance. For Lowe and Ward, God is hidden due to the limitations of the finite human condition. Insights concerning cultural anthropology such as the situated nature of all human knowledge and the limits of human language are developed to suggest the inadequacy of all human knowledge of God and so to "decenter" theology primarily on *anthropological* grounds. Johnson moves beyond this claim by asserting that for Barth it is *God himself* who decenters theology.

---

[23] Graham Ward, "Postmodern Theology," in David Ford ed. *The Modern Theologians: An Introduction to Christian Theology in the Twnetieth Century*, second ed. (Oxford, UK: Blackwell Publishers, 1996), p. 593.

The "foundations" of the theological task are not to be sought in anthropological, linguistic, or philosophical categories but only in the being-in-act of the triune God in his self-revelation. However, these foundations are construed as postmodern in that they are not to be understood as a means of providing self-evident, non-inferential, or incorrigible grounds for theological claims.

Johnson maintains that for Barth the God who is revealed in Jesus Christ nevertheless remains an unfathomable and ultimate mystery to human creatures. The reality of this divine mysteriousness means that to study the living God of Christian theology is to "converge upon the untamed and uncoercible" being who calls human beings "fundamentally into question" and overturns "all that was previously stable and secure."[24] According to Johnson, Barth's understanding of the mystery of God, even in the act of revelation, unsettles all doctrinal affirmations and suggests that such statements be viewed as open-ended and subject to continual revision in accordance with the nature of the God to whom they seek to bear witness. In this conception, theology becomes a fragile venture in which no claims of certainty can prevail and no one can have the final word in the face of the intractable mystery of the living God.

Now each of the works mentioned here seek not simply to interpret Barth for the sake of interpreting Barth, but to make use of his work to further a particular approach to theology in the postmodern situation, along the lines of the linguistic turn or the nonfoundational turn or both. As stated at the outset, these various efforts at making use of Barth have provided fresh and compelling reasons to engage in the study of his theology with renewed interest. However, while these appropriations of Barth are fueling new theological paradigms aimed at addressing the postmodern context, other interpreters have been suggesting that before Barth is pressed into the service of such proposals, theologians would do well to gain a greater purchase on the actual contours of his thought. These thinkers maintain that Barth's theology has been largely misunderstood in the English-speaking world by his supporters as well as his critics. As a result, much of the potential significance of Barth's thought for the current theological situation has been, and continues to be, obscured.

---

[24] William Stacy Johnson, *The Mystery of God: Karl Barth and the Postmodern Foundations of Theology* (Louisville, KY: Westminster John Knox Press, 1997), p. 14.

In particular, Bruce McCormack is concerned that in the postmodern interpretations of Barth on offer, Barth's dialectical approach to theology is broken, albeit broken in different directions. In the case of the particular nonfoundational, postliberal reading of Barth offered by Frei and Lindbeck, the givenness of God in revelation is emphasized in such a way that Barth is potentially made into a revelational positivist who collapses the whole of revelation into the text of the biblical witness. This approach can also lead to the bracketing of questions concerning reality-reference in a way foreign to Barth's concerns. Such a conception bears striking similarities to standard neo-orthodox interpretations of Barth's theology and has sometimes been viewed as merely an updated and refurbished version. In the case of the readings of wholly otherness advanced in different ways by Lowe, Ward, and Johnson, the nongivenness and hiddenness of God in revelation is emphasized in such a way as to potentially turn Barth into a theological skeptic. McCormack points out that the difficulty of both approaches is that they end up with an utterly and completely nondialectical Barth.[25]

Such nondialectical readings can be accounted for in part due to the long-standing paradigm for interpreting his work. According to what was for a long time regarded as the most definitive account of Barth's theological development, articulated by the Swiss Catholic theologian Hans Urs von Balthasar in his work on Barth's theology first published in German in 1951, there were two major shifts in his thinking.[26] The first occurred in 1918 with his rejection of liberalism and move to a dialectical method of setting theological statements over against counter-statements without allowing a synthesis of the two to emerge. This approach led to Barth's highly influential commentaries on Romans (first edition, 1919; second edition, 1922) and is said to characterize his thinking until 1931.

The publication of his work on Anselm in 1931 is then viewed as marking a second shift, this time from dialectic to analogy. The so-called "turn to analogy" marks the point at which Barth abandons his dialectical method and adopts a more "objective"

---

[25] For a detailed discussion of this critique, see Bruce L. McCormack, "Beyond Nonfoundational and Postmodern Readings of Barth: Critically Realistic Dialectical Theology," part I, *Zeitschrift für dialektische Theologie* 13:1 (1997), pp. 67–95; part II, *ZDTh* 13:2 (1997), pp. 170–94.

[26] Hans Urs von Balthasar, *Karl Barth: Darstellung und Deutung Seiner Theologie* (Köln: Verlag Jakob Hegner, 1951). English Translation: *The Theology of Karl Barth: Exposition and Interpretation*, Edward T. Oakes, S.J. tr. (San Francisco, CA: Ignatius, 1992).

and "positivistic" approach to theology that comes to be known as neo-orthodoxy. Thus, we are presented with three phases in Barth's intellectual pilgrimage: the early, liberal Barth; the dialectical Barth; and the mature, neo-orthodox Barth of the *Church Dogmatics* who repudiated the dialectical method of his earlier work. While this overall sequence has been nuanced in various ways, its basic form became established as the standard account of Barth's historical development and as the crucial background for interpreting the shape and content of his definitive theological statement in the *Church Dogmatics*.

This reading of Barth has dominated the Anglo-American reception of his thought in fundamental ways, and may be said to be largely responsible for the labeling of Barth as a neo-orthodox theologian. However, the question may be raised as to the legitimacy of this interpretive scheme and its influence on the interpretation of Barth. However, in what is perhaps the most groundbreaking study of Barth in English-language scholarship, Bruce McCormack has produced a detailed, meticulous, and erudite exposition of Barth's early works and the context in which they emerged that has the potential to significantly reshape the discipline of Barth studies.[27] McCormack, building on the work of several German scholars, argues that after Barth's break with liberalism and the development of his dialectical conception of theology there were no subsequent major shifts or turning points in his thinking. Dialectic was never simply left behind as the formula suggesting a "turn from dialectic to analogy" implies. McCormack maintains that the great weakness of the von Balthasarian formula is that it conceals the extent to which Karl Barth remained a truly dialectical theologian, even in the *Church Dogmatics*. Thus, while Barth's theology certainly developed as he took on genuinely fresh material insights, these were always maintained in the context of a fundamentally dialectical theology.

The work of George Hunsinger has also provided a thorough demonstration of the dialectical character of Barth's thought.[28] Hunsinger suggests an approach to reading Barth's *Church Dogmatics* that diverges from previous attempts to set forth and analyze Barth with its focus on "pattern recognition" rather than the explication

---

[27] Bruce L. McCormack, *Karl Barth's Critically Realistic Dialectical Theology: Its Genesis and Development 1909–1936* (Oxford, UK: Oxford University Press, 1995).

[28] George Hunsinger, *How to Read Karl Barth: The Shape of His Theology* (Oxford, UK: Oxford University Press, 1991).

of his theology by means of a "single overriding conception" that functions as the interpretive key to his thought. Hunsinger's aim is to help readers of Barth develop a "set of skills" which will enable them to more effectively discern the argument of the *Church Dogmatics*. He suggests that Barth's theology is shaped by the recurrence of several "dialectical and often counterintuitive" patterns or motifs that interlace the argument of the *Church Dogmatics*.[29] While these are often experienced as elusive and strange to readers of Barth, Hunsinger maintains that they are "fully capable of clear and distinct formulation" and can serve as "felicitous categories of discernment" in the reading of the *Dogmatics*.[30]

Since these motifs recur in various contexts and combinations in Barth, the reader who has come to recognize and master them will be better able to grasp the nuances of Barth's argument throughout the *Church Dogmatics* and will also be in a position to more fully appreciate the distinctiveness of his theology. The significance of this is that Hunsinger's approach preserves the truly dialectical character of Barth's work and avoids the flattening tendency of systematization characteristic in many interpretations that tend to place emphasis on a particular aspect of his thought while distorting its general shape. It is the dialectical character of Barth's thought that makes him seem, at various turns, frustratingly complex, slippery, and even incoherent. Indeed, Hunsinger maintains that nothing is more likely to lead readers of Barth astray than a "nondialectical imagination."[31] The great strength of his book lies in his ability to explicate the dialectical patterns of Barth's theology in ways that show those patterns to be both comprehensible and coherent.

Failure to recognize these dialectical patterns has often led to the domestication of Barth in the direction of overly positivistic neo-orthodox readings of his theology. Rather than neo-orthodox, McCormack labels Barth as a "critically realistic dialectical theologian" by which he means that the content of Barth's theology is governed by the notion of "indirect identity" with respect to the doctrine of revelation. This means that in his self-revelation God makes himself to be indirectly identical with the creaturely medium of that revelation. Such revelation is *indirect* because God's use of

---

[29] The motifs are: actualism, particularism, objectivism, personalism, realism, and rationalism.

[30] Hunsinger, *How to Read*, p. vii.

[31] Hunsinger, *How to Read*, p. ix.

the creaturely medium entails no "divinization" of the medium; and yet at the same time God is indirectly *identical* with the creaturely medium in that God chooses to truly *reveal* himself through such mediums.

This is the dialectic of veiling and unveiling which says that God unveils (reveals) himself in and through creaturely veils, and that these veils, although they be used of God for the purposes of unveiling himself, remain veils. Further, the self-revelation of God means that the whole of God, complete and entire, and not simply a part, is made known in revelation, but nevertheless remains hidden within the veil of the creaturely medium through which he chooses to unveil himself. For McCormack, it is this dialectic of veiling and unveiling that drives Barth's entire approach to theology to such an extent that failure to recognize it will inevitably lead to significant interpretive distortions.

However, this dialectical approach to theology coupled with the vastness and complexity of Barth's writings serve to make the interpretation of his theology a challenging undertaking that is resistant to neat summarization. John Webster notes that one of the implications of his approach to theology is that no single stage of the argument is definitive and that it is only the whole that conveys the substance of what he is attempting to communicate. The result is that "Barth's views on any given topic cannot be comprehended in a single statement (even if the statement is one of his own), but only in the interplay of a range of articulations of a theme."[32]

Put another way, it is very easy to misread Barth, particularly without careful attention to the shape and style of his work as a whole. What McCormack asserts is that the postmodern readings of Barth examined here have failed at the task of taking adequate account of the whole, especially its dialectical character, in spite of the fact that they can indeed appeal to particular aspects of Barth's thought in support of the programs they seek to initiate. However, in spite of the criticisms that may be made concerning the details of these particular postmodern readings of Barth with respect to their neglect of the dialectical character of his thought, it does seem clear that several of the themes in his theology do, in fact, have affinities with a number of postmodern concerns, such as the linguistic and nonfoundational turns mentioned previously.

---

32 John Webster, *Karl Barth* (London: Continuum, 2000), pp. 13–14.

3. Karl Barth, postmodern thought, and evangelical theology

What is the significance of this discussion of Barth for evangelical theology? On the one hand, he has generally been viewed with a jaundiced eye by evangelicals for a number of reasons such as his perceived failure to provide an adequate account of biblical authority, his openness to the possibility of universalism, and the suspicion that in spite of his break with liberalism his thought remained far too much indebted to that theological movement to be of use to those with more conservative convictions.

On the other hand, a few evangelicals have defended Barth and insisted that his theology provides a way forward beyond the standard liberal-conservative impasse that shaped so much of evangelical theology in the twentieth century. However, both Barth's defenders and his detractors in the evangelical community have generally relied upon and assumed the standard neo-orthodox reading of Barth with the effect of negating the dialectical character of his thought. Recent Barth scholarship suggests that the common evangelical interpretations of his thought are considerably flawed and do not provide an accurate account of his views. This is evidenced in both influential older studies such as those of the highly critical Cornelius Van Til and the more accommodating Bernard Ramm as well as in the presentation of his ideas in more recent evangelical textbooks on theology. evangelicals must correct this shortcoming if they are to engage in intelligent conversation with Barth for either critical or constructive purposes.

This discussion is also significant for evangelicals in that it suggests why such an engagement might be worthwhile. As we have noted, the postmodern context has triggered a quest for new theological paradigms that might more effectively address the contemporary situation in the aftermath of modernity. This state of affairs has not passed by the evangelical theological community and has resulted in an ongoing conversation concerning the implications of postmodern culture for theology. In this discussion one of the central questions has to do with the compatibility of a biblical, confessional theology with the concerns of postmodernity. In short, is the idea of a robustly confessional and postmodern theology simply oxymoronic or is it a genuine possibility? Barth's thought is highly suggestive of the potential contours of such a theology and may be taken to imply that it is not only possible but also desirable.

For instance, in seeking to articulate a construal of revelation in the context of postmodern thought and orthodox faith we return to the linguistic turn in postmodern thought and the assertion that rather than inhabiting a prefabricated, given world, we live in linguistically construed social-cultural worlds of our own creation. This notion of the linguistically and socially constructed nature of the world raises a concern for evangelical theology and the doctrine of revelation due to the corresponding conclusion of the inadequacy of human language to provide immediate access to ultimate reality.

This "crisis of representation" raises the question of God and the very possibility of theology for many postmodern thinkers, and poses a challenge for evangelical thought to provide a theological account of the meaningfulness of language in general and to address specifically the question concerning the way in which the Word of God comes to expression in human words. If we are immersed and imbedded in language, how can we speak of truth beyond our linguistic contexts? Some have suggested that the evangelical position on revelation simply negates postmodern thought in that revelation must entail the notion that God "breaks through" language in order to provide access to "ultimate reality."[33] How might we address the challenge posed by the linguistic turn in postmodern thought without sacrificing the evangelical commitment to revelation?

From the perspective of Barth's theology, we might begin by asserting that God does not break through language and situatedness, but rather enters into the linguistic setting and uses language in the act of revelation as a means of accommodation to the situation and situatedness of human beings. This position arises out of theological commitments that are Christian and Reformed. The church has long maintained the distinction between finite human knowledge and divine knowledge. Even revelation does not provide human beings with a knowledge that exactly corresponds to that of God. The infinite qualitative distinction between God and human beings suggests the accommodated character of all human knowledge of God. For John Calvin, this means that in the process of revelation God "adjusts" and "descends" to the capacities of human beings in order to reveal the infinite mysteries of divine reality, which by their very nature are beyond the capabilities of human creatures to grasp,

---

[33] R. Scott Smith, "Christian Postmodernism and the Linguistic Turn," in Myron Penner ed. *Christianity and the Postmodern Turn* (Grand Rapids, MI: Brazos, 2005), pp. 53–69.

due to the limitations that arise from their finite character.[34] These observations give rise to the theological adage, *finitum non capax infiniti*, the finite cannot comprehend the infinite.

The natural limitations of human beings with respect to the knowledge of God made known in the process of revelation extend not only to the cognitive and imaginative faculties but also to the creaturely mediums by which revelation is communicated. In other words, the very means used by God in revelation, the mediums of human nature, language and speech, bear the inherent limitations of their creaturely character in spite of the use God makes of them as the bearers of revelation. In Chalcedonian Christology, the divine and human natures of Christ remain distinct and unimpaired even after their union in Jesus of Nazareth. Reformed theological formulations of Christology consistently maintained that one of the implications of the Chalcedonian definition was the denial of the "divinization" of the human nature of Christ in spite of its relationship to the divine nature. With respect to the revelation of God in Christ, this means that the creaturely medium of revelation, in this case the human nature of Christ, is not divinized through union with the divine nature but remains subject to the limitations and contingencies of its creaturely character. Yet in spite of these limitations, God is truly revealed through the appointed creaturely medium.

This dynamic is captured in the previously discussed dialectic of veiling and unveiling that animates the theology of Karl Barth and his notion of "indirect identity" with respect to the doctrine of revelation. In christological terms, as Bruce McCormack observes, this means that the process by which God takes on human nature and becomes the subject of a human life in human history entails no impartation or communication of divine attributes and perfections to that human nature. This in turn means that "revelation is not made a predicate of the human nature of Jesus; revelation may not be read directly 'off the face of Jesus'. And yet, it remains true that God (complete, whole, and entire) is the Subject of this human life. God, without ceasing to be God, becomes human and lives a human life, suffers and dies."[35] The consequence of this notion of

---

[34] On Calvin's understanding of the accommodated character of all human knowledge of God, see Edward A. Dowey, Jr. *The Knowledge of God in Calvin's Theology*, third ed. (Grand Rapids, MI: Eerdmans, 1994), pp. 3–24.

[35] McCormack, "Readings," 68.

indirect revelation is that it remains hidden to outward, normal, or "natural" human perception and requires that human beings be given "the eyes and ears of faith" in order to perceive the unveiling of God that remains hidden in the creaturely veil. In this conception revelation has both an objective moment, when God reveals himself through the veil of a creaturely medium, and a subjective moment, when God gives human beings the faith to understand what is hidden in the veil. In this instance, the objective moment is christological while the subjective moment is pneumatological.

Another entailment of this position is its affirmation of the contextual character of revelation. Since the creaturely mediums God employs in revelation are not divinized, they remain subject to their historically and culturally conditioned character. It simply needs to be added that what is true of the human nature of Jesus Christ with respect to divinization is also true of the words of the prophets and apostles in canonical Scripture. The use that God makes of the creaturely medium of human language in the inspiration and witness of Scripture does not entail its divinization. Language, like the human nature of Jesus, remains subject to the historical, social, and cultural limitations and contingencies inherent in its creaturely character. Yet, this does not in any way negate the reality of biblical inspiration as a gracious act of the Holy Spirit or detract from the authority of Scripture. It simply means that in approaching the text of Scripture, we do so with an understanding of the infinite wisdom and majesty of God, the limitations of our finite and fallen nature, the economy of God in revelation, and a corresponding awareness of our complete and ongoing epistemic dependence on God for our knowledge of God.

In the framework of indirect identity, we are able to affirm God's use of language in the act of revelation without denying our theological and existential awareness of its inherent limitations and contingencies as a contextually situated creaturely medium. It should be added that Barth secures the divine primacy in God's epistemic relations with human beings by maintaining the "actualistc" character of revelation. In other words, revelation in this conception is not simply a past event that requires nothing further from God. This would imply that God had ceased to act and become directly identical with the medium of revelation. If this were the case, the epistemic relationship between God and human beings would be static rather than dynamic with the result that human beings would be able to move from a position of epistemic dependency to one of epistemic mastery. Instead, continual divine action is required in the knowing process, securing the ongoing epistemic dependency of human beings with respect to the knowledge of God.[36]

This epistemic dependency that is the natural outworking of indirect revelation points to the nonfoundational character of theological epistemology. For Barth, theology is, humanly speaking, an impossibility. Where it nevertheless becomes possible in spite of its impossibility from the human side, it does so only as a divine possibility. An approach to theology that takes these insights on board will be one that finds its ongoing basis in the dialectic of the divine veiling and unveiling in revelation. For Barth, this construal of revelation demands a theology that takes seriously the ongoing reality of divine action not only on the level of the theological epistemology it presupposes but also on the level of the theological method it employs. Apart from this, theology is reduced to something that is humanly achievable and subject to human manipulation and control in which it becomes "a regular, bourgeois science alongside all the other sciences."[37]

Some evangelicals fear that such a nonfoundational approach to theology presupposes a denial of Truth. This is another of the ways in which postmodern thought is viewed as antithetical to, and therefore incompatible with, Christian faith; that is that the assumption that the affirmation of finitude and the denial of foundationalism imply a corresponding denial of Truth. It is certainly true that some postmodern theorists move in this direction and express their commitment to the finitude of human knowledge in a statement such as: the truth is that Truth does not exist. Thus, the assertion is made that postmodern thought denies the reality of Truth per se. However, Merold Westphal maintains that such a claim

> stems not from analyzing the interpretive character of human thought but from placing that analysis in an atheistic context. If our thinking never merits the triumphalist title of Truth *and* there is no other knower whose knowledge is the Truth, then the truth is that there is no Truth. But if the first premise is combined with a theistic premise, the result will be: The truth is that there is Truth, but not for us, only for God."[38]

---

[36] McCormack, "Readings," 69.
[37] McCormack, "Readings," 70.
[38] Westphal, *Onto-theology*, p. xvii.

Here, an important distinction is made between epistemological and ontological foundations. While nonfoundational theology means the end of foundationalism, it does not signal the denial of "foundations" or Truth.

However, these "foundations" are not "given" to human beings. Rather, they "always elude the grasp of the human attempt to know and to establish them from the human side" and they cannot be demonstrated or secured "philosophically or in any other way."[39] Hence, human beings are always in a position of dependence and in need of grace with respect to epistemic relations with God. Attempts on the part of humans to seize control of these relations are all too common throughout the history of the church and, no matter how well intentioned, inevitably lead to forms of oppression and conceptual idolatry.

A Barthian nonfoundationalist theology seeks to oppose such seizure through the promotion of a form of theology and a theological ethos that humbly acknowledges the human condition of finitude and fallenness and that, by grace if at all, does not belie the subject of theology to which it seeks to bear faithful witness. On this basis Karl Barth concludes that the focal point and "foundation" of Christian faith, the God revealed in Jesus Christ, determines that in the work and practice of theology "there are no comprehensive views, no final conclusions and results. There is only the investigation and teaching which take place in the act of dogmatic work and which, strictly speaking, must continually begin again at the beginning in every point. The best and most significant thing that is done in this matter is that again and again we are directed to look back to the center and foundation of it all."[40]

4. Conclusion

Karl Barth did his work as a confessional theologian in the Reformed tradition who was chiefly concerned with exegetical and dogmatic questions. As John Webster notes, he thought and wrote as "a biblical dogmatician."[41] Yet, as we have seen, Barth's theology

---

[39] Bruce L. McCormack, "What Has Basel to Do with Berlin? The Return of 'Church Dogmatics' in the Schleiermacherian Tradition," *The Princeton Seminary Bulletin* 23:2 (2002), p. 172.

[40] Karl Barth, *Church Dogmatics*, I/2, G. W. Bromiley and T. F. Torrance, eds. (Edinburgh, UK: T&T Clark, 1956), p. 868.

[41] Webster, *Karl Barth*, p. 173.

has also been appropriated to address various postmodern concerns, and while the precise ways in which his thought has been developed in some of the works mentioned may be subject to criticism, the postmodern concerns identified in these works are found in Barth. His thought does raise major challenges concerning the legitimacy of epistemological foundationalism for the theological enterprise. The hiddenness of God and the non-givenness of revelation are themes that recur in his thought. He does raise questions concerning the nature of theological language that serve to unsettle both liberal and conservative approaches to theology. Further, the conclusions Barth draws in his explication of these topics do have commonality with aspects of postmodern thought. What must be remembered is that Barth's primary focus is theological rather than philosophical. This means that his development of these themes and his approach in addressing them is driven primarily by his concern to produce a biblical dogmatics that faithfully bears witness to the self-revelation of the living God.

The assertion that Barth's theology articulates some concerns held in common with postmodern theorists should not, however, lead to the conclusion that Barth was himself a postmodern thinker. While he certainly challenged aspects of modernity, it is also true that in many ways he remained a thoroughly modern theologian whose thought resonates with themes from the nineteenth century as well as with some of those of the late twentieth. Barth is best viewed as a thinker who is able to speak to the postmodern situation not because he was a postmodern theologian but rather because he *anticipated* certain postmodern questions and concerns *within the framework of a biblical dogmatics*. Again, the problem with many of the postmodern readings of Barth on offer is not that postmodern themes and concerns have been found in Barth where they do not exist, but rather that they have not been articulated and developed within the method and framework of Barth's theology as a whole. Nevertheless, the presence of these themes suggests that their re-articulation within the context of Barth's dialectically conceived biblical dogmatics is a project brimming with constructive possibilities for a confessional evangelical theology that seeks to address the intellectual challenges raised by the emerging postmodern ethos.